Writing In-House Medical Device Software in Compliance with EU, UK, and US Regulations

This book is a comprehensive guide to producing medical software for routine clinical use. It is a practical guidebook for medical professionals developing software to ensure compliance with medical device regulations for software products intended to be sold commercially, shared with healthcare colleagues in other hospitals, or simply used in-house.

It compares requirements and latest regulations in different global territories, including the most recent EU regulations as well as UK and US regulations.

This book is a valuable resource for practising clinical scientists producing medical software in-house, in addition to other medical staff writing small apps for clinical use, clinical scientist trainees, and software engineers considering a move into healthcare. The academic level is post-graduate, as readers will require a basic knowledge of software engineering principles and practice.

Key Features:

- Up to date with the latest regulations in the UK, the EU, and the US
- Useful for those producing medical software for routine clinical use
- Contains best practice

Philip S. Cosgriff worked as a clinical scientist (medical physicist) in the UK National Health Service for nearly 40 years, specialising mainly in nuclear medicine. He produced in-house data analysis software for that whole period, with an emphasis on software quality assurance. He was a UK delegate on a pioneering EU project (COST-B2) on quality assurance of nuclear medicine software, and he has contributed to numerous reports published by the UK Institute of Physics and Engineering in Medicine (IPEM). He retired from the NHS in 2016 but has remained professionally active, with continued contributions to IPEM publications and a chapter in a recently published book entitled *Diagnostic Radiology Physics with MATLAB®*. He is a recognised expert on the application of EU and US medical device legislation, as well as other consumer protection legislation that may affect the in-house medical software developer. His current interests include the application of AI methodologies to diagnostic imaging and the future role of medical apps.

Matthew J. Memmott is a consultant medical physicist based at Manchester University NHS Foundation Trust, with experience working as a clinical scientist in the UK National Health Service for over 15 years. He has previously published journal articles, book chapters and delivered talks at national and international conferences on topics ranging from Monte Carlo image generation, computational phantoms and cardiac positron emission tomography (PET-CT) optimisation to dosimetry for radiation accident scenarios. He has a long-standing interest in scientific programming, utilising various languages for analysis and simulation of ground truth quality assurance data; and commercial platforms for the development of in-house clinical applications. He was a previous Chair of the UK Institute of Physics and Engineering in Medicine (IPEM) Nuclear Medicine Software Quality Group (NMSQG); a group which develops national audits to promote quality standards across departments utilising in-house developed software, as well as commercial packages. His current interests are in modelling exposure scenarios from radiation accidents, developing ground-truth computational phantoms for software quality assurance, investigating novel quantitative methods in PET-CT studies and the potential applications of AI in nuclear medicine.

Writing In-House Medical Device Software in Compliance with EU, UK, and US Regulations

Philip S. Cosgriff and Matthew J. Memmott

CRC Press
Taylor & Francis Group
Boca Raton London New York

CRC Press is an imprint of the
Taylor & Francis Group, an **informa** business

MATLAB® is a trademark of The MathWorks, Inc. and is used with permission. The MathWorks does not warrant the accuracy of the text or exercises in this book. This book's use or discussion of MATLAB® software or related products does not constitute endorsement or sponsorship by The MathWorks of a particular pedagogical approach or particular use of the MATLAB® software.

Designed cover image: © Shutterstock

First edition published 2024
by CRC Press
2385 NW Executive Center Drive, Suite 320, Boca Raton FL 33431

and by CRC Press
4 Park Square, Milton Park, Abingdon, Oxon, OX14 4RN

CRC Press is an imprint of Taylor & Francis Group, LLC

© 2024 Philip S. Cosgriff and Matthew J. Memmott

ISBN: 9781032293486 (hbk)
ISBN: 9781032293509 (pbk)
ISBN: 9781003301202 (ebk)

DOI: 10.1201/9781003301202

Typeset in Times
by codeMantra

Access the Support Material: www.routledge.com/9781032293509

Dedication

To our respective partners, Natalie and Sarah,
without whose support and forbearance none
of this would have been possible.

Contents

Contents

Preface

This book was produced in response to a perceived need to bring together the various technical, professional, and legal strands associated with the development and certification of medical device software. It represented an opportunity to delve into the relevant legislation, to describe and recommend relevant software development techniques, and to discuss the possible impact of new technologies.

At its core, it is an attempt to demystify a process that has undoubtedly deterred many highly skilled scientists/engineers from embarking on a much-needed local software development project due to concerns about the complexity of the process, an unease about additional costs and/or worries about legal liability. For the same reasons, it has undoubtedly deterred some small software start-ups from entering the medical devices market. For some organisations, those concerns will remain after reading this book, but they will at least have a better understanding of what is required.

It is appreciated that a book about regulatory compliance is not exactly bedtime reading, but a knowledge of the subject has nonetheless become an essential part of the professional development of established or aspiring software developers working in the healthcare sector.

Any book dealing with regulations runs the risk of gradually becoming out of date as regulations change, but the basic principles of the medical device regulations in the US and in the EU/UK are now reasonably well established. Amendments will undoubtedly occur over the coming years, but the basic recommendations contained in this book should remain valid for the foreseeable future.

MATLAB® is a registered trademark of The MathWorks, Inc. For product information, please contact:

The MathWorks, Inc.
3 Apple Hill Drive

Natick, MA 01760-2098 USA
Tel: 508-647-7000
Fax: 508-647-7001
E-mail: info@mathworks.com
Web: www.mathworks.com

Acknowledgements

The authors wish to thank the International Electrotechnical Commission (IEC) for permission to reproduce several diagrams (our Figures 5.6–5.10 and 5.13 and Tables 5.2–5.4) from its International Standards IEC 62304:2006+AMD1:2015 CSV and IEC 82304-1:2016. All such extracts are copyright of IEC, Geneva, Switzerland, and all rights are reserved. Further information on the IEC is available from www.iec.ch. IEC has no responsibility for the placement or context in which the extracts and contents were reproduced by us, nor is IEC in any way responsible for the other content or accuracy therein.

Figures used or adapted from Medical Device Coordination Group (MDCG) publications (our Figure 6.1 and Tables 6.2 and 6.4) are reproduced with permission, subject to the general copyright notice published on the European Commission website (https://commission.europa.eu/legal-notice_en).

Material on the FDA website is not copyrighted, so specific permission to reproduce content is not required. Nonetheless, we followed the informal guidelines on re-use issued by the FDA (https://www.fda.gov/about-fda/about-website/website-policies) and are grateful for access to this invaluable resource.

Permission to reproduce extracts from British and ISO Standards is granted by BSI Standards Limited (BSI). No other use of this material is permitted. British Standards can be obtained from BSI Knowledge (www.knowledge.bsigroup.com).

Other acknowledgements regarding permission to republish materials are contained in the legends of the respective figures and tables.

Finally, and most importantly, we would like to thank Rebecca Hodges-Davies (Commissioning Editor for Physics at CRC Press) for the initial invitation to produce this work, and Danny Kielty (Senior Editorial Assistant at CRC Press) for his constant encouragement and timely reminders about looming deadlines that helped keep the whole thing on track.

1 Introduction

1.1 AIMS AND SCOPE

The primary aim of this book is to provide would-be medical software developers with the knowledge and tools to guide them through the maze of regulatory compliance steps that are now required prior to clinical deployment, whether the application is intended purely for in-house use, for sharing with the wider healthcare community, or for commercial exploitation. To this end, we have endeavoured to distil the vast amount of information available in official and unofficial guidance documents down to the essentials of what the developer needs to know and understand in order to produce "medical-grade software" [1]. Relevant regulations are considered *in the round*, but this book is written mainly from the perspective of the in-house software developer.

We focus on *what* needs to be done to comply with the existing medical device regulations. General guidance is provided, but a detailed discussion on how each of the hundreds of specific requirements can be met is beyond the scope of this book.

Coding standards are discussed, but this is not a book about computer programming. There is an obligatory focus on required documentation, but this is not about checklists, rather an explanation of the inter-relationships between regulatory clauses, international standards, and other publicly available documents, as well as a measure of pragmatism to hold it all together.

The latest developments in software engineering and quality management systems are discussed, primarily because a system based purely on regulations does not guarantee safe or reliable working practices or products. This has been demonstrated many times in the medical devices arena, as well as in other safety-critical industries. For example, the following paragraph is taken from an analysis of the events that led up to the Piper Alpha oil rig disaster in 1988; words that, sadly, could easily have been cut and pasted into the report of the Deepwater Horizon disaster that occurred 22 years later.

> When the disaster occurred, offshore safety was governed through the use of prescriptive regulations. Such regulations have their uses, provided all eventualities have been considered. But a regulations-bound system falls down because practices not covered by regulations are simply not addressed. People become complacent when they are encouraged to think that safety can be ensured by rules enforced by inspectors: it is impossible to cover all eventualities in a set of general rules [2].

As with many other regulations that scientists and engineers encounter in their daily working lives, medical device regulations are primarily concerned with basic safety, which is why there is now so much focus on risk management. Achieving regulatory compliance is unquestionably a significant achievement, especially for a small group, but it is just the beginning and, in many ways, could be considered analogous to professional registration. Pursuing this comparison, we also emphasise the benefits that

DOI: 10.1201/9781003301202-1

regulatory compliance can bring (Section 6.6), both for the individual developers and for the establishments in which they work.

1.2   A BRIEF HISTORY OF MEDICAL DEVICE REGULATION

Regulation of medical devices goes back quite a long way, but not quite as far back as you might imagine. In Europe, the type of regulation that we have today only began in 1990, following the European Commission's adoption of the so-called *new approach* concept (covering most consumer goods) in 1985. Regulation in the United States goes back considerably further, with its current methodology traceable to the 1976 medical devices amendments to the 1938 Food, Drug, and Cosmetic Act.

It is important to appreciate that medical device regulations effectively stipulate a set of minimum requirements for device safety and performance, so do not represent the "last word" in design, manufacture, or testing. For this reason, updates and amendments are often reactionary, making regulation essentially a catch-up operation.

By the early 2000s it was becoming clear that the increasing number and complexity of medical devices, combined with a lack of robust clinical evaluation, had reduced the effectiveness of medical device legislation in both the EU and the US. In the EU there was an additional problem of variable implementation of the old Medical Device Directives in member states, which was also a growing cause for concern. Two public consultations were conducted (in 2008 and 2010), seeking feedback from industry, national regulatory authorities, professionals, and others regarding the existing regulations and possible targets for reform. At around the same time, two high-profile scandals involving metal-on-metal hip prostheses [3] and silicone breast implants [4] prompted strong criticism of EU medical device regulation in leading medical journals [5,6].

Although the US had managed to avoid such scandals, there were also calls for a radical overhaul of the regulatory process due to delays in the FDA's approval systems, the relatively large number of recalls of 'high-risk' devices, and the fact that many of these devices had been approved via the less stringent pre-market notification scheme [7,8]. In the EU, the European Commission responded by accelerating the reform process, resulting in the adoption (in September 2012) of a proposal to replace all three Medical Devices Directives with two new regulations. The complicated ratification process took another five years, concluding with the publication of the EU Medical Devices Regulations in May 2017 (herein MDR17). In the US, changes have been more piecemeal, but all regulators now agree on the need for greater harmonisation, given the global nature of the medical device market.

The current UK Medical Devices Regulations came into force in 2002, implementing three European directives focusing on general, active-implantable, and in-vitro medical devices [9]. However, medical devices manufactured and used within the same health institution were exempt. Whilst only explicitly stated in relation to in-vitro medical devices, this exemption has been interpreted as applying equally to general medical devices. The consequence was that many

UK clinical departments developed sizeable libraries of software medical devices in the form of spreadsheets, macros, and other clinical programs using commercial application programming interfaces (APIs). The superseding EU MDR17 regulations formalised and increased the regulation around in-house developed software, requiring adherence to the general safety performance requirements (GSPR) and the implementation of a quality management system for the duration of the software's life cycle; the ramifications of which are still being felt in many clinical departments. This book will cover the requirements for purely in-house manufacture and use (IHMU) as well as full regulatory compliance in the EU, the UK, and the US.

The vast scope of current EU and US medical device legislation – which some industry commentators have referred to as a "regulatory tsunami" – will undoubtedly be regarded as "overkill" by many small-scale medical software developers, especially those working in public sector healthcare who "only" produce spreadsheet or database applications. The regulations are, of course, primarily aimed at commercial medical equipment manufacturers but, with recent regulatory changes in the EU, small in-house teams developing software for use within their own hospitals have also been brought under regulatory control. For such teams, a pragmatic approach is required given the step-wise increase in production overheads that the regulations mandate.

There are certainly many requirements to address, but many require a relatively small investment of time and effort to fulfil. Some, however, such as detailed risk analysis, undoubtedly need a much larger commitment (throughout the life cycle of the product), but this now has to be accepted as the cost of remaining active in this field of work. The main purpose of regulation is to protect the public and/or the environment, but the intended *effect* of regulation is to set the bar high enough to discourage all except those organisations with the expertise and resources to operate compliantly. Medical device regulations in all jurisdictions now have a heavy dependence on specific quality and risk management systems, so commercial organisations and health institutions that have already adopted a generic quality management standard to assist them with the day-to-day organisation of their other work have a distinct advantage.

1.3   THE PROBLEM WITH SOFTWARE

Software allows developers to build extremely powerful and flexible systems, but the resultant complexity makes the quality assurance of software-based systems a considerable challenge. Ironically, the huge increase in raw computing power (i.e., transistor density in microprocessors and memory chips) that we have witnessed since the 1970s has made the "software quality issue" much more difficult to manage, as it has allowed ever larger and more complex applications to be built. For example, Google's web browser ("Chrome") currently contains about 5 million lines of code (LoC), spread over more than 20,000 unique files, written in over 30 different programming languages [10].

The exponential growth in microprocessor speed and memory capacity over the last 50 years[1] has served to mask the issue of bloated, inefficient code. This has resulted in the widely held view that increasing computer power is never *quite* enough to outweigh the huge increase in software size and complexity that it has facilitated; a situation succinctly expressed more than 20 years ago by Reiser, who stated that "software is getting slower faster than hardware is getting faster", adding that "the hope is that the progress in hardware will cure all software ills" [11]. Unfortunately, this optimistic prediction has not materialised.

Several landmark papers have been published over the last 40 years highlighting fundamental problems with software development, including an article by Gibbs in 1994 in which he described what he called a "software crisis" [12]. Calls for the more rigorous application of software engineering techniques have continued to appear with regularity over the intervening years, from both computer science academics and industry insiders [13,14].

Back in the world of medical devices, a typical module of medical device software does not usually contain more than a few thousand LoC, but the potential still exists for it to be overly complex and convoluted. Indeed, even a small 100 LoC program can be built inefficiently and erroneously, so the need to deploy software engineering principles and practices remains. Of course, the major difference between general commercial software and medical device software is that the development of the latter is a regulated activity and this has enormous implications.

1.4   STRUCTURE OF THE BOOK

The chapters are ordered in a similar way to a course curriculum: fundamentals first, leading progressively to more complex ideas and concepts. Medical device regulations do not pause to elaborate on every requirement (far from it!) and therefore assume a basic knowledge of risk management, quality management, and software engineering. This book aims to provide at least some of the necessary background information, but software developers familiar with these techniques may wish to start at Chapter 6, which contains cross-references to earlier chapters dealing with basic concepts. The main regularity requirements of the EU, UK, and US systems are covered, but more detail is provided on the EU regulations.

The sections of Chapter 6 are jurisdiction-based, as software practitioners will generally be interested in one set of regulations. However, readers are encouraged to investigate how a particular issue is approached by a different regulatory authority as guidance documents produced by the FDA, EU MDCG, and UK MHRA should be regarded as valuable sources of information for *all* medical device manufacturers.

A comprehensive discussion of software engineering techniques is outside the scope of this book but we have provided direction on the most suitable methods and procedures for in-house developers. The situation regarding quality management systems is more straightforward, in principle at least, as the adoption of a small number of

---

[1] In 1971 a state-of-the-art microprocessor chip contained about 3,000 transistors; in 2021 the figure is close to 3 *billion*, confirming "Moore's law" that microprocessor performance (i.e., transistor density on an integrated circuit) doubles about every two years.

international standards has been recognised as an effective means of achieving compliance with the relevant aspects of the regulations.

Artificial intelligence (AI) is already having a big impact on medical device technology and is also presenting a big challenge for regulators. The basics of AI-enabled medical software are covered in Chapter 3, with the regulatory aspects covered in Chapter 6. Health apps for mobile devices also present a challenge for medical device regulators, and we consider the numerous issues associated with their use in routine clinical practice. A separate chapter is devoted to the cybersecurity of medical devices, due to its increasing importance in terms of internet-connected devices and the sensitivity of corporate IT departments within large health establishments to open-source software.

1.5   INTENDED AUDIENCE

The intended audience is primarily clinical scientists and engineers who develop (or are interested in developing) medical software for routine clinical use. However, the book's wide scope means that it should also be of interest to commercial software companies – especially small startups – that are considering entering the medical device market in either Europe or the United States.

Basic knowledge of software engineering (SE) and software quality assurance (SQA) principles and practice is essential for a thorough understanding of this book, but it is appreciated that (a) software development is not a primary role for most graduate scientists and engineers working in clinical departments and (b) that few have formal qualifications in this area. Most in-house developers will be skilled self-taught programmers who have encountered and used one or more SE models in the course of their work. In any event, most will benefit from an awareness of the specific SE standards and guidelines covered in Chapter 5, as this knowledge is a prerequisite to producing safe, reliable, and clinically useful software.

Due to the largely informal/organic way that the software industry has developed, there are also many software developers in commercial organisations who will not have been required to obtain formal qualifications in either SE or SQA. As such, the principles and concepts described in Chapters 3–5 should be of interest to those working in software companies with limited or no experience of the medical device market.

Finally, the book should also be of interest to post-graduate clinical scientist trainees (as part of the computer science element of their structured training programme), tech-savvy medical staff who are interested in writing medical apps for use in clinical areas such as intensive care, radiology, anaesthetics and surgery, and qualified software engineers working in industry and commerce who are considering a career move into the medical field.

1.6   SUPPLEMENTARY MATERIAL

Not all the prepared content would fit within the tight constraints of a printed publication, so the extra material has been made available as an online resource at www.routledge.com/9781032293509. It also contains all the online references as clickable hyperlinks, thus avoiding the need to type complex URLs into web browsers.

REFERENCES

[1] M. Jonsson, "2021 predictions for medical device product and systems development," Jama Software, December 2020. [Online]. Available: https://www.jamasoftware.com/blog/2021-predictions-medical-device/. [Accessed 13 October 2023].

[2] F. Macleod and S. Richardson, "Piper alpha: The disaster in detail," 6 July 2018. [Online]. Available: https://www.thechemicalengineer.com/features/piper-alpha-the-disaster-in-detail/. [Accessed 10 January 2022].

[3] M. Wienroth, P. McCormack and T. Joyce, "Precaution, governance and the failure of medical implants: the ASR(TM) hip in the UK," *Life Sciences, Society and Policy,* vol. 10, p. 19, 2014.

[4] V. Martindale and A. Menache, "The PIP scandal: An analysis of the process of quality control that failed to safeguard women from the health risks," *Journal of the Royal Society of Medicine,* vol. 106, no. 5, pp. 173–177, 2013.

[5] R. Horton, "Offline: A serious regulatory failure, with urgent implications," *The Lancet,* vol. 379, no. 9811, p. 106, 11 January 2012.

[6] M. Eikermann, C. Gludd and C. Perleth, "Commentary: Europe needs a central, transparent, and evidence based regulation process for devices," *British Medical Journal,* vol. 346, p. f2771, 2013.

[7] B. Kramer, S. Xu and A. Kesselheim, "How does medical device regulation perform in the United States and the European union? A systematic review," *PLoS Medicine,* vol. 9, no. 7, p. e1001276, 2012.

[8] D. Zuckerman, P. Brown and S. Nissen, "Medical device recalls and the FDA approval process," *Archives of Internal Medicine,* vol. 171, no. 11, pp. 1006–1011, 2011.

[9] "Regulating medical devices in the UK," July 2023. [Online]. Available: https://www.gov.uk/guidance/regulating-medical-devices-in-the-uk. [Accessed 13 October 2023].

[10] S. Anand, "How many lines of code is Google Chrome," 24 August 2012. [Online]. Available: https://www.quora.com/How-many-lines-of-code-is-Google-Chrome. [Accessed 12 October 2023].

[11] M. Reiser, *The Oberon System User Guide and Programmer's Manual,* New York: ACM Press, 1991.

[12] W. Gibbs, "Software's chronic crisis," *Scientific American,* vol. 271, no. 3, pp. 86–95, 1994.

[13] R. Somers, "The coming software apocalypse," *The Atlantic,* 26 September 2017. [Online]. Available: https://www.theatlantic.com/technology/archive/2017/09/saving-the-world-from-code/540393/. [Accessed 21 January 2022].

[14] A. Barr, *The problem with software: why smart engineers write bad code,* Boston: MIT Press, 2018.

2 The Need for In-House Development of Medical Software

2.1 PREAMBLE

This book is obviously based on the premise that there is a continuing need for the in-house development of medical software within healthcare institutions, but it is important to consider both the advantages and disadvantages of such development. Each organisation/department will be different, in terms of the resources at its disposal, so each potential project needs to be justified by reference to an organisational policy on software development (Section 2.7).

The term "in-house software development" simply means "developing software within your own organisation for your own purposes"; the main requirement being the availability of staff with the required knowledge and skills to undertake such projects. This book can help with the "knowledge part", but the computer programming (coding) skills will need to already be in place. In this regard, a clear distinction is made between bespoke software development and relatively simple software configuration that the end-user may also perform.

When a healthcare institution is considering an in-house development project, the alternative is usually the outright purchase of commercial off-the-shelf (COTS) software – usually from a medical equipment manufacturer. For custom software development generally, outsourcing the project to a software house would usually be an alternative, but this is rarely an option in the medical sector. Apart, that is, from the burgeoning area of mobile apps (Chapter 3).

2.2 TYPES OF IN-HOUSE SOFTWARE DEVELOPMENT

There are several means by which in-house software may be developed. The most obvious is to develop the software completely in-house using the tools and resources available internally ("writing software from scratch"). The second option is to share the development with another healthcare establishment interested in solving the same problem. The third option is to modify software developed elsewhere, which might be proprietary commercial software or open-source software. Finally, direct collaboration with a medical equipment manufacturer provides a possible means by which software developed in-house may be formally adopted by the commercial supplier.

DOI: 10.1201/9781003301202-2

⚠ WARNING

Validation of Aladdin protocols that are not part of the Xeleris release is the sole
responsibility of the customer.

FIGURE 2.1   Disclaimer included in the Reference Guide for General Electric's Xeleris™ 3
Functional Imaging Processing and Review System.

2.2.1   Writing Software From Scratch

Some medical equipment manufacturers offer a *user programming environment*
(usually as an extra cost option) for departmental staff with the skills to write their
own software. There will generally be an associated training package if such a facility is offered. Software developed in this way is the sole responsibility of the staff
who produced it and the manufacturer/supplier will usually include a written disclaimer to that effect in the user documentation (Figure 2.1).

The fact that software will mainly use library modules, functions, and sub-
routines supplied by the medical equipment manufacturer/supplier is immaterial as
far as legal responsibility is concerned. In any such development, the person(s) who
assembled the various components into a dedicated computer program becomes the
"manufacturer" of the new device under current medical device regulations.

The phrase "writing software from scratch" is somewhat misleading as all software
is an assembly of pre-existing building blocks that are supplied with the "programming environment", whether obtained from a medical equipment manufacturer, from
a third-party commercial source, or from a free and open-source software (FOSS).

Medical software produced using a manufacturer-supplied scripting language
constitutes a common form of end-user programming and would certainly fall within
the definition of bespoke software development. Although the supplied functionality
may be considered part of the commercial medical device (i.e., the device is *designed*
to host scripts) this does not mean that the manufacturer is legally responsible for all
or any of the software produced/assembled using them.

At its simplest, "scripting" is a way of automating the execution of discrete tasks
that could be performed manually (by the computer operator), but a scripting language will also contain many features and functions (e.g., mathematical operators)
found in common high-level languages. And, even without additional data processing, pre-existing code elements ("primitives") could easily be linked in a way that
produced an undesirable result. A script can thus provide additional functionality
that may not be covered by the manufacturer's statement of intended purpose, so
should be considered a medical device in its own right [1]. A CE mark associated
with a medical equipment manufacturer's clinical software package will only apply
to the documented programs described in the supplied user manual.

2.2.2   Writing Spreadsheet Applications

Spreadsheets offer the in-house developer an attractive means of building powerful
medical software tools relatively quickly but there is a problem: General-purpose

commercial spreadsheets such as Microsoft Excel™ (or the many free or open-source alternatives, such as Google Sheets and Calc[1]) were not *designed* to be used in a regulated environment. Nonetheless, as described below, custom spreadsheets can be made compliant with GMP-based medical device regulatory requirements if certain software validation procedures are followed. Best practice guidelines for spreadsheet development are covered in Section 5.4.5.

Spreadsheets are commonly used in a *supporting* capacity in the MedTech and pharmaceutical industries (e.g., as part of the quality management system), but a spreadsheet having a medical purpose can qualify as a medical device (i.e., SaMD) in its own right (Sections 6.3.4 and 6.5.2).

2.2.2.1 Regulatory Requirements in the EU and the UK

Within the EU/UK such a spreadsheet qualifying as SaMD will generally be straightforward to justify as an in-house project – at least in principle – as there will usually be no existing CE-marked alternative on the market (Section 6.3.12).

Under current UK regulations, not all "clinical calculators" (such as custom spreadsheets) that qualify as medical devices need to be UKCA marked. Until revised, UK regulations still refer to MEDDEV 2.1/6 (*Guidelines on the qualification and classification of standalone software used in healthcare within the framework of medical devices*), which allows some regulatory discretion for medical device software that performs a "simple action" [2]. However, if the result of the clinical calculator's output cannot be easily verified by the *intended user* (e.g., by a qualified nurse using a handheld calculator) then it is likely to be defined as a medical device.

2.2.2.2 Regulatory Requirements in the US

The regulatory position in the US is complicated by the fact that a custom-designed spreadsheet is covered by the software validation requirements of 21 CFR Part 820 (Section 6.5.6.2) as well as federal regulation 21 CFR Part 11 (herein "Part 11") covering electronic records and electronic signatures.

Part 11 caused considerable confusion and misunderstanding in FDA-regulated industries following its publication in 1997. In response, the FDA issued guidance (in 2003) stating that, as part of a narrow interpretation of scope, it considered Part 11 to be applicable to "records that are required to be maintained under predicate rules, that are maintained in electronic format in addition to paper format, and that are relied on to perform regulated activities". The references to paper records in the regulations are nowadays someone redundant but the basic principle remains. More specifically, Part 11 applies to FDA-regulated activities where electronic records[2] are (a) maintained to meet predicate rules, (b) produced as part of a submission to the FDA,[3] or (c) subject to FDA inspection [3].

---

[1] We concentrate here on Microsoft Excel™ as an exemplar as it is still overwhelmingly the most commonly used spreadsheet within the general business community, and even more so within the science/engineering community [44].

[2] Electronic record means "any combination of text, graphics, data, audio, pictorial, or other information representation in digital form that is created, modified, maintained, archived, retrieved, or distributed by a computer system".

[3] The FDA moved to electronic submission of all pre-market notifications from October 2023 (Section 6.5.4.1)

Part 11 works in tandem with predicate rules, which refer to *any* FDA regulation that requires organisations to maintain records. For example, 21 CFR Part 820 requires medical device manufacturers to maintain records pertaining to design history, quality system, complaint investigation, training, etc. Part 11 requirements are most often applied to supporting "non-product software" (Section 3.3.6) associated with the quality management system,[4] but the regulation also covers software that controls or processes GxP data,[5] which would certainly include SaMD) [4].

FDA guidance states that the Agency will exercise enforcement discretion regarding Part 11 requirements for the validation of computerised systems (§ 11.10(a) and corresponding requirements in §11.30), given that a company must still comply with all applicable predicate rule requirements for software validation (e.g., 21 CFR 820.70(i)). In short, most electronic record-keeping systems used in FDA-regulated industries need to be appropriately validated.

A custom spreadsheet clearly meets the Part 11 definition of an electronic record and several groups have translated its generic requirements into the language of spreadsheet design. Briefly, the developer needs to implement built-in spreadsheet functions/facilities associated with access and security, as well as install approved third-party add-ins to provide features missing from general-purpose spreadsheet apps such as Microsoft Excel™ and Google Sheets™ [5] [6]. The developer does not need to validate the spreadsheet app *per se* but needs to validate *how* it is used [7].

Part 11 is a comprehensive regulation that requires the manufacturer to address the following topics in its documented procedures: Computer systems validation (CSV), record rendering, document storage and record retention, system access, audit trails, workflows, authority checks, device checks, personnel qualifications, personnel accountability, and document control. There are additional requirements for "open systems" (e.g., file encryption) in order to ensure the security and confidentiality of electronic records in circumstances where system access is controlled by persons other than those responsible for system contents and maintenance [8].

A basic gap analysis exercise based on the use of MS Excel™ reveals that the built-in "track changes" feature (used for shared workbooks) is not sufficient to meet the respective audit trail/change traceability requirements of 21 CFR 11.10(e) and IEC 62304 (Section 5.4.1.5), so approved third-party add-ins must be used [9].

Also, the relatively weak (file/sheet) password protection does not meet the strict security requirements of 21 CFR 11.10(d) [10]. Most of the security requirements can be met by making the spreadsheet a network (client/server) application that is only available to selected users via a secure two-level (user ID, strong password encryption) authentication process [5].

Individual spreadsheet cells can be locked and/or hidden (subject to worksheet protection), thus avoiding inadvertent corruption of formulae, code, or instructions. Many other features of good spreadsheet design, such as read-only file opening, logical sheet separation/layout, and data input verification (Section 5.4.5) are also expected by the FDA (Section 6.5.8.2).

---

[4] If the software is used to "support a quality decision", or produce data for management review it must be controlled and validated [7].

[5] Data produced in the process of following good practice guidelines and/or regulations.

The European equivalent of 21 CFR Part 11 is simply called EU Annex 11 (not to be confused with Annex XI of MDR 17/745), which is part of the "EudraLex" – the rules governing medicinal products in the European Union. Annex 11 was added to Volume 4 (*Good Manufacturing Practice: Medicinal Products for Human and Veterinary Use*) in 2011 due to the growing use of software for clinical trials [11].

In contrast to 21 CFR Part 11, *Annex 11* is a *guideline* that only applies to medicinal products or combinational devices.[6] Although not strictly applicable to medical device manufacturing, many European manufacturers have chosen to adopt some of the practices described in Annex 11 (as a supplement to MDR 17 GSPRs) for their clinical evaluation/investigation activities [12].

2.2.3 MODIFYING SOFTWARE

In everyday language, "modify" means "to alter slightly" or "to change some parts (of something) while not changing other parts". There are several scenarios that may be considered under the general heading of "software modification". As it requires coding, software modification is a form of customisation (Section 2.2.7).

The term "modification" is not defined in IEC 62304 (Section 5.4.1), but the standard contains numerous references to modifications – mostly in connection with software maintenance. For example, in Appendix B.1.2 (*Field of application*) it is stated that:

> The maintenance of released health software applies to the post-production experience with the health software. Software maintenance includes the combination of all technical and administrative means, including supervision actions, to act on problem reports to retain an item in, or restore it to, a state in which it can perform a required function as well as *modification requests* related to released health software. For example, this includes problem rectification, regulatory reporting, re-validation, and preventive action.

ISO/IEC/IEEE 14764:2022 (Chapter 5, A.1.3.4) defines the term "modification request" simply as "a generic term used to identify proposed modifications to a software product that is being maintained". A modification request (or change request) has two classifications that, in turn, lead to four basic types of maintenance (Figure 2.2).

Although IEC 62304 refers to modification mainly in terms of maintenance of the final (released) product *by the original developer*, the steps required also apply to modifications made by third parties (e.g., end-users). The standard dictates (in Appendix B.6.1) that the established *software maintenance process* be activated whenever the health software "undergoes modifications to program code and/or associated documentation, due to a reported problem *or* the need for improvement or adaptation" (Section 5.4.1).

Obviously, modifying a single line of code can completely change the way in which a computer program works, so, if such a change is made, the person who

---

[6] A medical device that achieves its intended use through the incorporation of a medicinal product or substance (e.g., insulin pump).

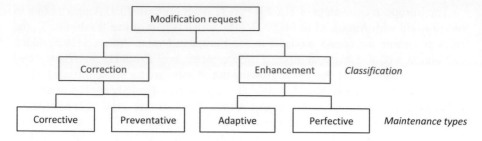

FIGURE 2.2 The relationship between modification requests and maintenance types. Adapted with permission from Figure 1 of ISO 14764:2022.

introduced it takes responsibility for the *whole program* as it is then considered to be a new entity (Section 5.4.1.11).

2.2.3.1 The EU MDR View on Software Modification

Although not specifically defined in MDR 17/745, a good indication of what EU regulators consider to be major and minor modifications of a medical device can be found in Part C of Annex VI of the regulations, which describes the unique device identifier (UDI) system. It is stated (in Section 6.5.2) that a new UDI device identifier (UDI-DI) is required for a previously certified device if there has been a modification that changes any one of the following:

a. the original performance;
b. the safety or the intended use of the software;
c. the interpretation of data.

Examples of such *major* modifications include new or modified algorithms, database structures, operating platforms, system architecture, new user interfaces, or new methods of interoperability.

It is added (in Section 6.5.3) that "minor" software revisions require a new UDI production identifier (UDI-PI) but not a new UDI-DI (Section 6.3.15). Minor software revisions are generally associated with bug fixes, usability enhancements, security patches, or operating efficiency improvements. Of course, the details of *all* software revisions (pre-release and post-release) should be fully documented by the manufacturer as part of a system of software quality assurance (Sections 6.3.6.3 and 6.5.8.3).

2.2.3.2 The FDA View on Modification

The FDA has produced guidance on 510(k) clearance of modified devices that have been previously cleared. [13]. The guidance contains links to two more specific documents, one of which (dated 2017) relates to software [14].

The guidance on the sort of software changes that would require a new 510(K) submission gives a clear indication of what the FDA considers to constitute a "major modification". The criteria are similar in principle to those used in the EU, but the wording is slightly different. In summary, a new 510(k) submission is only required if either of the following two circumstances apply:

1. A change is made with the intent to significantly affect the safety or effectiveness of a device.
2. A change is made that could significantly affect the clinical functionality or performance specifications that are directly associated with the intended use of the device.

The guidance document usefully provides advice to help manufacturers decide whether or not the above criteria have been met.

For more minor changes to medical device software (e.g., to the user interface), the FDA states that submission of a new 510(k) is not generally required and that the manufacturer should instead refer to its existing quality systems requirements as the "least burdensome approach to assuring the safety and effectiveness of the modified device". Simple bug fixes can therefore usually be handled internally (including an update to the device master record, 21 CFR 820.181), but each change should be considered on its own merits since all repairs are considered to be "design changes" under the FDA quality system regulation 21 CFR Part 820 [15].

The FDA has produced new guidance on the development of AI software, which, by its nature, is in a constant state of change as the system learns from the data with which it is presented. For entry into the US market, manufacturers incorporating AI/ML software in their medical devices can now take advantage of a new FDA mechanism called *Predetermined Change Control Plan (PCCP)*, which takes account of the type of iterative future modifications inherent in AI-based systems (Section 6.5.8.9)

2.2.3.3 Modifying Commercial Software

The only simple means to change the default way in which clinical software behaves is to change the configuration options (Section 2.2.7). However, some manufacturers may provide a facility to make more fundamental changes (using a programming tool) that would then effectively result in a new program. This is not a commonly available option (most compiled proprietary software is "locked") but is mentioned here as a reminder that legal responsibility would be transferred if a change other than routine configuration (i.e., involving coding) was made by the end-user.

2.2.4 COLLABORATING WITH ANOTHER HEALTH ESTABLISHMENT OR UNIVERSITY

Collaborating with another hospital or university department is an attractive proposition in principle as it provides access to additional knowledge and expertise. The software to be developed obviously must be of interest to both parties and it is helpful if a professional relationship already exists. Such a development would be subject to all the rules of IHMU that apply to a single centre but would bring additional communication issues. Although such arrangements may be viewed as informal, it is important to have a written agreement in place to clarify roles and responsibilities. The vexed issue of intellectual property rights (Section 7.6) should also be addressed at the outset.

The natural extension of this type of private arrangement is active participation in regional or national open-source projects. The legal aspects of using open-source software components in medical device development are discussed in Section 7.6.1.

It is also possible for clinical/scientific staff to formally contract with software engineering staff within a university computer science department, but this is generally a form of outsourcing that requires research funding [16].

2.2.5 COLLABORATING WITH YOUR MEDICAL EQUIPMENT SUPPLIER

This section relates to software intended to run on typically proprietary systems using the facilities and resources supplied by the manufacturer. Medical software designed in-house to run on general-purpose (e.g., UNIX, Windows, MacOS) PCs / workstations is covered in Section 2.2.1 above.

If a user develops (or part-develops) a new software product that sparks the interest of a medical equipment manufacturer, there is the possibility of making a formal arrangement (sometimes called a *software collaboration* agreement). This may be seen as a natural extension of the informal sharing system described in Section 2.5.1, but here the manufacturer effectively adopts user-written software and subjects it to its own development standards. Indeed, there are several examples of commercial medical image processing software packages that started out life as user-written programs.

The nature of such contracts varies, but would typically allow the company to modify the code as deemed necessary and distribute the final product to its customers. The user-developer would be required to sign a contract setting out the respective duties and obligations of the user and manufacturer, including clauses covering confidentiality, intellectual property, user-supplied documentation, and feedback.

This "active collaboration" route may be an option for complex medical software having genuine commercial possibilities, but this would not be the case for most medical software developed in-house.

2.2.6 CUSTOM-MADE DEVICES

The phrase *"custom-made device"* has a specific meaning under EU medical devices regulations, as it relates to the manufacture of a *one-off* device for an individual patient. The procedure for the manufacture of such devices is covered in Annex VIII of MDR 17/745. Article 2.3 of MDR 17/745 makes it clear that the responsibility for custom-made devices lies with the prescribing medical practitioner, and that "mass-produced devices that are adapted to meet the specific requirements of any professional user are *not* considered to be custom-made devices". In this context, commercial software provided by a medical equipment company would qualify as "mass-produced" and the sort of configuration described in the next section would not be subject to the manufacturing requirements of custom-made devices.

2.2.7 CONFIGURATION OF COMMERCIAL SOFTWARE BY THE USER

The terms "software customisation" and "software configuration" are often used interchangeably by medical device users, but have different meanings in software engineering generally [17]. Software configuration can usually be achieved by simply clicking or unclicking checkboxes in the "settings" part of the program. This may

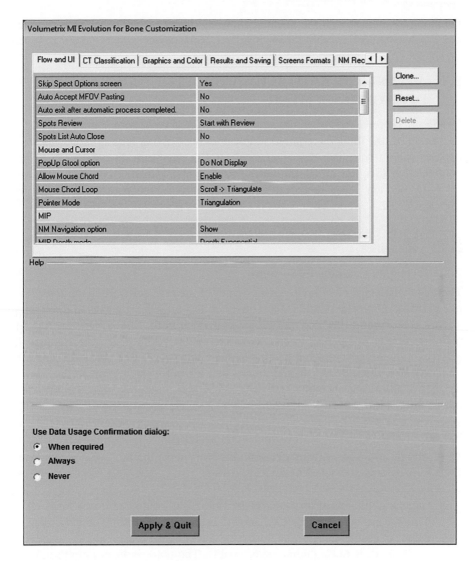

FIGURE 2.3   Flow and User Interface tab from the configuration options available within GE's XelerisTM 3 Functional Imaging Processing and Review System, demonstrating how the user experience can be customised without modification of the code base.

change the appearance of the user interface but may also change the flow control (and therefore outputs) of the program. Software customisation, on the other hand, requires the user to perform some coding, which has more far-reaching implications (Section 4.2.3; Figure 2.3).

It is advisable to read any "small print" regarding user configuration/customisations, to check whether the manufacturer claims any explicit or implied transfer of legal liability, as is normally the case for user-written applications or modifications. However, if the manufacturer has enabled the software to be configured, some liability may remain with the manufacturer, regardless of any general disclaimers, since such use may be within the intended use of the device.

2.3   ADVANTAGES AND DISADVANTAGES OF IN-HOUSE DEVELOPED SOFTWARE

Healthcare professionals often attempt to "fill gaps" in commercial clinical software packages (i.e., the function required simply does not exist) or redesign "sub-optimal" commercial software that the department already possesses. In contrast to simple configuration (Section 2.2.7), the latter could involve *modification* of the existing software (Section 2.2.3) or redesigning some or all of the package from scratch (Section 2.2.1).

2.3.1   BENEFITS

2.3.1.1   Highly Customised Systems

The main advantage of in-house development of medical software is the *total control* of the development process that it offers. It also provides a means of developing a clinical procedure that may not be possible otherwise. This is the same advantage that attracts companies in commerce and industry, but their choice is usually between in-house development and outsourcing the project to a specialist software company [18]. Outsourcing should ensure that the software is built to the client's detailed requirements specification (assuming perfect communication), but the client has no direct control over the schedule and timescales.

2.3.1.2   Better Quality than Commercial Systems?

Advocates of in-house software development often make the following points about commercially available medical device software:

1. Commercial medical software can become rapidly outdated if new research demonstrates a better way (e.g., a new data analysis algorithm) of addressing a clinical problem.
2. A CE mark is not a guarantee of quality. The mark indicates conformity with relevant EU regulations covering the type of product, but the regulations generally refer to process standards, as is the case for the EU medical device regulations. It is not an independent verification of product quality or safety.
3. Bespoke software developed in-house can potentially be of better quality than commercial software – provided it is developed to the same standards as medical equipment manufacturers [1].

There is undoubtedly a place for in-house medical software development alongside the commercial offerings of medical equipment manufacturers. Such software will always be developed to fulfil a local need but a greater benefit could be realised if the software could be shared with departments in other hospitals (i.e., different legal entities) faced with the same issue. Otherwise, enormous duplication of effort results (especially in situations where no commercial product exists), as has been the case for glomerular filtration rate (GFR) spreadsheet analysis software within UK nuclear medicine departments. At present, however, such sharing (within the EU/UK) requires full CE marking, so represents a considerable barrier.

Producing high quality software in-house is certainly possible, but considerable variability is to be expected amongst clinical departments currently undertaking it. This book attempts to outline a roadmap for current and future developers, but strong input from the relevant professional bodies is also required, especially in terms of training at both pre-registration and post-registration levels. The fact that in-house medical software development is now a regulated activity (in the EU/UK at least) effectively obliges participating departments/organisations to work to the same process standards (Chapter 5), so it is expected that although the number of centres undertaking software development may reduce (at least initially), the general standard will be raised. This is certainly the intention of the regulators. It would be helpful if national surveys could be organised by relevant professional bodies (or Competent Authorities) to establish the number of health institutions engaged in software development activities, the number of staff involved, and the types of medical software projects they are undertaking. The details of a survey of UK nuclear medicine departments are discussed in Section 2.6.2.

2.3.1.3   The Concept of the User/Developer

Experienced clinical users are obviously the best people to write the user requirements document for a medical device. In an outsourcing scenario, the user requirements would be translated into a detailed functional specification by an external software company that may have a limited understanding of the operating environment, which is particularly true in a medical context. Communication errors often arise due to misunderstandings and incorrect assumptions, which can lead to significant problems later in the project. In contrast, when the users and developers are the same people (or, more accurately, the developers are a subset of users) such misunderstandings cannot arise, so the only issue (at this early stage of the development life cycle) is a purely technical one of faithfully translating the detailed user requirements into a functional specification/design.

In-house developed medical software is covered in MDR 17 (Section 6.3.11) but is not subject to all of its requirements. The regulations (Article 5.5) make clear which requirements do *not* apply to "devices, manufactured and used only within health institutions established in the Union", subject to various conditions. This has been referred to as the health institution exemption (HIE) by the UK MHRA, but this term is slightly misleading as it is only a partial exemption.

It has been suggested [19] that Article 5.5 may cause problems in some hospitals due to the phrase "manufactured *and* used" [emphasis added] in relation to the quality management system (QMS) requirement. As it stands, in addition to the QMS implemented by the staff who developed the software, the clinical department in which it is *used* must also operate under an "appropriate quality management system". Many clinical departments now operate under a recognised QMS, but this is something that needs to be considered prior to device release/clinical use. Also, if the finished software is transferred to staff in another department (within the same hospital/health institution) post-deployment surveillance and clinical follow-up must take place. This would apply, for example, if staff in a medical physics department produced an item of medical software for use by colleagues in radiology (i.e., a separately managed department).

2.3.2 POTENTIAL ISSUES

The fear of potential litigation, however remote the possibility, under medical device regulations or product liability legislation was a factor that caused something of a pause amongst in-house medical software developers during the early 2000s when the meaning of phrases such as "placing on the market" (in the old Medical Devices Directives) and the general regulatory position of standalone software was still to be clarified. Most of those issues have now been resolved, but some reservations remain. Some of the practical issues faced by small development teams, as is nearly always the case for in-house development within healthcare institutions, are discussed in Section 2.7.1.

2.4 ADVANTAGES AND DISADVANTAGES OF COMMERCIAL SOFTWARE

2.4.1 BENEFITS

The software will have been developed to a quality standard, as prescribed by EU, UK, or US medical device regulations.

Ongoing support and bug fixes (patches) are usually free, but full updates (containing new/improved features) are usually a cost option unless included in the annual maintenance contract.

There are no issues of legal liability for the user, *provided* that the software is used strictly in accordance with the manufacturer's instructions. For example, the wording in the user manual (Safety section) for General Electric's "Xeleris" nuclear medicine image processing system states that:

> The images and calculations provided by this system are intended as tools for the competent user. They are explicitly not to be regarded as a sole incontrovertible basis for clinical diagnosis. Users are encouraged to study the literature and reach their own professional conclusions regarding the clinical utility of the system. The skill, knowledge and experience of the users are the primary defences against misdiagnosis. The system is not designed to substitute for these defences. Use of the system as such a substitute is strictly prohibited. The user should be aware of the product specifications and of system accuracy and stability limitations. These limitations must be considered before making any decision based on quantitative values. In case of doubt, please consult your sales representative.

There may also be the possibility of undertaking a formal collaborative venture with a commercial manufacturer (Section 2.2.5).

2.4.2 POTENTIAL ISSUES

For business software, a COTS product is designed for a "mass market" where the number of potential purchasers runs into thousands or tens of thousands. In specialised areas of medical practice, the market is much smaller but software products are still designed to appeal to a wide user base. This may mean having to pay for features and functions that are not needed but will have to be paid for and installed. On the other hand, in-house designed ("custom") software will tend to be less "bloated" (i.e., more efficient) and only contain the required features.

To mitigate this issue, some commercial medical software is designed to be configurable (i.e., options within the program can be included or excluded, see Section 2.2.7) but the whole package must still be purchased. More complex customisation typically involves some degree of user programming (typically using a scripting language, see Section 2.2.1), which means that the discipline of regulated in-house software development will apply.

2.5　OTHER MEANS OF UPGRADING EXISTING SOFTWARE

There are a couple of easily overlooked methods for upgrading existing medical device software that do not involve any user programming or financial expenditure. First, a clinical department can still benefit from a software sharing scheme provided the medical device software in question is CE-marked and, second, a software change request can be submitted to the medical device manufacturer.

2.5.1 SHARING SOFTWARE DEVELOPED BY OTHER USERS

Historically, some medical equipment manufacturers provided a facility whereby user-written software could be "made available" to other users of their equipment by simply placing the program in a central "user library", to be downloaded and used by customers at their own risk. Such use would typically be covered by an "evaluation agreement", which was similar to the one used for the company's own pre-release software. Namely,

> The Recipient [user] understands that the Product has only been received preliminary testing and takes full responsibility for the use of the Product. [Company name] is therefore not liable for any damages resulting from incorrect results, diagnosis or loss of data arising from the use of the software.

Manufacturer-based user libraries started to disappear when it became clear (under the old EU Medical Device Directives) that sharing software with colleagues outside of the developer's own health establishment constituted a "placing on the market", which requires the software to be fully CE-marked in the EU (or UKCA-marked in the UK). As explained later, user-written software for purely in-house use does not have to be CE-marked (Section 6.3.12), but the rules change as soon as it is released to an outside party. A department that has gone to the lengths of achieving a

CE-mark for its user-written software will probably have the intention of sharing (or selling) it, so such software may become available in the future.

2.5.2 Submitting a Change Request to the Manufacturer

If a module within a purchased clinical software package no longer meets the user requirements, a "change request" can be made to the software supplier to redesign the program/module in the manner required. However, if the change requires a significant redesign (and therefore extensive retesting), the company will be reluctant to accept the request unless there is sufficient supporting demand from other users. As a result, it may take a long time to achieve the desired result, and users with the requisite skills may decide to undertake the project themselves in those circumstances.

This sort of "development request" may be considered an extension of simple bug reporting, where users notify the manufacturer about errors in the software. A successful conclusion to a change request does *not* constitute in-house development, but should at least be considered as a possible (and generally cost-free) initial means of addressing a perceived deficiency with existing commercial software.

2.6 PROFESSIONAL STANDARDS

The general lack of professionalism and professional standards has long been the subject of debate in the wider software development industry, most of which is unregulated.

Indeed, there is an apparent "disconnect" between academic institutions and other authorities trying to impose voluntary regulation on the software development industry. Many commercial software developers are largely self-taught and simply do not accept the need for formal entry qualifications. With giant software companies adopting the current business trend of de-emphasising academic qualifications in favour of proven skills/experience [20], the "computer programmer vs software engineer" debate is set to continue. However, the discussion is largely irrelevant in the world of medical devices as the application of software engineering standards is a mandatory requirement (Chapter 5).

2.6.1 Training and Formal Qualifications in Computer Science

EU MDR17 contains no specific requirements for the competency and training of staff engaged in medical device manufacturing, but Section 6.2 of harmonised standard ISO 13485:2016 (Section 5.2) requires that organisations (a) determine the necessary competence for personnel performing work affecting product quality and (b) provide training or take other actions to achieve or maintain the necessary competence.

The MDR is, however, quite specific about the training and qualification requirements for staff employed by notified bodies (Annex VII, 3.2), staff carrying out clinical investigations of medical devices (Article 62.6), and persons responsible for regulatory compliance (Section 6.3.7). Manufacturers must also keep *records* of staff training as these data are part of the information that must be supplied to notified bodies as part of QMS surveillance assessment (Annex IX, Section 3.2).

Staff training is a regulatory requirement for medical device manufacturers in the US. 21 CFR 820.25 (subsection of the QSR) requires that personnel have the "necessary education, background, training and experience" to ensure that all activities required by the QSR are correctly performed. More specifically, each manufacturer must "establish procedures for identifying training needs and ensure that all personnel are trained to adequately perform their assigned responsibilities". More detail is available on the FDA's training requirements, plus a comparison with the human resources requirements of ISO 13485:2016 [21].

The lack of formal educational qualifications held by many programmers working in the wider (unregulated) IT industry is also true of most in-house software developers working in healthcare institutions. Those trained in the last 20 years will have probably covered some elements of software development in basic training, but this would have been insufficient to embark on medical software projects. As in the commercial world, many in-house developers have acquired their programming skills purely from experience over a long period of time. However, in-house medical software developers must work within a strict framework dictated by relevant national/regional regulations, so much of the activity is prescribed.

The standards and frameworks certainly represent a lot to learn, but this is well within the capabilities of scientific/technical staff with qualifications ranging from honours degree to PhD.

Some of the associated standards require familiarity with software engineering practice, but this does not equate to a university degree in software engineering. Nevertheless, it is hoped that software engineering and associated regulatory compliance will become more prominent components of postgraduate clinical scientist training in the future.

Knowledge of software engineering techniques amongst graduate scientists/engineers entering the medical physics/clinical engineering profession varies considerably. Most undergraduate physics/biomedical engineering courses will contain computer science modules, but course content varies. Also, Master's degree courses in medical physics tend to focus on the applications of ionising and non-ionising radiation in medicine. For new-entrant graduate trainees, there are various routes to gaining professional registration as a UK-qualified clinical scientist [22], the most common being completion of the three-year work-based Scientist Training Programme (STP) run by the UK National School of Healthcare Science [23].

The STP comprises 29 courses covering the different healthcare specialties, grouped under the headings of life sciences (e.g., clinical biochemistry, histopathology, cancer genomics), physical sciences (e.g., clinical engineering, nuclear medicine, clinical scientific computing) and physiological sciences (e.g., audiology, neurophysiology, urodynamics science) [24], but (since 2022) only trainees following the *Clinical Scientific Computing* (CSC) and *Clinical Bioinformatics Genomics* courses have received any training in software engineering [25].

It is, therefore, the responsibility of mainstream clinical departments such as nuclear medicine, radiology, and radiotherapy to facilitate and fund the training of clinical scientists engaged in the development of medical device software – as part of mandatory continuing professional development (CPD). This will usually be by the attendance of short courses organised by professional bodies and STP training centres [26], or by enrolling in online courses run by university computer science departments [27, 28].

At the next level of formalised in-service training, the European Federation of Organisations for Medical Physics (EFOMP) has defined a core curriculum for the postgraduate training of medical physicists wishing to become recognised as Medical Physics Experts (MPEs) in various sub-specialties. For example, the core curriculum (CC) for physicists working as MPEs in nuclear medicine requires a level of SE knowledge and skill that enables the candidate to "take responsibility for the development of new devices (including software) or modification of existing devices (including software) in response to clinical needs in Nuclear Medicine" [29].

At a national level, the UK Institute of Physics and Engineering in Medicine (IPEM) collaborated with the British Nuclear Medicine Society (BNMS) and the British Institute of Radiology (BIR) to produce a policy statement on "Medical Physics Expert Support for Nuclear Medicine" [30]. It includes a brief reference to the quality management of, and ongoing support for, clinical software used for patient data analysis but does not mention software development specifically.

However, a more recent (unpublished) UK report on scientific support to nuclear medicine lists the following amongst the core duties of the medical physicist:

- Provision of software for analysis of tests (possibly including in-house solutions); construction and review of clinical procedures and protocols; checking and reporting individual studies; liaison with referrers for troubleshooting; provision of reports of individual tests; carry out and support clinical audit
- Advise on procurement, implementation, and QA of advanced IT applications (particularly involving quantification and/or advanced image processing); Advice and troubleshoot issues associated with advanced IT applications; specification of bespoke software (including in-house programmes)

The corresponding EFOMP CC for physicists working as MPEs in radiotherapy departments contains the following statement under the heading of information and communication technology (ICT): "The MPE is also responsible for [the] safe (and legal) use of in-house developed software, in line with MDR"; the corresponding CC item being "GDPR and MDR, National regulations regarding the use of medical software, both developed in-house and commercially" [31].

The minimum qualification for the MPE programme is a B.Sc. degree in physics *and* an M.Sc. degree in Physics or Medical Physics. EFOMP assumes that candidates with these qualifications would have a "solid basis in computing and programming skills", but this is a questionable assumption.

However unlikely, it must be accepted that in the event of litigation resulting from a software medical device developed in-house, the first question asked by a claimant's lawyer would probably relate to the competency (i.e., formal qualifications and professional affiliations) of the person(s) writing and testing the software (see Chapter 7).

It is expected that medical staff will be increasingly involved in the development of medical apps, although how this will be controlled is currently uncertain. The level of computer literacy amongst people entering the medical profession (as for every other profession) is now significantly higher than it was 20 years ago, simply due to the massively increased exposure to computer technology at home, at school, and at university.

2.6.2 CURRENT LEVEL OF SOFTWARE DEVELOPMENT IN UK MEDICAL PHYSICS/CLINICAL ENGINEERING DEPARTMENTS

Medical physicists working in mainstream clinical specialties such as radiology, nuclear medicine, and radiotherapy have historically produced in-house medical software to supplement that available from commercial suppliers. Although the use of in-house developed software has reduced as the quality of commercial software has improved, a survey of 67 UK nuclear medicine centres conducted in 2019 showed that in-house software development still plays a crucial role in the maintenance of routine clinical services [32].

The survey confirmed that in-house developed software is still almost exclusively used for data analysis of quantitative *non*-imaging tests (e.g., measurement of GFR, plasma volume) but also showed that about 25% of imaging examinations requiring quantitative assessment were also processed using software developed in-house. Overall, it was reported that about 50% of all nuclear medicine exam types are quantified using in-house software in most UK centres.

In terms of software development processes, it was also reported that only 25% of the departments undertaking in-house software development/maintenance had a formal QMS in place. Of the remaining 75%, most centres quoted a lack of resources and/or a lack of knowledge in how to set up and maintain a software QMS. In Europe generally, there is still a significant amount of in-house development of medical software in diagnostic radiology [33].

Through its Scientific Computing Special Interest Group, the UK IPEM is attempting to raise the profile of scientific computing within medical physics and clinical engineering departments [34]. The first annual Clinical and Scientific Computing Symposium took place online in July 2022, with the aim of "establishing the current state of Scientific Computing as an IPEM discipline".

A recent trend in larger UK MP/CE departments is the establishment of scientific computing sections within departments such as Radiotherapy Physics, staffed by clinical scientists who have generally gone through the CSC STP training programme (or equivalent) and are dedicated to the development and use of *clinical* software in those areas. The extent to which this expertise can be shared with other clinical departments in need of scientific computing support is yet to be established. The factors driving the move to more centralised clinical computing in the UK include clinical scientist staffing shortages and the realisation of how much work is required to take a department from a position of producing ad-hoc software in an essentially uncontrolled environment to producing robust medical software to regulatory standards.

2.6.3 WHAT CAN HEALTH PROFESSIONALS BRING TO THE PROCESS?

Healthcare staff will typically exhibit a high level of professionalism, as working to mandatory professional standards is part and parcel of everyday working life. Most staff are also well used to dealing with safety-related issues and working in highly regulated environments. This type of knowledge and experience represents a good background for software development since it needs to be performed as a disciplined and well-documented activity. Most staff will also have useful relevant experience in managing complex medical equipment, project management, writing technical documentation (e.g., clinical procedures, laboratory procedures) as well as undertaking risk assessments for potentially hazardous aspects of their work.

Apart from relevant knowledge and skills, the main thing that healthcare professionals bring to the software development process is an intimate local knowledge of the clinical environment in which the software will be used. This includes detailed knowledge about potential users (hence training requirements) and how the results (i.e., software output) may be used in routine clinical practice. A commercial medical equipment manufacturer producing medical devices for a specialised area (e.g., Radiology) will have a good general idea about most of those things, but won't have a detailed knowledge of the local environment. This is not usually a problem for "general purpose" medical software (e.g., PACS software used in Radiology) but might be more of an issue for a more customised system. As previously stated, in-house development may be the *only* practical option if a commercially available system cannot be customised or modified to the required extent, or is simply not available.

2.7   JUSTIFICATION OF AN IN-HOUSE DEVELOPMENT PROJECT

Justification of each individual in-house medical device development project is required by Article 5.5 (c) of MDR 17 (Section 6.3.12), which states that:

> "The health institution justifies in its documentation that the target patient group's specific needs cannot be met, or cannot be met at the appropriate level of performance by an equivalent device available on the market". Article 5.5(d) adds that "The health institution provides information upon request on the use of such devices to its competent authority, which shall include a justification of their manufacturing, modification and use".

Justification of in-house development projects should be considered on a case-by-case basis, by reference to a written departmental policy on in-house software development. The policy needs to be kept up to date and should include sections on the general types of software projects undertaken as well as their size/complexity (Appendix 1). The ability to undertake such projects will clearly depend on the number and skill levels of the staff who may be involved, so the policy may state minimum staffing requirements for a project of a given size.

The policy will help determine whether a given software development project could be undertaken *in principle*, but the final decision should always be approved by senior departmental staff (perhaps after taking advice from the organisation's risk manager for large projects), based on the current clinical priorities within the department and the general strength of the staffing establishment.

The justification decision should be fully documented in the Project Assessment Report (PAR), regardless of the outcome. Also, if the proposal is rejected purely due to more important departmental priorities it may be possible to revisit it at some future date.

2.7.1 ISSUES FOR SMALL DEVELOPMENT TEAMS

The issues discussed here apply to in-house software development teams but some would equally apply to any small team trying to assess its capability to develop medical software to the standards required by European or US medical device regulations.

There are numerous formal staffing requirements embedded in the regulations themselves or the associated international standards, any one of which has the potential to represent a large "stumbling block" to a small in-house development team. Of course, regulations concerned with manufacturing are designed to produce a 'high barrier to entry' so in-house teams will need to organise themselves accordingly.

2.7.1.1 QMS Implementation

One of the biggest hurdles to be overcome is the establishment of a suitable QMS, which is almost certain to be ISO 13485:2016 (Section 5.2.1.5). Some large UK Medical Physics and Clinical Engineering departments have successfully implemented ISO 13485, but it requires a large amount of planning and dedicated resources. For example, a department that managed to obtain funding for a regulatory compliance post completed the implementation process in about 18 months [35].

Depending on department size, it may be possible to implement ISO 13485 using existing personnel, but it will take a lot longer if the staff concerned cannot be released from most of their other routine duties. In any event, the department will need to nominate a quality manager to oversee all the ISO 13485-related activities once certification has been achieved. In a large rehabilitation engineering department, this ongoing commitment was estimated at two full days per week [35], but would obviously be somewhat less for a much smaller development team producing or modifying a relatively small number of devices.

The only practical route for very small units is likely to be the formation of alliances with other departments impacted by the new medical device regulations, whereby an additional post may be justifiable if shared across several departments. This corresponds to the person responsible for best practice compliance discussed in Section 6.4.2.

The implementation of ISO 13485 involves some particular organisational challenges, the first of which is the need to identify "top management" and for those individuals to "ensure that responsibilities and authorities are defined, documented and communicated within the organization". There are further requirements under Section 6 of ISO 13485 concerned with the education, competence, and training of all staff directly involved with the production processes (Sections 2.6.1 and 5.2.1.2).

Another requirement of ISO 13485 is a mandatory internal audit of the QMS (Section 5.2.1.5), with Clause 8.2.4 specifying that "the selection of auditors and conduct of audits shall ensure objectivity and impartiality of the audit process" and that "auditors shall not audit their own work". This is an example where it may be worth in-house development teams collaborating with a neighbouring health institution, with a view to establishing a reciprocal arrangement for an "internal" audit of the respective quality management systems. Collaboration can also help facilitate independent code reviews, which not only represents the most effective way of finding bugs but is also a good method for spreading knowledge and good practice around the team [36].

These are some of the staffing issues arising purely from the implementation of ISO 13485. Further staffing and resource requirements are contained in ISO 14971 and IEC 62304 (Chapter 5), so gap analyses in respect of these standards play an important role in determining whether an organisation is prepared to invest the time, money, and effort in establishing a team structure that is capable of regulatory compliance (Sections 6.3.6.3 and 6.3.7).

A generic software engineering quality process standard (based on ISO/IEC 12207) has been developed for "very small entities" (VSEs); a VSE being defined as an organisation with less than 25 staff. The term "micro-enterprise" is used for organisations comprising less than nine staff, but even a (medical software development) team of this size would be considered large by most hospitals' standards. Nonetheless, the ISO TR 29110 standard (Chapter 5, A.1.3.13) has some useful ideas for "scaling down" international software engineering standards aimed at large organisations [37].

2.7.1.2   The Implications of Staff Leaving

Key staff leaving an organisation is usually disruptive in the short term but is particularly so in typically small development teams working in healthcare institutions. The anticipated completion date for ongoing projects will usually be adversely affected, and may even cause projects to be suspended indefinitely or cancelled. In very small organisations, the departure of a single experienced member of the team may even have an immediate effect on the viability of the team. Replacement of those software development skills is also likely to be an issue, at least in the short term, since recruitment to the vacant post may prioritise other core aspects of the job description that are unrelated to software development.

Pre-registration trainees can form part of the software development team (as supernumeraries) provided all their work is supervised and checked by a senior member of the team. Trainees completing the software engineering module of the STP programme (Section 2.6.1) need to complete small projects as well as undertake a programme of mentored learning.

The maintenance of in-house developed medical software is often an issue in clinical departments when the member(s) of staff who produced the software leaves. Sometimes due to poor documentation, but more often because the technical expertise required to maintain and develop the code is simply lost. In contrast, software maintenance provided by a commercial supplier is usually covered by a formal contract, in a similar way to the hardware, which will cover telephone support, response times, bug fixes, regular software updates, etc.

2.7.1.3   Dedicated Clinical Computing Posts

In recent years some large UK medical imaging departments have managed to create dedicated full-time posts for clinical data scientists, with person specifications typically referencing experience with Python, structured query language (SQL), and hypertext markup language (HTML). Although there are usually established professional links to scientific staff in other departments (e.g., medical physics, local university computer science department) these dedicated software development posts often report directly to a consultant radiologist. Due to the relative isolation of this type of post, the recent trend is towards the establishment of more centralised CSC departments associated with, or part of, MP/CE departments (Section 2.6.2).

2.7.1.4 Conflicts with Other Duties

While dedicated clinical computing posts are on the increase, software development tasks in clinical departments such as radiology and radiotherapy are often undertaken by clinical scientists who have a wide range of other clinical and technical responsibilities [38]. Staff authorised to undertake software development projects (Appendix 1) should have this clearly expressed in their job descriptions, but it will be difficult to put an accurate time commitment against it.

If estimated at all, this will simply be the "best guess" averaged over a whole year (e.g., 0.2 whole-time equivalents, WTE). The problem with software development, of course, is that the time commitment may be required in short bursts (or one long burst for a major project) with relatively little commitment in between. This activity is therefore unlike the other duties itemised in the job description, which will tend to be both routine and predictable.

If a relatively large project is undertaken, it may be necessary to release the required staff from some of their other routine duties, which may require adjustment to clinical work or other covering measures. It should also be borne in mind by the Head of Department that a software project is "never finished", as the release of version 1.0 is simply the first step of the post market process.

In general, software projects should be completed in the shortest possible time (i.e., a concerted effort by all those involved), so development staff should be released from their other duties to the maximum extent possible. An intense period of work will tend to produce a better end product than performing the same amount of work over a much longer period – simply due to the inherent nature of the software development process. If delays are allowed to occur between the different phases of the project, momentum will be lost and staff will waste time catching up on where they left off, which increases the chance of errors and results in more time being spent on bug fixing. It is thus a false economy to spread to work over a much longer period, but a focused effort requires the support of everyone in the department so there is a management task in "selling it" as a worthwhile venture.

In summary, in-house medical software development is never a cheap option when the full costs are considered, but it may be the only practical option if a specialised piece of software is required to fulfil an urgent local clinical need and/or capital funding is simply not available. Note that software developed locally to support a clinical research project is *not* covered by the EU medical device regulations (Section 6.3.4.7).

2.7.2 In-House Developed Vs Commercial Software

As a general rule, software should only be developed in-house if there is no commercially available product (Section 6.3.12). Even if the commercial software appears expensive, it is rarely cost-effective to develop an equivalent product in-house when all the costs are considered. And even if the software could be produced more cheaply, hospital management may not welcome the possible exposure to litigation (Chapter 7), which would tend to outweigh any modest cost savings. More importantly, commercial software will generally offer the type of technical support/upgrades that cannot be guaranteed from within publicly-funded health departments, where in-house software development may not be a core duty of the clinical/scientific staff undertaking it (Section 2.6.1).

Commercial medical software will be subject to the company's internal quality assurance programme and should be CE marked under the Medical Devices Regulations (Section 6.3). If also marketed in the US, the software will have gone through the equivalent FDA approval procedure (Section 6.5).

Situations in which in-house development may be considered include completely new clinical applications (where there is simply no commercially available product) and commercial products that are under development but have very long lead times (i.e., years). Patients are increasingly demanding access to leading-edge medical devices (especially medical apps) and may not be prepared to wait for a fully regulated product to become available [39]. This issue is of growing concern to medical device consultancy companies because getting a *finished* medical device approved for the market has become an increasingly lengthy and complicated process, sometimes adding up to two years to the overall product development time.

2.7.3 ASSESSING PROJECT SIZE

A key question for any software project is "how many person-hours – roughly – will it take and what will be the total duration of the project?" Even large commercial organisations are notoriously poor at estimating such things with any degree of accuracy, and for some it is still no more than an "educated guess". As previously stated, software development is extremely time-consuming, so estimating labour-intensive projects with many variables is difficult.

Formalised methods (e.g., functional size measurements, FSM) have been developed for sizing software projects but they are quite complex and require considerable expertise to implement [40]. More importantly, they generally require a system to be partially built before any reasonably accurate prediction of final size can be made. They are thus unsuitable for the situation in which a "reasonable estimate" needs to be made based on user requirements alone.

The implementation of formalised methods for software sizing may be justified by large commercial organisations undertaking very large projects (where significant over-runs could cost hundreds of thousands of dollars) but many are still searching for a simpler, more cost-effective way of estimating software size. Their usefulness for the type of in-house development described in this book is untried and unproven.

Most public-funded healthcare organisations will rely on size/cost estimations based on previous experience and an *outline* specification. The specification would include a top-level flow diagram to indicate the type and number of logical/functional elements required to implement the user requirements. An experienced development team should then be able to (roughly) estimate the amount of time required to perform the various stages of the software development life cycle. In this context, "experience" means referencing data on how long it took to develop previous software products in-house, which depends on recording accurate person-hours input to all such projects.

Depending on the accuracy of previous estimates, department management may wish to add an arbitrary percentage (i.e., "contingency") to cover unexpected problems or delays. Embarking on a new type of software development (e.g., using neural networks) would obviously make any size estimation more difficult, so including a larger contingency would seem prudent in those circumstances. Health establishments are not normally involved in competing for external software contracts so there is no significant downside to overestimation. The project would be finished earlier than expected, which would simply be seen as a benefit. These data would feed into the experiential database, providing more accurate size estimates for future projects.

Significant *underestimation* of a project's anticipated duration can have serious consequences for private companies with tight delivery schedules but can be managed more easily within a hospital-type environment. When (or before) the total allocated project time is reached, the projected overrun would be reviewed by senior staff, and the project either be allowed to continue at its current pace, allowed to continue at a reduced pace or suspended until such time that the required staffing resources could again be freed up.

It is crucial that, if approved, staff working on an in-house project accurately record their time input at the end of every day (organised and overseen by an appointed project manager), so that a comparison of estimated resources be compared to the actual figure at project "completion" (i.e., the point at which version 1 of the software is released). This helps determine the actual total cost of the project and also helps improve future estimates.

There are also useful checkpoints that can be used (by the project manager) whilst the project is in progress to determine whether the project is "on track" or not. For example, the time/resources needing to be spent on the separate phases of a typical software development project (almost regardless of type) is reasonably well established. Assuming, that is, that the relevant standards and guidelines are followed. According to these reference data, the combined user requirements and technical specification phases should typically consume about 15% of the total project time (TPT), so, if the TPT had been originally estimated at 500 person-hours, the project would be declared behind schedule if the two phases had taken more than 100 person-hours to complete. It is also useful to know, past on metrics from past projects, the amount of software engineering effort expended on each phase of a typical project [41], shown in Figure 2.4.

The total labour cost of the project must take into account the differing costs of employing the various staff involved, but "total person-hours" is an adequate measure for project monitoring purposes. Project management software (or a shared Excel spreadsheet) can help considerably with the recording of "time and motion" data.

2.7.4 Assessing Software Complexity

As mentioned in the *Introduction*, the management of ever-increasing software complexity is one of the current major challenges in software engineering, so attempting to predict (with any degree of accuracy) how complex a software project will become

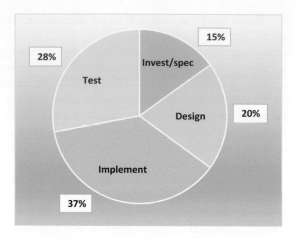

FIGURE 2.4 Typical amounts of software engineering effort (in-person-hours) expended during the main phases of the traditional software development life cycle (see text). Invest/spec: Investigation & specification.

(prior to any actual coding being performed) is a near-impossible task. The difficulty is generally proportional to project size, which is somewhat easier to estimate. A subjective estimate of complexity for a small software project will therefore be more reliable than for a very large one.

All quantitative measures are based on analysing constructed source code, so the methods are essentially retrospective. The alternative approach is to establish the *capability* of the department (according to an established model) and to decide whether the proposed project lies within those capabilities. In this regard, estimating the complexity of any proposed software is bound to be subjective but the accuracy will improve with experience.

Software capability models and associated *software complexity levels* (SCLs) were originally proposed as a means of either (a) grading software companies bidding for large government contracts [42] or (b) deciding the appropriate degree software engineering rigour to provide adequate quality assurance, but they may also be used in the general context of software complexity assessment.

Self-assessment of capability level is also subject to significant bias (how many departments would admit to their current development method being "chaotic"?) so established assessment methodologies should be employed. Clearly, given different capabilities levels, a proposed project graded as "simple" by a very experienced and highly skilled team of developers may be regarded as "complex" by another.

In summary, several factors need to be considered when attempting to predict software complexity from functional requirements.

- The quality/reliability of the functional requirements
- Estimated code volume
- Familiarity with the required programming tools and methods

- The need to incorporate new types of software technology (e.g., AI)
- Availability of key staff (especially the project manager) for the whole duration of the project

Software complexity is a difficult attribute to estimate in advance, but a department can at least establish the nature and type of software project that it would consider undertaking. The well-known phrase "complexity is the enemy of safety" is particularly apt for software-based systems and this is a key consideration in the risk-based justification decision process for in-house developed medical software.

2.7.5 COSTING

The true cost of the development should be estimated. This will mainly be the estimated time input (based on daily log books) of the respective members of the development teams (covering all aspects of the product life cycle) but should also include the cost of any new computer hardware and/or software development tools needed for the project. It should also include the time spent by prospective clinical users in setting/refining the user requirements, testing prototypes, checking the suitability of user documentation, and testing the finished product.

2.7.6 SUMMARY

It is rarely cost-effective to develop software in-house when a suitable commercial product is available. However, if, after careful consideration, a decision is made to proceed with an in-house software development project, the processes and procedures that need to be followed for regulatory compliance are described in Chapters 5 and 6. This guidance relates mainly to the 'writing software from scratch' option, in which case the user/developer takes responsibility for the whole project.

Appendix 1

An outline department policy on in-house medical software development

A department policy should include at least the following sections:

1. Roles and responsibilities

   This would include the person responsible for best practice compliance (PRBPC) if an organisation has more than one department engaged in the production of medical devices [43]. It would also include the person responsible for standards compliance (PRSC) in departments that have adopted national or international standards to support their development activities and regulatory obligations (see Chapter 5). In small CSC teams, individuals will usually have more than one role.

2. Staffing training and CPD

   To include Head of Section, Project Manager, development staff (software engineers), support staff (technical & administration), PRBPC/PRSC.

3. Adoption of best practice guides

   This should include an assessment of the relevant best practice guides (BPG) on in-house medical device manufacture and the rationale behind the one(s) adopted. BPGs may refer to different aspects of the overall development process. Any parts of the referenced BPG not adopted should be listed and justified. Other parts of this policy should refer to the adopted BPG(s) where appropriate.

4. Types of software project undertaken

   This will be dependent on local expertise, previous experience, and other factors. It may refer to the software safety classification levels in IEC 62304:2015 (Section 5.4.1.4).

5. Justification criteria

   To include assessment of available expertise and current staffing levels (ref: project type, size, and complexity) and assessment of existing commercial products (or products developed by other NHS departments) that may be suitable (Section 2.7.2).

6. Methods for estimating project size and complexity

   Based on detailed user requirements and outline software specification (Section 2.7.3)

7. Methods for estimating resources required to complete a project to the point of release
8. Project assessment report
An initial assessment by the appointed project manager, based on viability and potential usefulness of the project in clinical practice or research. The PAR should clearly state the outcome of the assessment. For example: (1) Not possible/appropriate (with reasons), (2) Not possible at this time but will be reviewed in x months, (3) Recommended for authorisation. The PAR may have to be elaborated into a full business case (according to the Trust's template) for large projects requiring additional resources.
9. Project authorisation
This section should describe the process by which the PAR is submitted for authorisation/sign off by senior department management and/or senior hospital management where appropriate.
10. Quality management and risk management procedures
11. House rules for software engineering
This section would refer to a separate software development procedure manual describing procedures to be followed for each project, including the following (non-exhaustive list):

- Software development process methodology (SDLC)
- Programming languages and tools
- Coding standards
- Use of open-source components and other SOUP
- Policy for re-use of previously developed code
- Configuration management (version control)
- Testing strategy
- Required documentation, including the Project Technical File

12. Collaboration with other Trust departments
13. Collaboration with centres and commercial organisations outside the Trust
14. Arrangements for user training and ongoing technical support
15. Arrangements for maintenance and surveillance
16. Participation in external audit schemes run by professional bodies
These schemes typically involve to use of test data to assist with clinical validation.
17. Arrangements for product registration with MHRA
This would be overseen by the PRBPC where appointed.

The Head of Department and, possibly, the Trust's Risk Manager should approve the policy. The issue of qualification and training is a difficult one because many excellent programmers are self-taught. However, such staff often lack awareness of the wider management issues involved in software development, and training should initially concentrate on these areas. Many such courses are available, but they are usually organised by non-NHS bodies (e.g., the British Computer Society) and can be costly.

REFERENCES

[1] "The big debate: Defining medical devices," *Scope,* vol. 29, no. 3, pp. 14–17, 2000.

[2] MHRA, "Software flowchart: Appendix 2 - Clinical calculators," 2020. [Online]. Available: https://assets.publishing.service.gov.uk/government/uploads/system/uploads/attachment_data/file/1103567/Appendix_2_-_clinical_calculators.pdf. [Accessed 12 September 2023].

[3] FDA, "Part 11, Electronic records; electronic signatures - scope and application," September 2003. [Online]. Available: https://www.fda.gov/regulatory-information/search-fda-guidance-documents/part-11-electronic-records-electronic-signatures-scope-and-application. [Accessed 14 September 2023].

[4] Johner Institute, "21 CFR Part 11: You should know these requirements," 6 June 2018. [Online]. Available: https://www.johner-institute.com/articles/regulatory-affairs/and-more/21-cfr-part-11/. [Accessed 12 September 2023].

[5] T. Phan, "Validation of electronic spreadsheets for complying with 21 CFR Part 11," *Pharmaceutical Technology,* Vol 27, No 1, pp. 50–62, January 2003.

[6] QIMacros, "21 CFR 11 compliance for the FDA," [Online]. Available: https://www.qimacros.com/support/21cfr11-compliance/. [Accessed 12 September 2023].

[7] N. Hrgarer, "A management approach to software validation requirements," in *Central European Conference on Information and Intelligent Systems (CECIIS)*, Varazdin, Croatia, 2008.

[8] Perficient, "The ultimate guide to CFR part 11," [Online]. Available: https://www.perficient.com/-/media/files/guide-pdf-links/the-ultimate-guide-to-21-cfr-part-11.pdf. [Accessed 12 September 2023].

[9] CSV Compliance, "Spreadsheet validation of 21 CFR Part 11," [Online]. Available: https://www.spreadsheetvalidation.com/. [Accessed 12 September 2023].

[10] Greenlight Guru, "CSA vs. CSV: Modern validation for modern MedTech," 7 July 2023. [Online]. Available: https://www.greenlight.guru/blog/computer-systems-validation-vs-computer-software-assurance-medtech. [Accessed 12 September 2023].

[11] European Commission, "Good manufacturing practice: Annex 11: Computerised systems," 30 June 2011. [Online]. Available: https://health.ec.europa.eu/system/files/2016-11/annex11_01-2011_en_0.pdf. [Accessed 12 September 2023].

[12] Florence Healthcare, "EU Annex 11: How to stay compliant," [Online]. Available: https://florencehc.com/blog-post/eu-annex-11-how-to-stay-compliant/. [Accessed 12 September 2023].

[13] FDA, "Is a new 510(k) required for a modification to the device?," 31 October 2017. [Online]. Available: https://www.fda.gov/medical-devices/premarket notification-510k/new-510k-required-modification-device. [Accessed 12 September 2023].

[14] FDA, "Deciding when to submit a 510(k) for a software change to an existing device," 25 October 2017. [Online]. Available: https://www.fda.gov/media/99785/download. [Accessed 12 September 2023].

[15] FDA, "Artificial intelligence and machine learning in software as a medical device," 22 September 2021. [Online]. Available: https://www.fda.gov/medical-devices/software-medical-device-samd/artificial-intelligence-and-machine-learning-software-medical-device. [Accessed 12 September 2023].

[16] University of Sheffield, UK, "Research software engineering," [Online]. Available: https://rse.shef.ac.uk/. [Accessed 13 September 2023].

[17] Mitratech, "Configuration vs customization – What's the difference and why does it matter?," 20 June 2017. [Online]. Available: https://mitratech.com/en_gb/resource-hub/blog/configuration-vs-customization-whats-difference-matter/. [Accessed 12 September 2023].

[18] Distillery, "In-house or outsourcing software development: A strategic guide," 29 October 2019. [Online]. Available: https://distillery.com/blog/in-house-or-outsourced-which-software-development-path-is-right-for-you/. [Accessed 12 September 2023].

[19] J. McCarthy, "MDR: The health institution exemption and MHRA draft guidelines," *Scope,* vol. 27, no. 3, pp. 24–27, 2018.

[20] S. Morrin, "Did you need a degree to land your job?," LinkedIn, July 2023. [Online]. Available: https://www.linkedin.com/posts/linkedin-news-uk_did-you-need-a-degree-to-land-your-job-activity-7097618976519704576-t-rV/. [Accessed 12 September 2023].

[21] T. Brown, "Ultimate guide to training management for medical device companies," Greenlight Guru, 7 February 2021. [Online]. Available: https://www.greenlight.guru/blog/training-management-medical-device. [Accessed 12 September 2023].

[22] IPEM, "Becoming a clinical scientist," [Online]. Available: https://www.ipem.ac.uk/your-career/getting-started-on-a-career-in-mpce/becoming-a-clinical-scientist/. [Accessed 10 September 2023].

[23] National School of Healthcare Science, "Scientists training programme," NHS England, [Online]. Available: https://nshcs.hee.nhs.uk/programmes/stp/. [Accessed 10 September 2023].

[24] National School of Healthcare Science, "Clinical scientific computing curriculum," NHS England, [Online]. Available: https://curriculumlibrary.nshcs.org.uk/stp/specialty/SBI1-2-22/#specialist-modules. [Accessed 10 September 2023].

[25] National School of Healthcare Science, "Software module S-BG-S2 curriculum," NHS England, [Online]. Available: https://curriculumlibrary.nshcs.org.uk/stp/module/S-BG-S2/. [Accessed 10 September 2023].

[26] Royal Surrey County Hospital, "STP computing in healthcare course," [Online]. Available: https://medphys.royalsurrey.nhs.uk/courses/ [Accessed 10 September 2023].

[27] University of Nottingham, "Software engineer online bootcamp," [Online]. Available: https://coding-bootcamps.nottingham.ac.uk/nott-software-engineering/. [Accessed 10 September 2023].

[28] Software Engineering Institute, "Courses," Carnegie Mellon University, [Online]. Available: https://www.sei.cmu.edu/education outreach/courses/index.cfm. [Accessed 10 September 2023].

[29] A. Del Guerra and M. Bardies, "Curriculum for education and training of medical physicists in nuclear medicine: Recommendations from the EANM Physics Committee, the EANM Dosimetry Committee and EFOMP," *European Journal of Medical Physics,* vol. 29, no. 2, pp. 139–162, 2013.

[30] L. Fraser, N. Parkar, K. Adamson et al, "Policy statement: Medical physics Expert support for nuclear medicine," IPEM, BIR, 2022. [Online]. Available: https://www.ipem.ac.uk/media/2wgox5uy/mpesup-2.pdf. [Accessed 10 September 2023].

[31] European Federation for Organisations for Medical Physics (EFOMP), "Core curriculum for medical physics experts in Radiotherapy (Revised 3rd Edition)," [Online]. Available: https://www.efomp.org/uploads/595e3c8a-52d9-440f-b50b-183c3a00cb00/Radiotherapy_cc_2022.pdf. [Accessed 10 September 2023].

[32] J. Price, M. Barnfield and J. Cullis, "Variation in software platforms including the use of in-house analysis in nuclear medicine – results from a UK survey (abstract)," *Nuclear Medicine Communications,* vol. 42, pp. 1162–1185, 2021.

[33] J. Helmenkamp, R. Bujila and G. Poludniowski, *Diagnostic Radiology Physics with MATLAB,* London: CRC Press, 2021.

[34] Institute of Physics and Engineering in Medicine, "Clinical and scientific computing special interest group," [Online]. Available: https://www.ipem.ac.uk/about/special-interest-groups/clinical-and-scientific-computing-group/. [Accessed 10 September 2023].

[35] L. Tasker and R. Nix, "Medical device regulatory compliance: Swansea's experience," *Scope,* vol. 33, no. 2, pp. 32–35, 2023.

[36] G. Wilson, D. Aruliah and C. Brown, "Best Practices for Scientific Computing," *PLoS Biology,* vol. 12, no. 1, 2014: e1001745.

[37] C. Laporte, R. O'Connor and L. García Paucar, "The implementation of ISO/ IEC 29110 software engineering standards and guides in very small entities," in *Evaluation of Novel Approaches to Software Engineering*, L. Maciaszek, Ed., Springer, Cham, 2015, pp. 162–179. [Online]. Available: https://link.springer.com/ chapter/10.1007/978-3-319-30243-0_9. [Accessed 25 November 2023].

[38] W. Tindale, P. Thornley and T. Nunan, "A survey of the role of the UK physicist in nuclear medicine: A report of a joint working group of the BIR, BNMS and IPEM," *Nuclear Medicine Communications,* vol. 24, no. 1, pp. 91–100, 2003.

[39] IPEM, "Why and how to regulate software in the healthcare setting - Part 1," 2022. [Online]. Available: https://www.ipem.ac.uk/resources/other-resources/webinars/ why-and-how-to-regulate-software-in-the-healthcare-setting-part-1/. [Accessed 10 September 2023].

[40] E. Ng'An'ga and I. Tonui, "A survey on software sizing for project estimation," *International Journal of Software Engineering,* vol. 5, no. 4, pp. 56–58, 2015.

[41] R. Grade and D. Caswell, "The need for tools," in *Software metrics: Establishing a Company-Wide Program*, New Jersey, Prentice-Hall, 1987, pp. 112–114.

[42] Wikipedia, "Capability maturity model," [Online]. Available: https://en.wikipedia.org/ wiki/Capability_Maturity_Model. [Accessed 10 September 2023].

[43] IPEM, "Best-practice guidance for the in-house manufacture of medical devices and non-medical devices, including software in both cases, for use within the same health institution," 25 July 2022. [Online]. Available: https://www.ipem.ac.uk/media/ vp0ewy01/ipembe-1.pdf. [Accessed 10 September 2023].

[44] H. Gislasen, "Excel vs. Google Sheets usage — nature and numbers," GRID, 28 August 2018. [Online]. Available: https://medium.grid.is/excel-vs-google-sheets-usage-nature-and-numbers-9dfa5d1cadbd. [Accessed 13 September 2023].

3 Types of Health Software

3.1 PREAMBLE

The purpose of this chapter is to describe and define what is meant by "health software", in preparation for the discussion of qualification and classification of medical device software in Chapter 6.

However, it is important to first explain some terminology that will be used later in the book. Digital health is the new all-embracing term for the application of information technology (IT) in healthcare, encompassing mobile health (mHealth), wearable devices, telehealth, telemedicine, and personalised medicine. Corresponding digital health *technologies* use computing platforms, software, connectivity, and sensors [1].

From a regulatory perspective, it is helpful to first consider "embedded" and "standalone" software since the "health" and "medical device" tags are applied later. Embedded software is an integral part of a hardware device (e.g., washing machine, infusion pump, fire alarm system, modern car) that runs on an embedded *system*. The software (often known as firmware) is typically specialised for a particular device and is usually designed for hardware control. It is essentially invisible to the user. In contrast, standalone software is software designed to run on general-purpose computers and workstations, where the presence of complex software is generally much more obvious.

Using terminology from EU MDR *guidelines,* software that meets the definition of a medical device is called medical device software (MDSW). Embedded software that meets the definition is called *software in a medical device* (SiMD), whereas qualifying standalone software is called *software as a medical device* (SaMD).

The term "health software" is now used as a general term to include *all* software used in a healthcare setting that could have an impact on an individual's health or general well-being. Health software is defined in IEC 82304-1:2016 (*Health software: general requirements for product safety*) as "software intended to be used specifically for managing, maintaining or improving the health of individual persons, or the delivery of care". By this definition, the health software spectrum is very wide, ranging from well-being apps aimed at lay people to safety-critical software controlling surgical robots.

The EU MDR does not use specific terminology such as "medical device software" or "software as a medical device", prompting the publication of guidance documents by regulators themselves, standards organisations, and other bodies involved in the regulatory process. For example, a guidance document published by the Medical Device Coordination Group (MDCG)[1] defines *medical device software* as "software that is intended to be used, alone or in combination, for a purpose as

---

[1] This is not an *official* EC document. However, the MDCG was specifically established by Article 103 of EU MDR 17 to produce approved guidance on the interpretation of the regulation.

DOI: 10.1201/9781003301202-3

specified in the definition of a 'medical device' in the MDR or IVDR, regardless of whether the software is independent or driving or influencing the use of a device" [2].

MDCG guide 2019–11 mainly discusses MDSW in general, referring to SaMD only briefly, in connection with the interpretation of classification Rule 11 in MDR 17.

Note that the US FDA tends to use the term "software function" instead of "software" and uses the term *device software functions* (instead of "medical device software") to describe software that meets the definition of [medical] "device" under Section 201(h) of the FD&C Act (Section 6.5.8.1). Device software functions (DSF) therefore include SiMD and SaMD. Qualification of software as *device software* is platform-independent, but the FDA uses the term "mobile medical app" (MMA) to describe software specifically designed to run on mobile devices (Section 6.5.8.5).

3.2   SOFTWARE AS A MEDICAL DEVICE

The term *software as a medical device* (SaMD) was first coined by the International Medical Device Regulators Forum (IMDRF), defined as "software intended to be used for one or more medical purposes that perform these purposes without being part of a hardware medical device"; a definition that has subsequently been widely adopted by medical device regulators worldwide.

In the context of medical devices, "standalone software"[2] and SaMD are effectively synonymous, so SaMD can be thought of as standalone software that meets the definition of a medical device. The FDA previously used the term "standalone medical device software" but has since adopted the IMDRF definition of SaMD [3].

The key point is that SaMD is a sub-class of *any* type of standalone health software, ranging from mobile apps to complex diagnostic or treatment software. However, the regulatory position of some types of standalone health software (including apps) in some jurisdictions is still in a state of flux, with some products previously deemed not to be medical devices now falling into the SaMD category.

3.2.1   RISK CATEGORISATION OF SaMD

The IMDRF's four-level risk categorisation framework for SaMD (usually referred to as SaMD N12) is based on the criticality of usage and the significance of the information provided [4].

The document's objective was to introduce a foundational approach, harmonise vocabulary, and address the challenges associated with SaMD. It was not intended to replace or modify existing regulatory classification schemes or requirements (Table 3.1).

Two factors are involved in the risk categorisation process:

1. The significance of the information provided by SaMD to the subsequent healthcare decision
2. The degree of criticality of the patient's healthcare condition

---

[2] As defined, for example, in MEDDEV 2.1/6.

TABLE 3.1

Assignment of SaMD risk category. Adapted with permission from the table provided on page 14 of the IMDRF SaMD guidance document [4], but with the significance scale reversed to produce a more conventional risk matrix. (Management = Clinical management)

Healthcare condition	Significance of information provided by SaMD		
	Inform management	Drive management	Treat or diagnose
Critical	2	3	4
Serious	1	2	3
Non-serious	1	1	2

The risk categories are expressed as "impact levels". That is, the level of impact of the SaMD output on an individual patient's clinical management or the wider potential impact on public health:

Category 1: Low impact
Category 2: Medium impact
Category 3: High impact
Category 4: Very high impact

Factor 1: Significance of the information provided
The significance of the information provided by the SaMD to clinical management is subdivided into three headings: *Inform, Drive,* and *Treat or Diagnose.*

To *inform* clinical management means that the SaMD output will (only) be used for providing options for diagnosis or treatment, or for aggregating data from relevant sources, based on the patient's symptoms, lifestyle, etc. Such information will not be used to trigger any immediate or short-term treatment of the patient.

To *drive* clinical management infers that the information provided by the SaMD will be used to aid in the diagnosis or treatment of disease. Specific examples include (a) triage systems to identify early signs of a disease or conditions (i.e., information that might be used to guide subsequent diagnostic or treatment interventions), (b) providing information support on the safe and effective use of medicinal products or other medical devices and (c) analysing relevant information to help predict the future risk of a disease or condition. SaMD systems that drive clinical management may thus be thought of as *high-level* clinical decision support (CDS) systems, which would typically include systems based on complex mathematical models and/or AI-based technology.

Information used to *treat or diagnose* is used to diagnose (or screen for) a disease or condition or to make immediate or short-term treatment decisions to manage the patient's illness.

Factor 2: Healthcare conditions
The 'healthcare situation or condition' in the IMDRF scheme describes the criticality of the clinical situation in which the SaMD is to be deployed. Three states are identified and defined: *critical, serious,* and *non-serious.*

Critical situations are those for which accurate and/or timely diagnosis or treatment action is vital to avoid death, long-term disability, or other serious deterioration in the health of an individual patient, or to mitigate the impact on public health. SaMD is used in a critical situation where (a) the type of disease or condition is life-threatening, (b) requires major therapeutic interventions, (c) is time-critical, where the patient population at risk is especially vulnerable to the disease (e.g., elderly people, infants), or (d) where the SaMD interpretation requires highly trained users.

Serious situations are those for which an accurate diagnosis or treatment is of vital importance to avoid unnecessary interventions (e.g., biopsy) or where timely interventions are important to mitigate long-term irreversible consequences on an individual patient's health condition or public health. SaMD is used in a serious condition when the (often curable) disease progression is moderate and does not require major therapeutic interventions. Moreover, any necessary interventions are not expected to be time-critical in order to avoid death, long-term disability, or other serious deterioration of health, thereby providing the medical practitioner with the opportunity to detect erroneous results/commendations. Also, where the intended target population is not vulnerable ("fragile" in IMDRF guidance) with respect to the disease or condition in question and the medical device is intended to be used by either specialised trained practitioners or lay people.[3]

Non-serious situations are those in which an accurate diagnosis and treatment are important but not critical for determining interventions to mitigate long-term irreversible consequences on an individual patient's health condition or public health. SaMD is used in a non-serious situation or condition when the type of disease or condition has a slow or predictable progression, can be effectively managed (even if incurable), or requires only minor therapeutic interventions that are generally non-invasive in nature.

As with risk matrices (see Chapter 4), there is an element of subjectivity associated with the assignment of variables such as "critical situation" and "serious situation" so external expert advice should always be sought where appropriate.

The IMDRF document provides several "worked examples" of SaMD that fall into each of the four categories. It also provides advice on various types of "environmental conditions" that may affect the operation of the SaMD, including purely technical considerations (e.g., hardware, network connections, information security) as well as human factors.

3.2.1.1 Adoption of IMDRF SAMD Framework Proposal by Regulatory Authorities

The IMDRF risk categorisation scheme for SaMD has been adopted by several national regulatory authorities. In the US, the FDA used it to refine its draft guidance on CDS software (Section 6.5.8.6), which includes a scheme similar to the EU MDR classification Rule 11 to categorise different types of SaMD [5]. MDCG guidance document 2019-11 provides information on how the IMDRF's SaMD categorisation scheme may be used for the risk classification of medical device software under MDR 17 [2].

---

[3] SaMD intended to be used by laypersons (e.g., patients) in a "serious situation or condition" (as defined above) without the support from specialised medical professionals, should be "upgraded" and treated as SaMD used in a *critical* situation.

TABLE 3.2

The degree of independent oversight required for SaMD in the various IMDRF risk categories, including reference to risk management and software engineering standards

Summary of controls		IMDRF SaMD risk category			
		Type I	Type II	Type III	Type IV
Risk management – ISO 14971		X	X	X	X
SDLC requirements – IEC 62304	Class A	X	X		
SDLC requirements – IEC 62304	Class B			X	
SDLC requirements – IEC 62304	Class C				X
Labelling the device		X	X	X	X
Clinical effectiveness					X
Clinical safety and performance				X	X
Clinical efficacy statement		X	X		
MDR 17 classification		IIa	IIa	IIb	III

In assessing the place of the IMDRF categorisation scheme within medical device regulation, it is important to distinguish between the proposed SaMD risk *categories* and SaMD *classification* under MDR 17 and other regulations. The MDR 17 *device* classification scheme is also risk-based, but the criteria are different. The IMDRF proposals contain a mapping of the IMDRF risk categories to the corresponding EU MDR 17 risk classes according to Rule 11 (Chapter 6).

The IMDRF categorisation scheme can also be used to establish the level of risk management and software engineering required to assure the safety and effectiveness of a device of each risk *type* (Table 3.2). However, this needs to be viewed against the actual regulatory requirements (Chapter 6).

3.3   SUBCLASSES OF HEALTH SOFTWARE

Health software may be classified either according to the type of hardware platform on which it operates (e.g., mobile app), its intended purpose (CDS, health and well-being software), the nature of the software (functional document), or the technology on which it depends (e.g., AI software). As a result, the subclasses are not mutually exclusive. For example, most clinical decision support software is implemented as a mobile app. Of the tens of thousands of "health-related software products", relatively few will be qualified as SaMD (Chapter 6).

3.3.1   MOBILE APPS

A mobile application ("app") is a software product designed to run on a mobile hardware platform, such as tablet computers, mobile phones, and wearable devices. Mobile apps are seen as an important vehicle for getting health advice directly to patients, especially in countries where access to primary care is difficult. A whole new area of healthcare has thus grown over the last ten years, referred to as "mHealth", and defined as "the use of mobile and wireless technologies for health" [6].

If a mobile app has a health-related application it may be variously described as a health app, a wellbeing app, a lifestyle app (or any combination thereof), or a medical app, depending on the intended use. A health app can only be described as SaMD if it meets the criteria for a medical device.

The vast majority of health apps are of the well-being/lifestyle variety, including the popular (Fitbit-type) activity trackers. It is unlikely that health apps of this type would be classified as MDSW, but apps designed to display and/or interpret radiological or pathological images on mobile phones almost certainly would be. The slightly different approaches being taken to the regulation of health apps by EU and US authorities are discussed in Chapter 6.

3.3.2   CDS Software

There is no universally accepted *definition* of a CDS system, but a description is provided by the MDCG: *computer-based tools which combine general medical information databases and algorithms with patient-specific data. They are intended to provide healthcare professionals (HCP) and/or users with recommendations for diagnosis, prognosis, monitoring, and treatment of individual patients* [2].

Within the medical profession, CDS software usually refers to tools to assist doctors in making clinical management decisions about their patients, with some definitions relating specifically to software "that improves physicians' adherence to a recommended guideline or process of care" [7]. More general descriptions of CDS systems state that they should be usable by "clinicians, patients and others" to inform decisions about healthcare [8].

The issue with CDS software, at least in terms of regulation, is that its scope is very wide, ranging from software that simply provides reference information (e.g., a software implementation of an established clinical guideline) to a fully AI-enabled application that makes an automatic diagnosis from some form of medical image. Other examples include order sets (e.g., recommended diagnostic tests for a particular set of symptoms) and individually tailored software designed to provide reminders and alerts about medication and other treatments. Software that simply monitors physical activity and/or makes lifestyle suggestions is considered separately under *health and well-being software* (Section 3.3.5).

Much of modern CDS software is designed to run as an app on a mobile device but CDS software may equally run on a general-purpose computer (PC) or a dedicated workstation. It increasingly utilises AI technology to make clinical management suggestions/recommendations based on a patient's symptoms, medical history, and demographic, so may be subject to different regulatory oversight than non-AI software (Sections 3.3.4 and 6.5.8.9).

3.3.2.1   International Perspective

The IMDRF proposal for a framework for risk categorisation of SaMD (Section 3.2.1) does not mention CDS software by name, but the "significance of the information provided by the SaMD to the healthcare decision" is one of the two key factors in deciding the risk category (Table 3.1). For CDS software, the information provided will usually fall within the "inform clinical management" category.

3.3.2.2 US Perspective

The uptake of CDS software has been particularly high in the US, with strong support coming from the Centres for Disease Control and Prevention (CDC) [9], the Agency for Healthcare Research and Quality (AHRQ) [8] and the Office of the National Coordinator for Health IT (ONC) [10]. A wide-ranging review of CDS was published under the auspices of the US National Academy of Medicine in 2017 [11]. The FDA issued guidance on how it intends to regulate CDS software in 2022 (Section 6.5.8.6).

3.3.2.3 EU perspective

EU MDR 17 makes no specific reference to CDS software, but the MDCG guideline on the qualification and classification of software under MDR 17 [2] describes CDS software as "computer-based tools that combine general medical information databases and algorithms with patient-specific data"; the stated purpose being to "provide healthcare professionals and/or users with recommendations for diagnosis, prognosis, monitoring and treatment of individual patients". As with US regulation, some types of CDS software will qualify as SaMD and some types will remain unregulated (Chapter 6).

3.3.2.4 UK Perspective

CDS software is briefly discussed under the heading "non-medical functions" (along with "monitors fitness/health/wellbeing" and "databases") in the MHRA's latest guidance on standalone software and apps [12]. Due to Brexit, the guidance still relates to the UK Medical Device Regulations 2002, which are based on the old EU Medical Device Directives. This guidance will be updated when new UK medical device regulations become law in 2025.

Existing MHRA guidance states that CDS software will generally only be considered a medical device if it "applies automated reasoning such as a simple calculation, an algorithm, or a more complex series of calculations". For example, dose calculations, symptom tracking, and recommendations based on established clinical guidelines. CDS software will *not* generally be considered a medical device if it only provides "reference information" to enable a healthcare professional to make a clinical decision, as the HCP will ultimately rely on his/her own knowledge/judgement.

However, if the software/app performs a calculation or interprets or interpolates data and the healthcare professional does not (or cannot) review the raw data, then this software may be considered a medical device. Apps are increasingly being used by clinicians who will rely on the outputs from this type of software and may not review the source/raw data.

3.3.3 SPREADSHEETS AND OTHER FUNCTIONAL DOCUMENTS

There is no question that custom-built spreadsheets qualify as software [13]. Furthermore, complex spreadsheets can be produced using only the built-in *functions* (i.e., without using the built-in programming language), so *all* spreadsheets with a medical purpose should be regarded as potential SaMD. With the addition of the new LAMBDA function (announced in January 2021), Microsoft Excel™ is now considered a Turing-complete language, which is one of the hallmarks of a fully-fledged programming language [14].

The UK MHRA includes spreadsheets in a category of software called a "functional document"[4] defined as "software that requires separate software to perform its function, which will often be a general-purpose application" [12]. A functional document is regarded in the same way as conventional software as far as device qualification is concerned; the first decision point in the MHRA flowchart is "Computer program *or* functional document?" Other types of functional documents include script-enabled portable document format (PDF) files and Interactive web pages.

Regulatory requirements for custom-made spreadsheet software that qualifies as a medical device are discussed in Section 2.2.

3.3.4   AI SOFTWARE

Health-related software that includes AI technology is usually described as AI-enabled (e.g., AI-enabled ECG analysis software). In this section, we briefly explain some of the basics of AI technology, a knowledge of which is important to understand current approaches to the regulation of such software.

Artificial intelligence can be defined as "the science and engineering of making intelligent machines, especially intelligent computer programs". Different AI techniques such as machine learning (ML) can be leveraged on large datasets to "learn" complex systems based on task-based training through a process of validation and feedback. The information "learned" from the data can then go on to inform clinical decisions, assist in and even provide a definitive clinical diagnosis.

AI-based medical devices present unique issues due to their complexity and the iterative and data-driven nature of their development. They can operate in a very abstract way, using multiple layers of analysis and neural networks. As such there is often little transparency in their operation, so the reasoning behind a particular decision or recommendation will not be readily apparent to clinicians, or patients – a characteristic feature that has particular significance in the classification of AI-enabled medical devices.

Data-driven ML systems can be generally divided into "locked" models and continuous learning models

- Systems using locked models are developed using training data and ML, which are then fixed so the core method and associated outputs do not change automatically.
- Systems using continuous learning (adaptive) models automatically update their internal algorithms (i.e., network weights, thresholds, etc.) and outputs when new data is found to improve the model.

---

[4] The term "functional document" is not used in EU MDR 17 (or associated MDGC guidance) or FDA guidance.

TABLE 3.3

The main differences between rules-based AI systems and data-driven ML systems. Adapted with permission from Figure 1 of BSI-AAMI white paper on *ML AI in Medical Devices* [15]

Rules-based AI systems	Data-driven/ML AI systems	
	Locked ML models	**Continuous learning/adaptive models**
• Mimic human behaviour-making decisions by applying static rules to arrive at predicable decisions.	• Neither the internal algorithms nor system outputs change automatically	• Utilise newly received data to test assumptions that underlie their operation in real-world use.
• Often visualised as a decision tree.		
• May be originally developed based on a set of rules provided by human experts or can be based on training data.	• Further ML can be implemented through external approval, or in a stepwise manner	• Programmed to automatically modify internal algorithms and update external outputs in response to improvements being identified.
• The logic used to make decisions is usually clear and reproducible.		

Note that the term 'locked' may also be used to describe any ML-enabled device that does not perform continuous learning, so a clarifying statement should always be included in technical documents (Table 3.3).

AI/ML-enabled medical device software is a sub-type of SaMD, but is afforded a special term – *AI as a medical device* (AIaMD) – due to its unique features.

With AIaMD regulation, there are all the usual software change controls that apply to conventional SaMD (specifics covered by IEC 62304), but with the added issue of ongoing monitoring and validation of an adaptive system.

The notion that approved/certified medical device software can subsequently change or adapt automatically "in the field" poses a significant problem to regulators and, as a result, somewhat different approaches are being taken to the regulation of AI-enabled health software in the EU, UK, and US (Chapter 6).

Appropriate standards for validation of AI systems are still to be developed so regulators are attempting to adapt existing medical device regulations in ways that will not stifle innovation (Chapter 9).

3.3.5 HEALTH AND WELL-BEING SOFTWARE

Health and wellbeing software tends to be thought of in terms of commonplace fitness and diet-related programs/devices, but the modern definition of a "health and wellness app" means that a growing percentage of "consumer health apps" may be qualified as medical devices. Indeed, apps targeting specific health conditions, including mental health, diabetes, and cardiovascular disease, now account for about half of the widely used apps [16]. FDA guidance on mobile apps (Section 6.5.8.5) provides several examples of what would be considered wellness and lifestyle apps in the US, most of which will be implemented as mobile apps.

In response to the huge number of health apps appearing in online app stores over recent years, many countries have set up schemes to evaluate their quality, resulting in a multitude of "approved app libraries" run by government agencies and private "app evaluation" companies [17].

ISO/TS 82304-2:2021 (Chapter 5, A.1.3.7) addresses the quality and reliability of health and wellness apps that are intended to be used by healthcare organisations and health app assessment organisations as a basis on which to recommend health apps to healthcare professionals and the general public.

The ISO *technical specification* defines a health and wellness app as an "app intended to be used specifically for managing, maintaining or improving the health of individual persons, or the delivery of care" – essentially the same definition as "health software" given IEC 82304-1:2016 with "app" replacing "software". Although the publication of ISO/TS 82304-2 has been welcomed, it has also received criticism from sections of the medical profession due to its focus on software design [18].

Compliance with the ISO TS is not considered sufficient to provide the required level of quality assurance, reliability and, particularly, usability, so other standards are being actively developed. In the UK, for example, a standard called DTAC (Digital Technology Assessment Criteria) has been developed by an IT branch of NHS England (Section 5.4.6).

App evaluation companies such as the Organisation for the Review of Health and Care Apps (ORCHA) typically use several standards (including ISO/TR 82304-2 and NHS DTAC) to compile comprehensive checklists of app "quality criteria". At the end of the assessment process, a score is assigned to each app in the library, with guidance on how scores should be interpreted [19].

3.3.6 NON-PRODUCT SOFTWARE (NPS)

NPS is defined as any software (in-house produced or purchased off-the-shelf) used in the design, development, and production of medical devices and software tools used to implement the quality system itself [20]. NPS software, by definition, does not meet the criteria for a medical device but needs to be validated for its intended use [20]. Sections 4.1.6, 6.3, 7.5.6, and 7.6 of ISO 13485:2016 are relevant and ISO 80002-2:2017 provides guidance on their application. Manufacturers of devices intended for the US market also need to comply with FDA 21 CFR 820.70(i) and 21 CFR Part 11 (Section 2.2.2.2).

REFERENCES

[1] Jama software, "The rapid rise of digital health technology- Challenges and keys to success," 22 November 2021. [Online]. Available: https://resources.jamasoftware.com/shared-content/the-rapid-rise-of-digital-health-technology-challenges-and-keys-to-success. [Accessed 10 September 2023].

[2] MDCG, "MDCG 2019-11. Guidance on qualification and classification of software in regulation (EU) 2017/745 – MDR and regulation (EU) 2017/746 – IVDR," October 2019. [Online]. Available: https://ec.europa.eu/docsroom/documents/37581. [Accessed 10 September 2023].

[3] FDA, "Software as a Medical Device (SaMD)," 4 December 2018. [Online]. Available: https://www.fda.gov/medical-devices/digital-health-center-excellence/software-medical-device-samd. [Accessed 8 September 2023].

[4] IMDRF, ""Software as a Medical Device": Possible framework for risk categorization and corresponding considerations," 18 September 2014. [Online]. Available: https://www.imdrf.org/sites/default/files/docs/imdrf/final/technical/imdrf-tech-140918-samd-framework-risk-categorization-141013.pdf. [Accessed 10 September 2023].

[5] Ropes and Gray, "FDA overhauls its draft guidance on Clinical Decision Support ("CDS") software," 7 October 2019. [Online]. Available: https://www.ropesgray.com/en/newsroom/alerts/2019/10/FDA-Overhauls-its-Draft-Guidance-on-Clinical-Decision-Support-CDS-Software. [Accessed 9 September 2023].

[6] S. Agarwal, A. LeFevre and L. Jaime, "Guidelines for reporting of health interventions using mobile phones: Mobile health (mHealth) evidence reporting and assessment (mERA) checklist," *British Medical Journal,* vol. 352, p. 1174, 2016.

[7] J. Kwan, L. Lo and J. Ferguson, "Computerised clinical decision support systems and absolute improvements in care: meta-analysis of controlled clinical trials," *British Medical Journal,* vol. 320, p. 3216, 2020.

[8] Agency for Healthcare Research and Quality, "Clinical decision support," June 2019. [Online]. Available: https://www.ahrq.gov/cpi/about/otherwebsites/clinical-decision-support/index.html. [Accessed 8 September 2023].

[9] Centers for Disease Control and Prevention, "What is clinical decision support?," 22 August 2022. [Online]. Available: https://www.cdc.gov/opioids/healthcare-admins/ehr/clinical-decision-support.html. [Accessed 8 September 2023].

[10] The Office of the National Coordinator for Health Information Technology (ONC), "Clinical decision support," [Online]. Available: https://www.healthit.gov/topic/safety/clinical-decision-support. [Accessed 8 September 2023].

[11] US National Academy of Medicine, "Clinical decision support," 2017. [Online]. Available: https://www.healthit.gov/sites/default/files/page/2018-04/Optimizing_Strategies_508.pdf. [Accessed 8 September 2023].

[12] MHRA, "Guidance: Medical device stand-alone software including apps (including IVDMDs)," 1 July 2023. [Online]. Available: https://www.gov.uk/government/publications/medical-devices-software-applications-apps. [Accessed 8 September 2023].

[13] Wikipedia, "Spreadsheet," [Online]. Available: https://en.wikipedia.org/wiki/Spreadsheet. [Accessed 8 September 2023].

[14] Visual Studio Magazine, "Microsoft's new programming language for Excel now Turing complete," [Online]. Available: https://visualstudiomagazine.com/articles/2021/01/27/excel-lambda.aspx. [Accessed 8 September 2023].

[15] BSI/AAMI, "Machine learning AI in medical devices: Adapting regulatory frameworks and standards to ensure safety and performance," 2020. [Online]. Available: https://www.ethos.co.im/wp-content/uploads/2020/11/MACHINE-LEARNING-AI-IN-MEDICAL-DEVICES-ADAPTING-REGULATORY-FRAMEWORKS-AND-STANDARDS-TO-ENSURE-SAFETY-AND-PERFORMANCE-2020-AAMI-and-BSI.pdf. [Accessed 10 September 2023].

[16] J. Diao, K. Venkatesh, M. Raza and J. Kvedar, "Multinational landscape of health app policy: Toward regulatory consensus on digital health," *NPJ Digital Medicine,* vol. 5, p. 61, 2022.

[17] FDA, "Device software functions including mobile medical applications," 29 September 2022. [Online]. Available: https://www.fda.gov/medical-devices/digital-health-center-excellence/device-software-functions-including-mobile-medical-applications. [Accessed 10 September 2023].

[18] D. Neal, T. Engelsma and J. Tan, "Limitations of the new ISO standard for health and wellness apps," *The Lancet Digital Health,* vol. 4, no. 2, pp. E80–E82, 2022.

[19] ORCHA, "Check your app against NHS DTAC," 17 February 2021. [Online]. Available: https://orchahealth.com/check-your-apps-against-dtac/. [Accessed 11 September 2023].

[20] OrielStat, "Medical device production, QMS and NPS software risk assessment, validation, and protocols," 25 May 2023. [Online]. Available: https://www.orielstat.com/blog/nps-non-product-software-risk-assessment/. [Accessed 10 September 2023].

4 Basic Concepts of Risk and Safety

"Safety doesn't happen by accident."

Anon

4.1 OVERVIEW

Risk management is a cornerstone of US and EU medical device regulations (see Chapter 6), so a clear understanding of the terminology is essential for successful compliance. However, such knowledge is assumed as key concepts such as "hazard" and "risk" are generally limited to one-sentence definitions, and some other terms used in the regulations are not defined. Furthermore, some terms that do not appear in the regulations themselves are important to the understanding of associated risk management standards, with ISO 14971:2019 (*Application of risk management to medical devices*) being the key reference standard for compliance with the risk management requirements of both EU and US medical device regulations. To understand how the various terms relate to each other, we briefly discuss the circumstances giving rise to the risk and a management process that aims to control it.

4.2 THE RELATIONSHIP BETWEEN HAZARD, RISK, AND HARM

The estimation of P_1 and P_2 in the context of medical device software is discussed in Section 5.4.1.8 (Figure 4.1).

4.3 THE RISK MANAGEMENT PROCESS

Viewed as a conventional project, the basic steps in the medical device risk management process are as follows (Figure 4.2):

1. Create a risk management plan (Section 4.4.10)
2. Perform risk management activities (e.g., risk estimation, risk evaluation)
3. Review the risk management outcomes and produce a report

ISO 14971:2019 elaborates the process into six steps and provides guidance on how each step should be performed. The detailed requirements of ISO 14971:2019 are covered in Section 5.3, but it is useful at this stage to illustrate the basic flow diagram (Figure 4.3) and the terminology.

DOI: 10.1201/9781003301202-4

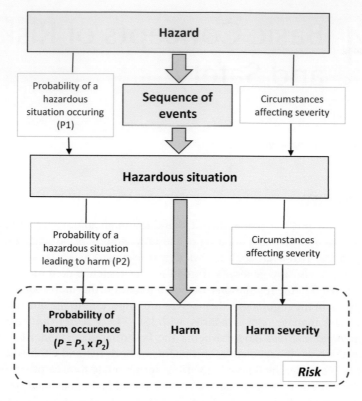

FIGURE 4.1 The relationship between hazard and harm. The thin arrows represent elements of risk analysis. Note that (a) a specific hazard may or may not lead to a hazardous situation and (b) that a hazardous situation may or may not lead to harm. Adapted with permission from Figure 1 of ISO Guide 63:2019.

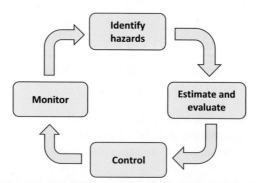

FIGURE 4.2 The risk management process. The "estimate and evaluate" step refers to risks associated with the identified hazards; "monitor" refers to monitoring the effectiveness of implemented risk control measures throughout the product life cycle.

FIGURE 4.3 The six main risk management process steps outlined in ISO 14971:2019. Adapted with permission from Figure 1 of BSI White Paper on *Risk management for medical devices and the new BS EN ISO 14971* (2022).

4.4   DEFINITIONS AND TERMINOLOGY

It is particularly important to understand the jargon and terminology used in risk management, as many common terms (e.g., risk, safety) do not have standard dictionary definitions. As a result, some terms are misused, leading to confusion and misunderstanding.

The format of each subsection comprises the term, the definition, the source of the definition, any *relevant* notes added to the definition, and a further explanatory comment where required. If the term is defined in Chapter I, Article 2 of MDR 17/745 then that definition is given; otherwise, the source is either an international standard or an academic reference.

4.4.1   SAFETY

Definition: Freedom from unacceptable risk.

Source: ISO Guide 63:2019. *Guide to the development and inclusion of aspects of safety in International Standards for medical devices.*

Comment: The general public understands the term "safe" to mean a state "free from harm or danger", but this standard dictionary definition is not applicable to medical devices. Even after the implementation of the most stringent production process, there will always be a residual risk (Section 4.4.21) associated with the use of a medical device, which means that there is no such thing as absolute safety in this context. The other key message from the health and safety world is that safety is a *systems* issue [1], so the term "software safety" is somewhat misleading.

In relation to medical devices, the word 'safe' should be used to indicate a state where the risks (of harm to patients or users) from recognised hazardous situations have been reduced to an acceptable level. It is therefore important to understand the precise meaning of the terms "hazardous situation", "risk", and, particularly, "acceptable risk".

4.4.2   HAZARD

Definition: a potential source of harm.

Source: ISO 14971:2019 (refers to ISO/IEC Guide 63).

Comment: This is effectively the standard dictionary definition. ISO 31000:2018 uses the term "risk sources" rather than "hazard" but these may be regarded as synonymous (Section 4.3.12).

4.4.3   HAZARDOUS SITUATION

Definition: a circumstance in which people, property, or the environment are exposed to one or more hazards.

Source: ISO 14971:2019 (refers to ISO/IEC Guide 63).

Comment: The expression "hazardous situation" is not used in the regulations themselves, but is very much a part of relevant ISO guides and ISO 14971. See Annex C of ISO 14971:2019 for further details on the relationship between "hazard" and "hazardous situation".

4.4.4   HARM

Definition: injury or damage to the health of people, or damage to property or the environment.

Source: ISO 14971:2019 (refers to ISO/IEC Guide 63).

Comment: The definition of harm used in the previous (2009) version of ISO 14971 referred to *physical* injury, but that has now been omitted, so "injury", by implication, now means either physical or mental injury. The Implantation Guidance (version 3.2) associated with the NHS Digital standard DCB0129 (Chapter 5, A.1.2.6) defines harm as "death, physical injury, psychological trauma and/or damage to the health or wellbeing of a patient". Other safety-related definitions used in the above UK standard are stated to be "broadly consistent with ISO 14971".

4.4.5   RISK

Definition: the combination of the probability of occurrence of harm (P) and the severity of that harm (S).

Source: MDR 17/745: Chapter I, Article 2 (23).

Comment: The word "combination" here is normally taken to mean [mathematical] product, so an attempt must be made to quantify or at least classify both the probability of occurrence and the severity of resultant harm (see Section 4.3.18, risk matrix). Annex D of ISO Technical Report 24971:2020 (Chapter 5, A.1.2.3) provides some useful guidance on risk analysis concepts, including risk estimation, but the medical device manufacturer is free to use his own measures and descriptors as long as they are defined in the risk management plan (Section 4.4.10).

By definition, the probability of occurrence of harm, P, is composed of two separate probabilities: the probability that an identified hazard will lead to a hazardous situation (P_1) and the probability that the hazardous situation will lead to harm (P_2).

If P_1 and P_2 can be estimated, then $P = P_1*P_2$. However, in situations where only P_1 or P_2 can be estimated, it is conventional to set the unknown probability to unity, thus adopting a worst-case scenario. The risk estimate is then based on the severity and a conservative estimate of the probability of occurrence of harm. If neither P_1 nor P_2 can be confidently estimated then the risk must be based purely on the severity of harm (i.e., $P = 1$). The process used to assign values to the probability of occurrence of harm and the severity of that harm is called *risk estimation.*

It should be noted that as with "safety", this definition of "risk" is quite different from the standard dictionary meaning, which is generally defined purely in terms of probability: "the chance of injury, damage or loss".

ISO 31000:2018 (Risk Management – *Guidelines*) defines risk in a more abstract fashion ("effect of uncertainty on objectives") but this effectively represents a different way of looking at the same problem; the MDR 17 approach is event-orientated whilst the ISO 31000 approach is goal-orientated. A note attached to the ISO 31000 definition acknowledges that "risk is usually expressed in terms of *risk sources*, potential *events*, their consequences and their *likelihood*". Some have argued that the reference to 'objectives' in this definition enables a closer link between risk management and corporate governance [2] but we will adhere to the MDR 17 definition.

ISO Guide 63:2019 suggests that the term 'effective safety' be used to indicate that "a balance has been achieved [by the manufacturer] between the state where risks have been reduced to an acceptable level and the product achieving its intended purpose". It also recommends that other uses of the word "safe" should be replaced, whenever possible, with an indication of the objective (e.g., "slip-resistant floor covering" rather than "safe floor covering")

The main *purpose* of risk management, expressed in Annex I of MDR 17, is to "reduce risks as far as possible" (AFAP), which means only taking measures that do not adversely affect the risk-benefit ratio (i.e., reduce the benefit). This phrase has officially replaced the ALARP (as low as reasonably practical) concept, but they mean effectively the same thing in practice, leading to the idea of acceptable or tolerable risk.

4.4.6 EVENT

Definition: occurrence or change of a particular set of circumstances.
  Source: ISO 31000:2018.
  Notes added to definition:

1. An event can be one or more occurrences and can have several causes and several consequences.
2. An event can also be something that is expected which does not happen, or something that is not expected which *does* happen.
3. An event can also be a risk source

Comment: Under this definition, "event" can be read as "unexpected event". According to ISO Guide 73:2009 (*Risk management vocabulary*), an event occurrence without [safety] consequences may be referred to as a "near-miss", "close call" or simply an "incident".

4.4.7   CONSEQUENCE

Definition: outcome of an event affecting objectives.
    Source: ISO Guide 73:2009- *Risk management vocabulary.*
    Notes added to definition:

1. An event can lead to a range of consequences.
2. A consequence can be certain or uncertain and can have positive or negative effects on objectives.
3. Consequences can be expressed qualitatively or quantitatively.
4. Initial consequences can escalate through knock-on effects.

4.4.8   LIKELIHOOD

Definition: the chance of something happening.
    Source: ISO Guide 73:2009- *Risk management vocabulary.*
    Notes added to definition:

1. the word "likelihood" is used here to refer to the chance of something happening, whether defined, measured, or determined objectively or subjectively, qualitatively, or quantitatively, and described using general terms or mathematically (such as a probability or a frequency over a given time period).
2. The English term "likelihood" does not have a direct equivalent in some languages; instead, the equivalent of the term "probability" is often used. However, in English, "probability" is often narrowly interpreted as a mathematical term (i.e., having a value between 0–1). Therefore, in risk management terminology, "likelihood" is used with the intent that it should have the same broad interpretation as the term "probability" has in many languages other than English.

4.4.9   RISK MANAGEMENT

Definition: the systematic application of management policies, procedures, and practices to the tasks of analysing, evaluating, controlling, and monitoring risk.
    Source: ISO 14971:2019 (refers to ISO/IEC Guide 63).

4.4.10   RISK MANAGEMENT PLAN (RMP)

Definition: a document that describes *how* your project's risk management process will be executed.
    Source: https://www.projectmanager.com/blog/risk-management-plan.
    Comment: ISO 14971:2019 specifies that the *RMP* contains at least the following:

a. the scope of the planned risk management activities, identifying and describing the medical device and the life cycle phases for which each element of the plan is applicable;
b. assignment of responsibilities and authorities;

c. requirements for review of risk management activities;
d. criteria for risk acceptability (Sections 4.3.12 and 4.3.21);
e. a method to evaluate the overall residual risk and the criteria for acceptability of the overall residual risk (Section 4.3.20);
f. verification activities; and
g. activities related to the collection and review of relevant production and
   post-production information.

Notes

1. Verification in (f) refers to both the "verification of the implementation of
   risk control measures" (i.e., completeness) *and* verification of the *effectiveness* of the control measures (ISO/TR 24971:2020, 4.4.7), so reference to the
   risk management review (Section 4.4.11) is appropriate.
2. ISO/TR 24971:2020 contains guidance on developing an RMP and on
   establishing criteria for risk acceptability. This ISO *Technical Report* also
   points out that the RMP requirements in ISO 14971:2019 represent a set
   of *minimum* requirements and adds that manufacturers may include other
   content, such as details of risk analysis tools, or a rationale for the choice
   of specific risk acceptability criteria. On a similar theme, it is stated (clause
   4.4.1) that "the extent of planned activities and the level of detail of the RMP
   should be commensurate with the level of risk associated with the medical
   device" – a particularly important point for most in-house medical software
   developers, who tend to produce low-risk applications.
3. All changes to the plan must be referenced in the RMF (using suitable
   change control notation) as compliance with ISO 14971 is initially checked
   by inspection of the risk management file (Section 4.4.12).
4. The RMP may be derived from a generic risk management procedure (typically covering different types of medical devices) if one exists [3]. The plan
   is bound to evolve and should be kept up to date, even after the finished
   product has been released.

4.4.11 RISK MANAGEMENT REVIEW (RMR)

Definition: a process to ensure that the RMP was properly executed.
   Source: "Risk management for medical devices and the new BS EN ISO 14971".
Medical device white paper series. British Standards Institute, 2020.
   Comment: The risk management review process is essentially one of assessing the
risk management activities undertaken against the RMP. The results of this review
are documented as the risk management report, which should contain a statement
about the acceptability of the overall residual risk. The risk management report
forms an important part of the risk management file.

4.4.12 RISK MANAGEMENT FILE (RMF)

Definition: a set of records and other documents that are produced by risk management.
   Source: ISO 14971:2019.

Comment: The RMF will refer to the RMP and the risk management review, and contain records plus evidence of risk analysis, risk evaluation, risk control, assessment of residual risk acceptability, as well as consideration of post-production risks [4].

The manufacturer is required to establish *and maintain* an RMF, which contains records and key documents (RMP, RMR) created throughout the life cycle of the device, from initial conception through to decommissioning and disposal. It should therefore contain evidence of risk analysis, risk evaluation, risk control, assessment of residual risk acceptability, as well as consideration of post-production risks

The individual clauses in ISO 14971:2019 specify which records and related documents are to be maintained as part of the RMF (Section 5.3.11). The RMF is a logical construct; it is not necessary that it physically contain the required records and documents as they may reasonably be stored elsewhere. However, it must be possible to assemble the required components in an efficient and timely fashion. The file itself can exist in printed or purely electronic form.

4.4.13 RISK CRITERIA

Definition: terms of reference against which the significance of a [particular] risk is evaluated.

Source: ISO Guide 73:2009- *Risk management vocabulary.*

Note added to definition: risk criteria are based on organisational objectives, and external and internal context (defined terms) and can be derived from standards, laws, policies, and other requirements.

Comment: The term is synonymous with "criteria for risk acceptability" (Section 4.4.22) used in ISO 14971:2019, described as "essential for [demonstrating the] ultimate effectiveness of the risk management process". Note that the standard *also* requires that medical device manufacturers establish criteria for the acceptability of the overall *residual* risk (Section 4.4.21). It is important to establish the criteria for risk acceptability *before* starting the risk assessment; otherwise, the outcome of the latter could unduly influence the former. For each RMP (Section 4.4.10), the manufacturer needs to establish risk acceptability criteria that are appropriate for the particular medical device.

ISO/TR 24971:2020 (Annex C.3) states that risk criteria should be based on the manufacturer's policy for determining acceptable risk, and include criteria for accepting risks when the probability of occurrence of harm (Section 4.4.8) cannot be estimated. The criteria for risk acceptability should be recorded in the RMP (Section 4.4.10). Specific criteria may be established for each type of medical device, dependent on its characteristics and intended use, or the same criteria may be applied to all medical devices. The criteria can include combinations of qualitative measures and quantitative limits for specific properties, preferably based on international standards. ISO Guide 63:2019 (*Guide to the development and inclusion of aspects of safety in International Standards for medical devices*) also lists some general factors to be considered when establishing risk criteria. Clearly, the criteria for acceptability of an estimated risk must be expressed in the same terms as that used to estimate it.

4.4.14   LEVEL OF RISK

Definition: the *magnitude* of a risk or combination of risks, expressed in terms of the combination of consequences and their likelihood.
Source: ISO Guide 73:2009- *Risk management vocabulary.*
Comment: In normal parlance, this would simply be referred to as "the risk". It may be estimated by the use of a risk matrix (Sections 4.4.19 and 4.5) or by other methods.

4.4.15   RISK ANALYSIS

Definition: the systematic use of available information to identify hazards and to estimate the risk.
Source: ISO 14971:2019 (refers to ISO/IEC Guide 63)

4.4.16   RISK ESTIMATION

Definition: the *process* used to assign values to the probability of occurrence of harm and the severity of that harm.
Source: ISO 14971:2019 (refers to ISO/IEC Guide 63).
Comment: Note the difference to "level of risk" (Section 4.4.14).

4.4.17   RISK EVALUATION

Definition: the process of comparing the estimated risk against given risk criteria to determine the acceptability of the risk.
Source: ISO 14971:2019 (refers to ISO/IEC Guide 63)

4.4.18   RISK ASSESSMENT

Definition: the overall process of risk analysis and risk evaluation.
Source: ISO 14971:2019 (refers to ISO Guide 51:2014).

4.4.19   RISK MATRIX

Definition: a tool for ranking and displaying risks by defining ranges for consequence and likelihood.
Source: ISO Guide 73:2009- *Risk management vocabulary.*
Comment: A somewhat more specific definition is given in IEC 31010:2019 (Chapter 5, A.1.2.1): "a means of combining qualitative or semi-quantitative ratings of consequence and probability to produce a level of risk (Section 4.4.14) or risk rating". The use of a risk matrix-type tool may be useful in risk estimation but is not obligatory. Beyond its basic definition, the subject of risk matrices is discussed further in Section 2.4, due to the widespread misunderstanding and confusion surrounding its use in risk evaluation.

4.4.20 Risk Control

Definition: a process in which decisions are made and measures implemented by which risks are reduced to, or maintained within, specified levels.

Source: ISO 14971:2019 (refers to ISO/IEC Guide 63).

4.4.21 Residual Risk

Definition: the risk remaining after risk control measures have been implemented.

Source: ISO 14971:2019 (refers to ISO/IEC Guide 63).

Comment: Clauses 7.4 and 8 of ISO 14971:2019 emphasise the need to evaluate residual risk. The standard also specifies that the manufacturer establishes defined criteria for the acceptability of the overall residual risk, which should be part of the RMP. The estimation of residual risk is a difficult procedure since it involves combining different individual risks associated with different hazardous situations.

The criteria used for the acceptability of individual risks usually include placing limits on the probability of occurrence of harm of a given severity. In contrast, the criteria used to evaluate the overall *residual* risk are often based on additional considerations, such as the clinical benefits of the intended use of the medical device. In short, there is no well-defined way of evaluating the overall residual risk. ISO 14971:2019 specifies that decisions about the acceptability of residual risk should be made by persons with the knowledge, experience, and authority to perform such tasks, but it is the responsibility of the manufacturer to establish an appropriate method. ISO/TR 24971:2020 (clause 8.2) provides some examples of how residual risk may be evaluated. Annex D.3 of the same document also provides information on the *disclosure* of residual risk to medical device users.

If the overall residual risk is not judged acceptable using the criteria established – and a further reduction in individual component risks is not possible or practicable – the manufacturer may gather clinical evidence data to determine if the medical benefits of the intended use outweigh this residual risk. If this evidence does not support this conclusion the manufacturer's only recourse is to modify the medical device or change its intended use.

4.4.22 Acceptable Risk

Definition: A level of risk that is accepted in a given context based on the current values of society.

Source: ISO Guide 51:2014. *Safety aspects – Guidelines for their inclusion in standards.*

Comment: the above is the definition of *tolerable risk*, but the term is stated to be synonymous with acceptable risk. Some safety organisations (e.g., HSE) make a subtle distinction between "acceptable risk" and "tolerable risk", but key ISO standards consider the terms synonymous. Safety is defined (Section 4.3.1) as "freedom from unacceptable risks", so a safe product has been produced when the associated risks have been reduced to an acceptable level. ISO Guide 51:2014 (*Safety aspects – Guidelines for their inclusion in standards*) contains additional information on tolerable risk.

ISO 14971:2019 (*Application of risk management to medical devices*) does not specify acceptable risk levels but does require manufacturers to establish objective criteria for risk acceptability (Section 4.4.13), based on the type and complexity of the medical device in question. A medical device with potentially high clinical benefits may therefore justify the acceptance of a higher level of risk than a device with lower benefits. The process of comparing the estimated risk (P*S) against previously established risk criteria to determine the acceptability of the estimated risk is called risk evaluation (Section 4.4.17).

Annex C of ISO 14971:2019 describes the relationship between the manufacturer's policy for determining acceptable risk (as defined by top management) and the criteria for risk acceptability based on that policy.

MDR 17/745 (Annex I, Chapter 1[8]) refers to acceptable risk as follows: "All known and foreseeable risks, and any undesirable side-effects, shall be minimised and be acceptable when weighed against the evaluated benefits to the patient and/or user arising from the achieved performance of the device during normal conditions of use".

ISO Guide 63:2019 (*Guide to the development and inclusion of aspects of safety in International Standards for medical devices*) lists the following methods for determining acceptable risk:

- use of applicable basic and group standards representing the generally acknowledged state of the art, and including requirements for the demonstration of acceptable risk, balanced towards clinical risk-to-benefit ratio;
- comparing levels of risk evident from medical devices already in use, being considered generally acknowledged state of the art;
- use of expert opinion;
- use of scientific research results, including clinical data;
- stakeholder concerns and societal expectations;
- applicable national or regional regulations (Figure 4.4).

4.4.23 BENEFIT

Definition: positive impact or desirable outcome of the use of a medical device on the health of an individual, or a positive impact on patient management or public health.

Source: ISO 14971:2019 (refers to ISO/IEC Guide 63)

Note added to definition: benefits can include positive impact on clinical outcome, the patient's quality of life, outcomes related to diagnosis, positive impact from diagnostic devices on clinical outcomes, or public health impact.

4.4.24 BENEFIT-RISK DETERMINATION

Definition: the analysis of all assessments of benefit and risk of possible relevance for the use of the device for the intended purpose, when used in accordance with the intended purpose given by the manufacturer.

Source: MDR 17/745: Chapter I, Article 2 (24).

Comment: The term is synonymous with benefit-risk analysis. Note that benefit-risk analysis does not yield a calculable ratio. There is no set formula for determining the correct balance, so this must be driven by the *intended use* of the medical device [3].

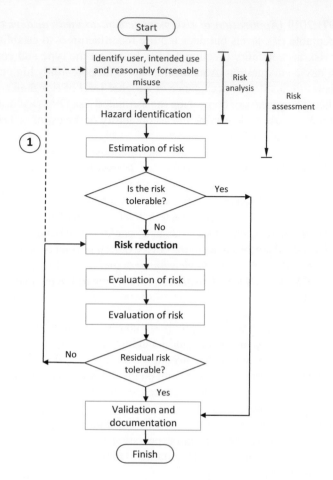

FIGURE 4.4 The iterative process of risk assessment and risk reduction, in the context of tolerable/acceptable risk (adapted with permission from Figure 2 of ISO Guide 51:2014). The dashed-line limb (1) is only relevant if the tolerable risk cannot be achieved by risk reduction (i.e., implementation of risk control measures).

4.4.25 LIFE CYCLE

Definition: all phases in the life of a medical device, from the initial conception to final decommissioning and disposal.

Source: ISO 14971:2019 (refers to ISO/IEC Guide 63).

4.4.26 STATE OF THE ART

Definition: developed stage of technical capability at a given time as regards products, processes, and services, based on the relevant consolidated findings of science, technology, and experience.

Source: ISO 14971:2019 (refers to ISO/IEC Guide 63).

Comment: The term is used extensively in MDR17 but is not defined. It embodies what is currently and generally accepted as good practice in technology and medicine. It does not necessarily imply the most technologically advanced solution. It is also sometimes referred to as the "generally acknowledged state of the art".

4.4.27 ALARP

Definition: as low as reasonably practicable.

Source: UK Health and Safety Executive (HSE).

https://www.hse.gov.uk/managing/theory/alarpglance.htm

Comment: Note the use of the word "practicable" rather than "practical", meaning "something that can be put into practice".

Although the ALARP concept has been replaced by AFAP (4.4.28) for medical device manufacture in Europe, it is still used in other jurisdictions. ALARP is a form of risk acceptance criteria that was developed by the UK Health and Safety Executive. It has two components: technical (risk reduction without affecting the effectiveness of the machine/equipment) and economic (ensuring that risk control measures do not make the equipment too costly to produce, and therefore too expensive for potential users to purchase) [3] (Figure 4.5).

Risks in the unacceptable (red) zone must be reduced to the point where they fall into the acceptable (or tolerable) zone. Risks in the tolerable zone must be reduced further *unless* the measures required to do so are either impractical or disproportionate (in terms of time, effort, and cost) to the risk reduction achievable. This is the essence of the ALARP concept, so this is also called the "ALARP zone". For risks initially classified as "broadly acceptable", no specific additional risk reduction measures are deemed necessary.

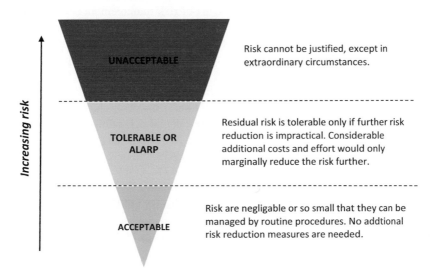

FIGURE 4.5 A typical "carrot diagram" illustrating risk classification using the ALARP principle, where the width of the triangle conveys increasing risk.

4.4.28 AFAP

Definition: as far as possible (i.e., without adversely impacting the benefit-risk ratio).
Source: MDR 17/745.

Comment: The regulation clarifies that reducing risks *as far as possible* (AFAP) means "without adversely impacting the benefit-risk ratio"; an approach that should take into account the generally acknowledged state of the art for the type of device/clinical application in question. In contrast to ALARP, the benefits refer only to clinical benefits and, in particular, that *all* risks should be reduced as far as possible.

The term "AFAP" has been around for a long time and guidance on its use was issued by the Notified Bodies Recommendation Group (NBRG) as far back as 2014, in relation to ISO 14971:2012 and the old EU Medical Devices Directive [5]. At that time ISO 14971 allowed the use of ALARP whilst the MDD stated that "... essential requirements require risks to be reduced as far as possible without there being room for economic considerations". The European Commission was concerned that the use of ALARP could lead to economic considerations overriding safety issues whilst, on the other hand, acknowledged that strict interpretation of the phrase "as far as possible" could mean "risk reduction without limits", resulting in very expensive devices that might no longer be affordable to potential users.

In response to the confusion, the report stated that "Although economic considerations will always be relevant in decision-making processes, the safety of the product must not be traded off against business perspectives", adding that "...the manufacturer must document the end-point criteria of risk reduction based on his risk policy". Although the statement was intended to offer Notified Bodies and manufacturers an interpretation of AFAP that was "clear, easy to understand and unambiguous" it still left room for debate. In general terms, a reasonable end-point may be the point at which all practical risk control measures have been implemented, reflecting the current state of the art of risk management and the intended application of the device. In that sense, the "spirit" of ALARP and ALARA (as low as reasonably achievable) can be incorporated into AFAP. As with many standards, provided that a method is cleared documented and adhered to, compliance will be achieved.

Although ISO 14971:2019 makes a passing reference to ALARP when describing the manufacturer's risk policy, Annex ZD (Note 1) makes it clear that, for compliance with EU MDR 17/745, risks should be reduced according to the wording of the contained General Safety and Performance Requirements (Section 6.3.2). Since MDR 17/745 does not mention ALARP (only AFAP), the new overarching risk control criteria for medical device producers in Europe is AFAP.

Medical device producers in the US should also adopt the AFAP approach to risk control (Section 6.5.7). The FDA has produced a useful guidance document on what it refers to as *patient-focused* benefit-risk assessment for medical devices [6], which recommends consideration of seven different aspects of *clinical* benefit (type, magnitude, likelihood, duration, patient perspective, caregiver perspective, and medical necessity).

4.4.29 INTENDED USE

Definition: use for which a product, process, or service is intended according to the specifications, instructions, and information provided by the manufacturer.

Source: ISO 14971:2019 (refers to ISO/IEC Guide 63).

Note added to definition: The intended medical indication, patient population, part of the body or type of tissue interacted with, user profile, use environment, and operating principle are typical elements of the intended use.

4.4.30 REASONABLY FORESEEABLE MISUSE

Definition: use of a product or system in a way not intended by the manufacturer, but which can result from readily predictable human behaviour.

Source: ISO 14971:2019 (refers to ISO/IEC Guide 63).

Notes added to definition:

1. Readily predictable human behaviour includes the behaviour of all types of users, e.g. lay and professional users [as appropriate].
2. Reasonably foreseeable misuse can be intentional or unintentional.

Comment: MDR 17/745 (Annex I, Chapter 1, 3c) requires the manufacturer to estimate and evaluate the risks associated with, and occurring during, the intended use and during reasonably foreseeable misuse. ISO 14971:2019 (Section 5.3.1) states that risk analysis of identified hazards should consider that medical devices may be used in situations other than those intended (so-called "off-label" uses). These requirements are in addition to what is normally understood as "user error" when a professional user operates the device incorrectly. For example, by accidentally pressing two buttons simultaneously (inadvertent misuse) or by randomly pressing keys on a keyboard (deliberate misuse).

It requires that the manufacturer attempts to "look into the future to see the hazards due to potential [unintended] uses of their medical device and also the reasonably foreseeable misuse". This is obviously difficult to predict but requires a statement to show that the potential problems have been given some consideration.

4.5 THE RISK MATRIX – FURTHER INFORMATION

Risk matrices are not mentioned in either MDR17, ISO 14971:2019, or ISO Guide 63:2019, but are discussed in ISO 24971:2020 (Chapter 5, A.1.2.3) and IEC 31010:2019 (Chapter 5, A.1.2.1).

4.5.1 GENERAL DISCUSSION

The term risk matrix has a defined meaning (Section 4.4.19) but variations can be found in the literature. Although often incorrectly referred to as a risk evaluation tool, the risk matrix is essentially a technique for *assigning* a level of risk (Section 4.3.13) to the outcomes of an (untoward) event [7]. Note that this is different from risk estimation (Section 4.4.16), which is concerned with determining the separate components of risk.

The risk matrix provides a means of *combining* these components to produce a risk level (see IEC 31010:2019). Although the graphical nature of risk matrices is appealing to those attempting to communicate risk issues to colleagues, there are some fundamental problems associated with them, especially if used in isolation [2].

A typical risk matrix is shown in Figure 4.6. It shows a mapping of the likelihood of harm occurrence against its severity, resulting in a "risk rating" that is used by management to guide action on risk reduction. The problem is that the assignment of risk ratings is subjective and has little if any scientific basis. Also, given the hard boundaries between the risk level categories, it is quite likely for the same risk to be rated differently by different observers.

Many variations on the risk matrix can be found in the literature, with matrix sizes varying from 3 × 3 to 6 × 6, and differing scales used for both likelihood and severity (Figure 4.7).

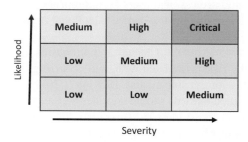

Medium	High	Critical
Low	Medium	High
Low	Low	Medium

Likelihood (vertical axis) → *Severity* (horizontal axis)

FIGURE 4.6 An example of a 3 × 3 risk matrix, with risk levels graded as low, medium, high, or critical, depending on the combination of the likelihood of the hazardous situation leading to harm and the severity of the consequence.

		1 Insignificant	2 Minor	3 Moderate	4 Major	5 Critical
1	Rare	3	4	5	4	5
2	Unlikely	2	4	6	8	10
3	Possible	3	6	9	12	15
4	Likely	4	8	12	16	20
5	Certain	5	10	15	20	25

FIGURE 4.7 A 5 × 5 risk matrix using numerical risk scoring.

4.5.2 RISK MATRICES IN THE CONTEXT OF MEDICAL DEVICE RISK MANAGEMENT

ISO 24971:2020 discusses risk matrices (as a development of risk charts) in the context of risk estimation (Section 5.5), evaluation of overall residual risk (Section 8.3), and risk control (Annex C.4). In Section 5.5.1 of the standard, it is simply stated that "if a risk chart or risk matrix is used for ranking risks, the particular risk chart or risk matrix and the interpretation used should be justified for that application" and (in Section 5.5.5) that "rationales for the selection of matrices and their outcome scores should be documented".

In the discussion of the *evaluation of overall residual risk* (Section 8.3), it is stated that "visual representations of the residual risks can be useful. Each individual residual risk can be shown in a risk chart or risk matrix giving a graphic view of the distribution of the risks. If many of the risks are in the higher severity regions or in the higher probability regions of the risk matrix then the distribution of the risks may indicate that the overall residual risk might *not* (emphasis added) be acceptable, even if each individual risk has been judged acceptable".

Several different *graphical* alternatives to risk matrices ("heat maps") have been suggested but most are subject to the same limitations. The use of *S-curves* is discussed in IEC 31010:2019 (Chapter 5, A.1.2.1) for situations where a risk has a *range* of consequence values, so can be plotted as a probability distribution.

Full quantitative risk assessment (QRA), as practiced in safety-critical process engineering [8], is beyond the scope and expertise of most medical device software manufacturers and would not, in any event, represent a cost-effective methodology. However, there is a "middle ground" occupied by semi-quantitative techniques that are simpler to learn /implement than fully quantitative methods, but offer improved objectivity over risk matrices [9].

REFERENCES

[1] F. Redmill, "Software in safety critical applications - A review of current issues," in *Safety critical systems: Current issues, techniques and standards*, London, Chapman and Hall, 1993, pp. 3–15.

[2] C. Peace, "The risk matrix: Uncertain results?," *Policy and Practice in Health and Safety,* vol. 15, no. 2, pp. 131–144, 2017.

[3] OrielStat, "How medical device risk management and ISO 14971:2019 work," 21 March 2023. [Online]. Available: https://www.orielstat.com/blog/iso-14971-risk-management-basics/. [Accessed 13 September 2023].

[4] Greenlight Guru, "ISO 14971 risk management for medical devices: The definitive guide," 11 May 2023. [Online]. Available: https://www.greenlight.guru/blog/iso-14971-risk-management. [Accessed 11 September 2023].

[5] Notified Bodies Recommendation Group, "Consensus paper for the interpretation and application of Annexes Z in EN ISO 14971:2012," 13 October 2014. [Online]. Available: http://www.team-nb.org/wp-content/uploads/2015/05/nbmeddocuments/NBRG_WG%20RM_Interim_NBmed_Consensus_Version_140812_1_1.pdf. [Accessed 8 September 2023].

[6] FDA, "Factors to consider regarding benefit-risk in medical device product availability, compliance, and enforcement decisions," 27 December 2016. [Online]. Available: https://www.fda.gov/files/medical%20devices/published/Factors-to-Consider-Regarding-Benefit-Risk-in-Medical-Device-Product-Availability--Compliance--and-Enforcement-

Decisions---Guidance-for-Industry-and-Food-and-Drug-Administration-Staff.pdf. [Accessed 11 September 2023].

[7] L. Cox, "What's wrong with risk matrices?," *Risk Analysis,* vol. 28, no. 2, pp. 497–512, 2008.

[8] Engineering Safety Consultants, "Quantitative Risk Assessment (QRA)," [Online]. Available: https://esc.uk.net/quantitative-risk-assessment/. [Accessed 14 September 2023].

[9] A. Sidorenko, "An alternative to risk matrices," Corporate Compliance Insights, 1 July 2019. [Online]. Available: https://www.corporatecomplianceinsights.com/alternative-risk-matrices/. [Accessed 12 September 2023].

5 Standards and Guidelines

"The good thing about standards is that there are so many to choose from"
Andrew Tanenbaum

5.1 OVERVIEW

Many international standards are relevant to medical device manufacture, but most are concerned with biological or electrical safety [1]. In this section, we discuss standards and guidelines that are relevant to the production of medical device software, based on the requirements for quality management, risk management, and software development contained in EU and US medical device regulations.

The relevant quality management standard is ISO 13485 (*Medical devices – quality management systems – requirements for regulatory purposes*), which applies to the manufacture of *all* medical devices. The associated risk management standard is ISO 14971 *Medical devices – Application of risk management to medical devices.*

ISO 13485 and ISO 14971 provide an essential management framework for medical software development but neither contains any specific information on software engineering practices. This is provided by IEC 62304 (*Medical devices software – life cycle processes*), which requires a knowledge of general quality management and risk management.

ISO 14791 and ISO 13485 are related because they are both designed to create a quality management system (QMS) that is risk-based. The focus of ISO 13485 is on quality and regulatory/user requirements, whereas ISO 14971 is concerned with safety, security, and risks associated with medical devices.

Other standards are important in the production of medical device software, but ISO 13485, ISO 14971, and IEC 62304 are *effectively* mandatory. The European ("EN") versions of ISO 13485 and ISO 14971 are harmonised standards under EU MDR 17/745 and IEC 62304 is expected to become harmonised in 2024 (Section 6.3.3).

In the US, ISO 14971 and IEC 62304 are both designated as *recognised consensus standards* in connection to the FDA's medical device regulation programme. ISO 13485 is not yet formally designated but the FDA has begun accepting ISO 13485 QMS audit reports from manufacturers under the Medical Device Single Audit Program (MDSAP), which is associated with the agency's proposed quality management system regulation (Section 6.5.6).

These main standards are discussed in the relevant sections below. However, for completeness, a more comprehensive list of standards that may be useful in the development of software medical devices is included in Appendix 1.

DOI: 10.1201/9781003301202-5

5.2   QUALITY MANAGEMENT

"Quality means doing it right when no one is looking".

Henry Ford

A QMS may be defined as "a formal system that documents the structure, processes, responsibilities and procedures required to achieve effective quality management". Such systems have become the cornerstone of many regulatory frameworks, including medical device regulations.

In principle, it is preferable to have a simple QMS that everyone understands and follows rather than a complicated system that only a select few understand, but medical device manufacturers have limited options in this regard as both EU and US medical device regulations prescribe very comprehensive systems (see Sections 6.3.8 and 6.5.6, respectively). It is possible to "start small" with a scalable QMS [2], but this requires careful coordination as the organisation develops.

Regulatory authorities make no distinction between very small and very large organisations, so the QMS requirements (at the point of seeking market approval) amount to a "one-size-fits-all" model. Although the EU MDR 17/745 regulations do not specify any particular QMS standard, many organisations have found from experience that implementation of ISO 13485 will ensure compliance with the QMS requirements of the regulations, so an expectation has developed amongst notified bodies that nearly all medical device manufacturers will follow this route. Furthermore, ISO 13485 is now a harmonised standard under MDR 17 (Section 6.3.7), which gives it special status. In summary, all medical device manufacturers, including those developing software for in-house use only, are advised to implement ISO 13485. The learning curve may be steep for departments with no experience with ISO 9001, but the effort will be beneficial in the long term and will make demonstrating compliance with MDR 17 relatively straightforward. The US *quality system regulation* (QSR) is quite flexible and is now aligned with ISO 13485 (Section 9.2.1).

Some organisations still use an ad-hoc QMS system – a combination of paper-based records, general-purpose software (e.g., MS Excel™, MS Sharepoint™, Google docs™, and Dropbox™) and a loose system of document control – but a single integrated system (eQMS) is preferable. Some are generic and support ISO 9001 (e.g., Q-Pulse™, Qualio™, MasterControl Quality Excellence™) while others (generally produced by medical device consultancies) are specific to medical device manufacturing and support ISO 13485 directly [3,4]. Organisations already using an IT system for general quality management may be able to adapt their procedures to accommodate the QMS requirements of MDR 17/ISO 13485.

As a logical extension of eQMS, a recent trend in the medical devices sector is the deployment of comprehensive Regulatory Information Management (RIM) systems, which have been used for many years in the pharmaceutical industry. RIM systems generally integrate existing commercial eQMS systems and add the necessary facilities required for interaction with the regulator (e.g., submission planning, UDI management, and product and registration tracking) [5].

5.2.1 ISO 13485. Medical Devices – Quality Management Systems – Requirements for Regulatory Purposes

Latest version of the standard: ISO 13485:2016
  Normative references: ISO 9000:2015

5.2.1.1 Overview

As its title suggests, ISO 13485:2016 is a quality management standard specifically developed for the medical devices sector, with an emphasis on regulatory compliance. It is based on the ISO 9001 generic quality management standard and has undergone significant changes since the previous edition in 2003.

A harmonised European version (EN ISO 13485:2016/A11:2021) was published in 2021 containing new annexes ZA and ZB, which provide a mapping between ISO 13485 and the quality management requirements of MDR 17/745 and MDR 17/746 respectively. Each Z Annex contains three tables detailing the relationship between the standard and the relevant parts of the regulations. Namely:

- The general obligations of the manufacturer described in Article 10
- The QMS requirements (Annex IX) on conformity assessment, based on a QMS and on assessment of technical documentation
- The QMS requirements (Annex XI) on conformity assessment, based on product conformity verification

Like the regulations it supports, the requirements of ISO 13485 are "applicable to organisations regardless of their size and type, except where explicitly stated".

5.2.1.2 Structure of EN ISO 13485:2016/A11:2021

The close relationship to ISO 9001 is evident from ISO 13485's emphasis on management responsibility and customer focus (Figure 5.1). As a result, several aspects of the standard (e.g., parts of Clauses 6, 7, and 8) are not relevant to software development, so do not need to be addressed. However, the quality manual (covered in Clause 4.2.2) should reference all standard clauses with a brief explanation of why a particular requirement (e.g., 6.4 contamination control) is *not* relevant. It is also possible to map some of the more abstract-sounding clauses to the more specific software requirements of IEC 62304 (Section 5.4.1.7).

5.2.1.3 Relationship to FDA QSR

Quality management requirements for medical device manufacturers intending to market their products in the US are described in the FDA's QSR; legally codified as CFR 21 Part 820. The current part 820 was introduced over 20 years ago and the FDA has recently proposed a move towards a more globally harmonised system based on ISO 13485. Unlike ISO 14971 and IEC 62304, the FDA has not previously designated ISO 13485 as a "recognised consensus standard", but the link between the two systems is set to become much closer. The proposed "adoption" of ISO 13485 by the FDA is discussed further in Section 9.2.1.

1. Scope

2. Normative references

3. Terms and definitions

4. Quality management system

    4.1 General requirements

    4.2 Documentation requirements

5. Management responsibility

    5.1 Management commitment

    5.2 Customer focus

    5.3 Quality policy

    5.4 Planning

    5.5 Responsibility, authority, and communication

    5.6 Management review

6. Resource management

    6.1 Provision of resources

    6.2 Human resources

    6.3 Infrastructure

    6.4 Work environment and contamination control

7. Product realisation

    7.1 Planning of product realisation

    7.2 Customer-related processes

    7.3 Design and development

    7.4 Purchasing

    7.5 Production and service provision

    7.6 Control of monitoring and measuring equipment

8. Measurement, analysis and improvement

    8.1 General

    8.2 Monitoring and measuring

    8.3 Control of non-conforming product

    8.4 Analysis of data

    8.5 Improvement

Annex A: Comparison of content between ISO 13485:2003 and ISO 13485:2016

Annex B: Correspondence between ISO 13485:2016 and ISO 9001:2015

Annex ZA: Relationship between this European standard and Regulation (EU) 2017/745.

Annex ZB: Relationship between this European standard and Regulation (EU) 2017/746.

FIGURE 5.1   The structure of ISO 13485:2016/A11:2021.

5.2.1.4   Relationship to ISO 9001

ISO 13485:2016 is based on ISO 9001:2008 (*Quality management systems –
Requirements*). It contains additional requirements relating to life cycle activities
while elements of ISO 9001 not relevant to regulatory compliance are omitted. The
clause mapping (given in Annex B) is to the latest (2015) version of ISO 9001, while
ISO 9000:2015 (*Quality management systems – Fundamentals and vocabulary*) is
also the only normative reference[1] for ISO 13485:2016. Due to the exclusions, organisations whose quality management systems conform (solely) to ISO 13485 cannot
claim conformity to ISO 9001.

5.2.1.5   Implementation

The implementation of ISO 13485 is best approached as a formal project, using
established project management principles and/or standards [6]. An initial gap analysis should reveal areas where work needs to be done prior to implementation [7].

A top-level project checklist for ISO 13485 implementation should include the
following:

1. Project initiation/preparation

   • Appoint a project manager and a small supporting implementation team
   • Do costings estimates depending on whether you intend to use external
     consultants or make use of available document templates

2. Obtain senior management support

   • Present a brief business case (using local corporate format) using the data
     obtained in step 1. Template project proposals are available online [8]

3. Identify the individual relevant requirements of the standard
4. Define and implement the processes and procedures necessary to meet the
   relevant requirements, including:

   • Quality Manual (Clause 4.2.1)
   • Document control procedure (Clause 4.2.4)
   • Internal audit procedure (Clause 8.2.4)
   • Procedure for corrective and preventative action (CAPA) (Clauses 8.5.2
     and 8.5.3)
   • Describe how the risk management requirements will be handled (i.e.,
     whether ISO 14971 will be used) within *Design and Development*

5. Undertake training of staff who will be involved with the implementation
   and evaluation of the QMS

   • This includes (initial) awareness training for all other staff in the organ-
     isation who will be involved with subsequent use of the QMS

---

[1] A normative reference is a document that is indispensable for the application of the standard.

6. Operate the QMS

- Use a planned software development project as a pilot scheme

7. Perform an internal audit
8. Perform the management review (Clause 5.6)
9. Choose a certification body

- A notified body (ref: EU MDR17) will perform an external audit of the QMS system as o part of the wider regulatory compliance audit

10. Perform certification audits

- Stage 1 certification audit
- Stage 2 certification audit

Further information on *how* to conduct these various activities can be found in the standard itself and in various online sources, some of which are free [8]. Full toolkits of document templates may also be purchased [9].

The standard (Clause 8.2.4) mandates that organisations carry out internal audits at "planned intervals" to ensure that their established QMS meets the requirements of the standard/applicable regulations, and is effectively maintained. ISO 13485 refers to ISO 19011 (*Guidelines for auditing management systems*), which contains a section on the evaluation and competence of auditors. Useful basic internal audit checklists can also be found online [10].

5.2.1.6   Reference to Software Development

ISO 13485 refers to software validation in connection with three distinct applications:

A: The quality management system itself (Clause 4.1.6)
B: Production and service provision (Clause 7.5.6 [g])
C: Monitoring and measuring equipment (Clause 7.6 [e])

The wording of the clauses is identical, apart from the insertion of the application type. Namely:

> The organization shall document procedures for the validation of the application of computer software used in [A/B/C]. Such software applications shall be validated prior to initial use and, as appropriate, after changes to such software or its application. The specific approach and activities associated with software validation and revalidation shall be proportionate to the risk associated with the use of the software. Records of such activities shall be maintained.

Clause 7.5.6 [e] (Production and service provision) applies to all medical device software manufacturers. Clause 7.6 [e] (Monitoring and measuring equipment) refers to equipment used to measure the *effectiveness* of the QMS, including the collection and analysis of field data designed to assess whether the product has met customer/ user requirements. Clause 4.1.6 (relating to the QMS itself) will be most relevant for organisations employing ad-hoc QM systems (Section 5.2).

The method used for software validation is not prescribed, but manufacturers adopting IEC 82304-1 (5.4.2) will be able to demonstrate compliance with Clauses 7.5.6 (g) and 7.6 (e). Guidance on the validation of software used in the QMS can be found in ISO/TR 80002-2: 2017 (*Medical device software – Part 2: Validation of software for medical device quality systems*). Useful background information on software validation can be found in the National Physical Laboratory (NPL) Best Practice Guide #1 [11].

5.2.2 QUALITY MANAGEMENT STANDARDS FOR UK CLINICAL DEPARTMENTS

This discussion is primarily aimed at UK NHS clinical departments that produce medical software, but it will be of interest to in-house developers in other countries that have similar clinical/technical accreditation schemes. In-house manufacturing and use (IHMU) is exempt from full compliance with MDR17 but departments must comply with all the general safety and performance requirements. One of the conditions of this exemption is that "the manufacture and use of devices occur under appropriate quality management systems" (Section 6.3.11).

BOX 5.1   ACCREDITATION AND CERTIFICATION.

These terms are closely related but have different meanings. *Certification* represents a third-party endorsement that an organisation's products or services meet specified requirements. *Accreditation*, on the other hand, represents confirmation by a recognised authority (i.e., an accreditation body) that an organisation has the competence to perform *specific technical activities* such as certification, inspection, and testing. Accreditation is thus an oversight role that "underpins the quality, impartiality, and competence of the certification process" [13].

An *accredited* certification body (e.g., BSI, Bureau Veritas) is an organisation that has been formally assessed by an accreditation body – usually a national government agency such as the UKAS. Simply put, accreditation legitimises certifications and certification legitimises the individual, organisation, product, or service. A company may quote that it is "accredited to ISO 9001", for example, but this generally means that it has achieved *accredited certification* to the standard.

Some of these departments will have historically achieved certification to ISO 9001 for their overall quality management, but the recent trend is towards specific accreditation schemes (Box 5.1) run by accreditation bodies. For example, some UK Medical Physics and Clinical Engineering (MPACE) departments have recently achieved *MPACE accreditation* in one or more sub-specialty areas through an audit process run by the UK Accreditation Service (UKAS) that involves assessment under BS 70000:2017 (*Medical physics, clinical engineering and associated scientific services in healthcare – Requirements for quality, safety, and competence*) [12].

This follows the establishment of similar UKAS accreditation schemes for Pathology Departments (ref: ISO 15189, *Medical laboratories. Requirements for quality and competence*), Radiology Departments (Quality Imaging Standard, QSI), and Physiological Measurement Departments (Improving Quality in Physiological Services Accreditation Scheme, IQIPS).

TABLE 5.1

Extract from a gap analysis between ISO 13485 and the UKAS Accredited Quality Standards for Imaging (QSI) Content from the QSI was reproduced with kind permission from the Royal College of Radiologists and College of Radiographers.

ISO 13485	QSI	Comments
4.2 Documentation requirements		
4.2.1 General		
The QMS documentation (see 4.2.4) shall include:		
a. documented statements of a quality policy and quality objectives;	A quality policy should define the service's quality objective and key performance indicators (KPI).	Partially met, need to include software processes in current documentation
b. a quality manual;	A quality manual should be in place to describe the service's QMS.	Partially met, need to include software processes in current documentation
c. documented procedures and records required by this International Standard;	–	Not met. Review ISO 13485 for required documentation
d. documents, including records, determined by the organisation to be necessary to ensure the effective planning, operation, and control of its processes;	A document management system should be in place. All policies, procedures, guidelines, and formally issued instructions should comply with the *wider organisation's* document control policy; th.s should include but not be limited to: a. Review dates and use authorisation b. An agreed list of who can write, change, amend, approve, and issue protocols, procedures, and instructions. Standardisation of protocols should be in place across the service and the protocols should be part of a QMS.	Partially met, need to include software processes in current documentation
e. other documentation specified by applicable regulatory requirements.	The service can provide evidence of compliance with national regulations on the use of radioactive materials and radiopharmaceuticals.	Not met. Would need to review documentation required by the medical device regulations when operating under the in-house exemptions – defined in the GSPR (Annex I)

BS 70000 is a specific type of standard known as an *accreditation standard*, which requires compliance with a formal QMS equivalent to ISO 9001:2015. ISO 9000 and ISO 13485 are both given as normative references. A note in Section 4.3 of BS 70000 states that for medical device development, the QMS "should be consistent with BS EN ISO 13485 and BS EN ISO 14971". If the design and manufacture of medical devices constitute a part of a department's routine work, certification to ISO 13485 and ISO 14971 would therefore be the simplest way of meeting this requirement.

Clearly, those departments engaging in the production of medical device software will also need to implement a suitable software engineering standard equivalent to IEC 62304. The detailed requirements for UK MPACE departments undertaking medical software development are covered in Annex A of IPEM's *Guidance for health institutions on in-house manufacture and use, including software* [14].

UKAS is in discussion with MHRA regarding the suitability of BS 70000 accreditation in meeting Article 5.5 (the so-called *Health Institutions Exemption*, see Section 6.3.11) of the current EU Medical Device Regulations, presumably on the assumption that a similar exemption will appear in the forthcoming revision of the UK Medical Device Regulations [15].

For organisations accredited to quality management standards other than those recommended for SaMD development (e.g., QSI), a gap analysis should be performed to determine the key differences. It is likely that the requirements for such standards will significantly overlap with those required for medical device development, so duplication can be avoided. This is important for smaller departments that may find the task of starting a new accreditation process daunting.

As an example of this gap analysis process, Table 5.1 shows a mapping of general documentation requirements between ISO 13485 and the QSI. Where brief statements exist in the QSI, such as "a quality manual should be in place", users can refer to the ISO standard for the detailed requirements (e.g., ISO 13485 part 4.2.2: *Quality manual*). The gaps identified should be collated to inform the development and implementation of a QMS suitable for medical device software production, which could be viewed (in this example) as an extension of the existing QSI. A similar process can be undertaken for ISO 14971 (Section 5.3.1) and IEC 62304 (Section 5.4.1)

5.3 RISK MANAGEMENT

"The essence of risk management lies in maximising the areas where we have some control over the outcome while minimising the areas where we have absolutely no control over the outcome."[2]

Peter L. Bernstein

---

[2] From his book "Against the Gods: The Remarkable Story of Risk". John Wiley & Sons, 1998.

5.3.1 ISO 14971. Medical Devices – Application of Risk Management to Medical Devices

Latest version of the standard: ISO 14971:2019/A11:2021

Normative references: None

Note: The above 2021 addendum to ISO 14971:2019 was published to harmonise ISO 14971 with the 2017 EU medical device regulations. Annex ZA harmonised ISO 14971 with the EU MDR (2017/745) and Annex ZB harmonised ISO 14971 with the EU IVDR (2017/746).

5.3.1.1 Overview

In both EU and US medical device regulations, risk management is addressed within the context of the wider QMS. Although ISO 14971:2019 states that "risk management *can* be an integral part of a quality management system" it does not actually require the manufacturer to have a QMS in place. This is somewhat academic as medical device manufacturers are bound to implement a recognised QMS for other regulatory reasons. It is therefore natural to use the ISO 14971 framework to address the risk management requirements of ISO 13485. There are specific references to risk management in ISO 13485:2016 (design and development, overall product realisation) [2].

ISO 14971:2019 provides a framework methodology by which the essential components of risk can be managed. In brief, the standard describes *processes* for (a) identifying the hazards associated with medical devices, (b) assessing the corresponding risks, (c) controlling the risks where needed, and (d) monitoring the effectiveness of the risk control measures introduced. The focus of ISO 14971 is thus on *product* safety risks, not organisational and business risks. The standard requires manufacturers to establish objective criteria for risk acceptability but does not specify acceptable risk levels.

Risk management of medical devices can be problematic due to the sparsity of real-world data to accurately quantify risks, especially for new or novel devices. Although risk management should be data-driven, some estimations are inevitably involved. The manufacturer must therefore follow the steps outlined in ISO 14971 and justify to use of estimated risk values and scores where necessary (Figure 5.2).

The structure of ISO 14971 is shown in Figure 5.3. Compared to the 2012 version of the standard, the main body of the ISO 14971:2019 standard is surprisingly short, with only 18 pages plus 3 annexes. However, the reason is that many annexes from the 2012 revision have been moved into the accompanying guidance document ISO/TR 24971:2020 (A.1.2.3), which has grown to nearly 100 pages with 8 annexes.

5.3.1.2 Relationship to EU MDR 17/745 and US Medical Device Regulation

ISO 14971:2019 is a harmonised standard under MDR 17/745 so compliance confers a presumption of conformity with the risk management requirements of the regulations. Annex ZA of the harmonised version contains a table showing the mapping of ISO 14971 clauses to specific MDR 17/745 requirements (Section 6.3.9). Note

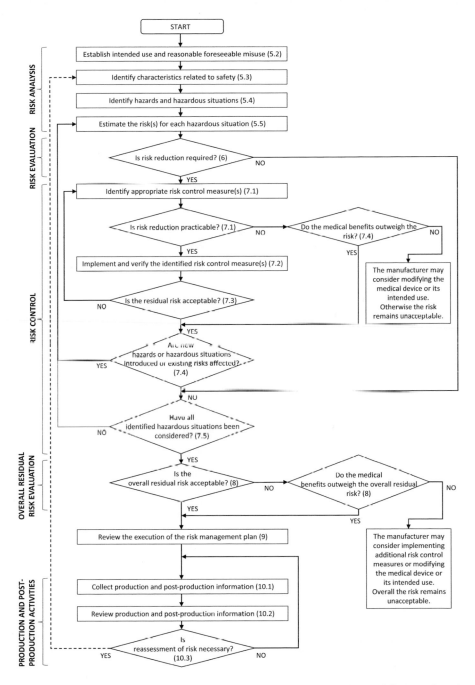

FIGURE 5.2 An overview of risk management activities applied to the manufacture of medical devices. Adapted with permission from Figure B.1 of ISO 14971:2019. Figures in brackets refer to clauses in ISO 14971. The activities covered need to go into the RMP (Clause 4.4, Section 4.4.10).

1. Scope

2. Normative references

3. Terms and definitions

4. General requirements for risk management system

    4.1 Risk management process

    4.2 Management responsibilities

    4.3 Competence of personnel

    4.4 Risk management plan

    4.5 Risk management file

5. Risk analysis

    5.1 Risk analysis process

    5.2 Intended use and reasonably foreseeable misuse

    5.3 Identification of hazards and hazardous situations

    5.4 Risk estimation

6. Risk evaluation

7. Risk control

    7.1 Risk control option analysis

    7.2 Implementation of risk control measures

    7.3 Residual risk evaluation

    7.4 Benefit-risk analysis

    7.5 Risks arising from risk control measures

    7.6 Completeness of risk control

8. Evaluation of overall residual risk

9. Risk management review

10. Production and post-production activities

    10.1 General

    10.2 Information collection

    10.3 Information review

    10.4 Actions

Annex A: Rational for requirements

Annex B: Risk management process for medical devices

Annex C: Fundamental risk concepts

Annex ZA: Relationship between this European standard and the GSPR requirements of Regulation (EU) 2017/745 (MDR)

Annex ZB: Relationship between this European standard and the GSPR requirements of Regulation (EU) 2017/746 (IVDR)

Bibliography

FIGURE 5.3   The structure of ISO 14971:2016/A11:2021

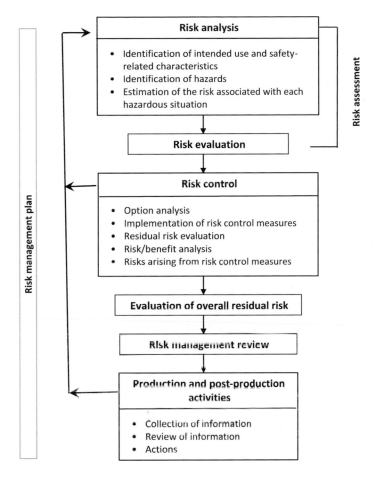

FIGURE 5.4   A schematic representation of the ISO 14971 risk management process (Clause 4.1). Adapted with permission from Figure 1 of ISO 14971:2019. A risk control measure (RCM) is simply an action taken to eliminate, prevent, or reduce the occurrence of an identified hazard.

that MDR 17/745 requires that risks be reduced 'as far as possible' (AFAP, Section 4.3.28), even though this is not a specific requirement of ISO 14971.

ISO 14971:2019 is also formally designated by the US FDA as a recognised consensus standard within the context of medical device regulation (Section 6.5.7).

5.3.1.3   Implementation of ISO 14971

This section describes the implementation of ISO 14971 itself. The use of ISO 14971 for meeting the risk management requirements of MDR 17/745 and the US medical device regulations is described in Sections 6.3.9 and 6.5.7 respectively.

The first thing to consider is how a department's risk management procedures fit within those of the parent organisation[3]. Management responsibility is a key component

---

[3] This assumes that medical software development is undertaken by a subsection of a larger organisation. For small start-ups, the development team may only have to consider their own risk policy.

of ISO 14971:2019 and it is made clear that *top management*[4] has the responsibility to (a) ensure the provision of adequate resources for conducting risk management activities, and (b) define and document a risk management policy describing criteria for risk acceptability.

Assuming top management 'buy-in', detailed procedures need to be produced describing how each of the four main processes in ISO 14971 will be addressed. One of the most important documents is the risk management plan (RMP), which includes details on how the plan itself, along with other key documents, will be reviewed and approved. Crucially, the criteria for risk acceptability must be defined (refer to the *organisational* risk management policy where appropriate), along with the methods used to verify the effectiveness of any risk control measures, and how information captured in post-production will the fed back into the risk management process.

Hazard identification should be based on the intended use of the device as well as "reasonably foreseeable misuse" (both terms are defined in ISO 14971), the latter requiring knowledge of the real-world environment in which the device will be used. The risks associated with any identified hazardous situations need to be assessed based on the probability that the hazardous situation will occur, the probability that the situation will lead to harm, and the potential severity of that harm. It is also useful to identify similar products already on the market (within the relevant jurisdiction) and attempt to obtain information on that device's risk profile (i.e., the sort of things that either have gone wrong or could go wrong, based on post-market information, product recalls, etc.). Even if there are similar products on the market, it is often difficult to estimate the overall risk with any accuracy, so reasonable estimates must be made and justified. The risk estimation steps are described in detail in ISO 14971:2019 and its accompanying technical report (ISO TR 24971:2020).

Annex A of ISO/TR 24971:2020 contains a list of questions/prompts designed to help the manufacturer identify basic safety characteristics and assist with preliminary hazard analysis in the design phase. Note that most of the questions are general and do not specifically address medical device software.

A score or value for 'severity of harm' (e.g., minor injury, major injury, death) must be assigned in order to estimate the overall risk. The effect can be viewed graphically by constructing a risk matrix, where individual combinations of probability and severity are assigned an appropriate risk action level. There is no mention of risk matrices in ISO 14971 (or ISO Guide 63:2019) but various guidance documents produced by standards organisations suggest how they might be used to satisfy some of the risk management requirements of the standard [16].

Risk matrices are also discussed in Annex C.5 of ISO TR 24971 in the context of risk evaluation, particularly for risks "for which no requirements or solutions in international standards exist".

Guidance on the application of ISO 14971 to medical device software is provided by IEC/TR 80002-1:2009. Although the TR refers to outdated versions of ISO 14971 and IEC 62304 (2007 and 2006, respectively) the report remains current and still offers good practical advice. Although the focus is on medical device software, the

---

[4] Defined as a person or group of people who directs and controls a manufacturer at the highest level.

report may be used to implement a risk management process for health-related software in general, regardless of whether it is classified as a medical device.

Annex B of IEC/TR 800002-1:2009 contains numerous examples of typical software hazards, so constitutes a helpful checklist. The common causes for hazards are grouped by software condition or function (e.g., data entry, user interface, shutdown) and are accompanied by a series of questions designed to prompt action. Suitable risk control measures are then suggested to eliminate or minimise the possible effects of the software hazards identified, which include algorithmic design measures and coding measures. Finally, the document provides advice on how to demonstrate the effectiveness of the selected risk control measures (i.e., verification testing), including different types of static and dynamic testing. It is emphasised that different types of tests be performed to ensure that the software continues to function (or fail-safe) under a range of conditions (including external interrupts such as power failure) rather than just focusing on requirement-based testing. The guidance also contains some basic advice in connection with "security" (mostly access control) but modern cybersecurity risks need more comprehensive controls (Chapter 8).

5.4   SOFTWARE ENGINEERING

"If builders built houses the way that programmers build programs, the first woodpecker that came along would destroy civilization."

Gerald M Weinberg

5.4.1   IEC 62304. MEDICAL DEVICES SOFTWARE – LIFE CYCLE PROCESSES

The latest version of the standard: IEC 62304:2006/AMD1:2015, referred to herein as IEC 62304:2015.

Normative references: ISO 14971

Note: when a normative reference is undated (as above), the latest edition of the referenced document (including any amendments) applies.

5.4.1.1   Overview

IEC 62304 (*Medical devices software – life cycle processes*) is a process standard that describes activities that occur as part of the software development life cycle. It applies whenever software is an integral part of a medical device (i.e., SiMD), is used in the production of the device, or is a medical device in its own right (i.e., SaMD). The wider topic of "health software", which includes health-related software not defined as a medical device, is covered in IEC 82304 (see below).

IEC 62304 is generally regarded as a medical sector derivative of IEC 61508 (*Functional safety of electrical/electronic/programmable electronic safety-related systems*), so shares some of its concepts of functional safety. It also makes extensive reference to ISO 12207:2017: *Systems and Software Engineering – Software Life Cycle Processes*.

It was developed from the perspective that a combination of a general medical device quality standard (i.e., ISO 13485) and end-product testing is insufficient to ensure patient safety in situations where complex software is involved. Most aspects of the software development life cycle are covered, but the main focus is on the design and maintenance phases.

The central theme of IEC 62304 is software *classification*, whereby medical software is grouped into one of three safety classes depending on the risk it presents to patients for whom it is intended to be used. The classification level then determines the degree of software engineering rigour to be applied to ensure an acceptable level of safety.

5.4.1.2   Structure and Scope of IEC 62304

IEC 62304 takes a classic "divide and conquer" approach to the issue of software complexity. It defines five high-level processes, each broken down into a set of activities, with each further broken down into one or more *tasks*.

A *software system* in IEC 62304 can be a sub-system of a traditional medical device or be a medical device in its own right (i.e., SaMD, see Section 3.2). It is composed of *software items* that, in turn, are composed of *software units*. The software unit is the lowest level of the hierarchy that cannot be further decomposed for the purposes of testing, etc.[5] (Figures 5.5 and 5.6).

1. Scope

2. Normative references

3. Terms and definitions

4. General requirements

    4.1 Quality management system

    4.2 Risk management

    4.3 Software safety classification

    4.4 Legacy software

5. Software development process

    5.1 Software development planning

    5.2 Software requirements analysis

    5.3 Software architectural design

    5.4 Software detailed design.

    5.5 Software unit implementation and verification

    5.6 Software integration and integration testing

    5.7 Software system testing

    5.8 Software release

6. Software maintenance process

7. Software risk management process

8. Software configuration management process

9. Software problem resolution process

Annexes

FIGURE 5.5   The structure of IEC 62304:2006 + AMD1:2015. For simplicity, only those activities associated with the software development process are shown.

---

[5] The definition of these terms was left deliberately vague to allow different software development methodologies to be used. IEC 62304 uses a V-model to explain the relationship between its component parts, but this is for illustrative purposes only.

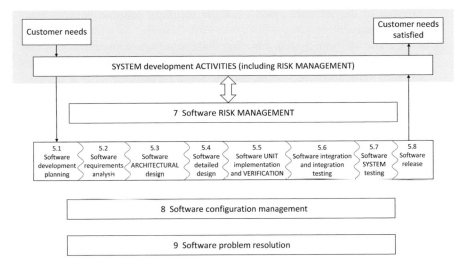

FIGURE 5.6 Overview of software development processes and activities described in IEC 62304:2006/AMD1:2015. Activities inside the grey shaded box are outside the scope of the standard. Adapted with permission from Figure 1 of the standard.

5.4.1.3 Relationship to EU MDR 17/745 and US Medical Device Regulations

ISO 62304:2006/AMD1:20015 has not yet been formally recognised as a harmonised standard under the EU MDR 17/745 but this is planned to occur by May 2024 (Section 6.3.3). It was adopted as a recognised consensus standard by the FDA in 2019 in relation to its regulation of medical device software [17] (Section 6.5.8.8).

ISO 62304 does not cover software validation so the EU MDR's general safety and performance requirements relating to software validation (of the finished software medical device) need to be addressed by reference to other standards or guidelines. For example, by the adoption of IEC 82304 (Section 5.4.2). The FDA has specific guidance covering the validation of medical device software [18].

Similarly, compliance with the MDR's cybersecurity requirements is aided by reference to IEC 8001-5-1:2021 (A.1.5.1), which constitutes a valuable supplement to IEC 62304 [19].

5.4.1.4 Software Safety Classification

Three software safety classes are defined according to the associated risk. The assignment of safety class for a particular software system (or item) is done by consideration of the potential severity of harm that could result from an identified hazardous situation and the risk acceptability.

Class A: This is the lowest class. Either (a) the software system cannot contribute to a hazardous situation, or (b) the software system can contribute to a hazardous situation which does not result in unacceptable risk after consideration of risk control measures external to the software system.

Class B: The software system can contribute to a hazardous situation which results in unacceptable risk after consideration of risk control measures external to the software system but the resulting possible harm is non-serious injury.

Class C: The software system can contribute to a hazardous situation which results in unacceptable risk after consideration of risk control measures external to the software system, and the resulting possible harm is death or serious injury.

These definitions of software safety classes are an improvement on the severity-only definitions found in the previous version of the standard, but the modifying criterion is acceptability, not the probability of occurrence. Also, the double-negative phraseology in the definition of Class A is confusing, so a simpler rule-of-thumb would be:

Class A: No risk or acceptable risk.
Class B: Unacceptable risk potentially leading to non-serious injury.
Class C: Unacceptable risk potentially leading to serious injury or death.

The classification scheme is shown in the form of a flowchart in Figure 5.7.

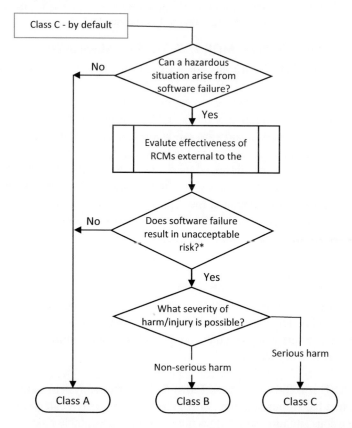

FIGURE 5.7   Software safety classification according to IEC 62304:2006 + AMD1:2015 (Adapted with permission from Figure 3 of IEC 62304).

Notes for Figure 5.7: In determining the *software safety classification*, the probability of a software failure shall be assumed to be unity,[6] so only risk control measures *external* to the software system shall be considered. Such risk control measures may reduce the probability that a software failure will cause harm, and/or the severity of that harm. Note that a software system that implements risk control measure(s) may fail, and this may contribute to a hazardous situation. Moreover, the resulting harm may include harm that the risk control measure is designed to prevent (Section 7.2.2b of IEC 62304).

The software safety classification of the system/item under consideration determines the processes and activities that need to be applied to achieve conformity with the standard. Clearly, the higher the software class, the greater the degree of software engineering rigour required to assure a similar level of safety. Some activities need to be applied to all classes of software, some only to classes B and C, and some only to class C. As a result, all IEC 62304 requirements apply to class C software, about 90% apply to class B and about 40% apply to class A. Table 5.2 shows the full mapping.

Related medical device classification schemes also use a risk-based approach, but IEC 62304's software safety classification system, the MDR's medical device classification system (Section 6.3.5), the IMDRF's SaMD risk categorisation system (Section 3.2.1) and the FDA's levels of concern were all developed independently of one another. Over time it is expected that these software classifications will become harmonised, including the replacement of the FDA's levels of concern with a simpler system (Section 6.5.3.4.2).

5.4.1.5 Version Control

Version control of individual software items (and the integrated product) is part of software configuration management. Tasks and activities that comprise the *software configuration management process* are described in Sections 5 and 8 of IEC 62304 (Figure 5.5).

In summary, information on configuration management to be included in the overall software development plan (SDP) should include a list of software items (or at least a list of the types of items) to be controlled, related activities and tasks, along with a clear indication of who is responsible for each activity. This software configuration plan should also indicate the circumstances in which the *problem resolution process* should be used.

For all software classes (A, B, C), there must be a formal scheme for the unique identification (e.g., version number) of the software items to be controlled. For SOUP items, this must also include the name of the item and the manufacturer (see *software bill of materials*, Sections 6.5.8.11 and 8.5.1).

At the system level, there should be a list of configuration items (i.e., those software items under configuration control) that comprise the software system. Clearly, this list (item name, version number) will grow as the system is developed.

Controlled software should only be changed in accordance with the change control procedure, which should describe the system for approving change requests, as

---

[6] Note that setting the probability of software failure to unity only relates to software safety classification; not to failure probability for risk management or other purposes.

TABLE 5.2
Summary of IEC 62304 requirements by safety class. Adapted with permission from Table A.1 of IEC 62304:2006. Clauses 4, 6, 8, and 9 are not broken down into their constituent sub-clauses as all the sub-clauses apply equally as indicated

Clause	Description	A	B	C
4	**General requirements (all)**	x	x	x
5	**Software development process**			
5.1	*Software development planning*			
5.1.1	SDP	x	x	x
5.1.2	Keep the software plan updated	x	x	x
5.1.3	SDP reference to system design and development	x	x	x
5.1.4	Software development standards, methods, and tools planning			x
5.1.5	Software integration and integration testing planning		x	x
5.1.6	Software verification planning	x	x	x
5.1.7	Software risk management planning	x	x	x
5.1.8	Documentation planning	x	x	x
5.1.9	Software configuration management planning	x	x	x
5.1.10	Supporting items to be controlled		x	x
5.1.11	Software configuration item control before verification		x	x
5.1.12	Identification and avoidance of common software defects		x	x
5.2	*Software requirements analysis*			
5.2.1	Define and document software requirements from system requirements	x	x	x
5.2.2	Software requirements content	x	x	x
5.2.3	Include RCMs in software requirements		x	x
5.2.4	Re-evaluate product risk analysis	x	x	x
5.2.5	Update system requirements	x	x	x
5.2.6	Verify software requirements	x	x	x
5.3	*Software architectural design*			
5.3.1	Transform software requirements into an architecture		x	x
5.3.2	Develop an architecture for the interfaces of software items		x	x
5.3.3	Specify functional and performance requirements of SOUP item		x	x
5.3.4	Specify system hardware and software required by SOUP item		x	x
5.3.5	Identify segregation necessary for risk control			x
5.3.6	Verify software architecture		x	x
5.4	*Software detailed design*			
5.4.1	Subdivide software into software units		x	x
5.4.2	Develop detailed design for each software unit			x
5.4.3	Develop detailed design for interfaces			x
5.4.4	Verify detailed design			x
5.5	*Software unit implementation*			
5.5.1	Implement each software unit	x	x	x

(Continued)

TABLE 5.2 (*Continued*)
Summary of IEC 62304 requirements by safety class. Adapted with permission from Table A.1 of IEC 62304:2006. Clauses 4, 6, 8, and 9 are not broken down into their constituent sub-clauses as all the sub-clauses apply equally as indicated

Clause	Description	A	B	C
5.5.2	Establish software unit verification process		x	x
5.5.3	Software unit acceptance criteria		x	x
5.5.4	Additional software unit acceptance criteria			x
5.5.5	Software unit verification		x	x
5.6	*Software integration and integration testing (all)*		x	x
5.7	*Software system testing (all)*	x	x	x
5.8	*Software release*			
5.8.1	Ensure software verification is complete	x	x	x
5.8.2	Document known residual anomalies	x	x	x
5.8.3	Evaluate known residual anomalies		x	x
5.8.4	Document released versions	x	x	x
5.8.5	Document on how released software was created		x	x
5.8.6	Ensure activities and tasks are complete		x	x
5.8.7	Archive software	x	x	x
5.8.8	Assure reliable delivery of released software	x	x	x
6	**Software maintenance process (all)**	x	x	x
7	**Software risk management process**			
7.1	Analysis of software contributing to hazardous situations		x	x
7.2	RCMs		x	x
7.3	Verification of RCMs		x	x
7.4.1	Analyse changes to health software with respect to safety	x	x	x
7.4.2	Analyse the impact of software changes on existing RCMs		x	x
7.4.3	Perform risk management activities based on analyses		x	x
8	**Software configuration management process (all)**	x	x	x
9	**Software problem resolution process (all)**	x	x	x

well as implementing and verifying the approved changes. The procedure should accommodate the various types of change requests received by members of the team or from the client/user. Bug fixes during the development stage should generally be dealt with using the problem resolution process described in Section 9 of the standard.

For significant design changes, a check should be made that the classification of the software has not been affected. Finally, there should also be a system for the tracking of changes, which can link the change request, problem report (if appropriate), and the implementation/verification of the approved change. This traceability requirement can be challenging for some software development platforms (Section 2.2.2.2) so is something that needs to be considered at the start of the project.

Configuration management is usually considered in connection with software items, but the same principles of change control apply to written documentation. However, the issue of "controlled documentation" is usually an integral part of any electronic QMS (Section 5.2).

The way in which change requests are generated and handled varies between software development methodologies (e.g., Waterfall or agile-based) but compliance with IEC 62304 is possible with either approach [20,21] (Section 5.4.1.12).

It is recommended that developers use some form of version control software (VCS) to automatically assign and keep track of version numbers. The Git open-source distributed VCS is commonly used for collaborative projects and is freely available under the GNU GPL version 2. The main use of Git is to manage source code, but it has other applications. If used with a central repository (not essential), the source code is hosted on GitHub (a cloud-based repository service) but all collaborators keep a local copy of the central repository, including its entire history [22]. Wang and Khopkar discuss version control systems, including Git, in the context of MATLAB® programming in radiology [23].

5.4.1.6   Software Partitioning

Software partitioning is a basic principle of software engineering that is embodied in IEC 62304. It provides for the segregation of system components with different safety classifications and allows more stringent code reviews and unit testing to be focused on the safety-related parts of the system. It is in the interests of the developer not to over-classify a software system as this will result in wasted effort/higher costs. Partitioning generally makes for a faster review process, ensures that code changes in one unit do not affect other units, and helps with certification.

Partitioning is advisable for Class B software but is mandatory for Class C (Table 5.2). The specific requirement (Clause 5.3.5) is that the manufacturer "identify any segregation between software items necessary for risk control and to state how to ensure that such segregation is effective".

All coding elements in the modular system shown in Figure 5.8 that could potentially result in hazardous situations that could lead to serious injury (or death) have

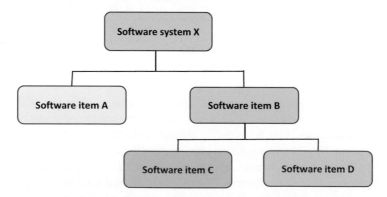

FIGURE 5.8   A software system (S) segregated into software items having different software safety classifications. Key: Pale green = Class A, Green = Class B, Orange = Class C. Adapted with permission from Figure B.1 in IEC 62304:2006/AMD1:2015

been segregated into item D, which is therefore designated software safety Class C. According to the inheritance condition specified in the standard (Clause 4.3d), software item B must therefore also be designated Class C. Similarly, the overall software system (X) will be classified as Class C since it contains at least one software item with a Class C designation. Software elements that, if they failed, could "only" lead to non-serious injury are placed in software item C and elements that could not lead to harm of any kind are placed in software item A.

5.4.1.7   Relationship to ISO 13485

It is a basic regulatory requirement (in the EU and the US) that medical devices (including software medical devices) are designed and manufactured in the context of a recognised QMS that has due regard to risk management.

IEC 62304 does not make a normative reference to ISO 13485, but compliance is the most straightforward way of complying with the QMS requirements of IEC 62304 [24]. It is therefore useful to relate the relevant requirements of IEC 62304 to those of ISO 13485 (Table 5.3).

TABLE 5.3

The correspondence between related clauses of IEC 62304:2006+AMD1:2015 and ISO 13485:2016. Adapted with permission from Table C.1 in IEC 62304:2006+AMD1:2015. Note that Table C.1 in IEC 62304:2006+AMD:2015 refers to the previous (2003) version of ISO 13485.

IEC 62304:2015 clause	Related clause of ISO 13485:2016
5. Software development process	
5.1 Software development planning	7.3.2 Design and development planning
5.2 Software requirements analysis	7.3.3 Design and development inputs
5.3 Software architectural design	
5.4 Software detailed design	
5.5 Software unit implementation	
5.6 Software integration and integration testing	
5.7 Software system testing	7.3.4 Design and development outputs 7.3.5 Design and development review
5.8 Software release	7.3.6 Design and development verification 7.3.7 Design and development validation
6. Software maintenance process	
6.1 Establish software maintenance plan	7.3.9 Control of design and development changes
6.2 Problem and modification analysis	
6.3 Modification implementation	7.3.6 Design and development verification 7.3.7 Design and development validation

(Continued)

TABLE 5.3 *(Continued)*
The correspondence between related clauses of IEC 62304:2006+AMD1:2015 and ISO 13485:2016. Adapted with permission from Table C.1 in IEC 62304:2006+AMD1:2015. Note that Table C.1 in IEC 62304:2006+AMD:2015 refers to the previous (2003) version of ISO 13485.

7. Software risk management process	
7.1 Analysis of software contributing to hazardous situations	
7.2 Risk control measures	
7.3 Verification of risk control measures	
7.4. Risk management of software changes	
8. Software configuration management process	
8.1 Configuration identification	7.5.8 Identification 7.5.9 Traceability
8.2 Change control	7.5.8 Identification 7.5.9 Traceability
8.3 Configuration status accounting	
9. Software problem resolution process	8.5.2 Corrective action 8.5.3 Preventative action

5.4.1.8   Relationship to ISO 14971

The risk management requirements of IEC 62304 are generally covered by a normative reference to ISO 14971; the correspondence between the clauses of the respective standards is shown in Table 5.4.

The information gleaned from the ISO 14971 risk management process (i.e., list of hazardous situations, associated risk control measures (RCM), harms, and severities) provides important input to the determination of the IEC 62304 software safety class. It is not necessary to perform separate additional procedures to collect information relevant to software safety classification. It can, and should, be done with the same information used to manage the overall risk of the product. Guidance on typical software-related risks is provided by IEC/TR 80002-1 (A.1.2.4).

Software risk management requirements of IEC 62304 are covered in Clause 7 (Section 5.4.1.2), which describes how software risk factors are managed, including those arising from software failure, software changes (including post-release upgrades and patches), user interaction and, of course, data protection and cybersecurity. The way that the separate risk management requirements of ISO 14971 may be integrated and aligned with IEC 62304 is shown in Figure 5.9.

As risk management continues into the post-release phases, the known risks continue to be monitored/refined and new risks may be identified. As a result, the software safety classification may need to be modified as the development cycle progresses.

Quantitative estimation of the probability of a specific software failure is generally difficult due to the variability of inputs, lack of historical data, and the complex

TABLE 5.4

The correspondence between related clauses of ISO 14971:2019 and IEC 62304:2006 + AMD1:2015. Adapted with permission from Table C.2 of IEC 62304:2006 + AMD1:2015, which refers to the previous (2007) edition of ISO 14971.

ISO 14971:2019 clause	IEC 62304:2006 + AMD1:2015 clause
5. Risk analysis	
5.1 Risk analysis process	
5.2 Intended use and reasonability foreseeable misuse	
5.4 Identification of hazards and hazardous situations	7.1 Analysis of software contributing to hazardous situations
5.5 Risk estimation	4.3 Software safety classification
6. Risk evaluation	
7. Risk control	
7.1 Risk control option analysis	7.2.1 Define RCMs
7.2 Implementation of RCMs	7.2.2 RCMs implemented in software
	7.3.1 Verify RCMs
7.3 Residual risk evaluation	
7.4 Benefit risk analysis	
7.5 Risks arising from RCMs	
7.6 Completeness of risk control	
8. Evaluation of overall residual risk	
9. Risk management review	7.3.3 Document traceability
10. Production and post-production activities	7.4 Risk management of software changes

nature of software. Therefore, the probability of software failure occurring should initially be set to 1. It is thereby assumed that if the software fails it does so catastrophically, thereby negating any software-based RCMs.

When assessing a *sequence* of events, the probability of other (non-software) events occurring can be used as the probability of the hazardous situation occurring (P1 in Figure 4.1). However, in many cases, it might not be possible to estimate the probability of the remaining events in the sequence, and the risk should then be evaluated based on the severity of harm alone (i.e., the overall probability of the hazardous situation *occurring* should be set to 1).

Estimates of the probability of a hazardous situation *leading to harm* (P2 in Figure 4.1) generally require system and clinical knowledge to take full account of mitigating factors external to the software. For example, the independent checking of a particular type of diagnostic image by a specialist clinical scientist and/or Radiologist prior to any decision being made about any further treatment of the patient – what the FDA refers to as "competent human intervention" (CHI) (Sections 6.2 and 6.3.6.4).

RCMs external to the software may thus include systems (separate hardware or software) as well as procedures performed by healthcare professionals that may

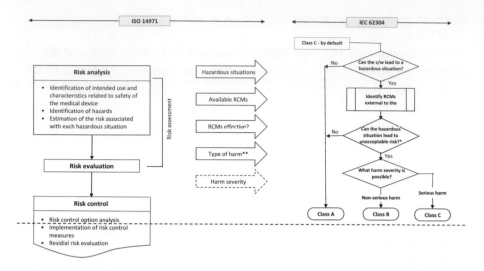

FIGURE 5.9 Integration of ISO 14971 practices with IEC 62304. Refer to Figures 5.4 and 5.7. Adapted with permission from Figure B.2 of IEC 62304:2006 + AMD1:2015). Key: RCM = risk control measure; *In consideration of the RCMs external to the software ("external RCMs"); **Type of harm that the product could potentially lead to. The dashed line indicates the point in the (ISO 14971) risk management process at which the IEC 62304 software safety classification should be finalised.

mitigate any harm caused by the failure/malfunction of the specific medical device software under consideration. This relates to documented intended use and intended users. For example, documentation associated with diagnostic software designed to assist in the diagnosis of disease X may state that it is not to be used as the sole means of making the diagnosis (see Section 2.4.1).

Other external RCMs would include systems and/or software that check the accuracy and usability of the software "in the field" (e.g., external audit schemes). Note that such systems are totally separate from any final product testing performed by the manufacturer, which is, part of the software development process. Of course, the overall safety risk management of SaMD comprises a combination of internal and external RCMs [25].

If external RCMs are comprehensive to the point where a software failure could not conceivably lead to unacceptable risk, then the software can be classified as Class A and be subject to less rigorous software engineering. However, if a manufacturer relies on an RCM-based "safety argument" to reduce the software safety classification he must be able to verify the *effectiveness* of such measures.

5.4.1.9 Relationship to Other Standards

IEC 82304-1 (A.1.3.6) is closely related to IEC 62304 and is discussed separately in Section 5.4.2. Other standards referenced by IEC 62304 include ISO 90003, IEC 14764, and IEC 61508, but there is a "stated relationship" (i.e., clause mapping) to the following:

ISO 13485:2003 (see Table 5.3)

ISO 14971:2007 (see Table 5.4)

ISO 12207:2017 (*Systems and software engineering – Software life cycle processes*)

IEC 60101-1:2005 (*Medical electrical equipment – Part 1: General requirements for basic safety and essential performance*)

Note that these are not the most recent versions of the respective standards. Tables 5.3 and 5.4 give the clause mapping to the most recent versions of ISO 13485 and ISO 14971 respectively.

Also, the latest version of IEC 60601-1 (IEC 60601-1:2005+AMD1:2012+ AMD2:2020 CSV) is only applicable if the software is part of a programmable electronic medical system (PEMS) and not if the software is itself a medical device. For SiMD manufacturers this effectively places *additional* requirements on the production processes, given that IEC 62304:2006 is a normative reference of IEC 60601-1:2005/AMD1:2012. A clause mapping between IEC 60601-1:2005/ AMD1:2012[7] and IEC 62304:2005/AMD1:2012 is given in Table C.3 of the latter.

5.4.1.10 Legacy Software

In this context, legacy software is medical software that was developed (and legally placed on the market) prior to the publication of the 2015 amendment to IEC 62304:2006. Indeed, the handling of legacy software was one of the key new features of the amendment.

Application of the legacy software procedure described in Clause 4.4 of the standard amounts to the retrospective application of IEC 62304, by way of specified risk management activities (associated with the continued use of the device), gap analysis, and possibly some reverse engineering. Suffice it to say that it is not a straightforward procedure and most organisations will need expert help for such an undertaking. The legacy software procedure (it is not one of the defined processes) is an alternative to applying Clauses 5–9, as would be performed for a new software system.

Though no consensus exists for the *prospective* quantitative estimation of software failure probability for a new software medical device, such information may be calculable, at least in principle, for legacy software, based on the evaluation of post-production data obtained from routine clinical use. If such historic data is available for one or more untoward events in the 'failure sequence' (software failure leading to patient harm very rarely has a single cause), it may be possible to derive a reasonable quantitative estimate for the probability of occurrence of the entire sequence. If such an estimation is not possible, the manufacturer is bound to consider the worst-case scenario, in which case the probability of occurrence of software failure is set to unity.

5.4.1.11 Commercial off-the-Shelf Software

The incorporation of commercial off-the-shelf (COTS) software into medical device software is an issue first highlighted in FDA guidance published in 1999, which was updated in 2023 [26]. It was made clear from the outset that the medical device

---

[7] The latest version of the standard (IEC 60601-1:2005/AMD1:2012/AMD2:2020 [aka IEC 60601-1 Edition 3.2]) post-dates the latest version of IEC 62304.

manufacturer must accept full responsibility for software assembled using third-party components.

In recognition of the 'COTS issue', IEC 62304:2006 introduced the concept of "software of unknown provenance" (SOUP) to cover all such general-purpose software, defining it as *"a software item that is already developed and generally available and that has not been developed for the purpose of being incorporated into the medical device (also known as "off-the-shelf software") or a software item previously developed for which adequate records of the development processes are not available"*.

All COTS software is thus effectively defined as SOUP, with several measures prescribed to ensure that such software is suitable for use in a safety-related environment [27]. SOUP does not appear as a chapter heading in IEC 62304 but is referred to in Chapters 3 (*Terms and definitions*), 5 (*Software development process*), 7 (*Software risk management process*), and Annex B (*Guidance of the provisions of the standard*).

Some suppliers of commercial programming environments have made the task of justifying the use of their software in safety-related applications somewhat easier by providing information on their development processes (usually in the form of a 'quality statement') and even sharing audit reports from independent testing bodies. Such commercial packages are referred to as "clear SOUP"; the MATLAB suite produced by MathWorks is one such example [28].

If unmodified open-source software is used in a software medical device it should be treated as SOUP, and if changes are made to the source code (however minor) they should then be treated as a software item that you developed yourself [29]. The legal and procedural aspects of using open-source software are discussed further in Section 7.6.1.

5.4.1.12   Iterative Development Techniques

IEC 62304 may be readily understood by reference to the V-model (e.g., as used in Table C.3 of the standard) but the use of other software life cycle models is possible.

Iterative/incremental techniques based on the general approach stated in the agile manifesto (e.g., agile, Kanban) are extensively used in the corporate IT world and are slowly gaining traction with medical device manufacturers. Although the "agile approach" has been very popular in general IT over the last decade, paradigm shifts happen frequently in the software industry and the way in which it has been implemented in some sectors has received criticism, due to the tendency to commence coding prematurely.

In any event, a "pure" agile approach is generally unsuitable in a highly regulated environment [30]. It is possible to adapt the agile approach to fit a regulated environment, but particular attention must be paid to the IEC 62304 requirement for extensive in-process documentation (to prove that each relevant clause in IEC 62304 was followed) and traceability of user requirements. This adaption generally involves the reinforcement/confirmation of key IEC 62304 requirements at the conclusion of each "sprint", and the automation of at least some of the testing and documentation production [31].

The system that most manufacturers end up with is usually a hybrid of an iterative technique and a traditional structured model (e.g., V or waterfall) – usually referred to as "structured agile". Whatever software development model/methodology is used, the manufacturer will still need to implement ISO 14971 and ISO 13485 (or an FDA-approved QMS in the US) *and* be able to demonstrate that the software development methodology employed meets the exacting requirements of IEC 62304.

Although the agile approach to software development is best suited to *relatively* small teams (5–10 people), such a team size would be considered large for in-house development teams working in public health bodies (e.g., large hospitals). Very small teams (2–3 people) may be able to adopt some of the principles of the agile approach, but they may find it somewhat cumbersome and artificial to use some of its methods (e.g., scrums, sprints).[8] The scrum system also assumes that the team members have separate roles, which is unlikely in a hospital department setting.

One of the few official guidance documents on the use of agile practices in the development of medical software is the recently updated Association for the Advancement of Medical Instrumentation (AAMI)[9] Technical Information Report 45 (AAMI TIR45:2023) [32]. Other general information is available on the challenges of deploying agile techniques in the medical device software domain [33,34].

The AAMI guidance document is written from a US perspective, so mainly references CFR Title 21 Part 820 (QSR) and associated FDA guidance documents. However, it also refers to ISO 13485, ISO 14971, and IEC 62304. Although not a standard, AAMI TIR45:2012 (the original publication) is designated as a voluntary recognised consensus standard by the FDA [35], so the new revision will be similarly recognised in due course. This should not be interpreted as implying that the FDA is favouring an agile approach to medical software development in preference to any other; simply that is allowing methodologies in compliance with AAMI TIR45 to be referenced in pre-market submissions [36].

In summary, the agile approach is not a natural fit for the highly disciplined approach to software development mandated by IEC 62304. It can be *made to fit*, but the adaption process is not straightforward. Unless development teams are already familiar (and successful) with the agile approach, it is recommended to stay with a traditional structured methodology for medical device software development.

5.4.1.13   Required Documents

IEC 62304 requires the following documents ("Deliverables"):

Risk Management File (Clause 4.2)
Software Safety Classification (Clause 4.3.c)
Software Development Plan (Clause 5.1.1)
Software System Requirements (5.2), including RCMs (Clause 5.2.3)
Software Architectural Design (Clauses 5.3 and 5.4)

---

[8] Guidance is available that attempts to express US medical device regulatory requirements using the language and terminology of agile development [65].

[9] AAMI: [American] Association for the Advancement of Medical Instrumentation.

Software Test Plan (Clauses 5.5, 5.6 and 5.7, especially 5.7.1 NOTE 1 and 2)
Traceability Overview (of test procedures to software requirements) (Clause 5.7.4)
Software Test Report (Clause 5.7.5)
Residual Anomalies (Clause 5.8)
Configuration Management (Clauses 5.8.4, 5.8.5, 8)

5.4.1.14 Missing Elements from IEC 62304

IEC 62304 is the most widely adopted process standard for medical software development but an update is now overdue. Most of the clauses relating to the various life cycle activities remain valid, but the requirements for change control do not reference artificial intelligence/machine learning systems. IEC 62304 also lacks requirements on software validation as this life cycle activity is included in IEC 60601 (for SiMD) and IEC 82304-1 (for SaMD). It is generally acknowledged that IEC 62304 and IEC 82304-1 both need updating to account for new developments in AI/ML systems [37].

5.4.2 IEC 82304-1: HEALTH SOFTWARE – PART 1: GENERAL REQUIREMENTS FOR PRODUCT SAFETY

Latest version of the standard: IEC 82304-1:2016
  Normative references: IEC 62304:2006; IEC 62304:2006/AMD1:2015
  IEC 82304-1:2016 applies to the safety and security of health software products designed to operate on general computing platforms and intended to be placed on the market without dedicated hardware (i.e., "standalone software", SaMD). The broad scope of IEC 82304-1 compared to that of IEC 62304 is indicated in Figure 5.10.
  IEC 82304-1 covers the entire software lifecycle including design, development, validation, installation, maintenance, and disposal of health software products, but its

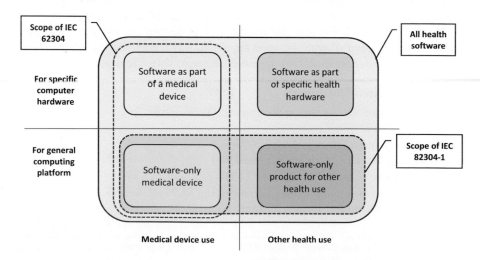

FIGURE 5.10 Scope of IEC 82304-1:2016 compared with IEC 62304:2006 + AMD1 2015. Adapted with permission from Figure A.1 of IEC 82304-1:2016.

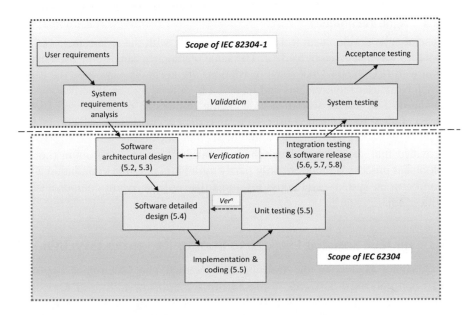

FIGURE 5.11 The *effective* SDLC coverage of IEC 62304:2006 + AMD1:2015 and IEC 82304-1:2016 (shown using the V-model). The figures in brackets refer to the relevant clause within IEC 62304. IEC 82304-1 covers the whole SDLC but defers to IEC 62304 for most of the low-level software activities.

emphasis is on system-level requirements and final product validation (Figure 5.11). It relies heavily on IEC 62304 for elaboration of the software development process. For example, Section 4.7 of IEC 82304-1 (*Updating system requirements*) refers to Section 5.2 of IEC 62304 and Section 5 (*Software life cycle processes*) states that "requirements in clauses 4.2, 4.3, 5, 6, 7, 8, and 9 of IEC 62304:2006/AMD1:2015 shall apply to health software *in addition to* [emphasis added] the other requirements of this document" (see Section 5.4.1.2).

For standalone software (i.e., SaMD), IEC 82304-1 and IEC 62304 dovetail together, since IEC 82304-1 provides guidance on software validation and other processes (including post-market activities) that are missing from IEC 62304 (Figure 5.11). For embedded software (i.e., SiMD), IEC 60601-1 (Appendix A.1.3.8) takes the place of IEC 82304-1 as far as validation is concerned.

In summary, IEC 82304-1 effectively fills the gap between the software verification procedures described in IEC 62304 and the software validation requirements of regulations when health software is regulated as a medical device. However, IEC 82304-1 also expands on the requirements of IEC 62304, and its guidance on defining and validating product use requirements is helpful to SaMD developers using IEC 62304.

Note that IEC 82304-1 uses the same (barely distinguishable) definitions of "validation" and "verification" as quoted in the US medical device QSR (Section 6.5.8.2); the source of both being ISO 9000:2015. Software product validation is covered in Section 6 of the IEC 62304-1 but the term "software validation" is not defined. However, a generally accepted meaning is provided in Section 6.5.8.2.

5.4.2.1 Agile Techniques

The use of agile development techniques that comply with the requirements of IEC 62304:2016 was discussed in 5.4.1.12. The same techniques can also be used in connection with IEC 82304-1 but some restrictions are normally placed on the degree to which basic user requirements and resultant high-level system specifications can be changed. The former would include "static immutable requirements" such as intended clinical use, intended user, general system security, etc., which represent a subset of high-level requirements found in Sections 4.2 and 4.5 of IEC 82304-1.

Provided that such system-level changes can be kept to a minimum (i.e., the development process is therefore only partly agile) it is possible to maintain a separation between system-level activities and fully agile software component-level activities [38].

5.4.3 The IEEE Software Engineering Body of Knowledge (SWEBOK)

The Computer Society of the Institute of Electrical and Electronics Engineers (IEEE) first published its *Guide to the Software Engineering Body of Knowledge* (SWEBOK) in 2004,[10] as the first of three "essential building blocks" considered for software engineering to "become a legitimate engineering discipline and a recognised profession"; the other two being defined educational curricula (for undergraduate, postgraduate, and continuing education) and defined ethical and professional standards [39].

Adoption of the *Guide* within the software development industry for in-service training has been mainly limited to large companies, but it has been widely used by universities in establishing curricula for software engineering degree courses [40].

Many parts of the (unregulated) software industry remain sceptical about the benefits of formalised software engineering, and the question of whether software engineering should be considered a branch of engineering – or even a profession – is still debated among practicing software developers [41].

5.4.4 Coding Standards

The software community tends to speak of "coding standards", but they are actually guidelines that can be divided into *style* guidelines (aimed at improved readability/ understandability by others) and *coding conventions* that minimise errors and simplify testing and future maintenance.

A coding guideline is only pertinent to the coding phase of the software development life cycle (SDLC), so it must be integrated into a wider system for managing the whole SDLC – specified by IEC 62304 in the case of medical device software. Most generic coding standards (i.e., those that apply to all high-level programming languages) cover the same basic principles so the choice is not critical. The important thing is that the chosen coding guideline is documented in the organisation's software development policy manual and is clearly understood and followed by all

---

[10] The IEEE SWEBOK was adopted as ISO/IEC TR 19759 in 2005, most recently updated in 2015.

members of the development team. Independent internal code reviews should reveal any divergence from the required standard.

Generic coding standards [42,43] are usually discussed under the following headings:

- Naming of variables, constants, and functions
- Variable declarations
- Format and content of module headers
- Code formatting (Indentation, spaces, etc.)
- Error handling
- Code complexity
- Commenting
- Metrics (Length of lines, functions, classes, etc.)
- Nested loops
- Statements/constructs to avoid

Many of the individual conditions/specifications will be familiar (and obvious) to experienced software developers, but it is easy for standards to slip if they are not enforced.

A recent best practice guide for scientific computing refers to many of the above requirements but also contains useful advice on collaboration within the software development team [44].

Ideas about making software as readable and as testable as possible have been brought together and elaborated into what is referred to as the "clean code move- ment" [45], which was a reaction to the "spaghetti code" that its original authors had witnessed over the last 30 years. Most of the examples are written in Java but will be readily understood by developers using other languages. The main "bullet points" of the clean code approach have been summarised by others [46]. The "clean code movement" is associated with the agile approach to software development but the basic principles and techniques are applicable to traditional structured development models [47]. The GNU coding standards offer detailed guidance on C programming, but most of the recommendations (especially those on source code formatting and commenting) are applicable to other high-level languages [48].

For developers working in truly safety-critical situations (e.g., embedded software in direct treatment devices) there are more prescriptive coding guidelines, including those developed by the Motor Industry Software Reliability Association (MISRA) [49]. The MISRA guidelines were originally developed for handwritten C/C++ code used in the automobile industry but were quickly adopted by other safety-critical sec- tors (e.g., aerospace, nuclear power generation, rail transport). MISRA C and MISRA C++ essentially comprise a "safe subset" of the C and C++ languages to protect against language syntax constructs that can compromise the safety and security of embedded systems. The guidelines have been recently revised to accommodate auto- matically generated C/C++ code as well as that produced by development tools such as MATLAB and Simulink [50].

Software partitioning is a particularly important part of software architectural design and is part of the IEC 62304 standard (Section 5.4.1.6).

5.4.4.1 Defensive Programming

Defensive programming is a combination of techniques aimed at (a) minimising bug insertion during coding and (b) mitigating the effects of any errors that may still be present in released code. The key principles are as follows:

1. Keep code as simple as possible
2. Use appropriate coding standards
3. Don't assume anything (in terms of program inputs)

User input validation is a key concern and there are specific programming constructs designed to trap invalid inputs and return the system to a safe state if something unanticipated happens. Programming constructs such as a guard clause represent a "second line of defence" for input validation [51]. An online search will reveal defensive programming examples for specific languages, such as Python [52].

Defensive programming fits well within the general philosophy of IEC 62304 since it represents a risk-based approach to coding. Note that hazard analysis performed as part of ISO 14971 forces the developer to think about "reasonably foreseeable misuse" (Section 5.3.1.3) but software failures also occur due to *unforeseen* issues. Defensive programming is an attempt to address that possibility.

IEC 62304 does not *prescribe* adherence to a coding standard but requires (in Clause 5.5.3) that manufacturers of class B and C software "establish acceptance criteria for software units prior to integration into larger software items as appropriate, and ensure that software items meet [the established] acceptance criteria". Although not mandatory, it is added in note form that an example of a suitable "acceptance criterion" would be whether the software code "conforms to programming procedures or coding standards".

FDA guidelines on general principles software validation [18] state that the software design specification should include *"development procedures and coding guidelines (or other programming procedures)"*, adding that

> software requirement specifications should identify clearly the potential hazards that can result from a software failure in the system as well as any safety requirements to be implemented in software. The consequences of software failure should be evaluated, along with means of mitigating such failures (e.g., hardware mitigation, defensive programming, etc.).

5.4.5 SPREADSHEET GUIDELINES

Spreadsheets have long been regarded as the "Cinderella" of the programming world, despite spreadsheet errors continuing to lead to huge losses in the finance industry, incorrect government election results, as well as lost healthcare records [53]. Reflecting ongoing concerns about the unprofessional use of spreadsheets in business generally, the theme of the 2023 European Spreadsheet Risk Interest Group (EuSpRIG) annual conference was *"The Spreadsheet Crisis: Regaining control"*.

Custom-built spreadsheet models qualify as *software* (Section 3.3) and qualify as SaMD if their intended purpose meets the definition of a medical device (Section 6.3.2.1). As such, an organisation producing medical spreadsheets for purely in-house use would need to implement framework standards ISO 13485 (Section 5.2) and IEC 62304 (Section 5.4.1). In the context of IEC 62304, commercial (or open source) general-purpose spreadsheets (e.g., Microsoft Excel™, Google Sheets™, Calc™) constitute SOUP and should be treated accordingly (Section 5.4.1.11).

This section focuses on spreadsheet-specific guidelines, which also follow basic principles of software engineering. If the developer uses the built-in programming language or macros (e.g., *Visual Basic for Applications* in Microsoft Excel™), the principles discussed under coding standards (Section 5.4.5) would also apply.

Spreadsheet guidelines are designed to reduce the likelihood of spreadsheet errors. The European Spreadsheet Risk Interest Group (EuSpRIG) has collated various good practice guides [54], including some recommendations by Microsoft for using Excel in a regulated environment [55]. This paper includes recommendations for mitigating common spreadsheet risks and cites references that could be used to support the case for justifying this SOUP in a clinical setting.

The UK NPL Best Practice Guide #7 on the development and testing of spreadsheet applications was last updated in 2006 [56] but its general recommendations remain valid. It contains a useful discussion on the issues associated with the validation of spreadsheet software applications that are pertinent to IEC 13485 (Section 5.2 1.6).

Finally, a comprehensive spreadsheet modelling guide aimed at the financial sector [57] contains basic principles and detailed design recommendations relating to Microsoft Excel™ that are equally applicable to the medical sector.

All guidelines contain recommendations for the separation of sheets (documentation, data input, complex calculations [e.g., pivot tables], results from output, references, etc.) consistent with the principles of software partitioning (Section 5.4.1.6). User input validation is a well-developed feature in both MS Excel™ (Figure 5.12) and Google Sheets™ and should be employed to its fullest extent. The workbook (i.e., the whole application) should be protected to prevent unauthorised structural changes, such as adding or deleting worksheets. Individual worksheets within the workbook also need to be protected to limit the user's ability to edit. In addition, cells containing formulae and associated lookup tables need to be locked and/or hidden in order to prevent inadvertent deletion/modification by the user.

Spreadsheet applications like Microsoft Excel™ are set to become even more powerful in future as generative AI capabilities such as LMM (large language models) are built into its functions and formulae [58].

5.4.6   Best Practice Guides for Mobile App Developers

The EU medical device regulations make no distinction between general standalone medical software and mobile medical apps, but there is specific guidance available on the latter that developers should be aware of regarding their obligation to use state-of-the-art techniques (see Chapter 6, Appendix 1).

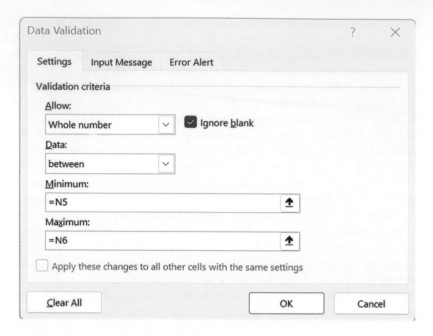

FIGURE 5.12   The main *Settings* options for Microsoft Excel's Data Validation feature. Number format can vary (whole number, decimal, date, etc.) and range limits can be constants or values held in cells (here N5 and N6) as variables.

The EC produced a draft code of conduct on the *privacy aspects* of mHealth apps in 2016 [59], which is based on EU data protection laws. It followed the publication of the Commission's Green Paper on mobile health (mHealth) in 2014.

The British Standards Institution (BSI) had previously produced a fast-track standardisation document called a Publicly Available Specification (PAS) on quality criteria for health and wellness apps (PAS 277), which covered most of the product life cycle [60].

The UK NHS subsequently developed its own best practice guide for "digital and data-driven healthcare technologies" [61]. It is meant to cover a range of health-related software but is aimed primarily at mobile health app developers.

There is an associated procurement questionnaire (comprising the Digital Technology Assessment Criteria, DTAC), which is intended to be used by NHS healthcare institutions when tendering for health IT systems [62]. It prompts users to check that suppliers meet certain standards, including DCB0129 and DCB0160 for risk management (Appendix 1). Only organisations that can meet the stated criteria would pass initial screening based on an assessment of clinical safety, cybersecurity, data protection, usability, interoperability, and accessibility [63]. The DTAC was also meant to be used to vet entry to the NHS Apps Library, but this facility closed in December 2021.

In the US, the FDA produced its first guidance document on the production of mobile medical apps in 2013. It has since been updated several times, most recently in 2022 [64]. It includes advice on the development process as well as detailed guidance on whether a given mobile app would qualify as a medical device under US regulations (Section 6.5.5.4).

5.5 RELATIONSHIPS BETWEEN THE MAIN STANDARDS

Figure 5.13 shows the relationship between standards used to manufacture medical devices in a regulatory setting. Medical device management standards such as ISO 13485 and ISO 14971 provide the management framework for product development. If the medical device includes software, IEC 62304 provides more detailed direction on what is required. Other standards such as ISO/IEC 12207, IEC 61508-3, and ISO/IEC 90003 can be used as a source of methods, tools, and techniques for implementing the requirements in IEC 62304.

In conclusion, medical software developers should use IEC 62304 for design. ISO 13485 and ISO 14971 provide the framework for quality management and risk management systems respectively. IEC 82304 supplements IEC 62304. IEC 81001-5-1 (Section 6.3.6.7) can be used to deal with security issues and IEC 62366-1 (Section 6.3.6.6) provides the necessary guidance on usability.

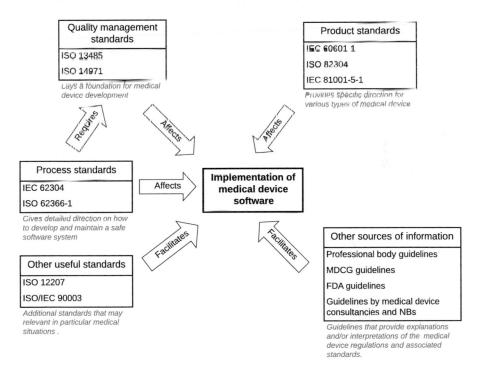

FIGURE 5.13 Relationships between standards relevant to the production of medical device software (adapted with permission from Figure C.1 in IEC 62304:2006/AMD1:2015). Note. IEC 62304 requires ISO 14971 and *effectively* requires ISO 13485. ISO 14971 has two accompanying technical reports, one general (ISO/TR 24971:2020) and one specific to software development (IEC/TR 80002-1:2009).

Appendix 1
List of standards and guidelines

This non-exhaustive list, grouped by topic, includes standards and guidelines specifically discussed in this chapter and elsewhere in the book, along with other standards that may be helpful to the medical device software developer. A brief description is added, where appropriate, for standards/guidelines not covered in the book. The current versions of the standards and guidelines should always be checked on the relevant website.

A.1.1 QUALITY MANAGEMENT SYSTEMS

A.1.1.1 ISO 9000:2015. Quality Management Systems – Fundamentals and Vocabulary

A.1.1.2 ISO 9000-1:2015. Quality Management Systems – Requirements

Application: General. Not directly applicable to software development.
Normative references: None
Derived standard or guideline: ISO 90003 (see below)

A.1.1.3 ISO 13485: 2016. Medical Devices – Quality Management Systems – Requirements for Regulatory Purposes

Application: Medical device manufacture
Normative references: ISO 9000:2015
Chapter reference: 5.2.1

A.1.1.4 ISPE GAMP 5 (second edition), 2022: A Risk-Based Approach to Compliant GxP Computerised Systems (Second Edition): 2022

Application: Guidance produced for the pharmaceutical industry but has general application to computerised systems. Relevant to NPS software validation (Section 3.3.6)

Brief description: The 2022 edition includes a discussion of FDA activity on computer software assurance (CSA), with cross-reference to ISPE/GAMP guidance on Data Integrity (DI). The appendices have been expanded to incorporate new and evolving topics in the life sciences industry such as blockchain, Artificial Intelligence/Machine Learning (AI/ML), cloud computing, and open-source software (OSS).

A.1.1.5   ISO 80002-2:2017. MEDICAL DEVICE SOFTWARE – VALIDATION OF SOFTWARE FOR MEDICAL DEVICE QUALITY SYSTEMS

Application: Software used in the quality management system
 Normative references: None
 Chapter reference: 5.2.1

A.1.2   RISK MANAGEMENT

A.1.2.1   IEC 31010:2019. RISK MANAGEMENT – RISK ASSESSMENT TECHNIQUES

Application: Generic
 Normative references: ISO Guide 73:2009 (Risk management – Vocabulary), ISO 31000:2018 (Risk management – Guidelines).
 Chapter references: 4.4.19 and 4.5

A.1.2.2   ISO 14971:2019/A11:2021. MEDICAL DEVICES – APPLICATION OF RISK MANAGEMENT TO MEDICAL DEVICES

Application: Medical device manufacture
 Normative references: ISO 14971
 Derived standard or guideline: ISO TR 24971:2020
 Chapter reference: 5.3.1

A.1.2.3   ISO TR 24971:2020. MEDICAL DEVICES – GUIDANCE ON THE APPLICATION OF ISO 14971

Application: Medical device manufacture
 Normative references: ISO 14971:2019
 Chapter reference: 5.3.1.3

A.1.2.4   IEC/TR 80002-1:2009: MEDICAL DEVICE SOFTWARE – PART 1: GUIDANCE ON THE APPLICATION OF ISO 14971 TO MEDICAL DEVICE SOFTWARE

Application: Medical device software
 Normative references: ISO 14971
 Chapter references: 5.3.1.3, 5.4.1.8

A.1.2.5   IEC 80001-1:2021. APPLICATION OF RISK MANAGEMENT FOR IT NETWORKS INCORPORATING MEDICAL DEVICES – PART 1: SAFETY, EFFECTIVENESS, AND SECURITY IN THE IMPLEMENTATION AND USE OF CONNECTED MEDICAL DEVICES OR CONNECTED HEALTH SOFTWARE

Application: IT networks that include connected medical devices.
 Normative references: None
 Chapter reference: 6.3.6.7

A.1.2.6   DCB0129: Amd 25/2018. Clinical Risk Management: its Application in the Manufacture of Health IT Systems

Application: Manufacture of health IT systems, including "medical device IT systems" for marketing in England
    Normative references: None
    Chapter references: 5.4.6 and 6.4.7

A.1.2.7   DCB0160: Amd 25/2018. Clinical Risk Management: its Application in the Deployment and Use of Health IT Systems

Application: Deployment of health IT systems, including "medical device IT systems" for application in England.
    Normative references: None
    Brief description: This is a companion standard to DC0129. Compliance with DC0129 and DCB 0160 is required for manufacturers to sell health IT products to the UK NHS.

A.1.2.8   BS AAMI 34971:2023. Application of ISO 14971 to Machine Learning in Artificial Intelligence. Guide

Application: Medical devices with AI/ML-enabled software
    Normative references: ISO 14971:2019.
    Brief description: Jointly developed by the BSI and the US AAMI. The standard is based on AAMI consensus report CR34971, which was recognised as a consensus standard by the FDA in 2022. It may be republished as ISO/IEC 34971.
    Chapter reference: 9.3.3

A.1.3   SOFTWARE ENGINEERING

A.1.3.1   ISO/IEC/IEEE 90003:2018. Software Engineering: Guidelines for the Application of ISO 9001:2015 to Computer Software

Application: Software development (generic)
    Normative references: ISO 9001:2015
    Derived standard or guideline: None

A.1.3.2   IEC 61508:2000. Functional Safety of Electrical/Electronic/ Programmable Electronic Safety-Related Systems

Application: Safety critical software systems (generic)
    Normative references: None
    Derived standard or guideline: IEC 62304
    Brief description: A huge (1,500 page) standard that is normally reserved for highly complex control software deployed in truly *safety-critical* situations (e.g., power distribution, public transport, military systems, aviation).

A.1.3.3 ISO/IEC 12207:2017. Systems and Software Engineering – Software Life Cycle Processes

Application: Generic
   Normative references: None
   Derived standard or guideline: ISO/IEC TR 29110:2016
   Brief description: The corresponding standard for system life cycle process (i.e., those with computer hardware elements) is ISO/IEC/IEEE 15288:2015 *(Systems and software engineering - System life cycle processes)*.
   Chapter reference: 5.4.1.1, 5.4.1.9

A.1.3.4 ISO/IEC 14764:2022. Software engineering – Software Life Cycle Processes – Maintenance

Application: Generic
   Normative references: ISO/IEC 12207
   Brief description: Provides guidance on the maintenance of software, based on the *maintenance process* and associated activities/task described in ISO/IEC 12207.
   Chapter reference: 2.2.3

A.1.3.5 IEC 62304:2006/AMD1:2015. Medical Device Software – Life Cycle Processes

Application: Medical software development
   Normative references: ISO 14971
   Brief description: based on ISO/IEC 12207
   Chapter reference: 5.4.1

A.1.3.6 IEC 82304-1:2016. Health software – Part 1: General Requirements for Product Safety

Application: Health software development
   Normative references: IEC 62304:2006/AMD1:2015
   Chapter reference: 5.4.2

A.1.3.7 ISO/TS 82304-2:2021. Health Software – Part 2. Health and Wellness Apps – Quality and Reliability

Application: Health and wellness apps
   Normative references: None
   Brief description: Refers to IEC 82304-1 for product safety requirements and to IEC 62304 for product development life cycle requirements. Its main purpose is to establish the Health App Quality Label (HAQL). It also contains information on product validation that is additional to that found in Section 6 of IEC 82304-1.
   Chapter references: 3.3.5 and 5.4.2.1.

A.1.3.8   IEC 60601-1:2005+AMD1:2012+AMD2:2020 CSV. Medical Electrical Equipment – Part 1: General Requirements for Basic Safety and Essential Performance

Application: Embedded software within medical devices
  Normative references: None
  Brief description: Section 14 of this standard refers to PEMS, so the old IEC 60101-4 has been withdrawn.
  Chapter references: 5.4.2

A.1.3.9   IEC 62366-1:2015/AMD1:2020. Medical Devices – Part 1: Application of Usability Engineering to Medical Devices

Application: All medical devices, but especially user interfaces.
  Normative references: None
  Derived standard or guideline: IEC/TR 62366-2:2016. Medical devices – Part 2: Guidance on the application of usability engineering to medical devices.
  Chapter references: 6.3.6.6, 6.4.4.4 and 6.5.8.10.

A.1.3.10   AAMI TIR45:2012 (R2018). Guidance on the use of Agile Practices in the Development of Medical Device Software

Application: Medical device software
  Normative references: None
  Chapter reference: 5.4.1.12
  Brief description: Refers to IEC 62304 and relevant FDA guidance documents.

A.1.3.11   ISO/TR 80002-2: 2017: Medical Device Software – Part 2: Validation of Software for Medical Device Quality Systems

Application: Software used in quality management systems, including that used for monitoring and measurement of user requirements. It does *not* apply to medical device software, or software that is a component of, or accessory to, a medical device.
  Normative references: N/A
  Chapter reference: Relevant to NPS software validation (Section 3.3.6)

A.1.3.12   FDA Guidance Document on Software Validation

Full title: General principles of software validation: Final guidance for industry and FDA staff.
  Application: Medical device software
  Chapter reference: 6.5.6.2.

A.1.3.13 ISO/IEC TR 29110: 2016: Software Engineering – Lifecycle Profiles for Very Small Entities (VSEs) – Part 1: Overview

Application: Generic. Useful for very small (or "micro") software organisations that are new to formalised quality management systems and who may want to progress in stages.

Based on: ISO/IEC 12207 and ISO/IEC 15288

Normative references: None

Brief description: The ISO/IEC 29110 series of standards and guides was developed mainly to provide a 'road map' for VSEs developing systems or software. The roadmap is composed of four profiles (i.e., Entry, Basic, Intermediate, and Advanced) to guide VSEs in moving from a start-up to an established manufacturer. The standard is intended to be used with any life cycle model, including waterfall, V, iterative/agile, or incremental.

A.1.4 ARTIFICIAL INTELLIGENCE

A.1.4.1 Good Practices for Health Applications of Machine Learning; Considerations for Manufacturers and Regulators. International Telecommunication Union Focus Group, January 2021

Application: All health-related software, including medical device software.

Normative references: N/A

Website reference: https://luisoala.net/assets/pdf/standards/FGAI4H-K-039.pdf

A.1.4.2 Machine Learning-Enabled Medical Devices: Key Terms and Definitions. IMDRF Guidance, 2022

Application: Medical devices containing AI technology

Normative references: N/A

Chapter reference: 9.5.5.1

A.1.4.3 Marketing Submission Recommendations for a Predetermined Change Control Plan for Artificial Intelligence/Machine Learning (AI/ML)-Enabled Device Software Functions (issued April 2023)

Application: Medical devices containing AI technology

Normative references: N/A

Brief description: Draft FDA guidance document on pre-market submission requirements.

Chapter reference: 9.2.3

A.1.4.4 MACHINE LEARNING AI IN MEDICAL DEVICES. ADAPTING REGULATORY FRAMEWORKS AND STANDARDS TO ENSURE SAFETY AND PERFORMANCE (ISSUED 2020)

Application: Medical devices containing AI technology

Normative references: N/A

Brief description: BSI/AAMI guidance document containing lots of useful background information on machine learning, with proposals for the adaption of medical device regulatory frameworks in both the EU and the US.

Chapter reference: 6.3.6.5

A.1.5 CYBERSECURITY

A.1.5.1 IEC 81001-5-1: 2021. HEALTH SOFTWARE AND HEALTH IT SYSTEMS SAFETY, EFFECTIVENESS, AND SECURITY – PART 5-1: SECURITY – ACTIVITIES IN THE PRODUCT LIFE CYCLE

Application: All health-related software, including medical device software.

Normative references: None

Brief description: The standard is based on IEC 62443-4-1 (*Security for industrial automation and control systems, Part 4-1: Secure product development lifecycle requirements*) and may be regarded as a supplement to IEC 62304 and IEC 82304-1. The five main processes described (software development, software maintenance, security risk management, software configuration management, and software problem resolution exactly match those in IEC 62304. The software development process focuses on security-related activities to be undertaken during specific life cycle phases, such as requirements analysis, architectural design, software design, and integration testing.

Chapter references: 6.3.6.7, 6.5.8.11, 8.2.6, 8.3.1, 8.3.3.

A.1.5.2 AAMI TIR57:2016 (R2023). PRINCIPLES FOR MEDICAL DEVICE SECURITY – RISK MANAGEMENT

Application: Medical devices

Normative references

Brief description: This Technical Information Report (TIR) provides guidance on methods to perform information security risk management for a medical device in the context of the risk management process required by ISO 14971. It also incorporates the same key properties found in IEC 80001-1 (relating to the security of IT networks incorporating medical devices, see A.1.2.5) and includes illustrative examples.

Chapter reference: 8.3.2.

A.1.5.3 AAMI TIR97:2019 (R2023). Principles for Medical Device Security – Post-Market Risk Management For Device Manufacturers

Application: Medical devices
Normative references: ISO 14971, IEC 80001-1.
Brief description: Designed to be used in conjunction with AAMI TIR57:2016.
Chapter reference: 8.4

A.1.5.4 MDCG 2019-16 Rev.1 Guidance on Cybersecurity for Medical Devices (last revised July 2020)

Normative references: N/A
Brief description: Provides advice on how to comply with the cybersecurity requirements of the current EU medical device regulations (745/2017 (MDR) and 746/2017 (IVDR))
Chapter reference: 6.3.6.7

A.1.5.5 Cybersecurity in Medical Devices: Quality System Considerations and Content of Remarket Submissions. Draft Guidance for Industry and Food and Drug Administration Staff (issued April 2022)

Normative references: N/A
Brief description: FDA guidance document describing the requirements for pre-market medical device submissions in the US.
Chapter reference: 6.5.8.11

A.1.5.6 Post-Market Management of Cybersecurity in Medical Devices (Issued December 2016)

Normative references: N/A
Brief description: FDA guidance document describing the post-market requirements for medical devices cleared for placement on the US market.
Chapter reference: 6.5.8.11

A.1.5.7 IMDRF/CYBER WG/N60:2020. Principles and Practices for Medical Device Cybersecurity

Normative references: N/A
Brief description: IMDRF guidance describing good practice for pre-market and post-market activities.
Chapter reference: 6.5.8.11

A.1.6 CLINICAL INVESTIGATIONS

A.1.6.1 ISO 14155:2020. CLINICAL INVESTIGATION OF MEDICAL DEVICES FOR HUMAN SUBJECTS – GOOD CLINICAL PRACTICE

Application: Clinical investigation of medical devices, including SaMD.
   Normative references: ISO 14971
   Chapter references: 6.3.10.2 and 6.5.5.

A.1.7 COMPETENCY

A.1.7.1 BS70000: 2017 – MEDICAL PHYSICS, CLINICAL ENGINEERING, AND ASSOCIATED SCIENTIFIC SERVICES IN HEALTHCARE. REQUIREMENTS FOR QUALITY, SAFETY, AND COMPETENCE

Application: Medical physics and clinical engineering departments engaged with in-house software development.
   Normative references: None
   Brief description: Based on ISO 15189:2012 (*Medical laboratories – Requirements for quality and competence*) and ISO/IEC 17025:2017 (*General requirements for the competence of testing and calibration laboratories*).

REFERENCES

[1] T. Rish, "Ultimate list of ISO standards for medical devices," Greenlight Guru, 14 July 2023. [Online]. Available: https://www.greenlight.guru/blog/iso-standards. [Accessed 11 September 2023].

[2] J. Speer, "Ultimate guide to ISO 13485 for medical device QMS," Greenlight Guru, 16 February 2023. [Online]. Available: https://www.greenlight.guru/blog/iso-13485-qms-medical-device. [Accessed 12 September 2023].

[3] E. Nichols, "Best QMS software: Ultimate guide to comparing quality management system solutions," Greenlight Guru, 17 March 2023. [Online]. Available: https://www.greenlight.guru/blog/best-qms-software-quality-management. [Accessed 12 September 2023].

[4] OrielStat, "Medical device quality management system (QMS): What it is, where it's required, and key regulations to know," 13 June 2018. [Online]. Available: https://www.orielstat.com/blog/medical-device-qms-overview/. [Accessed 15 September 2023].

[5] D. Lundy, "RIM vs eQMS software for medical device manufacturers," Rimsys, 20 January 2023. [Online]. Available: https://www.rimsys.io/blog/rim-vs-eqms-software-for-medical-device-manufacturers. [Accessed 14 September 2023].

[6] Advisera, "Project plan for ISO 13485 implementation," [Online]. Available: https://info.advisera.com/13485academy/free-download/project-plan-for-iso-13485-implementation-presentation. [Accessed 11 September 2023].

[7] Advisera, "Free ISO 13485:2016 gap analysis tool," [Online]. Available: https://advisera.com/13485academy/iso-13485-gap-analysis-tool/. [Accessed 10 September 2023].

[8] Advisera, "Project proposal for ISO 13485:2016 implementation," [Online]. Available: https://info.advisera.com/13485academy/free-download/project-proposal-for-iso-13485-2016-implementation. [Accessed 11 September 2023].

[9] Advisera, "ISO 13485 and MDR integrated documentation toolkit," [Online]. Available: https://advisera.com/13485academy/iso-13485-eu-mdr-documentation-toolkit/. [Accessed 11 September 2023].

[10] E. Nichols, "The ultimate internal audit checklist every medical device company needs," Greenlight Guru, 25 October 2022. [Online]. Available: https://www.greenlight.guru/blog/internal-audit-checklist-medical-device. [Accessed 12 September 2023].

[11] B. Wichman, G. Parkin and R. Barker, "NPL software support for Metrology: Validation of software in measurement systems," Software Support for Metrology 2007. [Online]. Available: https://eprintspublications.npl.co.uk/3922/1/DEM_ES14.pdf. [Accessed 11 September 2023].

[12] UKAS, "Medical physics and clinical engineering accreditation," [Online]. Available: https://www.ukas.com/accreditation/standards/mpace/. [Accessed 11 September 2023].

[13] UKAS, "Accreditation vs certification: What's the difference?," [Online]. Available: https://www.ukas.com/accreditation/about/accreditation-vs-certification/. [Accessed 19 September 2023].

[14] IPEM, "Guidance for health institutions on in-house manufacture and use, including software (2nd Edition)," 25 July 2022. [Online]. Available: https://www.ipem.ac.uk/resources/other-resources/statements-and-notices/guidance-for-in-house-manufacture-of-medical-devices-and-non-medical-devices-including-software-2nd-ed/. [Accessed 19 September 2023].

[15] UKAS, "Medical physics & clinical engineering accreditation: FAQs," [Online]. Available: https://www.ukas.com/wp-content/uploads/2022/02/MPACE-FAQ-Jan-2022.pdf. [Accessed 19 September 2023].

[16] R. Van Vroonhoven, "Risk management for medical devices and the new BS EN ISO 14971," BSI, July 2022. [Online]. Available: https://www.bsigroup.com/globalassets/localfiles/en-th/Medical%20devices/whitepapers/wp_risk_management-th.pdf. [Accessed 11 September 2023].

[17] FDA, "Recognized consensus standards: Medical devices," 14 January 2019. [Online]. Available: https://www.accessdata.fda.gov/scripts/cdrh/cfdocs/cfStandards/detail.cfm?standard__identification_no=38829. [Accessed 11 September 2023].

[18] FDA, "General principles of software validation," January 2022. [Online]. Available: https://www.fda.gov/regulatory-information/search-fda-guidance-documents/general-principles-software-validation. [Accessed 11 September 2023].

[19] Johner Institute, "IEC 81001-5-1: The standard for secure health software," [Online]. Available: https://www.johner-institute.com/articles/software-iec-62304/and-more/iec-81001-5-1-the-standard-for-secure-health-software/. [Accessed 11 September 2023].

[20] Medical Device HQ, "The IEC 62304 standard and configuration management," 25 June 2020. [Online]. Available: https://medicaldevicehq.com/articles/the-iec-62304-standard-and-configuration-management/. [Accessed 14 September 2023].

[21] A. Marinelli and H. Mann, "Agile software development in bio/pharma & medical devices, Part 3," Med Device Online, 25 July 2023. [Online]. Available: https://www.outsourcedpharma.com/doc/agile-software-development-in-bio-pharma-medical-devices-part-0001. [Accessed 11 September 2023].

[22] R. Sheldon, "What is Git?," Tech Target, February 2023. [Online]. Available: https://www.techtarget.com/searchitoperations/definition/Git. [Accessed 19 September 2023].

[23] Y. Wang and P. Khopkar, "Good programming practices.," in *Diagnostic Radiology Physics with MATLAB®*, J. Helmenkamp, Ed., London: CRC Press, 2021, pp. 79–87.

[24] i3cglobal, "IEC 62304/ISO 62304," [Online]. Available: https://www.i3cglobal.com/iso-iec-62304-procedures/. [Accessed 11 September 2023].

[25] M. Dahlke and R. Ginsberg, "Safety risk management of software," *RF Quarterly*, vol. 2, no. 1, pp. 35–54, 1 April 2022.

[26] FDA, "Off-the-shelf software use in medical devices," August 2023. [Online]. Available: https://www.fda.gov/regulatory-information/search-fda-guidance-documents/shelf-software-use-medical-devices. [Accessed 11 September 2023].

[27] MD101, "Got SOUP? - Part 1 - Because every good software starts with SOUP," 17 May 2013. [Online]. Available: https://blog.cm-dm.com/post/2013/05/10/Got-SOUP-Part-1-Because-every-good-software-starts-with-SOUP. [Accessed 11 September 2023].

[28] P. S. Cosgriff and J. Atting, "Regulatory considerations when deploying your software in a clinical environment," in *Diagnostic Radiology Physics with MATLAB*, London, CRC Press, 2021, pp. 105–126.

[29] Johner Institute, "SOUP – Software of Unknown Provenance," 10 December 2015. [Online]. Available: https://www.johner-institute.com/articles/software-iec-62304/soup-and-ots/. [Accessed 18 September 2023].

[30] M. Steck, "IEC 62304 software development methodologies," Integrated Scientific Services, 28 April 2020. [Online]. Available: https://www.aligned.ch/images/BlogPictures/Sharpen_2020/IEC62304.pdf. [Accessed 12 September 2023].

[31] P. Massey, "Making AAMI TIR45 work for your software teams," Bluefruit Software, 25 November 2020. [Online]. Available: https://www.linkedin.com/pulse/making-aami-tir45-work-your-software-teams-paul-massey/. [Accessed 11 September 2023].

[32] AAMI, "AAMI TIR45:2023," 2023. [Online]. Available: https://webstore.ansi.org/standards/aami/aamitir452023. [Accessed 19 September 2023].

[33] M. McHugh, F. McCaffery and V. Casey, "Adopting agile practices when developing software for use in the medical domain," *Journal of Software Evolution and Process,* vol. 26, no. 5, pp. 504–512, 2014.

[34] M. Kostić, "Challenges of agile practices implementation in the medical device software development methodologies," *European Project Management Journal,* vol. 7, no. 2, pp. 36–44, 2017.

[35] FDA, "Recognized consensus standards: Medical devices," 11 September 2023. [Online]. Available: https://www.accessdata.fda.gov/scripts/cdrh/cfdocs/cfstandards/detail.cfm?standard__identification_no=30575. [Accessed 20 September 2023].

[36] FDA, "Appropriate use of voluntary consensus standards in submissions for medical devices," 14 September 2018. [Online]. Available: https://www.fda.gov/media/71983/download. [Accessed 20 September 2023].

[37] COCIR, "Artificial intelligence in EU medical device legislation," May 2021. [Online]. Available: https://www.cocir.org/fileadmin/Publications_2021/COCIR_Analysis_on_AI_in_medical_Device_Legislation_-_May_2021.pdf. [Accessed 20 September 2023].

[38] MD101, "IEC 82304-1 - Consequences on agile software development processes," 8 April 2016. [Online]. Available: https://blog.cm-dm.com/post/2016/04/08/IEC-82304-1-Consequences-on-agile-software-development-processes. [Accessed 20 September 2023].

[39] IEEE Computer Society, "Software Engineering Body of Knowledge (SWEBOK)," [Online]. Available: https://www.computer.org/education/bodies-of-knowledge/software-engineering. [Accessed 20 September 2023].

[40] IEEE, "Software Engineering Body of Knowledge (SWEBOK)," [Online]. Available: https://www.ieee.org/about/ieee-india/ieee-computer-society-india/swebok.html. [Accessed 20 September 2023].

[41] Stack Exchange, "What needs to change for software engineering to become a formal profession," 2015. [Online]. Available: https://softwareengineering.stackexchange.com/questions/196829/what-needs-to-change-for-software-engineering-to-become-a-formal-profession. [Accessed 20 September 2023].

[42] S. Kumar Pal, "Coding standards and guidelines," Geeks for geeks, 28 June 2022. [Online]. Available: https://www.geeksforgeeks.org/coding-standards-and-guidelines/. [Accessed 20 September 2023].

[43] S. Bose, "Coding standards and best practices to follow," Browser Stack, 20 April 2023. [Online]. Available: https://www.browserstack.com/guide/coding-standards-best-practices. [Accessed 20 September 2023].

[44] G. Wilson, D. Aruliah and A. Brown, "Best practices for scientific computing," *PloS Biology,* vol. 12, no. 1, p. e1001745, 2014.

[45] R. Martin, *Clean Code: A Handbook of Agile Software Craftsmanship*, Boston, MA: Prentice Hall, 2008.

[46] W. Lukaszuk, "Clean code," GitHub, 2022. [Online]. Available: https://gist.github.com/wojteklu/73c6914cc446146b8b533c0988cf8d29. [Accessed 20 September 2023].

[47] R. Zain, "The clean code manifesto," 11 April 2022. [Online]. Available: https://medium.com/@RadhiansyaZ/the-clean-code-manifesto-4505605df83b. [Accessed 20 September 2023].

[48] GNU, "GNU coding standards," [Online]. Available: https://www.gnu.org/prep/standards/standards.html#Formatting. [Accessed 20 September 2023].

[49] MISRA, "MISRA main site," [Online]. Available: https://misra.org.uk/. [Accessed 20 September 2023].

[50] Mathworks, "What is MISRA C?," [Online]. Available: https://uk.mathworks.com/discovery/misra-c.html. [Accessed 20 September 2023].

[51] DevIQ, "Guard clause," [Online]. Available: https://deviq.com/design-patterns/guard-clause. [Accessed 20 September 2023].

[52] O. Yenigun, "Defensive programming in Python," 27 September 2022. [Online]. Available: https://python.plainenglish.io/defensive-programming-in-python-af0266e65dfd. [Accessed 20 September 2023].

[53] European Spreadsheet Risks Interests Group, "Horror stories," [Online]. Available: https://eusprig.org/research-info/horror-stories/. [Accessed 20 September 2023].

[54] European Spreadsheet Risk Interest Group, "Research and best practice," [Online]. Available: https://eusprig.org/research-info/research-and-best-practice/ [Accessed 20 September 2023].

[55] B. Weber, "Strategies for addressing spreadsheet compliance challenges," in *Proc. European Spreadsheet Risks Int. Grp.*, 2006.

[56] R. Barker, M. Harris and G. Parkin, "Software support for Metrology best practice guide no 7 - Development and testing of spreadsheet applications," 2006. [Online]. Available: https://eprintspublications.npl.co.uk/3878/. [Accessed 20 September 2023].

[57] PCW, "Global financial modelling guidelines (v3.0)," January 2020. [Online]. Available: https://www.pwc.com.au/deals/assets/pwc-global-financial-modeling-guidelines-booklet-live.pdf. [Accessed 20 September 2023].

[58] B. Dickson, "Microsoft and OpenAI get ahead in the LLM competition," TechTalks, 28 March 2023. [Online]. Available: https://bdtechtalks.com/2023/03/28/microsoft-openai-llm-competition/. [Accessed 20 September 2023].

[59] European Commission, "Code of conduct on privacy for mHealth apps has been finalised," 07 June 2016. [Online]. Available: https://digital-strategy.ec.europa.eu/en/library/code-conduct-privacy-mhealth-apps-has-been-finalised. [Accessed 20 September 2023].

[60] BSI, "Health and wellness apps. Quality criteria across the life cycle. Code of practice," 30 April 2015. [Online]. Available: https://knowledge.bsigroup.com/products/health-and-wellness-apps-quality-criteria-across-the-life-cycle-code-of-practice?version=standard. [Accessed 20 September 2023].

[61] NHS England, "A guide to good practice for digital and data-driven health technologies," 19 January 2021. [Online]. Available: https://www.gov.uk/government/publications/code-of-conduct-for-data-driven-health-and-care-technology/initial-code-of-conduct-for-data-driven-health-and-care-technology. [Accessed 20 September 2023].

[62] NHS England, "Digital Technology Assessment Criteria," [Online]. Available: https://transform.england.nhs.uk/key-tools-and-info/digital-technology-assessment-criteria-dtac/. [Accessed 20 September 2023].

[63] A. Downey, "NHSX launches assessment criteria for digital health tools," Digital Health, 26 October 2020. [Online]. Available: https://www.digitalhealth.net/2020/10/nhsx-launches-assessment-criteria-for-digital-health-tools/. [Accessed 20 September 2023].

[64] FDA, "Policy for device software functions and mobile medical applications," September 2022. [Online]. Available: https://www.fda.gov/regulatory-information/search-fda-guidance-documents/policy-device-software-functions-and-mobile-medical-applications. [Accessed 20 September 2023].

[65] A. Marinelli and H. Mann, "Agile software development in bio/pharma & medical devices, Part 1," Med Device Online, 27 July 2023. [Online]. Available: https://www.outsourcedpharma.com/doc/agile-software-development-in-bio-pharma-medical-devices-part-0001. [Accessed 11 September 2023].

6 Regulation of Medical Devices

6.1 OVERVIEW

This chapter aims to provide a general overview of how medical devices are regulated in the US, the EU, and the UK, and to explain how medical software fits into the overall picture. Software regulation has always presented a challenge to regulators and it is only relatively recently that it was recognised that software can be a medical device in its own right.

The nature of computer software means that advances in technology come very rapidly, so regulators struggle to keep up with the pace of development. This catch-up process tends to result in a largely reactive approach that can sometimes be too stringent and stifle innovation. Apart from attempting to keep pace with advances in technology, major adverse incidents tend to provoke an overreaction from regulators, especially if it was demonstrated in the aftermath that weak regulation was part of the problem. In fact, weak *enforcement* is often the main reason for most medical device scandals, but there is always an inclination to review and revise the regulations following such events.

Within the broad sweep of medical device software, the regulation of mobile health apps and AI-enabled medical software has presented particular issues to regulators worldwide. There are ongoing efforts to harmonise regulatory approaches to medical software, but significant differences remain, particularly for software developed in-house.

6.2 A COMPARISON OF EU AND US APPROACHES TO MEDICAL DEVICE REGULATION

The US and European approaches to medical device regulation are superficially similar but some of the systems are fundamentally different. Unlike in the US, no centralised agency in Europe is responsible for the approval of medical devices. Instead, it is the medical device manufacturers themselves who declare the conformity of their products, based on an appropriate conformity assessment procedure specified in the regulations. For most medical devices the assessment procedure requires the involvement of an independent Notified Body, but these bodies only issue certificates (the so-called "Annex certificates") confirming compliance with certain regulatory requirements; they do not issue or award CE marks.

In the US, the Food and Drug Administration (FDA)[1] was established to promote and protect public health whereas the European oversight system based on Notified Bodies (NB) developed as part of a broader initiative to strengthen innovation and industrial policy. As a result, NB were not designed to function as public health agencies. Instead, the responsibility for the protection of public health lies with the national competent authorities, whose duties include the initial appointment and subsequent supervision of NB (Section 7.2.1). Competent authorities are typically government departments or agencies whereas NB are usually private companies [1].

The centralised approvals system employed by the FDA has a clear benefit in terms of uniformity of approach but also puts strain on limited FDA resources, which has previously led to delays in getting devices to market in the US. In contrast, the EU employs a distributed system that effectively delegates approval responsibility to member states. The overall system may be better resourced but can lead to inconsistent approaches between NB. There are also fewer NB under the MDR regime than there were under the old MDD. The FDA has recently addressed the resource issue by allowing approved third-party organisations to review 510(k) submissions on its behalf (Section 6.5.4.1.4).

The EU and US device classification systems are similar in principle but there are significant differences. Both have three levels (I, II, and III) but EU MDR class II is subdivided into IIa and IIb. Both systems are risk-based (i.e., the risk posed to the patient if the device malfunctions or fails) but there are some differences in how the risk level is assessed, resulting in a tendency for some types of devices to be placed in a higher-risk class in the US system.

One of the most important factors in risk-based classification is the directness of the connection between the output of the device and the treatment of the patient. The FDA has previously used the term *"competent human intervention"* (CHI) to distinguish the various situations that arise when medical devices are used in routine clinical practice; high-risk software systems are those that give limited opportunities for competent human intervention [2]. The device classification determines the degree of regulatory oversight in both systems.

There are also some differences in the respective compliance procedures. For the lowest risk (Class I) devices, the manufacturer can make a self-declaration of conformity in both systems, without any reference to an external body. Devices in higher-risk classes are subject to varying levels of independent assessment. In the EU, all such assessments are handled by an approved Notified Body, with the submissions only varying in terms of detail and content. In the US, however, there are different *types* of submissions, depending on device classification.

In general, the US regulatory approach is more pragmatic and proactive than the EU system. There is also a clearly stated objective not to overburden manufacturers with regulations that have no proven impact on device safety or reliability. The US system is also generally more accessible and transparent, with the FDA regularly publishing

---

[1] The Food and Drug Administration is an agency within the US Department of Health and Human Services. Within the FDA, the Centre for Devices and Radiological Health (CDRH) is responsible for ensuring the safety and effectiveness of medical devices.

consultation documents to indicate the way it intends to regulate a new type of medical device in the future (Section 9.2).

In contrast, the EU regulatory system has been largely reactive since the publication of the Medical Devices Directives some 30 years ago. Indeed, the recent (2017) EU Medical Device Regulations can be traced back directly to the hip prosthesis and breast implant scandals, which came to light in around 2012 [3].

Compliance in the EU regulatory system is described in terms of conformity assessment procedures (CAP) and these are generally undertaken by NB, appointed by the Designating Authority (DA) in the relevant EU member state. This is in contrast to the system in the US where marketing approval of medical devices is centralised and is the sole responsibility of the FDA.

Getting a software medical device to market in the EU has become more difficult than in the US, where the FDA has removed some of the "red tape" associated with qualification and classification processes. Regarding supporting standards, however, a more globally harmonised approach is emerging as the FDA gradually adopts international (ISO/IEC) standards instead of its own standards. The British Standards Institution (BSI) produced a report in 2020 comparing the EU and US approaches to the regulation of medical device software [4].

The US is also leading the way on the regulatory oversight of AI-enabled medical device software, through the use of its Predetermined Change Control Plan (PCCP) programme and has also run a pilot scheme for a software pre-certification ("Pre-Cert") programme (Section 6.5.8.9).

6.3   MEDICAL DEVICE REGULATION IN THE EU

6.3.1   OVERVIEW

Regulation (EU) 2017/745 on medical devices, commonly known as the EU MDR, describes the requirements for marketing medical devices within the European Union. It replaced the Directive on general medical devices (MDD, 93/42/EEC) and the Directive on active implantable devices (90/385/EEC). The new MDR (herein MDR 17) is significantly more comprehensive and detailed than the MDD that it replaced. While the old MDD comprised 23 Articles and 12 annexes over 60 pages, MDR 17/745 has 123 Articles and 17 Annexes, running to 175 pages. Depending on how you count them, there are between 200 and 220 individual requirements.

There is an associated regulation (EU 2017/746) covering *in-vitro* diagnostic medical devices (IVDR), which replaced Directive 98/79/EC (IVDD). This book concentrates on MDR 17/745 since the main areas of application of medical device software are expected to be covered by that regulation. Corresponding sections on all the main regulatory requirements (device qualification/classification, conformity assessment, etc.) can be found in MDR 17/746, which is about the same length as MDR 17/745.

The EC's *New Approach*, of which the old Medical Device Directives were a part, has been replaced by what is now called the *New Legislative Framework* (NLF). The changes are described in the latest edition of the so-called *Blue Guide* [5]. Some of the top-level changes introduced by the NLF (e.g., increased focus on product life cycle, post-market surveillance, *and* emphasis on software) are reflected in MDR 17/745 and MDR 17/746. While the Blue Guide does not introduce new require- ments for medical devices or IVDs, it provides background information and includes examples that explain the rationale behind certain provisions in the 2017 EU medical device regulations.

There are essentially fifteen main steps to gaining approval to market a medical device within the European Economic Area (EEA), which includes the EU member states, plus Iceland, Liechtenstein, and Norway.

1. Establish a team and define roles
2. Gain a basic collective understanding of the regulations
3. Describe the intended purpose of the medical device
4. Determine the class of the device
5. Determine the relevant regulatory requirements for that class of device
6. Undertake a compliance audit to identify current weaknesses/ deficiencies
7. Formulate an action plan based on the compliance audit/gap analysis
8. Implement required standards
9. Systematically address each regulatory requirement and reference the docu- mentary evidence that proves that the requirement has been met
10. Undertake a clinical evaluation and compile a technical file as an ongoing process throughout the entire product life cycle
11. Undertake an appropriate conformity assessment procedure. For Class II and Class III devices, obtain a certificate of conformity ("CE certificate") from a Notified Body
12. Prepare and sign a declaration of conformity
13. Register the device and its unique device identifier (UDI) in the EUDAMED database
14. Affix CE mark and UDI
15. Place the device on the market and start post-market surveillance

6.3.1.1   Extension of transition deadlines

Following lobbying by EU member states, NB, and medical device manufacturers, the EC has extended the deadlines associated with the transition to the new MDR and IVDR regulations, effectively meaning an extension of the validity of certificates issued under the old MDD. The extensions are based on the risk class of the device, as follows:

- Class IIb implantable and class III: 31/12/2027
- Class Is, class Im, class IIa, and remaining class IIb: 31/12/2028
- Remaining Class I devices: 26/05/21 (no change)

The EC has published a flowchart to assist manufacturers in deciding whether a device is covered by the extended MDR transition period [6].

The extension will apply only to devices already deemed safe (i.e., certified under the old MDD) that have not undergone significant changes in design or intended purpose. In addition, the manufacturer must have already taken steps toward certifi- cation under the MDR.

6.3.2 THE STRUCTURE OF MDR 17/745

Before delving into the detailed requirements of MDR 17/745 it is important to have a clear overview of the regulation, especially as most web sources of the official text do not include a table of contents.

Preamble

Chapter I: Scope and definitions (Articles 1–4)

Chapter II: Making available on the market and putting into service of devices, obligations of economic operators, reprocessing, CE marking, and free movement (Articles 5–24)

Chapter III: Identification and traceability of devices, registration of devices and of economic operators, a summary of safety and clinical performance, European database on medical devices (Eudamed) (Articles 25–34)

Chapter IV: NB (Articles 35–50)

Chapter V: Classification and conformity assessment (Articles 51–60)

Chapter VI: Clinical evaluation and clinical investigations (Articles 61–82)

Chapter VII: Post-market surveillance, vigilance, and market surveillance (Articles 83–100)

Chapter VIII: Cooperation between member states, Medical Device Coordination Group (MDCG), expert laboratories, expert panels, and device registers (Articles 101–108)

Chapter IX: Confidentiality, data protection, funding, and penalties (Articles 109–113)

Chapter X: Final provisions (Articles 114–123)

Annexes

Annex I: General safety and performance requirements (GSPR)

Annex II: Technical documentation

Annex III: Technical documentation on post-market surveillance

Annex IV: EU Declaration of Conformity

Annex V: CE marking of conformity

Annex VI: Information to be submitted upon the registration of devices and economic operators in accordance with Articles 29(4) and 31, core data elements to be provided to the UDI database together with the UDI-DI in accordance with Articles 28 and 29, and the UDI system.

Annex VII: Requirements to be met by Notified Bodies

Annex VIII: Classification rules

Annex IX: Conformity assessment based on quality management system and on assessment of technical documentation

Annex X: Conformity assessment based on type-examination

Annex XI: Conformity assessment based on product conformity verification

Annex XII: Certificates issued by a Notified Body.

Annex XIII: Procedure for custom-made devices

Annex XIV: Clinical evaluation and post-market clinical follow-up

Annex XV: Clinical investigations

Annex XVI: List of groups of products without an intended medical purpose referred to in Article 1(2)

Annex XVII: Correlation table[2]

The chapters essentially describe *what* needs to be done and the annexes provide most of the detail on *how* to do it. Annex I outlines the general safety and performance requirements (GSPR), which represent the core of the regulation. Simply put, the GSPRs attempt to ensure that medical devices are (1) safe and effective when used as intended by the manufacturer, (2) have acceptable risks when weighed against the potential benefits to patients and (3) have the associated risks reduced as far as possible without adversely affecting the benefit-risk ratio.

The following gives an overview of the contents of Annex I, which will be referenced in the subsequent sections on specific aspects of the regulation.

Annex I: General safety and performance requirements

Chapter I: General requirements
1. Devices shall achieve their intended performance and be safe and effective
2. Explanation of the meaning of "reducing risks as far as possible"
3. Risk management system
4. Risk control measures
5. Reducing risks associated with "use error"
6. Performance of the device under stress
7. Performance of the device during changes in environmental conditions
8. Known and foreseeable risks, and undesirable side effects
9. Statement on devices without a medical purpose

Chapter II: Requirements regarding design and manufacture
10. Chemical, physical, and biological properties
11. Infection and microbial contamination
12. Devices incorporating a substance considered to be a medicinal product and devices that are composed of substances, or of combinations of substances, that are absorbed by or locally dispersed in the human body
13. Devices incorporating materials of biological origin
14. Construction of devices and interaction with their environment (Note 14.2(d) in relation to software)
15. Devices with a diagnostic or measuring function
16. Protection against radiation
17. Electronic programmable systems – devices that incorporate electronic programmable systems and software that are devices in themselves
18. Active devices and devices connected to them

---

[2] A table showing the mapping between the articles in MDR 17/745 and the corresponding articles in the superseded Directives 90/385/EEC and 93/42/EC.

19. Particular requirements for active *implantable* devices
20. Protection against mechanical and thermal risks
21. Protection against the risks posed to the patient or user by devices supplying energy or substances
22. Protection against the risks posed by medical devices intended by the manufacturer for use by lay persons

Chapter III: Requirements regarding the information supplied with the device
   23. Label and instructions for use
      23.1 General requirements regarding the information supplied by the manufacturer
      23.2 Information on the label
      23.3 Information on the packaging which maintains the sterile condition of a device
      23.4 Information in the instructions for use

Most of the requirements for any medical device are covered by a combination of quality management and risk management systems (Sections 6.3.8 and 6.3.9). Clearly, many of the above requirements will not be relevant to the production of medical software.

6.3.2.1 Definition of a Medical Device

The most important definition in Chapter I of MDR 17/745 is that of a *medical device*, as it determines whether or not the regulations apply:

Under the regulations, "medical device" means any instrument, apparatus, appliance, software, implant, reagent, material, or other article intended by the manufacturer to be used, alone or in combination, for human beings for one or more of the following specific medical purposes:

- Diagnosis, prevention, monitoring, prediction, prognosis, treatment or alleviation of disease
- Diagnosis, monitoring, treatment, alleviation of, or compensation for, an injury or disability
- Investigation, replacement, or modification of the anatomy or of a physiological or pathological process or state
- Providing information by means of *in vitro* examination of specimens derived from the human body, including organ, blood, and tissue donations

and which does not achieve its principal intended action by pharmacological, immunological, or metabolic means, in or on the human body, but which may be assisted in its function by such means.

6.3.3 Harmonised Standards and Official Guidance

The MDR provides two formal instruments to prove compliance: harmonised standards and common specifications. A harmonised standard is a European standard developed by a recognised European standards organisation (CEN, CENELEC, or ETSI) at the request of the European Commission.

The key point is that harmonised standards are regulation-specific. The process usually involves the formal adoption of an existing international standard and the addition of a European Foreword describing the background to the development of the standard. It also references the added "Z" annexes, which describe the mapping between individual GSPRs in the regulation and the clauses in the standard. When a harmonised standard is developed from an international standard, the prefix "EN" (European norm) is added to the designation to indicate formal adoption by the European Union (e.g., EN ISO 14971:2019).

Although the adoption of standards is strictly voluntary in the context of MDR17, the implementation of *harmonised* standards by the manufacturer represents the simplest way of demonstrating compliance with a particular aspect of the regulations since it confers a "presumption of conformity" with the statutory requirements to which the standard relates. In fact, the whole *raison d'être* behind harmonised standards effectively makes their implementation a *de facto requirement* for complying with the relevant aspects of the regulation. The harmonisation process is complete when the reference to the standard is published in the Official Journal of the European Union (OJEU), at which point it acquires its quasi-legal status. GSPRs that are not covered by a harmonised standard must be addressed by other means.

MDR 17/745 harmonised standards as of August 2023:

1. EN ISO 14971:2019/A11:2021 (Medical devices – Application of risk management to medical devices)
2. EN ISO 13485:2016/A11:2021 (Medical devices – Quality management systems – Requirements for regulatory purposes)

These are the only harmonised standards relevant to medical device *software*. There are numerous other harmonised standards related to the various aspects of *hardware* medical device production (e.g., sterilisation) [7].

IEC 62304:2006/AMD 1:2015 (Medical device software – life cycle processes) is not yet harmonised under the MDR, but IEC 62304:2006 was adopted as a harmonised standard under the old MDD. Medical software producers are therefore advised to proceed as if the 2015 amendment to IEC 62304 has been harmonised since this will occur soon. It is on the long list of standards previously harmonised under the MDD that the EC has formally requested CEN/CENELEC to revise to meet the requirements of MDR 17/745 and MDR 17/746 [8]. The target implementation date is 27 May 2024.

6.3.3.1 The Role of the Medical Devices Coordination Group

The Medical Devices Coordination Group (MDCG) was created by the enactment of MDR17 (Chapter VIII). It has eight defined roles under Article 105, which include the provision of official guidance to both NB and medical equipment manufacturers. The group is made up of one representative from each EU member state and is chaired by a representative of the European Commission. Its work is undertaken by

13 working groups that generally mirror the main aspects of the regulation. There is also a working group on "new technologies", which has specific responsibility for guidance on software, apps, and cybersecurity.

6.3.3.2   Common Specifications

The rationale behind common specifications (CS) is outlined in Article 9 of MDR 17. In short, they are intended to "fill a gap" in situations where either a harmonised standard does not exist or is considered insufficient to demonstrate compliance with the relevant GSPR. So far, CS relate only to the reprocessing of single-use devices and to groups of devices (listed in Annex XVI) without a strict medical purpose. It is the responsibility of the European Commission to produce or adopt such CS and to publish them in the form of an Implementing Regulation. At the present time, they have no relevance to the production of medical device software.

6.3.4   QUALIFICATION

6.3.4.1   Is My Software a Medical Device?

Qualification is the most fundamental regulatory process since it determines whether or not the software in question is a medical device. This is done by reference to the definition of a medical device in the relevant regulations (Section 6.3.2.1) and any accompanying guidance produced by the MDCG [9].

Figure 6.1 shows a flowchart depicting the key steps in determining whether the software in question is a medical device. In this section, we use the term medical device software (MDSW) as defined by the MDCG (Chapter 3), to include both standalone software and embedded software that is an integral part of a hardware medical device.

The following "clarifying statements" were added by the MDCG

1. Software that is intended to process, analyse, create, or modify medical information may be qualified as medical device software if the creation or modification of that information is governed by a medical intended purpose. For example, software that *alters the representation of data* for a medical purpose would qualify as medical device software. However, altering the representation of data for embellishment/cosmetic or compatibility purposes does not qualify the software as medical device software.
2. MDSW may be independent, by having its own intended medical purpose and thus meeting the definition of a medical device or *in vitro* diagnostic medical device on its own.
    Comment: Standalone software that is qualified as a medical device is now generally referred to as software as a medical device, SaMD (see Chapter 3)
3. If the software drives or influences a (hardware) medical device and also has a medical purpose, then it is qualified as MDSW.
    Comment: Software that "drives or influences a hardware medical device" is qualified as MDSW anyway, according to Figure 1 in MDCG 2019–11.

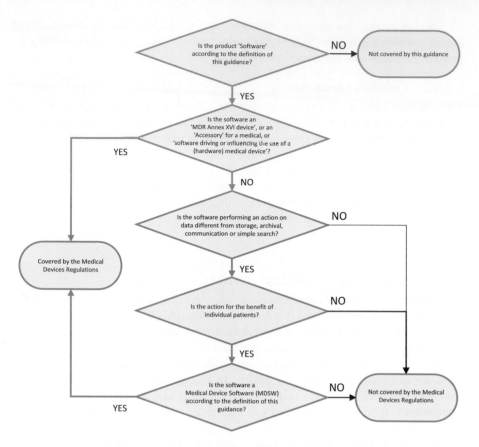

FIGURE 6.1 A flowchart for the qualification of medical device software under MDR 17/745 (Adapted with permission from Figure 1 of MDCG 2019-11) [9]).

4. Software may be qualified as MDSW regardless of its location (e.g., operating in the cloud, on a computer, on a mobile phone, or as an additional functionality on a hardware medical device).

5. MDSW may be intended to be used by healthcare professionals or laypersons (e.g., patients or other users). Where MDSW is intended to be used by a layperson, the manufacturer shall apply safety and performance requirements outlined in MDR Annex I. 22 and 23.4 (w); or IVDR Annex I. 9.4 and 20.4.2. MDSW in the form of an IVD for self-testing shall be considered a device intended to be used by laypersons.

6. Manufacturers must ensure that all regulatory requirements for placing on the market and conformity assessment have been fulfilled. As set out in Article 7 of MDR and IVDR, this also entails that any claims, relating to the intended medical purpose of their MDSW, are supported by clinical evidence.

  Comment: The MDCG has produced separate guidance on the clinical evidence requirements of MDR 17/745 in relation to legacy devices [10]

Returning to the MDR, Recital 19 makes a general comment about the qualification of software:

> It is necessary to clarify that software in its own right, when specifically intended by the manufacturer to be used for one or more of the medical purposes set out in the definition of a medical device, qualifies as a medical device, while software for *general purposes* [emphasis added], even when used in a healthcare setting, or software intended for life-style and well-being purposes, is not a medical device. The qualification of software, either as a device or an accessory, is independent of the software's location or the type of interconnection between the software and a device.

The above statement concerning general-purpose software used in a healthcare setting is slightly misleading since general-purpose software (such as spreadsheet software) can be used to produce a medical device (i.e., SaMD) (see Chapter 3 for more information on spreadsheets).

6.3.4.2 Clinical Database Systems

Apart from some types of "medical apps", the vast majority of software used in clinical diagnosis or treatment will be qualified as a medical device under MDR 17. The notable exceptions are the myriad of electronic healthcare record (EHR) systems[3] that simply store information about the patient. In a hospital setting, none of the large clinical database systems overseen by the corporate IT department would be regarded as medical devices.

Laboratory Information systems (LIS), as typically used in Pathology Departments, generally receive, store, organise and display data from various *in-vitro* medical devices designed to analyse blood or tissue samples. As such, LIS would not be qualified as *in vitro* medical devices under the terms of MDR 17/746.

6.3.4.3 Picture Archiving and Communication System (PACS)

The most recent official guidance on the qualification of PACS systems was produced in 2019 by an EC working group [11].

The guidance refers to the old MDD but MDCG 2019-11 [9], which refers to MDR 17, states that the transposition of this Directive Guidance to the Medical Device Regulations is in progress. In areas where the Directives and MDR remain aligned (e.g., PACS software) the guidance is still applicable.

If the PACS software is intended only for data archiving and storage (using a method that preserves the original data) it would not be considered a medical device. However, most modern PACS systems are designed to do much more than just store and display original image data, so will generally be qualified as medical devices. The classification of PACS systems is discussed in Section 6.3.5.2.

6.3.4.4 Mobile Apps

MDR 17/745 does not provide much detail on the qualification of mobile apps, but the accompanying guidance produced by the MDCG (Section 6.3.5.2) makes it clear that

---

[3] E.g., Electronic patient record (EPR), Hospital information system (HIS), Clinical information system (CIS).

the qualification and classification rules that apply to standalone software also apply to apps, whether they operate on a mobile phone, in the cloud or on other platforms.

Even when an app does not qualify as SaMD in its own right, it may still fall within the scope of the regulations if it qualifies as an *accessory* to a medical device (Section 6.3.5.2). That is, when it is "intended to *specifically enable* a device to be used in accordance with its intended purpose or to *specifically and directly assist* the medical functionality of the device". For example, an app linked wirelessly to a monitoring device to record data such as body temperature, heart rate, or blood pressure. In the FDA system, accessory software is certainly classified as a device (Section 6.5.8).

Definition of medical device accessory in MDR 17/745: An "accessory for a medical device" means an article which, whilst not being itself a medical device, is intended by its manufacturer to be used together with one or several particular medical device(s) to specifically enable the medical device(s) to be used in accordance with its/their intended purpose(s) or to specifically and directly assist the medical functionality of the medical device(s) in terms of its/their intended purpose(s).

6.3.4.5   Wearable Devices

Wearable devices such as "smart watches" have become extremely popular over the last few years as people's interest in monitoring health-related aspects of their daily lives has increased. The functionality of such devices is expanding rapidly, as ever-more sophisticated sensors are built into them. What started off as simple activity trackers (e.g., counting steps, measuring heart rate) have quickly become sophisticated gadgets capable of measuring blood oxygen level and body temperature, as well as performing a basic ECG [12]. And, of course, they all need complex embedded software to process large amounts of data and display the results. The regulatory issues surrounding the future supply and use of wearable devices are discussed further in Chapter 9.

6.3.4.6   Clinical Decision Support (CDS) Software

Based on Figure 6.1, software that meets the general description of a CDS given in Section 3.3.2 will be qualified as a medical device. Examples provided in MDCG 2019-11 [9] include a radiotherapy treatment planning application, a chemotherapy dose calculator, and systems that automatically analyse/interpret ECG recordings or X-ray images. This latter ("auto-diagnosis") type of CDS software would probably include some form of AI technology (Section 6.3.6.5).

The EU regulatory approach to CDS software is quite different from that being taken in other jurisdictions. In the US, the intended user is key. If the CDS software is intended only to be used by a healthcare professional (HCP), the software is not regulated by the FDA (Section 6.5.8.6). The same approach is being taken in Australia where certain types of CDS software are not subject to regulation by the Therapeutic Goods Administration (TGA) [13].

6.3.4.7   Software used for Clinical Research

A distinction needs to be made between software that constitutes an "investigational device" and software that is developed and used to *support* a local medical research project. An investigational device is defined in MDR17 as "a device that is assessed in a clinical investigation" (i.e., where the device itself is the subject of the clinical investigation [Section 6.3.10]). Many of the obligations specified in MDR 17 are thus directed to "manufacturers of devices, *other than* custom-made or investigational devices".

The meaning of investigational device is essential the same in the US, where the use of such a device to collect safety and effectiveness data (usually to provide evidence to support a pre-market approval (PMA), Section 6.5.4.3) is covered by an Investigational Device Exemption (IDE). According to 21 CFR 812.1, an approved IDE "permits a device that otherwise would be required to comply with a performance standard or to have PMA to be shipped lawfully for the purpose of conducting investigations of that device".

Software developed in-house to support a local clinical research project, where there is no intention for it to be placed on the market, is not an investigational device, and is not covered by EU or UK medical device regulations. Most examples of local research that may require the development of software for data analysis are covered by what the UK MHRA refers to as "health institution studies" [14]. Most examples in medical imaging involve further analysis of data collected as part of a routine scan, so does not usually involve any additional inconvenience or discomfort for the patient. If additional imaging (e.g., adding additional views to a routine examination) *is* required, this may require approval from the local ethics committee.

6.3.5   CLASSIFICATION OF MEDICAL DEVICES

6.3.5.1   Basic Principles and Implementation Rules

Medical devices are classified under MDR17 according to the following risk based schedule:

Class I: low risk
Class IIa: low-to-medium risk
Class IIb: medium-to-high risk
Class III: high risk

Class I is further sub-divided into Class Is (sterile), Class Im (measuring function), and Class Ir (reusable). The classification of a medical device determines the number and type of general quality assurance and other requirements that need to be applied during the production and post-production phases of the manufacturing process (Figure 6.2). It also dictates the rigour and formality associated with the conformity assessment (CA) procedure. For pure Class I devices, conformity can be done by self-declaration. For all other devices, the procedure requires the involvement of a Notified Body. For Class Is and Class Im devices, referral to a Notified Body is required for certification of the aspects of manufacture relating to sterility and metrology, respectively.

As might be expected, the GSPR described in Annex I of the regulations are grouped by device types rather than device class. For example, some requirements apply (only) to devices with a measuring function, some to devices containing chemicals, etc. The requirements that depend on device class apply mainly to clinical evaluation (Section 6.3.10.1), post-market activities (Section 6.3.15), and the summary of safety and clinical performance (SSCP, Section 6.3.13).

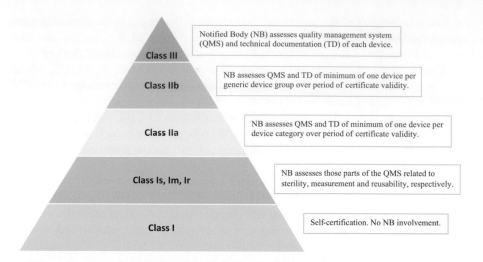

FIGURE 6.2 MDR 17/745 device classification related to the degree of external scrutiny for conformance assessment. Note: There are only four official device classes (I, IIa, IIb, and III) but the subdivision of Class I is shown here for clarity. Note: "Generic device group" is a set of devices having the same or similar intended purpose or commonality of technology, allowing them to be classified in a generic manner. Adapted with permission from Figure 9 in the COCIR document on AI in EU MDR [15].

TABLE 6.1

MDR general requirements by device class. Only the most significant requirements are shown

Obligations under MDR 17/745	Device classification				
	I	Is, Im, Ir	IIa	IIb	III
Quality management system (QMS)	Article 10			Article 10 & ISO 13485	
QMS assessment by Notified Body (NB)	NR	Annex IX (1)	Article 10 (2,3)		
Technical documentation	Annex II, III				
General safety and performance requirements	Annex I				
Risk management	Annex I, sections 3,4,5				
Clinical evaluation plan/report (CER)	Article 61 & Annex XIV Part A				
Clinical investigation file	Need is determined by the CER				Annex XV
Summary of safety and clinical performance	n/a		Article 32		
Post-market surveillance (PMS) plan	Article 84				
PMS report	Article 85			n/a	
Post-market clinical follow-up (PMCF) plan	Annex XIV Part B				
Periodic safety update report (PSUR)	n/a		Article 86		
Assessment of technical documentation by NB	NR	Annex IX (4)			
Declaration of conformity	Annex IV				
CE marking of medical device	Annex V				

6.3.5.2   Classification of Medical Device Software

The EU MDR classification rules are stated (Recital 58) to be based on the vulnerability of the human body and to take account of the potential risks associated with the technical design and manufacture of medical devices. The relevant classification rule for medical device software is Rule 11, which states that:

> Software intended to provide information which is used to take decisions with diagnosis or therapeutic purposes is classified as class IIa, except if such decisions have an impact that may cause: death or an irreversible deterioration of a person's state of health, in which case it is in class III; or a serious deterioration of a person's state of health or a surgical intervention, in which case it is classified as class IIb.
>
> Software intended to monitor physiological processes is classified as class IIa, except if it is intended for monitoring of 'vital physiological parameters', where the nature of variations of those parameters is such that it could result in immediate danger to the patient, in which case it is classified as class IIb. All other software (including most health and well-being apps) is classed as class I.

In this context "monitoring of vital physiological paraments" (ref: class IIb) means the *continuous surveillance* of parameters such as body temperature, heart rate, blood gases, respiration rate, and blood pressure in areas such as anaesthesia, intensive care, or emergency care [16]. In contrast, medical devices intended to measure one or more of these vital parameters in the context of a routine diagnostic work-up or follow-up visits are classed as class IIa – emphasising the importance of *intended use* in the EU regulation of medical devices.

Rule 11 was new to MDR 17/745 and has proved contentious, mainly because it focuses only on the potential severity of harm, with no account taken of its likelihood of occurrence [17]. Most SaMD is associated, directly or indirectly, with the diagnosis or treatment of disease, so is bound to be classified as either Class II or Class III according to Rule 11. Moreover, if Rule 11 were interpreted literally, all SaMD could be classified as a Class III device because it is always possible to think of a worst-case scenario in which the information provided by the software leads to death, no matter how unlikely. As a result, the situation regarding the classification of MDSW remains confused, with non-critical SaMD potentially being classified too highly, leading to over-regulation and increased costs for producers.

6.3.5.2.1   MDCG and International Medical Devices Regulators Forum (IMDRF) Guidance

Two MDGC guidance documents on medical device qualification/classification have been produced since the publication of MDR 17 [9,16], but neither directly addressed the central issue associated with Rule 11.

However, the reference to the IMDRF SaMD risk framework in MDCG 2019-11 (including a mapping table entitled "Classification guidance on Rule 11") clearly indicates that it is acceptable to use the IMDRF categorisation scheme as an aid to the classification of medical software under MDR 17.

The IMDRF scheme depends on the significance of the information provided *and* the criticality of the disease, condition, or intervention, so it effectively "moderates" the severity-only approach of Rule 11. The table in the guidance document relating

TABLE 6.2

Correspondence of MDR 17 medical device classes and IMDRF SaMD risk categories. Adapted with permission from Annex III of MDCG 2019-11 [9]

MDR device class	IMDRF risk category			
	I	II	III	IV
I	*Not applicable*			
IIa	✓	✓		
IIb			✓	
III				✓

TABLE 6.3

A MDSW classification system combining the effects of MDR Rule 111 and MDCG guidance document 2019-11 [9]. "Management" here refers to clinical management of the patient. See text for information on software that "drives or influences the use of the (hardware) device"

Healthcare Condition	Significance of information provided by SaMD		
	Inform management	Drive management	Treat or diagnose
Critical	Class IIa	Class IIb	Class III
Serious	Class IIa	Class IIa	Class IIb
Non-serious	Class IIa	Class IIa	Class IIa

the IMDRF risk category to the MDR device class is presented in a slightly confusing manner, so Table 6.2 is based on the accompanying wording.

Combining the information from MDR Rule 11 and MDCG 2019-11, a classification can be obtained that depends on the potential severity of the medical condition and the role played by the software. It is therefore advisable to determine the IMDRF SaMD risk category *first* (see Chapter 3) and then use Table 6.3 to determine the MDR *device* classification. Some groups have combined the MDR Rule 11 and MDCG requirements into one flowchart [18] but this can be confusing. The use of IMDRF's SaMD framework to help determine the MDR risk class for MDSW does not solve the fundamental problem with the wording of Rule 11 but it allows for a temporary "workaround".

The most recent MDCG classification guidance [16] does not mention the IMDRF SaMD framework proposal in connection with Rule 11 but makes the general statement (Section 3.2.1) that "in addition to the classification rules set out in Annex VIII of MDR, manufacturers must also take account of any applicable legal acts and consider guidance documents which may support the classification of their device". It is further added that:

for the classification of software, it is needed to consider the intended purpose, intended population (including e.g., diseases to be treated and/or diagnosed), the context of use (e.g., intensive care, emergency care, home use) and the information provided by the software, as well as the possible decisions to be taken.

6.3.5.2.2 Implications of Medical Device Software Classification

Notwithstanding the lack of clarity surrounding Rule 11, the actual requirements for software (in terms of design and production) are almost independent of its classification; the main consequences lie in CAP (Section 6.3.17) and post-market surveillance. In particular, the GSPR's related to software (Section 6.3.6.1) described in Annex I do not distinguish between products in different classes [19].

Although the general obligations and requirements for medical device software manufacturers are covered in the regulation itself, the detailed "how-to" software engineering procedures are mainly dictated by compliance with IEC 62304:2015, which is the standard recommended by NB and other industry observers to ensure conformity with the software development (i.e., life cycle) requirements of MDR 17/745 (see Chapter 5). It is inevitable that IEC 62304:2015 will become a harmonised standard under MDR 17/745 in due course (Section 6.3.3).

The *software safety* classification scheme used in IEC 62304 (giving rise to software classes A, B, and C) should not be confused with the medical device classification system described in MDR 17/745.

6.3.5.2.3 Is there Any Class I Medical Device Software?

The MDCG mapping given in Table 6.3 does not include medical device software in MDR Class I, giving the impression that nearly all MDSW is at least class IIa.

It is possible for MDSW software to fall into Class I (if none of the inclusion criteria for Class IIa and above apply), but this is only likely to include wellbeing apps (Section 3.3.5) that are intended only to be used by lay persons and are not designed to monitor any physiological processes [19].

The most recent (2021) MDCG guidance on classification of medical devices [16] includes some information on MDSW classification using Rule 11 but only includes one example of Class I software – an app for predicting a woman's fertility status based on body temperature and menstruation days. The example is very clear-cut so does not help with borderline cases. An example involving the prevention of disease (i.e., not directly associated with diagnosis or treatment) would have been helpful, but observers have inferred that such apps (e.g., "lifestyle apps" that suggest behavioural changes based on diet and body mass index) would be Class I [20].

The MDCG guidance further states that "a mobile app intended to analyse a user's heartbeat, detect abnormalities and inform a physician accordingly" would be classed as IIb, although some of these home-use devices for detecting cardiac arrhythmias such as atrial fibrillation (AF) have been classed as IIa [21].

6.3.5.2.4 Other Classification Rules

MDR 17 Classification rules 9–13 apply to "active devices", which are defined as "any device, the operation of which depends on a source of energy other than that generated by the human body for that purpose, or by gravity, and which acts by changing the density of or converting that energy" (Article 2[4]). For example, all electrically powered hardware devices are therefore active devices. It seems somewhat incongruous for software to be considered in this context but the definition nonetheless goes on to state that "software shall also be deemed to be an active device".

It may therefore appear that Rules 9, 10, 12, and 13 need to be scrutinised for any relevance to (standalone) software but MDCG guidance [MDCG 2019-11] makes it clear that software does not generally relate to the risks described in these rules but, rather, to the "consequences of indirect harm from failure to provide correct information". Nonetheless, by virtue of software being deemed an active device, if a hardware medical device contains software that provides information for patient management, then these other rules pertaining to active devices should be considered, along with special Rule 22.

6.3.5.2.5   Embedded or Accessory Software

In general, software that is an integral part of, or accessory to, a hardware medical device should be classified separately from the parent device. For example, it is quite possible for a high-risk class III device to contain software that only provides basic functionality that would place it in a lower class [22]. The low level of risk of the software component would also have a direct bearing on its software safety classification according to IEC 62304 (Section 5.4.1.4).

The exception to this general principle is expressed in Implementing Rule 3.3., which states that software, that "drives a device or influences the use of a device" shall fall within the same class as the device, thereby avoiding any confusion associated with interpretation of Rule 11 in this situation. Such software can include anything from direct control of a device to simply auto-selecting a device.

Such software is usually an integral part of the hardware medical device (e.g., embedded software or firmware) but can include other types of software. For example, current UK guidance on software and apps [23] contains several examples of third-party software that interfaces directly or indirectly with a medical device via a physical or wireless connection. In all cases, the third-party software assumes the classification of the "parent" device according to MDR Rule 3.3.[4] An accessory to a medical device is not a medical device (by definition) but still falls within the scope of MDR 17/745 [9].

6.3.5.2.6   PACS Systems

As discussed in Section 6.3.4.3, most modern PACS systems used in clinical radiology departments will qualify as medical devices. The qualification and classification of PACS systems under EU MDRs are based on EC guidance on "borderline" medical devices published in 2019 [24].

If the PACS software is intended for viewing, archiving, *and* transmitting patient data, it is considered a Class I medical device according to MDD Rule 12 (now MDR Rule 13). Above this level, things get complicated as the "current" guidance refers only to MDD classification rules and takes no account of the new classification rule for software (Rule 11, see Section 6.3.5.2) introduced by MDR 17/745.

---

[4] Current UK (MHRA) guidance refers to MEDDEV 2.1/6, which in turn refers to the old MDD. However, the relevant implementing rule in Annex IX (section 2.3) of the MDD is identical to rule 3.3 in the MDR.

However, PACS software that includes all the usual post-processing facilities (e.g., image filtering, multi-planar reconstruction, quantitative assessment) would be classified as Class IIa under either MDR Rule 11 or MDD Rule 10, provided it does not "drive or influence" a source device (e.g., CT scanner, MRI scanner, gamma camera) to which it is network connected. In the unlikely event that it was possible to drive or (directly) influence a source device from a PACS workstation (e.g., by controlling image data acquisition) then the PACS software would (according to Implementing Rule 3.3) fall automatically into the same class in the source device in question.

6.3.6 MEDICAL DEVICE SOFTWARE REQUIREMENTS

The recognition in EU MDR that software could be a medical device in its own right occurred relatively recently when Directive 2007/47/EC formally amended the definition of a medical device used in Directives 90/385/EEC (General MDD) and 93/42/EEC (Active Implantable MDD), on the basis that is was "...necessary to clarify that software in its own right, when specifically intended by the manufacturer to be used for one or more of the medical purposes set out in the definition of a medical device, is a medical device". The previous single *essential requirement* (ER) relating to software was thereby replaced by something more meaningful, which was subsequently transposed (with minor modification) into MDR 17/745 as GSPR 17.2 (Section 6.3.6.1).

There are numerous references to "software" in MDR 17 but the term is not defined. In what is considered official guidance, the MDCG defines software simply as "a set of instructions that processes input data and creates output data". For software to be considered medical device software (MDSW) it must (a) meet the definition of "software" in MDCG 2019-11 [9] and (b) meet the definition of a medical device in the regulations (see Section 6.3.2.1). Note that the term MDSW includes software used alone (i.e., SaMD) or in combination with a hardware medical device (see Chapter 3). To be considered as SaMD in an EU regulatory context, the software must also "perform an action on data for the medical benefit of individual patients" (figure 1 of MDCG 2019-11). Note that the MDR itself does not refer to the term "software as a medical device".

6.3.6.1 GSPRs Relating to Software

Having decided that the software under development is indeed a medical device (Section 6.3.4.1) and worked out its classification (Section 6.3.5.2), the specific tasks to be undertaken are largely dictated by the relevant GSPR in Annex I. Most of the GSPRs listed in Chapters I and III of Annex I are relevant to medical device software manufacture, but the specific requirements are detailed in the electronic programmable system (EPS) section (GSPR 17) of Chapter II (*Requirements regarding design and manufacture*):

> 17.1. Devices that incorporate electronic programmable systems, including software, or software that are devices in themselves, shall be designed to ensure repeatability, reliability and performance in line with their intended use. In the event of a single fault condition, appropriate means shall be adopted to eliminate or reduce as far as possible consequent risks or impairment of performance.

17.2. For devices that incorporate software or for software that are devices in themselves, the software shall be developed and manufactured in accordance with the state of the art taking into account the principles of development life cycle, risk management, including information security, verification and validation.

17.3. Software referred to in this Section [MDR 17, Annex I] that is intended to be used in combination with mobile computing platforms shall be designed and manufactured taking into account the specific features of the mobile platform (e.g., size and contrast ratio of the screen) and the external factors related to their use (varying environment as regards level of light or noise).

17.4. Manufacturers shall set out minimum requirements concerning hardware, IT networks characteristics and IT security measures, including protection against unauthorised access, necessary to run the software as intended.

GSPR 15.1 relating to devices with a diagnostic measuring function is also relevant to diagnostic software: *Diagnostic devices and devices with a measuring function, shall be designed and manufactured in such a way as to provide sufficient accuracy, precision, and stability for their intended purpose, based on appropriate scientific and technical methods. The limits of accuracy shall be indicated by the manufacturer.*

These GSPRs, combined with the *general* requirements detailed in Chapters I and III of Annex I, represent the basic tenets of MDR 17 for the manufacture and supply of medical device software in the EU. The *means* by which these wide-ranging requirements are satisfied are detailed in the following sub-sections, including the use of appropriate harmonised standards for software development (Section 6.3.3).

6.3.6.2   In-house Software Production

For in-house software production, the developer is only legally required to address a subset of the regulatory requirements relating to software (Section 6.3.11), but is encouraged to follow as many of the other relevant requirements as possible, for professional and general quality assurance reasons [25]. If in-house software is being used instead of commercially available software (see Chapter 3), then there is every reason to insist that it is developed to the same standards.

6.3.6.3   Reference to IEC 62304:2015

Having done all the planning and preparations described in the earlier sections, how do we go about actually producing the software? The simple answer is to identify every MDR17 article and GSPR relating to software and to ensure (i.e., be able to demonstrate through documentary and other evidence) that each has been considered and followed where appropriate.

Most of the *software* GSPRs will be addressed by compliance with a recognised international standard, some of which have been harmonised under the MDR (Section 6.3.3). For software production, the guiding *standard is IEC 62304 (Medical devices software – life cycle processes)*, which was most recently amended in 2015. IEC 62304 is a framework standard and, as such, does not prescribe any particular software development methodology. It lends itself to structured methodologies (e.g., V-model, waterfall variant) but modern iterative techniques (e.g., agile, Kanban) can, with some modification, also be used (Section 5.4.1.12).

The detailed requirements of IEC 62304 are described in detail in Chapter 5. The standard does not cover all aspects of the software development life cycle (SDLC), so some GSPR requirements need to be covered by other means.

IEC 62304:2006/AMD 1:2015 is not yet harmonised under MDR 17 (Section 6.3.3), but it is generally considered the current state of the art (see Appendix 1) for medical device software development. It does not include requirements for AI-enabled software but these are expected to be included in the next edition, which is now overdue [15].

A gap analysis tool for SaMD is available online that provides a useful checklist to assess an organisation's ability to meet the requirements of both IEC 62304 and MDR 17/745 [26].

6.3.6.4   Diagnostic Medical Software

For diagnostic medical software, there is usually considerable competent human intervention (CHI, Section 6.2) to mitigate the effects of software faults and thus protect the patient. In nuclear medicine, for example, the results of image data processing by a specifically trained technologist will usually be checked by a physicist before being passed to a radiologist for reporting. The referring clinician then considers the clinical report before deciding whether to implement a particular course of treatment based on the *suggested* diagnosis. And results from a particular scan will always be considered alongside other diagnostic tests (e.g., blood results, other types of scans) as well as physical examination of the patient and clinical history.

There is thus considerable "internal quality control" that should uncover the most obvious errors in data processing software, but it must be accepted that some types of systematic (e.g., algorithmic) errors in diagnostic software will be difficult to spot once in routine clinical use. Clinical software should therefore be subjected to external audit testing where such national or regional schemes exist [27,28]. Note that the notion of CHI relates to the concepts of Intended Purpose for Use (IPU) and adequate Instructions for Use (IFU) used in EU Medical Device Regulations.

For SaMD, *indirect* harm is therefore the most probable outcome of adverse incidents [29].

6.3.6.5   Devices Containing AI Technology

Medical devices containing AI/ML software present a special challenge to regulators due to the unique way in which the system can change and self-evolve (Section 3.3.4). MDR 17/745 contains no specific requirements for AI-based systems, but manufacturers of such systems must nonetheless adhere to general requirements for reliability, information security, elimination of bias and use error, as well as the all-embracing requirement that a device be developed and manufactured according to the current state of the art in terms of its intended purpose (GSPRs 1 and 17.2).

Possible future changes in medical device regulations and supporting European standards are discussed further in Section 9.3.3. Until such time as new regulations or official guidance become available, manufacturers of AI-enabled medical devices intending to sell into the EU market must work with what is currently available in terms of professional and industry guidance [30]. Manufacturers will also need to seek out a Notified Body with the specialist expertise required to deal with the certification of AI-based medical software, as the validation and verification of adaptive software will be different from traditional SaMD [31].

Current practice for AIaMD should be viewed within the context of what the MDCG defines as a "significant change" for medical device software generally [32].

Although focused on transitional arrangements for devices approved under the old MDD, the MDCG guidance lists five software design changes that would be considered "significant" in the context of MDR 17/745 (Article 120[3]). Amongst these is "a new or modified architecture or database structure, or change of an algorithm" and any change in which "required user input [was] replaced by a closed loop algorithm". It is expected that future MDCG guidance will address the issues of adaptive software in a more contemporary manner, akin to the approach being taken by the FDA (Section 6.5.5.8).

Guidance on the deployment of AI/ML software in the context of *current* EU MDR is also available on GitHub [33].

IEC 62304:2006/AMD1:2015 (Section 5.4.1) covers most aspects of the SDLC, including change management and configuration management, but does not reference artificial intelligence – an omission that will be addressed in the next edition of the standard. Issues surrounding the incorporation of AI-based chatbots are discussed in Section 9.5.5.5.

6.3.6.6 Usability Engineering

The term "usability" is not defined in MDR 17/745 but is defined elsewhere. For example, the BSI White Paper on *Human Factors and Usability Engineering* defines usability as "a multidimensional quality that refers to the ability of a human to interact easily and relatively error-free with a system or product" [34]. Terms such as "user-friendly" and "intuitive" have become associated with the concept of usability.

A search for the word "usability" in the text of MDR 17/745 produces only two "hits" (in connection with the UDI system and post-market surveillance, respectively) but the requirement for design and test processes to address usability issues are implied/inferred by statements about *intended purpose*. For example, paragraph 1 of Annex I states that "devices shall achieve the performance intended by their manufacturer and shall be designed and manufactured in such a way that, during normal conditions of use, they are suitable for their intended purpose".

The intended purpose is defined (Article 2[12]) as "the use for which a device is intended according to the data supplied by the manufacturer on the label, in the IFU or in promotional or sales materials or statements and as specified by the manufacturer in the clinical evaluation", but statements about "intended purpose" in the body of the regulation make it clear that the term refers to the intended medical purpose, the intended users and the environment in which the device is intended to be used.[5] As such, the user interface (UI) design of a software medical device is a key issue in avoiding use errors and other untoward effects.

Usability issues are also inferred by an explicit requirement for risk management activities to address intended use *and* "reasonably foreseeable misuse" (Annex I, Section 3). Good UI design will minimise use errors but they cannot be completely eliminated. Section 5 of Annex I describes specific actions for the elimination or at least reduction of risks related to use error. As a result, MDR17 makes it mandatory for manufacturers to design control measures for all identified risks relating to usability.

---

[5] This combination of requirements is referred to as the "use specification" in IEC 62366-1:2015 (Medical devices: Application of usability engineering to medical devices).

Section 14.6 of Annex I specifies that any measurement, monitoring, or display scale "must be designed and manufactured in line with ergonomic principles, taking account of the intended purpose, users, and the environmental conditions in which the devices are intended to be used". Such display scales may be implemented in software, so this requirement is relevant to software-based devices. The MDR does not elaborate on what is meant by "ergonomic principles" but good practice guidance can be found in the ISO 9241 (*Ergonomics of human-system interaction*) family of standards; the part dealing with GUI elements (e.g., buttons, checkboxes, collapsible containers) being ISO 9241-161:2016.

In a software context, exhaustive testing is key and prototype testing and beta testing of the final product should include testing by actual clinical users (e.g., doctors and/or nurses) as they tend to interact with the system rather differently than trained software testers. The envisaged different use scenarios (including those in which the device is used in combination with other devices) as well as the actual user environment (e.g., lighting conditions, types of input hardware devices) should also be considered. An external auditor would expect to see a description of this analysis in the risk management file (Section 6.3.9).

For organisations adopting IEC 62366-1 (see below), a full description and analysis of user scenarios, along with details of the use specification (and other items) should be documented in the usability engineering file (UEF), in which case a reference should be provided in the RMF.

Where manufacturers are designing devices (e.g., apps) for use by patients, the user should then be considered a layperson. The MDR defines a layperson (Article 2 [38]) and has specific requirements (Annex I, Section 22) for devices intended to be used by such persons. The requirements for simplicity, ease of use, and understandability will have a direct effect on the design of the device, the form of usability tests, and also on the production of user instructions (Annex I, Section 23.1 [a]) and any associated training materials.

In respect of technical documentation, Section 1.1(a) of Annex II specifies that the device description/specification should include the product name along with a general description of the device including its intended purpose and intended users. For test documentation relating to software validation and verification (Section (b) of Annex II), the manufacturer must produce evidence of testing performed "both in-house and in a simulated or actual user environment prior to final release".

In relation to post-market surveillance, it is specified (Article 83, Section 3[f]) that the information gathered by manufacturers should be used, amongst other things, "for the identification of options to improve the usability, performance and safety of the device".

Most of the above requirements are addressed by IEC 62366-1:2015/Amd1:2020 (Medical devices: Application of usability engineering to medical devices). IEC 62366:2007 was harmonised by the EC under the old medical device directives in 2008, but the latest version of the standard has not yet been harmonised under MDR 17/745. It nonetheless represents the current state of the art in this area and adoption is recommended to all manufacturers of medical device software. To assist manufacturers there is an accompanying technical report (IEC/TR 62366-2:2016 – Medical devices – Part 2: Guidance on the application of usability engineering to medical devices) that contains background information and examples, as well as guidance on the specific requirements of the standard. Compliance with IEC 62366-1 will certainly make conformance with the usability requirements of the EU MDR more straightforward and it is expected to become a harmonised standard in due course.

Unlike the EU MDR, the FDA is quite specific about usability regulations and has been addressing this issue for decades (Section 6.5.8.10).

6.3.6.7   Cybersecurity

The term "cybersecurity" is not mentioned in MDR 17/745 but there are many cyber-security issues referenced in sections of Annex I, including "information security" (GSPR 17.2), "IT security" (GSPR 17.4) (Section 6.3.6.1), the "interaction between software and the IT environment in which it operates" (GSPR 14.2.[d]), and information on "IT security measures" to be included in the IFU (GSPR 23.4 [ab]).

It follows from 14.2(d) that manufacturers of SaMD that runs on networked systems need to consider not only the risk posed by other networked systems but also the risk posed to those other systems by their software. The way to deal with this type of "reciprocal risk" is covered in IEC 80001-1:2021 (Chapter 5, A.1.2.5), which covers IT networks incorporating medical devices.

GSPR 18.8 also states that "devices shall be designed and manufactured in such a way as to protect, as far as possible, against unauthorised access that could hamper the device from functioning as intended". The identified cybersecurity issues should be included in the risk management plan (see Section 6.3.9). A useful checklist of typical software hazards, including unauthorised access issues, is included in IEC/TR 80002-1:2009 (Chapter 5, A.1.2.4).

The MDCG has produced useful guidance on cybersecurity-related aspects of MDR 17/745 [35], which includes a useful table showing relevant Articles and Annexes, broken down into pre-market and post-market activities (Table 6.4). In relation to GSPR 23.4 (ab), the MDCG guidance lists the types of information that could be included to satisfy the IFU requirement, including:

- Use environment (e.g., healthcare facility, home, both)
- Minimum hardware platform and operating system requirements (if provided as software-only product)
- Recommended IT security controls (anti-virus software, firewall, etc.)
- Description of backup and restore features for both software and data

It also describes information to be provided to the end-user in documentation other than the IFU, including provisions to ensure integrity/validation of software updates and security patches, user roles and respective privileges/permission on the device, operation of the system (fault) logging feature, and a software bill of materials (SBOM) [35].

Most cybersecurity issues discovered as part of post-market (vigilance) procedures would not qualify as "serious reportable incidents" (as defined in MDR Article 87) but would be subject to Trend Reporting (Article 88).

IT security standard IEC 81001-5-1:2021 (Chapter 5, A.1.5.1) was published after MDCG 2019-16 and now represents the state of the art for cybersecurity of health IT systems, including medical devices. According to GSPR 17.2, it should therefore be adopted with immediate effect, although it may not become a harmonised standard under MDR 17 until May 2024 [36].

TABLE 6.4

Cybersecurity-related requirements of EU MDR 17/745. Adapted with permission from Table 2 of MDCG 2019-16 (*Guidance on cybersecurity for medical devices*). Note: the EC's electronic system on vigilance contains information submitted by manufacturers on various post-market activities (serious incidents, trend analysis, etc.) and has links to the UDI database (6.3.14)

Pre-market activities	Post-market activities
Secure design (Annex I)	
Risk management (Annex I)	Risk management (Annex I)
Establish risk control measures (Annex I)	Modify risk control measures/corrective actions/patches (Annex I)
Validation, verification, risk assessment, benefit/risk analysis (Annex I)	Validation, verification, risk assessment, benefit/risk analysis (Annex I)
Technical documentation (Annex II and III)	Update technical documentation (Annex II and III)
CA (Article 52)	
Establish a PMS plan and a PMS system	Maintain and update a PMS plan and PMS system
Clinical evaluation process (Chapter VI)	PMSR (Article 85)
	PSUR (Article 86)
	Trend reporting (Article 88)
	Analysis of serious incidents (Article 89)
	Inform the electronic system on vigilance (Article 92)

Since 2021 there have been a plethora of articles and guidance documents about the cybersecurity of medical devices from national trade associations, legal firms, and other interested parties [37,38]. Such documents tend to offer a particular perspective on the security issues presented by networked medical devices, but the adoption of IEC 81001-5-1 alone will be sufficient for most EU medical device manufacturers.

Certification of products to cybersecurity standards must be undertaken according to the framework set out in Regulation (EU) 2019/881, otherwise known as the EU Cybersecurity Act 2019 [39].

6.3.6.8   Instructions for Use

IFU are the means by which a manufacturer informs the user about the intended purpose of a device and its proper use, including any precautions to be taken (Article 2[14]).

MDR 17/745 IFU requirements are covered in Annex I (23) under the general heading of "Requirements regarding information supplied with the device". In order to ensure a smooth transition from MDD to MDR, Legislative Act 97 states that Commission Regulation (EU) No 207/2012 (the EU IFU Regulations) [40] should remain in force and continue to apply unless and until repealed by implementing acts adopted by the Commission. The IFU regulations list the types of medical devices for which an electronic version of the IFU (eIFU) can be provided, which includes software-only medical devices,

Strictly speaking, IFU are not essential for Class I and Class IIa devices "if such devices can be used safely without any such instructions" (Annex I, GSPR 23.1[d]), but it would normally be considered good practice to provide comprehensive IFU for all medical devices.

When regulatory compliance has been achieved, the CE mark should appear in the IFU (Article 20). Once the medical device software is released, data gathered as part of post-market surveillance (Section 6.3.15) should be used to update various processes and documentation, including the IFU (Article 83).

6.3.6.9 Summary of Requirements for Medical Device Software Production

6.3.6.9.1 Basic Items
List all the GSPRs and indicate those that do *not* apply to software production

- Establish the class of the device
- Implement ISO 13485
- Implement ISO 14971
- Decide on the software development model/process
- Implement IEC 62304 and establish software safety class

The above list assumes that all the initial project initiation work concerning justification, senior management support, staffing resources, and training requirements has been successfully completed.

6.3.6.9.2 Detailed Items

6.3.6.9.2.1 Requirements Specification ("Phase 1")
The following checklist is designed to help manufacturers comply with the *requirements* specification of a software product that would qualify as a medical device under EU or US medical device regulations. It is primarily designed to ensure that the main user requirements are fully documented, and are both testable and individually traceable to a design feature- all requirements of ISO 62304:2015 (Section 5.4.1).

Formal aspects

- All key user requirements are documented
- All resultant software requirements are uniquely and individually identified
- The requirements specification document is under version control

General aspects

- All requirements are testable and that at least one test per requirement is specified.
- Software requirements cover all system or stakeholder requirements (to be proven by traceability matrix)

Detailed aspects

The software requirements specify the following:

- The UI (e.g., screens with UI elements (buttons, tables, menus)) including layout: position, colour, and size (or reference a style guide)
- How the UI responds to user actions (e.g., the panels that are shown, elements that are shown or hidden, other screens/hardware that are triggered)
- For all input fields, allowed values, value ranges, data types, and reaction of the system to incorrect/inappropriate user inputs
- Any interface to other systems and to hardware (e.g., actuators, sensors), addressing all interoperability levels (protocols, formats, value tables, authorisation, and data validation)
- For any technical/data interface the expected and maximum data volume, system behaviour if this volume is exceeded, or if data are corrupt, out of range, or missing
- For any technical/data interface, whether data are encrypted and, if so, how
- Response times for user interfaces and technical/data interfaces (based on load, number of network users, data volume, etc.)
- The computer hardware specification, including CPU, RAM, disc storage, screen size, resolution, and orientation
- Operating system requirements including version/patches and runtime environments (e.g., browser, Java Runtime, .NET Runtime)
- Compatibility of other software running in parallel (firewall, malware/virus protection, etc.)
- Basic system/network security measures
- Cybersecurity measures where appropriate

The above list is based on a published software system requirements specification (SSRS) [41].

6.3.7 WHERE TO START? – GAP ANALYSIS

Gap analysis is a benchmarking technique by which an organisation can measure its current performance against its desired or potential performance. It is perhaps the first task for any organisation wishing to assess the size of the task ahead when aiming to comply with medical devices and other relevant regulations, whether it be in the context of in-house manufacturing or full commercial development.

6.3.7.1 High-Level Gap Analysis

A top-level gap analysis should be performed first as there may be one or more fundamental issues that, if not overcome, would render further analysis of the dozens of detailed technical issues a waste of time and effort. An initial gap analysis should include:

6.3.7.1.1   Support and Commitment of Senior Management

The MDR generally refers to the 'responsibilities of the manufacturer', but some of the supporting standards (e.g., ISO 14971) are more specific in terms of commitment and responsibilities of senior or top management within the organisation. An outline plan[6] of the development, including staffing resources, capital expenditure, estimated timescales/milestones, etc. should be presented to senior management at the earliest opportunity. Specific individuals with responsibility for overall quality assurance, risk management, and regulatory affairs will need to be consulted.

In the context of in-house development, most large hospitals have a medical equipment committee that reports to the Board. This would be the sensible first port of call, especially as the business case would need to explain why no commercially available product is suitable.

6.3.7.1.2   Staffing and Other Resources

The development of a piece of medical device software should be regarded as an individual project since such software can take many forms and have different requirements (see Chapter 3). A project manager should be appointed to oversee the project and liaise with relevant senior managers outside of the developer's department. In particular, the project manager will be responsible for producing a business case (see above). Regarding staffing level requirements, due consideration will need to be given to the current staff's ability to undertake clinical evaluations (where appropriate) and effective post-market surveillance. For pure in-house development, the latter task is straightforward in principle since the device remains under the direct control of the developer/manufacturer.

6.3.7.1.3   Person Responsible for Regulatory Compliance

Article 15 of MDR 17 requires that the manufacturer appoint a Person Responsible for Regulatory Compliance (PRRC) having the requisite expertise in the field of medical devices. It is specified that the PRRC must hold a formal qualification equivalent to a university degree (in a relevant subject), plus at least one year of professional experience in regulatory affairs[7] or quality management systems related to medical devices *or* at least four years of professional experience in regulatory affairs or quality management systems related to medical devices.

There is, however, a caveat associated with the PRRC requirement. According to article 15(6), micro and small enterprises are not required to employ a PRRC within their organisation but must have such a person at their disposal. In other words, small organisations can outsource the role. According to EC Directive 2003/361/EC (*Commission recommendation of 6 May 2003 concerning the definition of micro, small, and medium-sized enterprises*), a "micro-enterprise" is one with has less than 10 employees and an annual turnover of less than 2 million euros, and a "small" enterprise is one with less than 50 employees and an annual turnover of less than 10 million euros. If the PRRC role is outsourced, a formal contract must exist between the manufacturer and the organisation employing the PRRC.

---

[6] Many organisations have business case templates that would be suitable for this type of application.
[7] This is understood to mean experience in *European* medical device regulations [MDCG 2019-7].

According to Article 15(3), the PRRC shall *at least* be responsible for ensuring that:

a. the conformity of the devices is appropriately checked, in accordance with the quality management system under which the devices are manufactured before a device is released;
b. the technical documentation and the EU Declaration of Conformity are drawn up and kept up to date;
c. the post-market surveillance obligations are complied with in accordance with Article 10(10);
d. the reporting obligations referred to in Articles 87 to 91 are fulfilled;
e. in the case of investigational devices, the statement referred to in Section 4.1 of Chapter II of Annex XV is issued.

Non-commercial organisations (e.g., publicly funded healthcare establishments) do not need to comply with the full PRRC requirements but still need to appoint someone with relevant experience to sign the declaration and take responsibility for regulatory compliance of exempted devices, including the supervision and control of manufacturing, and surveillance over the lifetime of the device [42].

6.3.7.1.4 Authorised Representative

Manufacturers based outside of the EU must appoint an Authorised Representative (AR) if they intend to market medical devices within the EU. No specific qualifications are required for this role, but the appointed person must take responsibility for overseeing key parts of the regulatory compliance process (CA procedure, declaration of conformity, etc.). A full list of responsibilities is given in Article 11(3) of MDR 17.

Article 15(6) refers to the relationship between the AR and the PRRC, stating that "authorised representatives shall have permanently and continuously at their disposal at least one person responsible for regulatory compliance who possesses the requisite expertise regarding the regulatory requirements for medical devices in the Union". In other words, for organisations based outside of the EU, the AR is the manufacturer's formal point of contact with the PRRC.

The MDR itself makes no comment about the geographical location of either the AR or the PRRC, but the relevant MDCG guidance (MDCG 2019-7: *Guidance on Article 15 of the Medical Device Regulation (MDR) and in vitro Diagnostic Device Regulation (IVDR) regarding a "person responsible for regulatory compliance"*) states that "taking into account that the AR is located in the EU, it must be assumed that any person to be permanently and continuously at its disposal (i.e., the PRRC) should be also located in the EU". Although the legal basis for this statement is unclear, manufacturers based outside of the EU have generally accepted that their AR ("EC Rep") and nominated PRRC must both reside in an EU member state [43]. The EU requirements are therefore similar to those for a US Agent within the FDA system (Section 6.5.10).

6.3.7.1.5 Quality Management System Considerations

Organisations/departments that have a recognised quality management system (QMS) already in place will find the process of achieving regulatory compliance for medical device manufacturing more straightforward than those that do not (Section

6.3.8.4). An organisation with ISO 9001:2015 certification will still need to implement ISO 13584:2016 for medical device manufacturing but the process should be straightforward, as ISO 13485 is based on ISO 9001.

Even transitioning from the old MDD to the new MDR has proved difficult for many established manufacturers, so starting from scratch represents a steep learning curve for small organisations and start-ups. A possible QMS strategy for would-be MDSW developers is suggested (Section 6.3.8) but every organisation is different in terms of skill-mix, leadership, and motivation.

Most organisations will be familiar with the general principles and processes of risk management, which is a key element of any QMS (Section 6.3.8). Implementation of ISO 14971 (which is effectively essential for MDR compliance, Section 6.3.9) represents a challenge but should not be too daunting for an organisation using risk assessments, risk registers, and risk scoring to manage other aspects of its work. Ironically perhaps, the biggest standards-related task for medical device software manufacturers is likely to be the implementation of IEC 62304 (Section 6.3.6.3).

6.3.7.2   Detailed Gap Analysis

The simplest way to conduct a systematic and detailed gap analysis is by reference to a checklist containing the key requirements contained in the numerous chapters and annexes of MDR17, including the GSPRs listed in Annex I. Several free MDR gap analysis checklists (usually in the form of Microsoft Excel™ spreadsheets) are available online, some covering the entire MDR [44] and some covering specific aspects such as technical documentation [45] and medical software development [46].

6.3.8   Quality Management System

6.3.8.1   The Quality Assurance Overhead

For software systems based on traditional programming techniques, the "quality assurance (QA) overhead" can be extremely time-consuming (i.e., expensive) and is not something that small organisations can usually implement cost-effectively. There is also a known issue with inadequate knowledge, skills, and professionalism, especially in the non-regulated parts of the software industry, where typically only half the staff will have been employed within an organisation for more than five years. For small teams, there are compromises to be struck in terms of the type and size of software project undertaken, the overall timescale for the development, and the amount of QA and testing that goes into the final product.

6.3.8.2   QMS Requirements

Manufacturers of devices (other than investigational devices, see Section 6.3.4.7) must establish, document, implement, and maintain (i.e., keep up to date and continually improve) a QMS that ensures regulatory compliance in a manner that is proportionate to the risk class of the device.

The QMS must cover all aspects of the manufacturer's organisation dealing with the quality of processes, procedures, and products, including:

a. a strategy for regulatory compliance, including compliance with CAP and procedures for the management of modifications to the devices covered by the system;
b. identification of applicable GSPR and exploration of options to address those requirements;
c. responsibility of the management;
d. resource management, including selection and control of suppliers and sub-contractors;
e. risk management as set out in Section 3 of Annex I;
f. clinical evaluation in accordance with Article 61 and Annex XIV, including post-market clinical follow-up (PMCF);
g. product realisation, including planning, design, development, production, and service provision;
h. verification of the UDI assignments made in accordance with Article 27(3) to all relevant devices and ensuring consistency and validity of information provided in accordance with Article 29;
i. setting-up, implementation, and maintenance of a post-market surveillance system, in accordance with Article 83;
j. handling communication with competent authorities, NB, other economic operators, customers, and/or other stakeholders;
k. processes for reporting serious incidents and field safety corrective actions in the context of vigilance;
l. management of corrective and preventive actions (CAPA) and verification of their effectiveness; (m) processes for monitoring and measurement of output, data analysis, and product improvement.

Note that point (e) effectively amounts to the adoption of ISO 14971 (Section 6.3.9), even though ISO 14971 itself does not mandate the presence of a general QMS.

6.3.8.3 Relationship to ISO 13485

ISO 13485 is an internationally recognised QMS standard for medical device manufacturing that has been adopted in Europe as a harmonised standard under MDR 17 (Section 6.3.3). Compliance with the standard therefore represents the most straightforward way of meeting the relevant quality management requirements of the regulation. The details of ISO 13485:2016 are discussed in Chapter 5.

ISO 13485 requirements are comprehensive and specific to medical device manufacture but do not cover all the QMS requirements of the EU MDR. For example, the technical file requirements specified in Annex II of MDR 17 are more comprehensive than the corresponding medical device file requirements listed in clause 4.2.3 of ISO 13485. The MDR also requires additional records to be kept for aspects of post-market surveillance and clinical evaluation. However, the *processes* described in ISO 13485 for creating, updating, and maintaining this documentation will not need to be changed.

TABLE 6.5

Correspondence between MDR 17/745 QMS requirements and clauses of ISO 13485:2016 (adapted with permission from Advisera.com blog [47]). "Product realisation" comprises planning, design, development, production, and maintenance. UDI: unique device identifier

EU MDR QMS requirements	ISO 13485 clause
A strategy for complying with regulations	4.1
Safety and performance	7.5
Management responsibility	5.1, 5.5
Resource management	7.4
Risk management	7.3
Clinical evaluation	7.3
Product realisation	7
Verification of UDI assignment	7.5.8, 7.5.9
PMS system	8.2.1, 8.2.2
Communication with authorities	8.2.3
Incident reporting	8.2.3
Verification of CAPA	8.5.2, 8.5.3
Monitoring and measurement, data analysis, product improvement	8.2

A mapping between the QMS requirements of MDR 17/745 and the relevant clauses of ISO 13485:2016 is included in Annex ZA of the standard. The table presented is, however, difficult to follow as the factors in MDR17/745 are not described *per se*; only referenced by article and paragraph number, and more than half (20/36) of the MDR requirements are listed as "partially covered". The more descriptive Table 6.5 may be more helpful (Note: number of requirements covered = 7, not covered = 9, partially covered = 20).

6.3.8.4   What About Organisations That Have Implemented ISO 9001?

Due to the close inter-relationships between ISO 14971, ISO 13485, and IEC 62304, departments/organisations already certified to ISO 9001 are advised to implement ISO 13485 (in addition) as the existing quality management system would require substantial modification in order to comply with the QMS requirements of MDR 17. Also, NB tend to expect medical device manufacturers to have implemented ISO 13485.

Organisations without an existing formal QMS for whom the main regulated activity will be medical device manufacture are advised to proceed directly to ISO 13485:2016 as this standard contains most of the (generic) requirements of ISO 9001:2015 and adds new ones for medical device manufacture.

For organisations with a broader range of activities, the decision of whether to implement (and maintain) both standards or develop a QMS that is a combination of the two depends on local circumstances and priorities [48].

For European medical device production, the QMS requirements of MDR 14/745 are paramount, whether met by the implementation of ISO 13485, a substantially modified version of ISO 9001, or a combination of the two. For software (in general) there is also ISO 90003:2018 (*Guidelines for the application of ISO 9001:2015 to computer software*).

6.3.9 RISK MANAGEMENT

Risk management is viewed as an essential part of the overall QMS requirements under MDR17, so the manufacturer's obligation to undertake formal risk management procedures is contained in the section (Chapter II, Article 10 (2)) dealing with the QMS: "Manufacturers shall establish, document, implement and maintain a system for risk management as described in Section 3 of Annex I" (*GSPR*). The regulations also state that risk management must be implemented as an iterative process throughout the entire life cycle of a device.

EN ISO 14971:2019/A11:2021 (*Medical devices – Application of risk management to medical devices*) is a harmonised standard under MDR 17/745 (Section 6.3.3) so compliance with its clauses represents a presumption of conformity with the relevant risk management requirements of the regulation. Note that ISO 14971 is not a normative reference for IEC 13485 but can be used to fulfil its risk management requirements (Section 6.3.9). It is, however, a normative reference of IEC 62304 (see Chapter 5).

For every device, the EU MDR mandates that the manufacturers must have a documented risk management plan, identify, and analyse the known and foreseeable hazards, estimate, and evaluate the associated risks and eliminate or control the risks. Additionally, in the "production phase", the manufacturer must evaluate the impact of new information and if necessary, amend risk control measures accordingly.

Annex ZA[8] of the harmonised standard (EN ISO 14971) contains a cross-reference table showing the relationship between the GSPR listed in Annex I of MDR 17/745 and the clauses of the standard. In particular, the table addresses:

- GSPR 3: the manufacturer's risk management system
- GSPR 4: risk control measures
- GSPR 5: eliminating or reducing risks
- GSPR 8: known and foreseeable risks, and undesirable side effects
- GSPR 9: devices without a medical purpose

GSPRs 1, 2, 7, and 10–22 (relating to *specific* design and manufacturing issues[9]) are not addressed by the standard, so these requirements must be met by other means, emphasising the need for a comprehensive "GSPR checklist", showing how every relevant GSPR listed in Annex I of MDR 17 will be met or justifiably ignored (Section 6.3.6.1) [44].

---

[8] Annex ZB shows the relationship between ISO 14971:2019+A11:2021 and MDR 17//46.

[9] Requirements relating to the mitigation of hazards associated with interaction with specific materials (e.g., chemicals, biological substances) and the environment (e.g., electrical fields, ionising radiation).

GSPR 1 basically specifies that devices must be designed and manufactured in such a way that they are suitable for their intended purpose, but also contains a requirement that the risks associated with the use of the device "constitute acceptable risks when weighed against the benefits to the patient [...], taking into account the generally acknowledged state of the art". GSPR 2 states that general risks must be reduced *as far as possible* (AFAP, see Section 4.4.28) so that, once identified, each and every risk must be formally assessed

Although numerous GSPRs and other risk-related requirements of MDR 17/745 are not *directly* covered by ISO 14971, the idea is that the framework established to address device-specific risks associated with requirements analysis, design, production, and maintenance should enable the manufacturer to tackle the "other" risk management requirements, such as those inherent in clinical evaluation, clinical investigations, SSCP, and post-market surveillance [49]. Device usability issues are also not covered by ISO 14971 but are fully addressed in IEC 62366-1:2015/AMD 1:2020 (Chapter 5, A.1.3.9), which is expected to become harmonised in due course. The details and practical implementation of ISO 14971 are discussed in Chapter 5.

6.3.9.1   Guidance on Software Hazard Identification

ISO 14971 provides useful assistance when identifying potential hazards through its annexes, but it lacks a strong identification catalogue for software hazards. More specific guidance is provided in Annex B of IEC TR 80002-1:2009 (*Medical device software – Part 1 Guidance on the application of ISO 14971 to medical device software*), which elaborates on possible software hazards and includes factors to consider when assessing whether they are applicable to a particular device [50].

6.3.10   CLINICAL EVALUATION AND CLINICAL INVESTIGATIONS

6.3.10.1   Clinical Evaluation and Sufficient Clinical Evidence

Clinical evaluation is defined (in Article 2{44}) as:

> "a systematic and planned process to continuously generate, collect, analyse and assess the clinical data pertaining to a device in order to verify the safety and performance, including clinical benefits, of the device when used as intended by the manufacturer."

The reference to clinical benefits was new to MDR 17/745 as the absence of such was perceived as a weakness of the old MDD.

The process of clinical evaluation should be based on a clinical evaluation plan (CEP), the essential content of which is detailed in Annex XIV (Part A, Section 1). Any questions that cannot be answered by the derived clinical evidence must be covered in the accompanying literature review. At least one member of the development team must therefore be familiar with conducting detailed literature searches using medical databases such as PubMed, MEDLINE, Google Scholar and Embase. Indeed, a Notified Body will generally want to see evidence of a literature search strategy (MDR Annex XII, Section 4.5.5).

The MDCG has published general advice on clinical evaluation under MDR 17 [51], which provides a framework for the determination of the appropriate level of clinical evidence for MDSW. The group has also published guidance on the use of clinical data related to an "equivalent device" already on the EU market [52], and on the issue of sufficient clinical evidence for legacy devices previously CE marked under the old MDD [53].

There should be a systematic and unbiased way of analysing the relevant literature that translates into the inclusion criteria and the evidence appraisal method. The evidence accumulated during the clinical evaluation process must be presented in a clinical evaluation report (CER) that forms part of the technical documentation referred to in Annex II of MDR 17 (Section 6.3.12). Guidance is available on the general process of clinical evaluation [54] and specifically on the structure and content of the CER [55]. Some of the supporting clinical evidence should also be referenced in the SSCP (Section 6.3.13).

6.3.10.2   Clinical Investigations

The EU MDR (Legislative Act 63) stipulates that class III and implantable devices are subject to a clinical investigation, defined in Article 2(45) as "any systematic investigation involving one or more human subjects, undertaken to assess the safety or performance of a device". Most clinical staff will be more familiar with the term "clinical study" (or "clinical trial"), which by its nature usually requires local ethics committee approval. In this context, it is a prospective study specifically designed to produce evidence relevant to the safety and *clinical* performance of the device. It is not required for class I or class II devices. If a clinical investigation is appropriate there must be a clinical investigation plan (CIP).

The procedures used for clinical investigations should be consistent with established international guidance in this field, such as the international standard ISO 14155:2020 (*Clinical investigation of medical devices for human subjects – Good clinical practice*), the EU General Data Protection Regulation (GDPR) 2016/679 and the World Medical Association's Declaration of Helsinki on ethical principles for medical research involving human subjects [56]. The US FDA recognises ISO 14155:2020 standard for medical device trials and accepts clinical data collected outside the US, under the condition that ISO 14155 good clinical practice (GCP) has been followed (Section 6.5.5).

The requirements of ISO 14155 are laid out under seven main headings:

- Summary of GCP principles
- Ethical considerations
- Clinical investigation planning
- Clinical investigation conduct
- Suspension, termination, and close-out
- Responsibilities of the sponsor
- Responsibilities of the principal investigator

The standard also specifically includes the clinical investigation of SaMD and defines several terms ("analytical validity", "scientific validity" and "clinical performance") connected with the clinical validation of medical devices. Compared to the previous (2011) version of the standard, the main change in ISO 14144:2020 is the emphasis on the application of risk management principles throughout the entire

TABLE 6.6

The application of the various clinical investigation types at different stages of development of a medical device. Adapted with permission from *Greenlight Guru's Ultimate Guide to ISO 14155:2020 for Medical Devices* [57]

	Pre-Market			Post-Market
Clinical development stage	Pre-clinical	Pilot	Pivotal	Post-market surveillance
Investigation type	Exploratory	Exploratory and confirmatory	Confirmatory	Observational

clinical investigation process. As such, there is a new Appendix H that outlines how ISO 14971 may be used for this purpose.

The section on GCP comprises a set of 14 ethical and scientific principles, which represent the essential checklist necessary to demonstrate compliance with the standard. It is also emphasised that clinical investigations are not restricted to the pre-market phase of the device development process, so *parts* of the standard are also applicable to any clinical investigations performed during the post-market surveillance stage. The standard defines four types of clinical investigation that may be applied at the different clinical development stages (Table 6.6).

According to Article 77(5) of MDR17, following the conclusion of a clinical investigation, and irrespective of its outcome, the sponsor of the clinical study is required to submit (to the relevant member state) a clinical investigation report (CIR) and a *summary* CIR, which should be "presented in terms that are easily understandable to the intended user".

The *minimum requirements* for the content of the CIR are outlined in Section 7 of Annex XV, Chapter III, but a more comprehensive description is given in Annex D of ISO 14155:2020. Section 7 of Chapter III of Annex XV also contains an outline of what should be covered in the *summary* CIR

- Title of the investigation
- Purpose of the investigation
- Description of the investigation, investigational design, and methods used
- Results of the investigation
- Conclusions of the investigation

However, due to a reported "lack of consistency among the summaries presented by different sponsors and, frequently, missing information...", the European Commission issued guidance (2023/C163/06) in May 2023 to address the issue. It provided further instruction and guidance on the content and structure of the *summary* CIR, aimed at "promoting harmonisation, ensuring completeness, and improving the quality of clinical data provided by manufacturers" [58].

6.3.11   THE HEALTH INSTITUTION EXEMPTION (HIE)

Legislative Act 30 of MDR 17/745 states that:

> Health institutions should have the possibility of manufacturing, modifying, and using devices in-house and thereby address, on a non-industrial scale, the specific needs of target patient groups which cannot be met at the appropriate level of performance by an equivalent device available on the market. In that context, it is appropriate to provide that certain rules of this Regulation, as regards medical devices manufactured and used only within health institutions, including hospitals as well as institutions, such as laboratories and public health institutes that support the healthcare system and/or address patient needs, but which do not treat or care for patients directly, should not apply, since the aims of this Regulation would still be met in a proportionate manner.

It is made clear that the term "health institutions" does not cover establishments primarily claiming to pursue health interests or healthy lifestyles, such as gyms, spas, wellness, and fitness centres. As a result, the so-called HIE does not apply to such establishments.

The detail of the HIE is provided in Articles 5.4 and 5.5 of the regulation. Article 5.4 simply states that "devices that are manufactured and used within health institutions shall be considered as having been put into service", while Article 5.5 describes the various conditions to be met for the exemption to apply. For medical devices manufactured and used only within health institutions established in the EU, the exemption applies to all regulatory requirements apart from the relevant GSPRs set out in Annex I. The conditions are crucial so are quoted verbatim:

a. the devices are not transferred to another legal entity;

b. manufacture and use of the devices occur under appropriate quality management systems;

c. the health institution justifies in its documentation that the target patient group's specific needs cannot be met, or cannot be met at the appropriate level of performance by an equivalent device available on the market;

d. the health institution provides information upon request on the use of such devices to its competent authority, which shall include a justification of their manufacturing, modification, and use;

e. the health institution draws up a declaration which it shall make publicly available, including the name and address of the manufacturing health institution; the details necessary to identify the devices; a declaration that the devices meet the GSPR set out in Annex I to this Regulation and, where applicable, information on which requirements are not fully met with a reasoned justification therefor[e];

f. the health institution draws up documentation that makes it possible to have an understanding of the manufacturing facility, the manufacturing process, the design and performance data of the devices, including the intended purpose, and that is sufficiently detailed to enable the competent authority to ascertain that the GSPR set out in Annex I to this Regulation are met;

g. the health institution takes all necessary measures to ensure that all devices are manufactured in accordance with the documentation referred to in point (f), and

h. the health institution reviews experience gained from clinical use of the devices and takes all necessary corrective actions. Member States may require that such health institutions submit to the competent authority any further relevant information about such devices which have been manufactured and used on their territory.

It was added that member states shall retain the right to restrict the manufacture and the use of any specific type of such devices and shall be permitted access to inspect the activities of the health institutions. The HIE does not apply to devices that are manufactured on an industrial scale.

A few terms used in Article 5.5 require clarification, as they are not defined in the MDR. In 5.5(a), "transferred" means any type of legal transfer (e.g., sale, loan, hire, lease, and gift). The common meaning of "legal entity" may be assumed,[10] but recent MDCG guidance (MDCG 2023-1, [59]) simply states that the national competent authority can clarify how the term is understood nationally. Guidance is offered on the meaning of "industrial scale" but it does not completely clarify the meaning. It is stated that the concept is "a combination of many factors to be considered on a case-by-case basis, including volume of production, commercial aspects and manufacturing process" and should be distinguished from "mass production". In any event, the exemption is intended to apply only to low-volume production medical devices.

The expression "manufacture and use" (Articles 5.4 and 5.5) has caused some debate [60] but no additional guidance is provided in MDCG 2023-1. Finally, Annex A of MDCG 2023-1 contains a basic template for the required public declaration described in Article 5.5(e). The current UK position regarding the HIE is discussed in Section 6.4.6.

6.3.12   TECHNICAL DOCUMENTATION

Technical documentation is one of the documentation types required by MDR 17 (Section 6.3.12) and is the means by which a medical device manufacturer provides evidence of compliance with the regulations. As such, the production and maintenance of technical documentation is one of the general obligations of manufacturers listed in Article 10, with specific elements detailed in Annex II (pre-market requirements) and Annex III (post-market requirements). This collection of required technical documents is usually referred to as a "technical file" even though this term is not used in MDR 17. Annex II describes the technical documentation requirements under six headings, which may be summarised as follows:

---

[10] Legal entity: "an association, corporation, partnership, proprietorship, trust or individual that has legal standing in the eyes of law". A legal entity has the capacity to enter into agreements or contracts, assume obligations, incur and pay debts, sue and be sued in its own right, and be held responsible for its actions.

6.3.12.1 Device Information and Specification

This section should contain a basic description of the products (to include trade name and UDI) and technical specifications. The basic description should include information about the intended purpose, indications for use, patient population to be served, novel features, and any other key functional elements to allow a broad understanding of the device. Any device accessories should also be described in this section.

6.3.12.2 Information Supplied by the Manufacturer

This section contains information provided to the intended user (IFU), including any relevant warnings/precautions or contraindications. It will also contain information on packaging and labelling (if software is supplied on a physical medium), release date (with version number), and expiry date (if relevant).

6.3.12.3 Design and Manufacturing Information

This section should include information on design and manufacturing processes (with reference to relevant standards used) and the various quality control procedures. It should also include information about the manufacturing site(s) and any sub-contractors/collaborating organisations. Clearly, design is a major part of software development process so it is appropriate to include some detail on the specific design processes employed.

6.3.12.4 General Safety and Performance Requirements

The technical documentation should contain the information necessary for the demonstration of conformity with those GSPR set out in Annex I of MDR 17 that are applicable to the device in question. This demonstration of conformity shall include:

a. the GSPRs that apply to the device and an explanation as to why others do not apply;
b. the method or methods used to demonstrate conformity with each applicable GSPR, including a justification where appropriate;
c. the harmonised standards and/or CS applied (Section 6.3.3);
d. if (c) is applicable, the identity of the controlled documents providing evidence of conformity with each harmonised standard, CS, or other certifiable method applied to demonstrate conformity with the GSPRs.

The reference to "controlled documents" serves as a reminder that *all* device documentation, technical or otherwise, should be controlled (password protected, etc.) as part of the QMS. The technical documentation should also include the CER (Section 6.3.10.1) and the post-market surveillance plan and reports (Section 6.3.15)

6.3.12.5 Benefit-Risk Analysis and Risk Management

Annex II (Section 5) is very brief on this topic, simply stating that the associated technical documentation must contain information on (a) the benefit-risk analysis referred to in Sections 1 and 8 of Annex I, and (b) the methods adopted and the results of the risk management referred to in Section 3 of Annex I.

The need for a risk management plan (RMP) for *each* device is the only specific documentation requirement mentioned in Section 3 of Annex I, but the adoption of ISO 14971 as a framework for the management of all identified risks will give rise to further top-level risk documents (risk management review, risk management file, etc.) and these should be cross-referenced. In particular, the risk management report (RMR) will include the results of the benefit-risk analysis ratio and the evaluation of any residual risks.

6.3.12.6 Product Verification and Validation

This section should contain the *results and critical analyses* of all verification and validation tests and/or studies undertaken to demonstrate the conformity of the device with the applicable GSPRs. Such evidence would typically take the form of records or results of test procedures (e.g., evidence that a given test procedure was followed and signed off).

Section (a) in MDR 17 Annex II (on *Pre-clinical and clinical data*), refers to "results of tests, such as engineering, laboratory, simulated use and animal tests, and evaluation of published literature applicable to the device, taking into account its intended purpose, or to similar devices, regarding the pre-clinical safety of the device and its conformity with the specifications", some of which applies to software.

Section (b) describes the need to produce detailed information regarding test design and test protocols relating to characteristics such as biocompatibility, and electromagnetic compatibility but also contains the following documentary evidence requirements for software validation /verification:

> Software verification and validation (describing the software design and development process and evidence of the validation of the software, as used in the finished device. This information shall typically include the summary results of all verification, validation and testing performed both in-house and in a simulated or actual user environment prior to final release. It shall also address all the different hardware configurations and, where applicable, operating systems identified in the information supplied by the manufacturer).

There is currently no official guidance that elaborates on this basic requirement, but a detailed technical documents checklist has been produced by the BSI [61] using the following headings:

- IEC 62304 checklist
- Software development plan
- Software requirements analysis
- Software architectural design
- Software detailed design
- Software unit implementation and verification
- Software integration and integration testing
- Software systems testing
- Software release
- Software risk assessment
- Cybersecurity documentation

A subset of the information contained in the technical documentation is used when submitting the device information (for class II and class III devices) to the notified body for pre-market or post-market CA activities. The format of the summary Technical Information (STED) was originally defined by the Global Harmonisation Task Force (GHTF).[11] However, the STED is slowly being replaced by a Table-of-Contents (ToC) format produced by the IMDRF [62].

A general provision of MDR17 (Recital 5) is that guidance developed at the international level, particularly by the GHTF or IMDRF should, where possible, be "taken into account to promote the global convergence of medical device regulations [....], in particular in the provisions on UDI, GSPR, documentation, classification rules, conformity assessment procedures and clinical investigations".

Submissions to NB must be in electronic form in order to satisfy the Annex II requirement that "the technical documentation and, if applicable, the summary thereof to be drawn up by the manufacturer shall be presented in a *clear, organised, readily searchable and unambiguous manner*", but most NB are quite flexible about the acceptance of different digital file formats (MS Office, PDF, JPEG, PNG, etc.) provided they do not require special software to read them.

The individual technical documents comprising the technical file (device description, information provided by manufacturer, etc.) will typically be compressed into a single zip file. The chosen Notified Body will provide their preferred method for receiving the technical documentation, which will *not* generally include email attachments. There are several approved file transfer tools that support the e-submission process.

Ensuring that the specified technical documentation is produced and maintained is one of the key duties of the person (or persons) responsible for regulatory compliance (Section 6.3.7.1) (Table 6.7).

6.3.13 Summary of Safety and Clinical Performance

The SSCP is a new requirement under MDR 17/745 that is applicable to Class III and implantable devices. It was introduced mainly as a result of the high-profile device failures that occurred around 2010, which were deemed to be due, in part, to a lack of transparency associated with the old MDD. The key point is that the SSCP is a *publicly available* document, uploaded to the EUDAMED database following approval by the Notified Body.

The document is designed to summarise the evidence for the safety, performance, *and* clinical benefit of the device in relation to its intended purpose, and to place this in the context of outcomes achievable with other diagnostic or therapeutic alternatives for the same patient population. The specific requirements are described in Article 32 of the MDR, with detailed guidance subsequently issued by the MDCG 2019-9 [63]. Although the MDCG guidance is careful to distinguish between regulatory requirements (usually designated as "shall be performed") and recommendations based on the MDCG's interpretation of that requirement ("should be performed"), it represents current best practice and NB will expect manufacturers to comply with its advice.

---

[11] The GHTF was the forerunner of the International Medical Device Regulators Forum (IMDRF).

TABLE 6.7

List of mandatory documents required to demonstrate compliance with MDR17, organised by development activity. Note that this list does not include the documentation requirements of supporting standards, such as ISO 13485, ISO 14971, and IEC 62304

Category	Required documents	MDR17 reference
General requirements	EU Declaration of Conformity	Article 10, para 8
	Quality management system	Article 10, para 9
	List of all UDI-DI	Article 27, para 7
	SSCP	Article 32, para 1
Risk management	Risk management plan	Annex I, Chapter I, item 3
	Risk management file	Annex I, Chapter I, item 3
	Risk management report	Annex I, Chapter I, item 3
Clinical evaluation	Clinical evaluation plan	Annex XIV, Part A, item 1(a)
	Clinical evaluation report	Chapter VI, Article 61, para 12; Annex XIV, Section 4, para 4
Clinical investigation	Informed consent	Article 63
	Application form	Annex XV, Chapter II, para 1
	Investigator brochure	Annex XV, Chapter II, para 2
	Clinical investigation plan	Article 72; Annex XV, Chapter II, para 3
	Safety and performance statement	Annex XV, Chapter II, para 4
	Proof of insurance	Annex XV, Chapter II, para 4
	Arrangements description	Annex XV, Chapter II, para 4
	Clinical investigation report	Annex XV, Chapter II, para 7
Post-market surveillance	PMS plan	Article 84; Annex III
	Post-market surveillance report	Article 85
	Periodic safety update report	Article 86
	PMCF plan	Annex XIV, Part B, para 6
Vigilance	Field safety corrective actions	Article 87
	Adverse event report	Article 87
Technical file	Device description and specification	Annex II, para 1
	Labels and IFU	Annex II, para 2
	Design information	Annex II, para 3
	Manufacturing process and validations	Annex II, para 3
	Manufacturing site(s) identification	Annex II, para 3
	Results of clinical and pre-clinical testing	Annex II, para 6

6.3.14   DEVICE LABELLING – THE UDI SYSTEM

6.3.14.1   The UDI System

The MDR regulations introduced a new EU identification system for medical devices, based on the framework produced by the IMDRF in 2013 [64]. It was designed to improve the traceability of medical devices, which was identified as a weakness under the old MDD regulations in the wake of the scandals involving faulty breast implants and metal-on-metal hip prostheses (Section 6.2). The UDI requirements apply to all medical devices *except* custom-made and investigational devices.[12] The UDI system has four key elements/processes:

1. Assignment of a UDI to a medical device
2. Placement of a UDI on a device or packaging via a UDI carrier
3. Storage of UDI information by "economic operators" (manufacturer, AR, etc.)
4. Data to be submitted by manufacturers to the UDI database through EUDAMED[13]

There are three components of the UDI:

1. Basic UDI-DI
2. UDI
3. Packaging UDI [65]

The various codes consist of a series of numeric or alphanumeric characters created through a widely accepted device identification and coding standard. It allows the unambiguous identification of a specific medical device on the market.

The *Basic UDI-DI* (often referred to as 'BUDI') identifies the group that a particular device belongs to. A device group is a group of products that all share the same intended purpose, risk class, essential design, and manufacturing characteristics, often referred to as a "Product Family" or "Product Category". The Basic UDI-DI functions as a "parent" or higher-level device descriptor. It is not printed on the product itself, nor on the packaging of a product, but it must be included in the relevant certificates, EU Declarations of Conformity, Technical Documentation, and the SSCP. The UDI itself is comprised of a Device Identifier (DI) and a Production Identifier (PI).

The *UDI-DI* is a "static" code that contains detailed information about the device. A change in any of several details will trigger the need for a new UDI-DI, but the ones relevant to software are the trade name of the device, the device version or model, and any critical warnings or contraindications. A UDI-DI should only be associated with one Basic UDI [66].

The *UDI-PI* is a "dynamic" code that contains manufacturing information (including serial number, lot/batch number, software identification, and manufacturing date and expiry date (if appropriate). It is used as an "access key" to core data (as defined in Part B of Annex VI) stored in the UDI database (EUDAMED).

6.3.14.2   EUDAMED Database

In conventional medical device manufacturing (e.g., syringes), a new lot will require and new UDI-PI. A medical device can thus contain various UDI-PIs. Along with the

---

[12] An "investigational device" is a device that is assessed in a clinical investigation (see Section 6.3.4.7).
[13] The UDI database is part of the European databank on medical devices (EUDAMED).

UDI-DI, they should appear on any device labels and the device itself (if physical). UDI-PIs are not part of the data set that needs to be registered in the EUDAMED database. Other descriptions/definitions relevant to the application of the UDI system are as follows:

- Automatic identification and data capture (AIDC). A technology used to automatically capture data. AIDC technologies include bar codes, smart cards, biometrics, and RFID
- Radio Frequency Identification (RFID): A technology that uses communication through the use of radio waves to exchange data between a reader and an electronic tag attached to an object, for the purpose of identification
- Human Readable Interpretation (HRI): A legible interpretation of the data characters encoded in the UDI carrier
- UDI carrier: The means of conveying the UDI by using AIDC and, if applicable, its HRI
- UDI carriers include ID/linear bar codes, 2D/Matrix bar codes, and RFID

MDR Article 10(9)(h) states that the verification of UDI assignments (according to Article 27(3)) and information provided (in accordance with Article 29) are amongst the requirements to be addressed by the manufacturer's QMS. The MDCG has recently produced a guidance note on the integration of the UDI system with an organisation's QMS [67], Appendix I of which outlines a process for implementing a UDI system at a manufacturer's site.

In respect of medical device registration (Article 29(1)), the UDI requirement is that the manufacturer assigns a Basic UDI-DI (as defined in Part C of Annex VI) to the device and provides it to the UDI database (Article 28), together with the other core data elements described in Part B of Annex VI that are relevant to the device in question. The details of how this should be done, in terms of the timing and communication with the Notified Body (where appropriate) are described in paragraphs 3 and 4 of Article 29.

As part of the post-market vigilance system, it is also the responsibility of the manufacturer to ensure that the device-specific information stored within the EUDAMED database is kept updated, as any changes to the software's device classification, intended purpose, or essential design and manufacturing characteristics could potentially trigger the need for a new Basic UDI-DI or UDI-DI [68].

All UDIs issued must conform to the requirements of a particular *Issuing Entity* that has been formally approved by the European Commission. The most commonly used organisation for issuing UDIs is GS1, whose global trade item number (GTIN) corresponds to the UDI-DI (see Figure 6.3)

The EU UDI system is fundamentally similar to the system used in the US as they are both based on the IMDRF framework [64]. The US FDA equivalent of EUDAMED is called the Global UDI Database (GUDID). The main coding difference between the two systems is that the EU UDI data model is split into three components (Basic UDI-DI, UDI, and Packaging UDI).

6.3.14.3 Application of the UDI System to Medical Software

The UDI system requirements relating to medical device software, are described in Part C (Section 6.5) of Annex VI. SaMD must comply with general UDI requirements

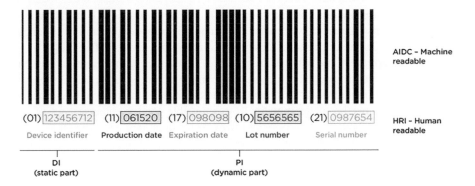

FIGURE 6.3 An example of a UDI barcode label produced by the GS1 organisation (identified by the (01) prefix). Reproduced with permission from the *Rimsys Guide to the EU MDR/IVDR UDI* [65].

for medical devices but some specific provisions/exemptions apply. Only the finished product is subject to UDI requirements (in both the EU and US) so software that is a component or accessory to a (hardware) medical device does not need a UDI.

All SaMD must display the full UDI value (Device Identifier + Production Identifier) in an easily readable plain text form each time the software is started, which could be on a start-up screen and/or in a menu command (e.g., Help/About page). The AIDC form of the UDI (i.e., barcode) is not required to be displayed upon start-up or in the menu.

Additional UDI labelling requirements depend on whether the SaMD is distributed in a packaged form (i.e., physical media such as a CD-ROM or USB memory drive), or in a non-packaged form (e.g., electronic download or cloud-based).

For software distributed in a *non-packaged* form, the UDI displayed as plain text on a start-up screen and/or in a menu command must include the software version number as the "Lot/Batch" value in the Product Identification (PI) portion of the UDI. Note: software lacking a graphical UI, such as middleware for image conversion, should be capable of transmitting the UDI through an application programming interface (API). For software distributed in a *packaged* form, the UDI must also appear on the product and packaging labels in both easily readable plain text *and* AIDC forms.

6.3.14.3.1 Software Changes that Require a New UDI

A new UDI-DI is required whenever there is a (major) modification that changes:

a. the original performance;
b. the safety or the intended use of the software; or
c. interpretation of data.

Such modifications include new or modified algorithms, database structures, operating platforms, architecture, new user interfaces, or new channels for interoperability. MDCG guidance document 2018-5 [68] describes such changes as "significant".

Minor software revisions require a new UDI-PI but not a new UDI-DI. Minor software revisions are generally associated with bug fixes, general usability enhancements, security patches, or changes designed to improve operating efficiency.

As will be apparent, the MDR UDI system is complicated and represents a considerable challenge for medical device software manufacturers, especially if the software is supplied on a physical medium and packaged. It is therefore recommended that a team member be made specifically responsible for the management of the UDI system throughout the development life cycle (as documented in the QMS). The responsibilities of the PRRC listed in Article 15(3) of the MDR (Section 6.3.7.1) do not include the UDI system, but it would seem reasonable to add it.

Official guidance on the application of the UDI system to medical device software [68] is very brief and does not contain sufficient information for an organisation new to GTIN-type systems to implement it. However, a free comprehensive guide produced by a commercial company is available [69].

6.3.15 POST-MARKET SURVEILLANCE

Post-market surveillance (PMS) is designed to monitor the performance of a marketed medical device by collecting and analysing field use data. It includes a specific activity called post-market clinical follow-up (PMCF). Post-market activities are a particularly important aspect of the EU MDR as this was deemed to be an area of relative weakness under the preceding Medical Devices Directive.

Article 10(10) of the EU MDR requires all device manufacturers to implement and keep up to date a PMS system, the main elements of which are laid out in Article 83. Additional requirements for low-risk and higher-risk devices are covered in Articles 85 and 86, respectively. In particular, the type and frequency of reporting varies depending on the device risk class.

In general, a PMS system consists of both proactive and reactive (vigilance) activities. PMS systems are used to collect and analyse data not only about the manufacturer's device but also about related devices on the market. Data collected through PMS procedures is then used to identify trends that may lead to, among other things, quality improvements, updates to user training and IFU, and identification of manufacturing issues.

6.3.15.1 PMS Plan

The PMS system is based on a PMS plan, which describes how surveillance data will be acquired and analysed to ensure that trends are identified and appropriate corrective actions taken. The detailed requirements are outlined in Section 1.1 of MDR Annex II (*Technical documentation on PMS*) and should include:

6.3.15.1.1   Data Sources
These will typically include adverse event reports, literature searches for similar devices, and data from EUDAMED (Section 6.3.14.2).

6.3.15.1.2   Data Analysis Methodology
This will comprise inclusion criteria and details of specific data analysis methods to be employed (regression analysis).

6.3.15.1.3   Benefit-Risk Indicators and Thresholds

PMS activities are used to re-evaluate and maintain the benefit-risk estimations made during the design and production phases. Information gained can lead to the identification of new/unexpected risk factors, and adjustments to risk frequency and/or severity values based on routine clinical use data.

6.3.15.1.4   Complaint and Feedback Handling Processes

To include a brief description of how data will be used for both vigilance and, when aggregated into trends, proactive surveillance activities.

6.3.15.1.5   Corrective Action Procedures

Corrective and preventative action (CAPA) processes should be detailed within the QMS (Section 6.3.8), but will be referred to in the PMS plan. Corrective action plans define procedures for identifying issues that need to be addressed immediately, often resulting from feedback from users. In a software context, a system for prioritising bug reports will need to be developed and implemented. Urgent bug fixes (including "workarounds") will not necessarily identify the root cause, so a CAPA plan should describe how trends will be identified that might lead to preventative actions or product design changes.

6.3.15.1.6   Device Tracking Methods

In order to evaluate the post-market performance of a device, a manufacturer must clearly be able to track and trace devices through the entire product life cycle. The UDI, a requirement under the MDR (Section 6.3.14), is the basis for PI, but a PMS system must reference the basic procedures for the tracing/tracking devices in the field.

6.3.15.1.7   Post-Market Clinical Follow-Up

A PMCF plan describes how data on the real-world clinical performance and device safety will be obtained; information that is used to update the PMS plan and the CER (Section 6.3.10.1). PMCF activities start when a device achieves a CE mark and are intended to supplement any pre-market clinical and non-clinical trial data. General activities include informal feedback from clinical users (and patients where appropriate) and screening of relevant medical literature. Such studies tend to produce subjective information that, in itself, is insufficient for MDR post-market requirements.

Specific PMCF activities are designed to produce datasets that can be used to scientifically support claims of clinical performance and device safety. Most examples would involve actual clinical use of the device in question (case studies, public registries, etc.), but a manufacturer may also refer to "equivalent devices" provided that "sufficient levels of access" (to the other manufacturer's clinical/safety data) can be clearly demonstrated.

There are advantages and disadvantages associated with each PMCF activity [70], so it is up to the manufacturer to select the ones most relevant for the device type in question. A basic template for the PMCF plan has been published by the MDCG [71].

As briefly explained in Section 6.3.5, the requirements for *reporting* PMS activities depend on device classification. Manufacturers of Class I devices are required to prepare a post-market surveillance report (PMSR) summarising the results and conclusions of the analyses of the post-market surveillance data gathered as a result of the PMS plan. The report should also include a rationale and description of any preventive and corrective actions taken during the reporting period. It should be updated when necessary (no minimum frequency is specified) and made available to the competent authority upon request.

Manufacturers of class IIa, class IIb, and class III devices are required to produce a periodic safety update report (PSUR), which is more detailed than the PMSR. It must be updated at least once per year and be submitted for review by the chosen Notified Body via the EUDAMED database. In addition to the documentation required for a PMSR, a PSUR should include the following:

- The main findings of the PMCF activities
- All conclusions from the reassessment of the benefit-risk determination
- Data on the estimated number of clinical users

In summary, the main steps in PMS are as follows:

1. Determine the type of surveillance and reporting that will be required for the device
2. Identify the sources of PMS data that will be used
3. Undertake the data analysis and reporting that will contribute to the re-evaluation of benefit-risk for the device(s)
4. Create a PMCF plan

6.3.16   Conformity Assessment (CA)

Conformity assessment (CA) is the process by which a manufacturer demonstrates compliance with the relevant parts of the medical device regulations. An appropriate CA procedure must be completed before a medical device is placed on the EU market or put into service (Article 52). Three CA procedures are described in annexes IX to XI, but X and XII are linked:

Annex IX: CA based on a QMS and on assessment of technical documentation.
Annex X: CA based on type-examination.
Annex XI: CA based on product conformity verification.

The type of CA procedure available to the manufacturer is dictated by the classification of the device in question [72]. The following section is written from a medical device software point of view, so excludes specific requirements for sterile devices, implantable devices, etc. It also excludes the separate CA requirements for custom-made and investigational devices (see Article 52).

Class I devices

Manufacturers of Class I devices (self) declare the conformity of their products by issuing an EU Declaration of Conformity (according to Article 19) after drawing up the required technical documentation set out in Annexes II and III. Class I devices that have a measuring function must use either the QMS and technical documentation procedures described in Chapters I and II of Annex IX or the production QA procedure described in Part A of Annex XI.

For Class I SaMD the involvement of a Notified Body is *not* required unless the device has a measuring function (Class Im), in which case certain metrological claims may have to be independently verified (contact Notified Body for advice).

Class II devices

Class IIa

Manufacturers of Class IIa devices may assess conformity by either:

a. Undertaking a QMS assessment (described in Sections I and III of Annex IX) as well as a technical documentation assessment (Section II*, Annex IX), or
b. Producing technical documentation according to Annexes II and III, coupled with the CA assessment procedure described in Section 10 or Section 18 of Annex XI.

Class IIb

Manufacturers of Class IIb devices may assess conformity by either:

a. Undertaking a QMS assessment (described in sections I and III of Annex IX) as well as a technical documentation assessment (Section II, Annex IX) or
b. Undertaking a type examination CA procedure (Annex X) in combination with a product conformity assessment (Annex XI).

Class III devices

Manufacturers of Class III devices may assess conformity by either:

a. Undertaking a QMS assessment (described in sections I and III of Annex IX) as well as a technical documentation assessment (Section II, Annex IX) or
b. Undertaking a type-examination CA procedure (Annex X) in combination with a product conformity assessment (Annex XI).

The involvement of a Notified Body is required for the CA of all class II and class III devices.

6.3.16.1　The Role of Notified Bodies and Competent Authorities

Notified Bodies play an essential role in conformity assessment (Section 6.3.16.1). They need to meet the strict requirements specified in Annex VII of MDR 17, including formal accreditation for their activities. The appointment and subsequent supervision of Notified Bodies is the responsibility of the national Competent Authority. A manufacturer is free to choose *any* Notified Body listed on the NANDO[14] database [73]. Documents and/or product samples are submitted to the chosen Notified Body for review. If successful, the Notified Body will issue a certificate of conformity, which is valid for a maximum of five years. An extension of the certificate is possible, subject to reassessment.

---

[14] NANDO = New approach notified and designated organisations.

On receipt of the required certificates, it is the responsibility of the manufacturer to make the actual declaration of conformity (as described in Annex IV). The CE mark that is then affixed to the device/packaging bears a four-digit code that identifies the Notified Body that was involved in the conformity assessment procedure.

All Notified Bodies previously designated under the old MDD had to be reassessed in order to act as authorised review bodies under MDR 17. The number of Notified Bodies is therefore now significantly lower than it was under the MDD and this has led to assessment backlogs in most EU states. Also, some Notified Bodies have reduced their scope, so do not offer a full range of assessment services. Various initiatives are underway to speed up the independent assessment process [74].

Once the manufacturer has been awarded a certificate of conformity by the Notified Body and subsequently placed the medical device on the EU market, the organisation will be subject to site inspections as part of the surveillance assessment (MDR Annex IX, clause 3). For manufacturers of Class II and Class III devices, the appointed Notified Body is required to carry out appropriate audits and assessments to make sure that the manufacturer is applying the previously approved QMS.

These regular audits (to be performed at least annually) are planned, so the manufacturer will generally receive notice of such a visit. The Notified Body is also required to undertake an *unannounced* site visit at least once every five years, which may be combined with, or quite separate from, the regular surveillance assessment visit. For Class II device manufacturers, the regular surveillance visit will also include an audit of other selected technical documentation, including the CER (Section 6.3.10) and the PMS plan (Section 6.3.15.1) (MDR Annex IX, clause 3.5).

6.4   MEDICAL DEVICE REGULATION IN THE UK

6.4.1   BACKGROUND AND OVERVIEW

In the UK, medical devices are currently regulated under the Medical Devices Regulations 2002 (UK MDR 2002), which gave effect in UK law to the following EU Directives (that have since been repealed and replaced at the EU level):

- Directive 90/385/EEC on active implantable medical devices (AIMDD)
- Directive 93/42/EEC on medical devices (MDD)
- Directive 98/79/EC on *in vitro* diagnostic medical devices (IVDD)

Following the UK's final exit from the European Union on 31 December 2020, the EU MDR 17/745 did not become retained law, but the Medicines and Medical Devices Act 2021 provided the UK government with the powers to amend the UK MDR 2002 through *secondary* legislation. This should be regarded as a temporary measure pending a comprehensive review of the 2002 regulations. As a result, the UK legislation that came into force on 1 January 2021 was the Medical Devices (Amendment, etc.) (EU Exit) Regulations 2020, also referred to as "UK MDR 2002+" [60].

These new regulations describe how the regulatory position of Northern Ireland is now different from the rest of the UK but make no substantial changes to the technical content of UK MDR 2002, which still applies in England, Scotland, and Wales (i.e., Great Britain, GB). Under the terms of the *Northern Ireland Protocol*, the EU

TABLE 6.8
EU and GB regulatory equivalents

Term or system	EU	GB
Approval/audit body	Notified body	Approved body
Approval mark	CE	UKCA
Registration system	EUDAMED database	MHRA database

MDR 17/745 became fully applicable in Northern Ireland on the same date (26 May 2021) as in EU member states.

A completely new set of UK medical device regulations were originally planned to come into force in July 2023 but this has now been delayed until July 2025 [75,76].

The "as amended" reference in the full title of the current UK medical device regulations[15] is important as the regulations originally issued in 2002 have been amended several times over the last 21 years to reflect changes in relevant EU Directives, to respond to serious problems with certain types of implantable medical devices, or to account for changes brought about by the UK's exit from the EU [77]. It is therefore important to realise that some relevant EU Directives issued after 2002 (for example, Directive 2007/47, which amended Directive 93/42/EEC [Section 6.3.1]) were also transposed into UK law using Statutory Instruments.

The basic *steps* involved in gaining approval to market a medical device in Great Britain are basically the same as for countries within the EU (Section 6.3.1), although the individual essential requirements (ER) in the UK Medical Device Regulations 2002 are different from the GSPR in EU MDR 17. Corresponding GB terms and systems are shown in Table 6.8

The one main procedural difference is that there is no mandatory requirement to affix a UDI since this was only added to EU regulations when MDR 17 was drafted. However, there is nothing to prevent a manufacturer from voluntarily placing devices on the market in the UK with a UDI. Other general UK regulations relevant to the manufacture of medical devices are discussed in Section 7.4.

6.4.2 UK RESPONSIBLE PERSON

In order to place a medical device on the GB market, manufacturers based *outside* of the UK must appoint a UK Responsible Person (UKRP) having a registered place of business in the UK. The role may be outsourced to a UK-based third-party organisation [78] and is equivalent to the Authorised Representative in the EU regulatory system (Section 6.3.7.1).

The UKRP is required to register devices with the MHRA and has responsibilities that include:

- Ensuring that the declaration of conformity and technical documentation has been drawn up where applicable, and an appropriate CA procedure has been carried out by the manufacturer

---

[15] Medical Devices Regulations 2002 (SI 2002 No 618, as amended).

- Keeping copies of the technical documentation, the declaration of conformity, and relevant compliance certificates available for inspection by the MHRA
- Cooperating with the MHRA on all matters relating to preventive or corrective actions necessary to eliminate or mitigate risks posed by the device(s)
- Immediately inform the manufacturer about complaints and reports from healthcare professionals, patients, and users about suspected adverse incidents related to a device

6.4.3 PERSON RESPONSIBLE FOR BEST PRACTICE COMPLIANCE

This UK requirement for *in-house* medical device development is analogous to the PRRC required by the EU MDR for commercial manufacturers[16] (Section 6.3.7). In a health institution where there are several unconnected departments impacted by the new medical device regulations, the institution should appoint a suitably qualified and experienced individual to be responsible for monitoring, advising, and reporting at an executive level on best practice compliance across the organisation [60]. Such a person would also be expected to help manage the transition to the new UK medical device regulations, coordinate expertise and compliance monitoring across the organisation, and take the lead in any dealings with the MHRA.

6.4.4 MEDICAL DEVICE SOFTWARE

The original classification rules described in MDD 93/42/EC (i.e., the old EU Directive on medical devices) did not account for standalone software and it was not until the Directive was amended by Directive 2007/47/EC in 2007 that an ER was written for software: "For devices which incorporate software or are medical software in themselves, the software must be validated according to the state of the art taking into account the principles of development lifecycle, risk management, validation and verification". This ER was subsequently underpinned by the development of a harmonised standard (IEC 62304:2006) covering *most* aspects of the software development life cycle (Section 5.4). The situation was further clarified in 2012 when the EC published a guidance document (MEDDEV 2.1/6) on the qualification and classification of standalone software [79].

6.4.4.1 Standalone Software and Apps

Current GB regulatory guidance on standalone software and health apps is essentially the UK MHRA interpretation of MEDDEV 2.1/6, which relates to the old MDD. The document is in the form of an interactive flowchart designed to assist with both qualification and classification issues. It also includes a list of "key words" that the MHRA may look for when deciding if an app is a medical device or not [23].

6.4.4.2 CDS Software

Decision support software is usually considered a medical device when it applies automated reasoning such as a simple calculation, an algorithm, or a more complex series of calculations, so is likely to fall within the scope of UK MDR 2002 (e.g., drug dose calculations, symptom tracking). Some decision support software may not be considered a medical device if it exists only to provide *reference information* to

---

[16] The PRRC was a new requirement in MDR 17 so it is not present in current UK regulations based on the old EU Medical Device Directives.

enable a healthcare professional (HCP) to make a clinical decision. However, if the software/app performs a calculation or interprets or interpolates data and the healthcare professional does not (or cannot) review the source/raw data, then this software may be considered a medical device. In summary, CDS software is *unlikely* to be a medical device if:

1. It reproduces a paper document in digital format, in which case it is down to the HCP to make the decisions based on the advice displayed
2. It follows the path of a procedure/treatment without any decision points
3. It provides options but the HCP decides which path to take
4. It offers only lifestyle treatment choices or referral advice (e.g., "see your family doctor")

Software is most *likely* to be deemed a medical device if:

1. It is closely linked to the operation of a hardware medical device (i.e., it is likely to be an accessory)
2. It is intended to influence the treatment of the patient (type of treatment, duration of treatment, dosage, etc.)
3. It produces a specific diagnosis or prognosis

6.4.4.3 Devices Containing AI Technology

Current MHRA guidance on *"Medical Device Stand-Alone Software including Apps (including IVDMDs)"* [23] makes passing reference to AI when discussing *in-vitro diagnostic medical devices* and "symptom checkers" but does not contain specific requirements. The MHRA's plans for the regulation of SaMD and AIaMD is discussed in Section 9.4.4.

6.4.4.4 Usability Engineering

The UK position on the application of usability engineering (UE) in the development of medical devices is summarised in MHRA guidance that is designed to be consistent with FDA guidelines (Section 6.5.8.10) and relevant standards [80].

EU Directive 2007/47 introduced several changes to the original MDD (93/42/EEC), including more specific requirements for consideration of ergonomic and human factors. These changes were subsequently transposed into UK law by Statutory Instrument 2008 No. 2936, which amended the UK MDR 2002.

Several changes to the essential requirements relate to usability (9.2, 10.2, 13.1), but a new general condition added to ER1 stated (in the context of patient safety and acceptable risk-benefit) that measures shall include (a) "reducing, as far as possible, the risk of use error due to the ergonomic features of the device and the environment in which the device is intended to be used (design for patient safety)", and (b) "consideration of the technical knowledge, experience, education and training and where applicable the medical and physical conditions of intended users (design for lay, professional, disabled or other users)".

MHRA guidance refers extensively to IEC 62366-1:2015 (*Medical devices – Part 1: Application of usability to medical devices*),[17] which is an FDA-recognised

---

[17] The standard was amended in 2020 (IEC 62366-1:2015/AMD1:2020), but no fundamental changes were made to the usability engineering process.

consensus standard (Section 6.5.8.10) and is expected to become a harmonised standard under EU MDR 17 (Section 6.3.6.6). There is also an accompanying technical report (IEC/TR 62366-2:2016) that provides more detailed guidance on the implementation of IEC 62366-1:2015.

The central point of the standard is the definition and description of a *software engineering process*, which includes use specification, hazard identification, and specification, planning, and implementation of the user interface. MHRA guidance and IEC TR 62366-2 provide more detail on these UE techniques. The manufacturer is also required to compile a concise UEF, which may be reviewed by regulatory authorities. It forms part of the overall technical documentation for the device (Section 6.3.12). A statement of "compliance with IEC 62366" is not sufficient without supporting evidence.

The MHRA guidance emphasises the importance of extending the UE approach to PMS as, despite pre-release testing, some types of use errors are only discovered through extensive use of the device in the field. The UE process is summarised in Figure 6.4. Pre-production prototypes are not subject to formal human factors studies as the "users" will generally be restricted to highly trained development personnel, but "final" versions are subject to test protocols involving representative users.

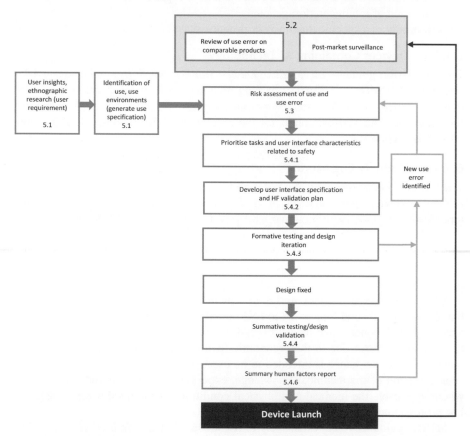

FIGURE 6.4   The UE process as defined in IEC 62366-1:2015, illustrating its iterative nature. Adapted with permission from MHRA guidelines on applying HFE to medical devices [80].

IEC/TR 62366-2:2016 goes beyond the safety-related considerations of IEC 62366-1:2015, to include general desirable features of graphical user interfaces that should be considered when designing medical device software.

6.4.5 REGISTRATION OF MEDICAL DEVICES

Following Brexit and the subsequent passing of The Medicines and Medical Devices Act 2021 (M&MD Act), the UK has a new framework for regulating medical devices. As part of this, from 1 January 2021, all medical devices placed on the market need to be registered by their suppliers on the MHRA's Device Online Registration System (DORS), as part of a UK-wide Medical Device Information System (MDIS) [81,82]. The resultant public database should provide valuable information to government departments, medtech companies, healthcare establishments and, most importantly, patients, and supports one of the key recommendations of the recent UK government review on effective MDR [83].

6.4.6 IN-HOUSE MANUFACTURING AND USE (IHMU)

EU MDR conditions for HIE (Section 6.3.11) only apply in Northern Ireland (Section 6.4.1) and medical device software developed within GB hospital Trusts for their own use is not subject to UK MDR 2002. However, in either case, if the software were transferred to another legal entity (e.g., a different hospital Trust) it would require full UKCA or CE marking.

The possible content of the new UK medical device regulations regarding IHMU is discussed in Section 9.4.1. Even in the absence of regulatory control of IHMU, best practice guidelines should be followed for both professional and *general* legal liability reasons. Such guidelines will typically represent a subset of regulatory requirements [60] and should be supplemented by specific guidance and applicable software engineering standards (see Chapter 5).

It is likely that in-house developed medical devices produced under the envisaged HIE will need to be registered with MHRA in the UK from July 2025 (Section 9.4.2).

6.4.7 RISK MANAGEMENT

The UK MDR contains several references to "risk analysis" but the term "risk management" is not mentioned. ISO 14971 (Section 5.3.1) was harmonised in support of Directive 93/42/EEC in 2009, so compliance with the currently harmonised version (ISO 14971:2012) is the most straightforward way of complying with the risk management requirements of UK MDR 2002.

When the UK exited the EU at the end of 2020 the link between the UK medical device regulations and the harmonised standards supporting the old EU medical device directive (93/42/EEC) was broken. As a result, the UK has recently published its own list of standards (termed "designated standards") that support the current UK medical device regulations. This list of designated standards is currently identical to the list of harmonised European standards associated with the old EU MDD [84].

Manufacturers of medical device software also need to be aware of NHS Digital standard DCB 0129:2018 *(Clinical risk management: its application in the manufacture of health IT systems)*, which is a mandatory standard (under Section 250 of the Health and Social Care Act 2012) for health IT systems used in the NHS in England [85].

Crucially, and somewhat controversially, the scope of the standard was extended in 2018 to include software medical devices subject to EU MDR 2017/745, but it subsequently became clear that NHS Digital only intended to include a small subset of software medical devices that are "implemented within a health IT system" [86]. Nonetheless, for such so-called "medical device IT systems", the manufacturer is obliged to comply with DCB0129 as well as ISO 14971, which is effectively a requirement of the UK Medical Device Regulations 2002. NHS Digital claims that DCB 0129 is "broadly consistent" with ISO 14971, but the DCB standard refers to an outdated (2012) version of ISO 14971 (Section 5.3.1).

AXREM, the UK trade association representing suppliers of medical equipment and healthcare IT, issued a "Problem Statement" regarding DCB 0129 that describes the difficulties that the standard is presenting to the UK medical device industry [87]. Its recommendations include a comprehensive revision of DCB 0129 and the associated DTAC procurement questionnaire (Section 5.4.6). Despite these concerns from industry, DCB0129 is gaining traction within the medical physics/clinical engineering (MP/CE) community and the Institute of Physics and Engineering in Medicine (IPEM) is running courses and webinars on "Clinical safety of health IT systems" based on DCB 0129 [88].

The current debate is focused on the appointment of Clinical Safety Officers (CSOs) within health institutions and ensuring that commercial health IT suppliers are compliant with DB0129, but the standard also has implications for scientific and technical staff who develop medical software in-house [89,90].

Unlike the European (EN) version of the recently amended standard, the current BSI version of ISO 14971 (BS EN ISO 14971:2019+A11:2021) does not yet include an annex describing the relationship of the standard to UK MDRs – what will be called a "national annex" – to be designated NZ – but this will follow in due course.

6.5 MEDICAL DEVICE REGULATION IN THE US

6.5.1 Overview

The regulation of medical devices in the US is broadly similar to that in the EU, but there are some important differences in the way that manufacturers gain approval to market their new products. Medical devices are regulated under the Federal Food, Drug, and Cosmetics Act (FD&C Act), as amended by the Medical Device Amendments 1976 and subsequent related amendments; the actual regulation of devices under this statute falling within the remit of US FDA. The basic regulatory requirements that manufacturers of medical devices marketed in the US must meet are:

- Registration of the manufacturing establishment
- Listing of manufactured medical devices

- Pre-market notification (PMN), unless exempt, or PMA
- IDE for clinical research studies
- Quality system regulation (QSR)
- Labelling requirements
- Medical device reporting

The specific requirements (type of pre-market submission, quality system adoption, labelling, and Medical device reporting) are determined by the regulatory classification assigned to the device [91,92]

There is a specific requirement for manufacturers based outside the US to appoint a *US Agent* (Section 6.5.10), which may present a problem for some SMEs. Nonetheless, it is an issue that needs to be resolved before undertaking any detailed technical planning.

The basic *device determination* steps to be taken by manufacturers of health-related equipment are the same as for most medical device regulatory systems. First, to determine whether the product meets the definition of a medical device and, second, to determine the device classification. The device classification then determines the type of pre-market application that the manufacturer needs to submit.

6.5.2   Qualification

Qualification is the process of establishing whether a given health product meets the US definition of a medical device, specified in Section 201(h) of the FD&C Act. Namely.

An instrument, apparatus, implement, machine, contrivance, implant, in vitro reagent, or other similar or related article, including a component part, or accessory which is:

a. recognised in the official National Formulary, or the United States Pharmacopoeia, or any supplement to them;
b. intended for use in the diagnosis of disease or other conditions, or in the cure, mitigation, treatment, or prevention of disease, in man or other animals; or
c. intended to affect the structure or any function of the body of man or other animals, and which does not achieve its primary intended purposes through chemical action within or on the body of man or other animals and which is not dependent upon being metabolised for the achievement of its primary intended purposes. The term "device" does not include software functions excluded pursuant to section 520(o).

Certain differences will be noted compared to the definition of a medical device contained in MDR 17/745 (Section 6.3.2.1) but the US definition, through points (b) and (c), will nonetheless capture all traditional medical devices and most types of medical software.

Section 520(o) of the FD&C Act (duly amended by the 21st Century Cures Act in 2016) describes types of software specifically excluded from the definition of a medical device. Examples include administrative IT systems used in healthcare facilities, electronic patient records (EPR) systems, most wellness mobile apps, most types of clinical support system (CDS) software (Section 6.5.6.5), and (database) software used only for storing, transferring, or displaying (clinical) data. However, software generally known as SaMD or software in a medical device (SiMD) certainly *is* included in the definition.

6.5.3 CLASSIFICATION AND ASSOCIATED CONTROLS

6.5.3.1 The Classification System

The FDA classifies medical devices based on the risks associated with the device, so the classification determines the level of regulatory control necessary to assure the safety and effectiveness of the device [93].

The US system has three classification levels (Class I, Class II, Class III), with Class I being the lowest risk and Class III the highest. Unlike the EU system, risk "labels" (low, medium, high) are not formally attached to the classes, but they are closely associated with the relevant control procedures.

Class I: General Controls
    With Exemptions
    Without Exemptions

Class II: General Controls and Special Controls
    With Exemptions
    Without Exemptions

Class III: General Controls and PMA

Device classification is strongly influenced by the intended use of the device and also by indications for use. The FDA's interpretation of "intended use" can be found in a guidance document covering PMN [94].

BOX 6.1   A NOTE ON FDA GUIDANCE DOCUMENTS

FDA guidance documents do not establish legally enforceable responsibilities. Instead, published guidance describes the Agency's current thinking on a topic and should be viewed only as recommendations, unless specific regulatory or statutory requirements are cited. They do not create or confer any rights for or on any person and do not operate to bind the FDA or the public. The use of the word "should" in Agency guidance means that something is suggested or recommended, but not required [94]. A manufacturer can use an alternative approach if it satisfies the requirements of the applicable statutes and regulations, but, in practice, it would need a very good reason not to follow FDA guidelines.

At this point, it is worth clarifying the difference between "intended use" and "indications for use". Briefly, the intended use [of a medical device] is what the manufacturer claims (in the user manual, accompanying promotional materials, etc.) the device *does* (i.e., its main purpose), and how it works.

Indications for use, on the other hand, describe the circumstances or conditions under which the device should be used (i.e., the clinical *reasons*). Intended use is thus device-specific and indications for use are patient population-specific. In diagnostic medicine is also common to speak of *clinical indications* for a given test, which has the same meaning. In FDA regulation, the terms are particularly important in the interpretation of substantial equivalence in connection with the 510(k) programme (Section 6.5.4.1).

6.5.3.2   The Effect of Classification on the Device Approval System

Device classification determines the type of pre-market submission/application required for FDA clearance. The route to market clearance for Class I and Class II devices is PMN, usually referred to as the 510(k) programme.[18] The traditional 510(k) process requires the manufacturer to demonstrate (by a written application) that the device in question is "substantially equivalent" to a legal device already on the US market – what the FDA calls a predicate device. If a predicate device type cannot be found, then an abbreviated 510(k) submission may be possible under certain circumstances. For new or novel devices, the *De Novo* classification process is also an option (Section 6.5.4.2).

Class III devices require full PMA, which is a much more stringent assessment process than PMN. In addition to the usual process controls deemed adequate for Class II devices, a Class III device applicant must provide the FDA with sufficient validated scientific evidence to assure that the device is safe *and* effective for its intended use [95].

6.5.3.3   Determining Device Classification

The first part of the classification process is to find out whether a generic product code already exists for the device in question. Unlike in the EU system, where devices are classified (using *classification rules*) on a case-by-case basis, the US system has pre-defined product codes for specific device categories [96].

Devices are grouped by medical specialty (cardiovascular, neurology, radiology, etc.), referred to as "panels". Selecting a particular generic device type (e.g., "positron camera" under "Radiology") in the FDA's product classification database will then reveal an identification (description) and classification [97]. If the appropriate panel is unknown or unclear, the manufacturer can conduct a keyword search of the product code classification database (PCCD) [98].

Selecting the "Go to Quick Search" feature (Figure 6.5) also allows input of a review panel (e.g., radiology) but is designed the facilitate narrower searches by inputting equipment-based terms such as "bone densitometer" or disease/condition terms such as "osteoporosis". An entry of "bone densitometer" reveals the output screen shown in Figure 6.6.

---

[18] So called because pre-market notification is covered in section 510(k) of the Federal Food, Drug and Cosmetic Act (FD&C Act).

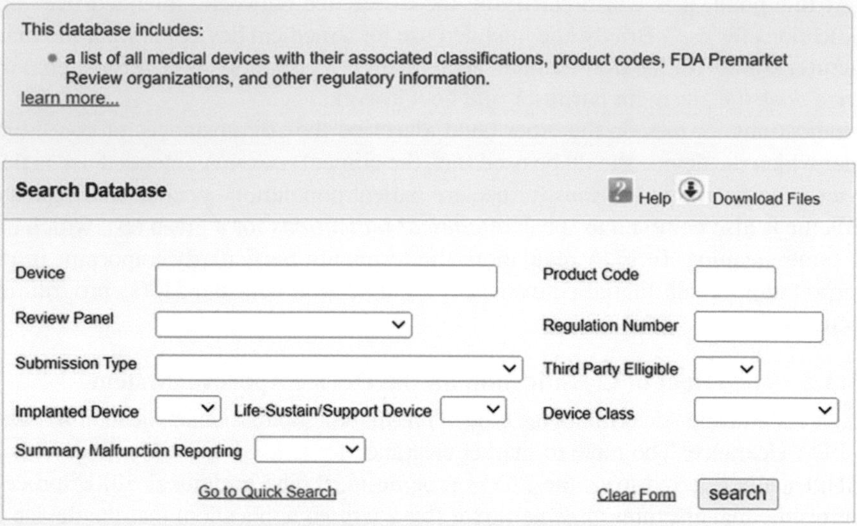

This database includes:
- a list of all medical devices with their associated classifications, product codes, FDA Premarket Review organizations, and other regulatory information.
learn more...

Search Database   ? Help ⬇ Download Files

Device		Product Code	
Review Panel	▾	Regulation Number	
Submission Type	▾	Third Party Elligible	▾
Implanted Device ▾ Life-Sustain/Support Device ▾	Device Class	▾
Summary Malfunction Reporting ▾		

Go to Quick Search   Clear Form   search

FIGURE 6.5   The input screen for the FDA's PCCD.

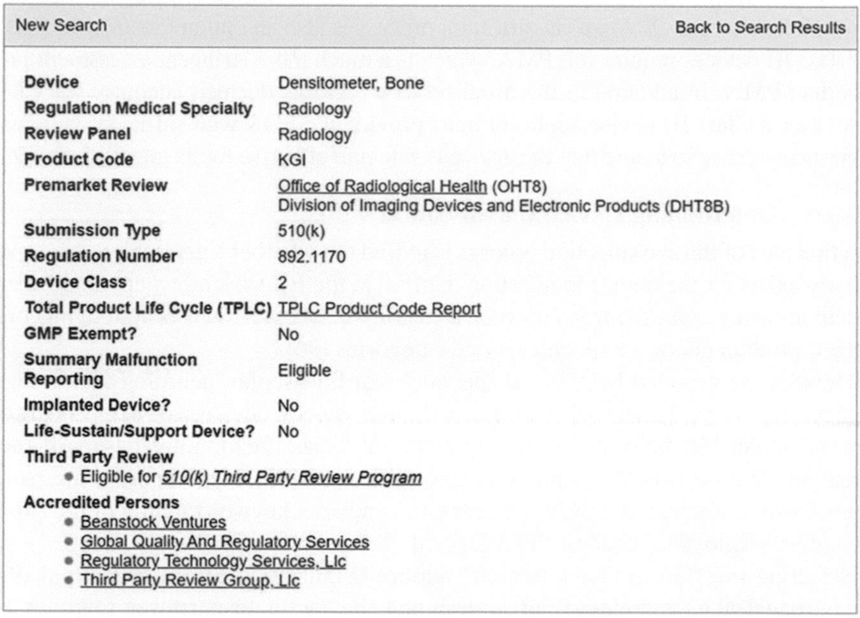

New Search   Back to Search Results

Device	Densitometer, Bone
Regulation Medical Specialty	Radiology
Review Panel	Radiology
Product Code	KGI
Premarket Review	Office of Radiological Health (OHT8)
	Division of Imaging Devices and Electronic Products (DHT8B)
Submission Type	510(k)
Regulation Number	892.1170
Device Class	2
Total Product Life Cycle (TPLC)	TPLC Product Code Report
GMP Exempt?	No
Summary Malfunction Reporting	Eligible
Implanted Device?	No
Life-Sustain/Support Device?	No
Third Party Review	

- Eligible for *510(k) Third Party Review Program*

Accredited Persons
- Beanstock Ventures
- Global Quality And Regulatory Services
- Regulatory Technology Services, Llc
- Third Party Review Group, Llc

FIGURE 6.6   Example output screen from the product classification database using a search of "bone densitometer". Data displayed include the generic product code, regulation number, and classification.

The output screen contains important information on the regulation number, device class, and submission type, along with other supporting information. The *regulation number* is the unique reference number for the device type within the Code of Federal Regulations (CFR) Title 21 database [99].

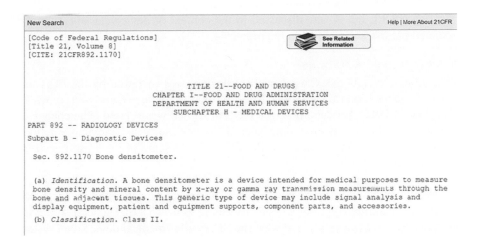

FIGURE 6.7 An example output screen from the CFR Title 21 database using the regulation number for bone densitometer (892.1170) as input.

It should be noted that text entered into the *quick search* part of the PCCD should be "device name orientated". For example, "bone densitometer" rather than "bone densitometry". Also, "bone densitometer" is not amongst the devices listed if "osteoporosis" is typed into the search field, so the cross-referencing between disease and associated medical devices is not always reliable. Nonetheless, the two main databases are comprehensive and provide fast online searches.

There is no direct link from the PCCD to the CFR database, but the regulation number (892.1170 in this case) obtained from the PCCD query can used to search the CFR database, the result of which is shown in Figure 6.7.

The output screen shown in Figure 6.6 can also be reached by selecting the appropriate regulation citation number on the device classification panels web page [97]. The first three digits of the regulation number (in this example 892) is the code for the specialty or panel, so clicking on "Part 892" (corresponding to radiology) reveals a long list of devices that includes "892.1170 Bone densitometer".

Once identified, the product code provides some of the information required for an FDA pre-market submission, including

- The type of pre-market submission required (e.g., 510(k), 510(k) Exempt, PMA)
- The device class (I, II, or III)
- The regulation number with the device description
- Recognised consensus standards for the device
- Requirements for any special controls

If a suitable product code does not exist, the option of a *De Novo* application is possible (Section 6.5.4.2)

6.5.3.4 Classification of Device Software

The term *Device Software Functions* (DSF) is used by the FDA to describe software functions that meet the definition of a medical device. It is considered more generally in Section 6.5.8.1, but is here discussed in the context of device classification and associated pre-market submission requirements.

6.5.3.4.1   Low-Risk Software

The regulation of low-risk Class I medical devices was reviewed by the FDA following the publication (in December 2016) of the 21st Century Cures Act, in which the previous FD&C Act definition of a medical device was revised. The change of definition (essentially removing some types of "low risk software" previously defined as medical devices) necessitated that the FDA update some of its software-related guidance documents.

The changes mainly concern types of health-related software that will no longer be defined as medical devices and thus will no longer be regulated by the FDA. This will include most types of CDS software (Section 6.5.8.6), "general wellness" apps (e.g., "activity trackers"), and what the FDA calls "medical device data system (MDDS) software". That is, software that passively transfers, stores, converts formats or displays existing medical device data [100,101], which brings the US system more in line with the EU regulations.

The FDA defines a "general wellness" product as one having an intended use that (a) relates to maintaining or encouraging a general state of health or a healthy activity, or (b) relates the role of a healthy lifestyle with helping to reduce the risk or impact of certain chronic diseases or conditions. Its policy on general wellness products contains numerous examples of the type of devices and apps (categorised by intended purpose) that would qualify as wellness products [102].

6.5.3.4.2   Documentation Levels

Device software is primarily classified according to general device classification criteria (Section 6.5.3) but the FDA specifies additional criteria to determine the amount of documentation required for pre-market submissions. As for hardware devices, the basic device classification determines the need for a QMS and many other requirements.

Until recently, the FDA used a system based on "levels of concern" (LoC) to determine the type of documentation to be submitted as part of the PMA process, but this system was replaced in June 2023 with the publication of the final version of guidance on the *Content of Pre-market Submissions for DSF* [103].

Unlike the previous 3-level LoC regime, the new "software classification" system has just two "documentation levels" (DL), based on the risk that the device presents to the patient or the user: Basic Documentation Level (BDL) and Enhanced Documentation Level (EDL).

Enhanced Documentation should be provided for any device software function(s) where a failure or flaw "could present a hazardous situation with a probable risk of death or serious injury, either to a patient, user of the device, or others in the environment of use". The risks should be assessed *prior* to implementation of risk control measures (i.e., mitigations) and should be considered in the context of the device's intended use (e.g., impacts to safety, treatment, and/or diagnosis), and any other relevant factors. BDL is required in situations where the EDL does not apply.

The use of the word "probable" in the above criterion is intended to exclude consideration of purely hypothetical risks, but includes analysis of "all known or

TABLE 6.9

FDA requirements for basic and enhanced documentation levels.

Document	Basic	Enhanced
Determination of the documentation level	✓	✓
Software description	✓	✓
System and software architecture design	✓	✓
Risk management file	✓	✓
Software Requirements Specification	✓	✓
Software design specification	note a	✓
Software development and maintenance practices	note b	note c
Software testing as part of verification and validation	note d	note e
Software version history	✓	✓
Unresolved software anomalies (e.g., "bugs", defects)	✓	✓

Notes for Table 6.9.
a. Not required for pre-market submission, but the manufacturer/sponsor should document this information in the design history file (DHF). During pre-market review, the FDA may request additional information to evaluate the safety and effectiveness of the device.
b. Declaration of Conformity to the FDA-recognised version of IEC 62304 (see guidance document for exact sub-clauses) *or* summaries of the life cycle development plan, the configuration management plan, and the planned maintenance activities.
c. Declaration of Conformity to the FDA-recognised version of IEC 62304 *or* BDL, plus *complete* configuration management and maintenance plans.
d. Summary description of the testing activities at the unit, integration, and system levels; *and* system level test protocol, including expected results, observed results, pass/fail determination, and system level test report.
e. BDL *plus* unit and integration test protocols, including expected results, observed results, pass/fail determination, and unit and integration test reports.

foreseeable software hazards and hazardous situations associated with the device, including those resulting from reasonably foreseeable misuse, whether intentional or unintentional, prior to the implementation of risk control measures". It also includes consideration of device functionality being compromised by inadequate device security.

As far as the actual documentation is concerned, the guidance describes information that would typically be generated during the SDLC, including verification, and validation (Section 6.5.8.2) (Table 6.9).

It will be noted that the only *major* difference between the basic and enhanced documentation levels is the lack of requirement for a software design specification for the BDL.

In summary, the FDA requires a form of additional classification for device software (SiMD and SaMD), which depends on the potential risk that it presents. The classification (documental level) of embedded software depends on whether it *controls* hardware functions of the device or is simply used to display and analyse data. The classification criteria reflect the FDA's ongoing alignment with IEC 62304 (Section 6.5.8.8).

The DL system determines the scope of the software development documentation to be *submitted* to the FDA for pre-market review. By contrast, the software classification system described in IEC 62304 determines the amount of documentation to be *prepared* (Section 5.4.1.13).

6.5.3.5   Controls

Controls are procedures applied to ensure safety and/or reliability. They are categorised as *general controls* or *special controls* and their application depends on the classification of the device (Section 6.5.3.1).

Controls include manufacturing procedures and PMN procedures. Design controls apply to all Class II and Class III devices, and also to Class I devices "automated using computer software" (21 CFR §820.30). With SaMD regulations evolving, it is important to consider that devices initially categorised as Class I may become Class II in the future [104].

6.5.3.5.1   General Controls

General controls require that all device manufacturers comply with the FDA's QSR, which represent current good manufacturing practices. General controls also require that all medical devices are properly labelled and that manufacturers and users report serious adverse incidents to the FDA (Section 6.5.9).

6.5.3.5.2   Special Controls

Special controls are required for Class II medical devices. A special control could be adherence to a particular standard or guideline, or a specific labelling procedure.

6.5.4   PRE-MARKET REQUIREMENTS

There are several routes to market approval of medical devices in the US. There are also several pre-market exemptions that apply to emergency/compassionate situations or that allow a device to be used in a clinical study in order to collect safety and effectiveness data, usually in connection with a PMA.

The main three conventional routes are PMN, PMA, and De Novo request, of which PMN is by far the most common. The exemptions, sometimes referred to as "special pathways" [105], are as follows:

- Class I/Class II exempt devices
- Investigational device exemption (IDE)
- Humanitarian device exemption (HDE)
- Custom device exemption (CDE)
- Expanded access pathway (EAP)

The EAP includes emergency use, compassionate use, and *treatment* IDE. More information on these exemptions can be found on the FDA website. The following discussion focuses on the three main types of pre-market submissions.

6.5.4.1   Pre-Market Notification

The PMN system is usually called the "510(k) clearance programme", named after the section of the Food, Drug, and Cosmetic Act to which it refers. Three types of

PNM may be submitted to the FDA: Traditional, Special, and Abbreviated [106]. The discussion below refers to the traditional programme unless otherwise indicated.

From October 2022 it has been possible to send 510(k) submissions electronically (eSTAR[19] system) using the Centre for Devices and Radiological Health's (CDRH) portal. And from 1 October 2023 all 510(k) submissions, unless exempted, *must* be submitted using eSTAR.

The 510(k) programme is a marketing clearance process that involves the submission of various documents to the FDA. The purpose of a 510(k) submission is to demonstrate that the device in question is "substantially equivalent" to another device already on the US market – a so-called predicate device. In general terms, "substantial equivalence" means that the new device is just as safe and effective as the predicate device. Finding a predicate device might appear to be a daunting task, but it is mostly based on *intended use* [107,108].

Specifically, a new device is substantially equivalent to a predicate if it meets either of the following two conditions:

1. Has the same intended use as the predicate *and* has the same technological characteristics as the predicate, or
2. Has the same intended use with different technological characteristics that do not raise questions of safety and effectiveness *and* that the information submitted to the FDA demonstrates that the device is as safe and effective as the legally marketed device. Note that the predicate must be a specific device, not a device type.

The FDA has recognised that the 510(k) process needs to be modernised and has issued further draft guidance on best practices for selecting a predicate device [109].

A manufacturer must back up any claim of substantial equivalence by providing evidence of the scientific methods used to evaluate differences in technological characteristics and performance data. For software-only products, the performance data would mainly comprise software validation.

If the FDA agrees with the manufacturer's claim of substantial equivalence, permission is then given to market the device, subject to compliance with relevant general and special control provisions of the FD&C Act (listed in the Approval Letter), since these will not have been inspected or verified by the FDA. A 510(K) clearance does not therefore mean that the FDA has determined that the device in question complies with other aspects of the FD&C Act since that responsibility is left with the manufacturer. If the FDA determines that a device is *not* substantially equivalent, the applicant has the following options:

- Resubmit another 510(k) with new data
- Request a Class I or II designation through the De Novo Classification process (see below)
- File a reclassification petition
- Submit a pre-market approval application (PMA)

---

[19] Electronic submission template and resource.

BOX 6.2   CRITICISM OF THE 510(K) PROCESS

The 510(k) programme has faced criticism from the medical establishment, government watchdogs, and patient advocacy groups; being perceived as a fast track mechanism that allows medium-risk (Class II) devices onto the US market without independent clinical testing [110,111]. In response, the FDA has defended the principle of the process and introduced some procedural changes. It remains the mainstay of FDA regulation of medical devices.

6.5.4.1.1   When is a 510(k) Submission Required?

Most Class II devices (about 90%) require a 510(K) submission, whereas most Class I devices are exempt [92]. Some devices in both categories are 510(k) exempt by statute. Class I devices exempt from 510(k) clearance are also usually exempt from quality system/GMP requirements, but manufacturers are still required to keep basic records and other compliance files. A complete list of exempt devices can be found in the FDA database [112]. The small percentage of class II devices that are 510(k) exempt are not exempt from GMP requirements.

A 510(k) submission will also be required if a manufacturer has made significant changes to a currently marketed device that may affect the safety and/or effectiveness of the device. Guidance is available to help manufacturers determine whether a particular modification requires a new 510(k) submission [113].

6.5.4.1.2   How to Make a 510(k) Submission

There is no proforma, but guidance is available on the content and format of submissions [107].

The main steps are as follows:

1. Define the intended use of the device
2. Search for predicate devices on the market and find the associated product codes in the FDA's PCCD [114]. If the reference device underwent a 510(k) procedure, a direct search of the 510(k) database can be made [115]
3. Search in the FDA database for product codes using the classification panels
4. Decide the most appropriate product code

6.5.4.1.3   Documentation Requirements for Device Software

Current FDA guidance on "device software functions" dates back to 2005 but was recently revised to reflect the change from LoC to DL [116] (Section 6.5.3.4).

6.5.4.1.4   Third-Party Review Programme

The third part review programme (TPRP) is a system by which authorised independent organisations can review 510(k) submissions on behalf of the FDA [117]. Most are within the US but some are outside. Third-party organisations review the submission and make recommendations to the FDA for review. The TPRP is also known as the FDA's Accredited Persons Programme (APP). It was designed to allow FDA staff to concentrate on the approval (PMA) of higher risk (Class III) devices.

On approval of the contents of the PMN 510(k) submission, the FDA issues an order in the form of a *Letter of Substantial Equivalence*, which confirms that the FDA finds the device to be substantially equivalent to the predicate device and can therefore be legally marketed in the US. This order "clears" the device for commercial distribution, hence the expression "510(k) clearance".

6.5.4.1.5   Abbreviated and Special 510(k) Submissions

An abbreviated 510(k) submission is an option for manufacturers who cannot find a predicate device but who can demonstrate compliance with a relevant FDA guidance document or standard [118]. More specially, such an application is possible when one of the following three conditions is met:

1. The FDA has published a specific guidance document for the relevant product or technology
2. The manufacturer applies the relevant special controls for Class I devices
3. The manufacturer is compliant with one or more relevant voluntary standards recognised by the FDA

Although the *format* of an abbreviated submission is the same as for a traditional one [119], the amount of documentation is reduced by the use of summary reports. As a result, Section 9 (*Declarations of Conformity and Summary Reports*) may therefore be longer than for a traditional submission but other sections (e.g., 14-19) will be shorter.

A Special 510(k) submission is designed for medical devices that have been previously cleared under the traditional 510(k) programme, but need to go through clearance again due to significant changes – now including those that have a bearing on the intended use or relate to the underlying technology. In this context, the FDA's focus is on the quality and robustness of the methods used to evaluate the changes [120].

6.5.4.1.6   Application Acceptance Criteria

The FDA has set out the reasons for which it may initially reject a 510(k) submission in its *Refuse to Accept (RTA) policy for 510(k)s* [121].

Despite this and other Agency guidance on the 510(k) submission process, a significant number of submissions do not get through the first stage of the review process without being subject to an Additional Information Request. Accurate official figures on initial rejection rates are difficult to obtain, although it is widely reported in non-peer-reviewed articles that the figure could be as high as 70% [122], with the majority of those being reported due to problems associated with the substantial equivalence condition [123]. Advice is available online on how to avoid a 510(k) submission being rejected [124].

6.5.4.1.7   Submission Process

Having collected all the information necessary to make a 510(K) submission, the administrative process is as follows:

1. Submit application
   Submit an application online to the CDRH document control centre (DCC) using the eSTAR system [125].
2. Acceptance review
   The DCC will forward the application to the Office of Product Evaluation and Quality (OPEQ) for acceptance review. A lead reviewer will be assigned. Contact information and application status will be provided within 15 days. Applications not accepted will be placed on "RTA hold" and applicants have 180 days to address the identified issues.
3. Substantive review
   The lead reviewer will contact the manufacturer within 60 days with information regarding readiness for the interactive review. Further information is often requested at this stage.
4. Notification of approval ("clearance") or rejection
   The FDA sends the manufacturer a "decision letter" notifying the outcome of the substantial review process and the whole process should take place within 100 days according to the FDA website.

6.5.4.2   De Novo Classification

De Novo classification[20] provides a marketing pathway for medical devices for which no predicate device can be found. It is applicable when either general controls alone or general and special controls combined, provide a reasonable assurance of safety and effectiveness for the intended use of the device [126]. Devices may only be classified into class I or class II using this procedure but may be used as predicates for future PMN [510(k)] submissions, where applicable.

There are two main situations in which a De Novo request to the FDA may be considered:

1. After receiving a high-level Not Substantially Equivalent (NSE) determination (that is, no predicate, new intended use, or different technological characteristics that raise different questions of safety and effectiveness) in response to a traditional 510(k) submission
2. Following the manufacturer's determination that there is no legally marketed device upon which to base a determination of substantial equivalence. That is, prior to submitting a 510(k) request

To avoid rejection, a De Novo request must include all the elements listed in Appendix A of the FDA acceptance review guidelines [126]. However, prior to submitting a De Novo request, the FDA recommends submitting a *Pre-Submission* in order to obtain initial feedback on the general suitability of the application.

---

[20] FDA sometimes uses the term "De Novo request" but it is a procedure leading to a device classification.

6.5.4.3 Pre-Market Approval

PMA is required for high-risk (class III) medical devices unsuitable for the PMN programme. There are four types of PMA submission [127] but we focus here on the traditional type. It is mainly intended for devices that the FDA has not previously encountered and/or involves the use of a technology that raises new questions about device safety and/or effectiveness.

The purpose of the PMA is to demonstrate to the FDA that, through valid scientific supporting evidence, the device is reasonably safe and effective *on its own merits*. Whereas the 510(k) procedure is essentially a comparison to a *similar* device, the PMA procedure requires specific clinical validation studies [95].

The PMA process is necessarily more complicated than a PMN (510(K)) submission so takes considerably longer, typically around 6 months from receipt of the application. The FDA assessment is essential a 4-stage review process that includes a pre-approval inspection of the QMS [127] (Section 6.5.6). Note that all pre-market application procedures (PMN, De Novo, PMA) involve fees payable to the FDA upon submission. The FDA has various procedures for notifying the application about the outcome of the PMA review, which include an "approvable letter" (if device will be approved subject to the stated conditions) and a "not approvable" letter, which is essentially a rejection [128].

6.5.4.4 Breakthrough Devices Programme

The *Breakthrough Devices Programme* (BDP) is a voluntary programme for certain medical devices that *may* provide a more effective treatment or diagnosis of life-threatening or irreversibly debilitating diseases or conditions than the current standard of care in the US. The purpose of the programme is thus to provide critically ill patients with timely access to state-of-the-art medical devices by speeding up their development, assessment, and review while preserving the statutory standards for PMA.

A breakthrough designation request must be sent prior to the associated pre-market submission so the manufacturer must convince the FDA that there is a "reasonable expectation" that this is indeed the case [129].

Devices intended for pre-market submission using any of the main three routes (PMN, PMA, De Novo) are eligible for breakthrough device designation, subject to certain conditions. Apart from the condition relating to "life threatening or irreversibly debilitating diseases", a novel device must also meet *at least one* of four additional criteria covering novelty, uniqueness, and clinical efficacy.

The BDP is effectively a pre-market prioritisation mechanism for devices with outstanding potential so the eligibility criteria are strict. Despite this, a surprising total of 688 devices were granted breakthrough device designations between 2018 and 2022 [130].

6.5.4.5 Obtaining FDA Feedback Prior to a Submission

The FDA has a structured process by which a medical device manufacturer/sponsor may obtain feedback and advice from the Agency prior to making a formal pre-market submission. The *Q-Submission Programme* was originally designed to support IDE applications but, over time, was extended to include PMA applications, HDE applications, De Novo requests, and 510(k) submissions [131].

A pre-submission ("Pre-Sub") should include specific questions regarding review topics relevant to a planned pre-marketing submission. Appendix 2 of the FDA guidance [131] provides examples of the type of questions that manufacturers may consider. A Pre-Sub is appropriate when FDA's feedback on specific questions would help guide product development and/or submission preparation but is not intended to be a pre-review of an intended submission or a pre-review of data to be provided in a submission.

When properly used, the Q-programme can be of benefit to both the manufacturer and the FDA. The Agency does not charge a fee for providing feedback through the Q-programme (nor does it put a limit on how many "Pre-Subs" a company can request) but manufacturers should use the service sparingly to get the greatest benefit [132].

6.5.5 CLINICAL INVESTIGATIONS

The requirements for clinical investigations of medical devices in the US are similar to those in the EU (see 6.3.10.2) but there are some differences.

The FDA allows manufacturers to use clinical data collected from outside the US to support pre-market applications but specifies that accepted principles of GCP must be followed. The FDA refers primarily to the definition of GCP given in 21 CFR 812.28 [134] but data collected by organisations following ISO 14155:2020 will also be accepted.[21] A statement that GCP criteria were met in the collection of the clinical data is required as part of the application.

For medical device clinical investigations conducted *within* the United States, the FDA's additional requirements for GCP compliance are covered in five 21 CFR parts:

21 CFR 812 – Investigational Device Exemptions
    Apart from the accuracy of results and the well-being of subjects, 21 CFR 812 also requires documentation on how investigators have been trained to comply with good clinical practices.

21 CFR 50 – Protection of Human Subjects
    This legislation is primarily concerned with the consent and well-being of human subjects in clinical trials (but is relevant to medical device investigations), and the specified roles played by sponsors, investigators, and institutional review boards.

21 CFR 56 – Institutional Review Boards
    Institutional Review Boards (IRB) are similar in principle and purpose to the independent oversight committees required by ISO 14155 (Section 6.3.10.2).

---

[21] ISO 14155:2020 is consistent with the FDA's own GCP guidelines and has the status of a recognised consensus standard.

21 CFR 54 – Financial Disclosure by Clinical Investigators

In order to ensure validity and exclude bias, 21 CFR 54 requires the disclosure of any financial arrangements/incentives that exist between sponsors and investigators.

21 CFR 11 – Electronic Records and Signatures

Compliance with 21 CFR Part 11 is essential in the conduct of clinical trials and medical device investigations. It specifies the criteria for the creation, modification, and maintenance of electronic records/signatures and ensures that the data generated during the clinical study is reliable and secure.

Further details are available on the FDA website [135].

6.5.6 Quality System Requirements

The US QSR for medical devices is described in part §820 of title 21 (relating to food and drugs) of the CFR. Quality systems for all FDA-regulated products (food, drugs, medical devices) are known as current good manufacturing practices (CGMPs) and the quality system GMP described in 21 CFR part §820[22] is given legal standing by section 520(f) of the FD&C Act. The QSR includes requirements relating to the design, manufacture, packaging, labelling, storing, installing, and servicing of medical devices [136].

Unlike some quality management standards, the FDA QSR is quite flexible in its approach. It defines the essential elements of a quality system but does not prescribe specific methods for their achievement. The regulation thus provides a framework that must be followed but requires manufacturers to use their own judgement when deciding which sections of the Quality System (QS) regulation are applicable to their products and operations (clause §820.5 of the QS regulation).

Furthermore, manufacturers are responsible for developing or following other related procedures (related to effectiveness and/or safety) as appropriate, given the current state-of-the-art manufacturing processes for the specific device type in question.

The US medical device approvals system involves a physical inspection of the manufacturer's premises in order to judge the suitability of the QMS. Such inspections cover a comprehensive audit of the documentation as well as "walk throughs" to assess whether a selection of documented procedures is followed in practice (Section 6.5.11). Manufacturers are also required (by law) to conduct an internal QMS audit at least once per year. It makes sense for manufacturers to employ quality system inspection techniques (QSIT) since they are used by the FDA inspectors [137]. A detailed internal audit checklist, based on QSIT, is also available online [138]. However, the FDA inspection regime is set to change under the proposed quality management system regulation (QMSR) but details are yet uncertain [139].

Certain types of medical devices are exempt from GMP requirements. These devices are exempted by FDA classification regulations published in the Federal

---

[22] 21 CFR part §820 is available free online as a searchable hypertext document [133]

Register and codified in 21 CFR 862-892. Exemption from the GMP requirements does not exempt manufacturers of finished devices from keeping complaint files (21 CFR §820.198) or from general requirements concerning records (21 CFR §820.180). Also, medical devices manufactured under an IDE are not exempt from design control requirements under 21 CFR §820.30 of the QS regulation. The planned alignment of the QSR with ISO 13485 is discussed in Section 9.2.1.

6.5.7   RISK MANAGEMENT

Although the current QSR only refers to risk analysis in the context of design validation (part 820.30[g]), the FDA argues that there has always been an (implicit) expectation that manufacturers integrate risk management throughout their QMS and across the product life cycle [140]. This is reflected in the numerous references to risk management techniques in the *preamble* to the 1996 version of the QSR; an appendage that is not part of the regulation but has traditionally provided valuable insight into its meaning and intent. Nonetheless, the FDA has recognised that ISO 13485's explicit references to risk management requirements make it highly suitable for incorporation into the revised QSR.

In January 2020 the FDA accepted ISO 14971:2019 as a *recognised consensus standard*. Conformance to ISO 14971 is thereby taken as sufficient proof of medical device safety (risk management aspects) by the FDA in support of pre-market submissions.

It has been common practice in the US to correlate the low-risk zone on a suitable risk matrix diagram (Section 4.5) with 'acceptable risk' and the high-risk zone with 'unacceptable risk' [141]. The medium-risk zone is often referred to as the ALARP zone (Figure 4.5). Risks in the high-risk and medium-risk zones are subject to risk reduction measures. Risk reduction in the US is generally based on the ALARP concept (Section 4.4.27) but manufacturers selling into both the US and EU markets are advised to follow the AFAP approach mandated by MDR 17/745 (Section 6.3.9) since it represents a stricter requirement [142].

6.5.8   MEDICAL DEVICE SOFTWARE

Medical device software is regulated in essentially the same way as any other type of medical device, the key initial steps being qualification (Section 6.5.2) and classification (Section 6.5.3.4). The purpose of this section is to describe how different *types* of medical software are classified and how the development processes and procedures are dictated by that classification. We also discuss the FDA's adoption of IEC 62304 (Section 5.4.1) as well as its approach to software-specific issues such as usability, cybersecurity, and artificial intelligence.

BOX 6.3   FDA DEFINITION OF MEDICAL SOFTWARE

"The set of electronic instructions used to control the actions or output of a medical device, to provide input to or output from a medical device, or to provide the actions of a medical device" [143].

The general regulatory position of health IT and mobile apps was outlined in a joint report issued by the FDA, the Office of the National Coordinator for Health Information Technology (ONC), and the Federal Communications Commission (FCC) in 2014 [144].

It was mandated by Section 618 of the Food and Drug Administration Safety and Innovation Act (FDASIA) and is therefore known as the FDASIA Report. The proposed strategy described three categories of health IT:

- Administrative health IT functions
- Health management health IT functions
- Medical device health IT functions

Full details and examples are given in the report, but a useful summary is available [145]. The medical device health IT functions were already regulated by the FDA, but it was clarified that the FDA does not intend to regulate administrative health IT and health management health IT.[23] However, products in these categories may be subject to regulatory oversight by other agencies. The report is described as a draft framework on the FDA website and is still open for comments.

The way in which the FDA approaches the regulation of various types of medical software is briefly described below.

6.5.8.1 Device Software Functions

Although most regulatory bodies use the general term "medical device software" to include SaMD *and* SiMD, the FDA prefers to use the term "device software functions" (DSF). The FDA policy document for DSF and mobile medical apps was last updated in September 2022 [100].

The guidance document explains the Agency's general oversight of DSFs (including mobile medical apps, MMA) and its focus on (a) software that presents the greatest risk to patients (if it does not work as intended) and (b) software that causes smartphones, computers, or other mobile platforms to impact the functionality or performance of traditional medical devices. It mainly seeks to clarify what types of software qualify as DSF and MMA, by way of specific criteria and numerous examples.

The associated guidance document on the content of pre-market submissions for DSF was published in June 2023 [103]. A significant change (compared to the 2021 draft guidance) is that the FDA now only differentiates between two "levels of concern", which translates to "basic" and "enhanced" documentation levels (Section 6.5.3.4.2).

6.5.8.2 Computer Software Validation

Software validation is a basic requirement of the QSR (Section 6.5.6) and applies to (a) software used as components in medical devices, (b) software that is itself a medical device, and (c) software used in the production of the device or in implementation of the device manufacturer's QS. These software validation requirements are similar to those stated in ISO 13485:2016 (Section 5.2.1.6).

---

[23] Most clinical decision support software was included in the health management health IT functions category (see 6.5.8.6).

The terms "validation" and "verification" are defined in 21 CFR §820.3, but the corresponding software terms are not. FDA guidance on software validation [146] acknowledges that some definitions used in the QSR may cause confusion when compared to commonly used terms in the software industry, so the Agency uses definitions of software verification and software validation that relate to the SDLC [146].

It is stated that *software verification* "provides objective evidence that the design outputs of a particular phase of the SDLC meet all of the specified requirements for that phase", and that *software validation* is "confirmation by examination and provision of objective evidence that software specifications conform to user needs and intended uses, and that the particular requirements implemented through software can be consistently fulfilled". The guidance further clarifies the Agency's interpretation of software verification and validation by listing and discussing their respective components.

BOX 6.4   SOFTWARE VERIFICATION AND VALIDATION

These software engineering terms are often confused to the point where some developers use them interchangeably. The FDA treats them separately, its definitions (above) being broadly consistent with the generally accepted industry view of "V&V"; namely that *software verification* is essentially an inward-looking activity that tests whether the *technical specification* derived from the detailed user requirements has been correctly implemented in the software architectural design and associated code ("*have we built the product right?*"). Software verification is therefore concerned with (internal) consistency, completeness, and correctness of the software (including documentation), as it is being developed, and provides support for a subsequent conclusion that the software is validated.

Software validation, on the other hand, is a more outward-looking activity (at least as far as the final integrated product is concerned) that tests whether the technical specification was indeed a correct interpretation of the user requirements/intended purpose ("*have we built the right product?*"). In practice, validation activities may occur during as well as at the end of the traditional SDLC process. If an agile approach to software development is taken, verification and validation are performed more as a linked activity, due to the way in which the user requirements ("User Stories") are frequently updated (Section 5.4.1.12).

Unless specifically exempted, any *device* software, irrespective of its device class, is subject to applicable design controls specified in 21 CFR §820.30. Design validation includes software validation, where appropriate, and other design controls applicable to medical device software include development planning, design input, and design verification [146]. The validation of any off-the-shelf (OTS) software incorporated into a software medical software is covered in separate FDA guidance (see Section 5.4.1.11).

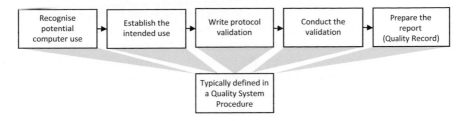

FIGURE 6.8   The basic steps in the FDA's computer system validation process

Software used to automate any part of the device production process or any part of the QS must be validated for its intended use, as required by 21 CFR §820.70(i). This includes any software used to automate device design, testing, component acceptance, manufacturing, labelling, packaging, distribution, complaint handling, or to automate other aspect of the QS. All software changes must be validated before the release of any revisions and these validation activities/results should be documented. More information on the QA of these types of *support* software is provided in the next section.

In addition, computer systems used to create, modify, and maintain electronic records and to manage electronic signatures are also subject to validation requirements under 21 CFR §11.10(a); a regulation that also applies to the validation of custom-made spreadsheets (Section 2.2.2.2). Such computer systems must be validated to ensure accuracy, reliability, consistent intended performance, and have the ability to detect invalid or altered records.

A flow chart describing the basic steps in the computer system validation (CSV) process is shown in Figure 6.8.

Although software validation remains a key principle of the FDA's approach to QA of *device* software, the Agency is slowly moving away from the term "computer software validation" in favour of the more general term compute software assurance (CSA), which aligns better with the term software QA widely used in the software industry [147]. It has therefore revised some of its software-related device standards to reflect this change (see next section).

6.5.8.3   Computer Software Assurance

At around the same time as the DSF policy update (Section 6.5.8.1), the FDA issued draft guidance on CSA of production and QS software [148].

The definition of CSA ("a risk-based approach for establishing and maintaining confidence that software is fit for its intended use") is *similar* to the definition of "validation" in §CFR 21 820[24] [149] but the activities described are broader. The general philosophy of the draft guidance is to reduce the regulatory burden of existing guidance by requiring that (only) *appropriate* assurance activities are undertaken for production and QS software that is commensurate with the risk of a given element/

---

[24] Validation means "confirmation by examination and provision of objective evidence that the particular requirements for a specific intended use can be consistently fulfilled" (21 CFR 820.3(z)). As an added note, "process validation" and "design validation" are separately defined.

module. The idea (supported by work done in pilot projects) is that this approach will significantly reduce the number of assurance activities and the amount of associated documentation compared to that required under the previous "validate everything" regime.

Apart from promoting a risk-based approach to software assurance, the FDA guidance on CSA also provides best practice advice for complying with the software validation requirements in 21 CFR Part 820.70(i) in relation to production and QS software (i.e., software used to support/automate the production *process* or software that is part of the QMS). It should be noted that the draft guidance does *not* apply to the verification or validation requirements (specified in 21 CFR §820.30) for *device* software (i.e. SiMD, SaMD), for which previous FDA guidance on the general principles of software validation (Section 6.5.8.2) continues to apply.

A useful guide is available on the basic planning and execution of verification and validation (V&V) activities in relation to FDA medical device requirements [150]. It does not address *software* V&V techniques specifically but provides useful background information.

Software covered by the CSA guidance is divided into that used *directly* as part of the product or QS and from that used in a *supporting* role. Supporting software carries a lower risk and is therefore subject to less rigorous validation requirements. Examples of "supporting software" include development tools that test or monitor software systems and software for automating general record-keeping that is not part of the quality record.

Software for general management activities, such as email or accounting applications, and software for supporting IT infrastructure that is unrelated to device production or the QS (e.g., networking software) is not defined as support software and is therefore not subject to software validation requirements.

The main process steps described in the CSA guidance are as follows:

1. Identify the intended use
2. Determine the risk-based approach
3. Determine the appropriate software assurance activities

In step 2 the FDA makes a distinction between a process risk and a medical device risk. A process risk refers to the potential to compromise device production or the QS, whereas medical device risk refers to the potential for a (finished) device to harm the patient or user. The focus is on medical device risk, but the two types of risk are inextricably linked. As with many FDA requirements, it is for the manufacturer to decide the appropriate assurance measures for the various software used, based on the criteria specified. In the following sections, we consider the different types of medical device software.

Under step 3 the guidance discusses a range of software assurance activities, which should be "commensurate with the medical device risk or the process risk" (as determined in step 2), including scripted and unscripted (or exploratory) software testing. The guidance suggests the use of scripted testing for high-risk software, and unscripted testing for lower risk software, but many software manufacturers use a combination of the two.

The FDA's new stance on validation of production and QS software does not change any regulations. It will, however, allow medical software manufacturers to take a more efficient and flexible approach to meeting the software validation requirements in its QSR. The FDA's CSA guidance also brings it more in line with ISO 13485:2016 (Section 5.2.1), which states that "the specific approach and activities associated with software validation and revalidation shall be proportionate to the risk associated with the use of the software".

The dramatic shift over recent years from customised software solutions to the widespread use of OTS commercial products to handle most of the production and quality systems issues is highly significant in this context. Clearly, such commercial QMS software[25] will have been quality assured by the provider (and have the latest FDA guidance built into them) so that the amount of additional assurance testing required by the end-user (i.e., the medical device manufacturer) is dramatically reduced. Furthermore, many of the requirements in the draft guidance are well covered in the GAMP®5 framework standard (Chapter 5, A.1.1.4), so any medical device manufacturers that have implemented GAMP®5 will have minimal work in ensuring compliance with the new FDA requirements.

It is emphasised that the CSA guidance is still in draft form and several changes are expected in the final document. When finalised, it will replace Section 6 of the FDA's guidance on the general principles of software validation [146].

6.5.8.4   Software as a Medical Device

As described in Chapter 3, the IMDRF defines SaMD as "software intended for one or more medical purposes that perform those purposes without being part of a hardware medical device". The FDA, on the other hand, defines SaMD as "software that meets the definition of a [medical] device in section 201(h) of the FD&C Act and is intended to be used for one or more medical purposes without being part of a hardware device", thereby referencing the legal definition of a medical device in the US.

Standalone software designed for analysis of pathophysiological data as an aid to disease diagnosis is a classic example of SaMD, but an FDA guidance document contains numerous examples of what is and what is not SaMD [151]. As in the EU regulatory system, once qualified as a medical device, the general requirements are dictated by the device classification (Section 6.5.3).

Most of the software defined as SaMD will be classified as either a Class I or Class II medical device, so will not need to go through the full PMA procedure. Most applications for FDA approval will be via the less onerous 510(k) PMN route (Section 6.5.4.1), but identifying a suitable predicate device may not be straightforward in all cases. Fortunately, the "substantial equivalence" sought relates mainly to the *intended use* and *indications for use* (see 6.5.3.1) rather than a side-by-side comparison of the respective device specifications.

However, if the new device contains a substantial amount of new technology a question will be raised as to whether its inclusion could significantly affect the device's safety or effectiveness [152]. For SaMD, this might be the use of a new programming language that has not been previously used in this context.

---

[25] Available from companies such as Greenlight Guru, MasterControl, and Jama Software, amongst others.

6.5.8.4.1   The Software Pre-Cert Pilot Programme (SPPP)

In July 2017 the FDA announced the software pre-certification (Pre-Cert) pilot programme as a means of evaluating a possible new mechanism for the pre-market review of SaMD products. A working model was subsequently published in January 2019 [153].

The focus of the Pre-Cert pilot programme is on the product developer rather than the product itself. If the developer could demonstrate a culture of quality, excellence, and responsiveness, FDA intended that a streamlined ("fast track") pre-market review process would be permitted. This planned shift to a more process-orientated approach would align more closely with the approach used within the EU. However, significant problems emerged during the pilot scheme and a different approach may therefore be needed (Section 9.2.2).

6.5.8.4.2   Clinical Evaluation of SaMD

Official FDA guidance on clinical evaluation of SaMD, published in 2017, essentially adopts the 2016 IMDRF report on the subject in its entirety [154]. In this document, clinical evaluation is defined to include analytical validation and clinical validation, so links to the FDA document on the general principles of software validation (Section 6.5.8.2). The procedure described covers both pre-market ("in-development") and post-market activities.

6.5.8.5   Mobile Medical Applications

The FDA first issued guidance on its intended regulation of mobile apps (entitled simply "Mobile Medical Applications") in 2013, subsequently updated in 2015, 2019, and 2022. The 2019 revision was produced to reflect changes made to the definition of "device" by the 21st Century Cures Act.[26] In short, some types of low-risk apps that were previously subject to FDA oversight were taken out of regulatory control. The 2022 revision was produced to reflect amended medical device classification regulation rules, as well as for consistency with the finalised version of the guidance on CDS software (Section 6.5.8.6)

Since the 2019 update, the document has been entitled "Policy for device software functions and mobile medical applications", to reflect the fact that the qualification criteria are independent of the platform on which the software runs [100]. A mobile app[27] that meets the definition of a medical device is called a *MMA*. Namely,

> an app that incorporates device software functionality that meets the definition of a 'device' in section 201(h) of the FD&C Act and is intended to be used (a) as an accessory to a regulated medical device or (b) to transform a mobile platform into a regulated medical device [155].

The types of apps that would be qualified as medical devices by the FDA are broadly similar to those that would qualify under EU MDR rules, but there are some notable

---

[26] The definition of a (medical) device in section 520 of the Federal Food, Drug and Cosmetic Act (herein FD&C Act, last amended in 2007) was amended by section 3060(b) of the 21st Century Cures Act (herein Cures Act) in 2016.

[27] A mobile app is defined by the FDA as "a software application that can be executed (run) on a mobile platform (i.e., a handheld commercial off-the-shelf computing platform, with or without wireless connectivity), or a web-based software application that is tailored to a mobile platform but is executed on a server".

differences. In particular, the FDA defines some categories of *software functions* (SF) that *may* meet the definition of a medical device but for which it intends to exercise "enforcement discretion". That is, it does not currently intend to enforce requirements under the FD&C Act. These are not "grey area" software in terms of qualification, but a general sub-class deemed to present a very low risk to the public. The types of software falling into this "enforcement discretion category" can be grouped under one of two main headings:

1. SF that help patients (i.e., users) self-manage their disease or condition without providing specific treatment or treatment suggestions; or
2. SF that automate simple tasks for healthcare providers.

The following sub-categories were also defined:

- SF that provide or facilitate supplemental clinical care, by coaching or prompting, to help patients manage their health in their daily environment
- SF that provide easy access to information related to patients' health conditions or treatments (beyond providing an electronic "copy" of a medical reference)
- SF that are specifically marketed to help patients communicate with healthcare providers by supplementing or augmenting the data or information by capturing an image for patients to convey to their healthcare providers about potential medical conditions
- SF that perform simple calculations are routinely used in clinical practice

Numerous examples of enforcement discretion-type software are given in Chapter V and Appendix B of the relevant FDA guidance [100]. Clearly, some of the SF will be mobile apps. Although the FDA guidance is completely general (re: software), it is stated that certain DSF may pose risks that are unique to the characteristics of the platform on which the software function is run. For example, the interpretation of radiological images on a mobile device could be adversely affected by the small screen size, lower contrast ratio, and uncontrolled ambient light of the mobile platform. The FDA takes these risks into account when assessing the appropriate regulatory oversight for these products. Many of these examples would not qualify as medical devices under EU MDR qualification rules (Section 6.3.4).

Manufacturers of "mobile health apps" for the US market should be aware that there are other Federal laws and regulations that may apply to the data security, data privacy, and data protection aspects of these devices. To increase awareness of these non-FDA regulations, the US Federal Trade Commission (FTC) has developed an online tool (flowchart) to help manufacturers decide which regulations apply to their application [156].

6.5.8.6   CDS Software

Recent FDA guidance on CDS software [157] concentrates mainly on CDS functions that do *not* meet the definition of a (medical) device under section 520(o)(1)(E) of the FD&C Act. It does, however, include some examples (in Chapter V, Section

C) of CDS software that *does* meet the definition of a medical device. The guidance applies only to standalone software and does not cover labelling requirements.

The FDA guidance quotes a general description of a CDS system from the HealthIT.gov website,[28] but its own definition of CDS software is based on device exclusion criteria listed in section 520(o)(1)(E) of the FD&C Act, duly amended by the 21st Century Cures Act in 2016. Under this amendment a software function is *not* a medical device if it meets *all four* of the following criteria:

1. Is *not* intended to acquire, process, or analyse a medical image or a signal from an *in vitro* diagnostic device or a pattern signal from a signal acquisition system
2. Is intended for the purpose of displaying, analysing, or printing medical information about a patient or other medical information (such as peer-reviewed clinical studies and clinical practice guidelines)
3. Is intended for the purpose of supporting or providing recommendations to a *healthcare professional* (HCP) about the prevention, diagnosis, or treatment of a disease or condition
4. Is intended for the purpose of enabling such *healthcare professionals* (HCP) to independently review the basis for such recommendations that such software presents so that it is *not* the intent that such healthcare professionals rely primarily on any of such recommendations to make a clinical diagnosis or treatment decision regarding an individual patient

These exclusion criteria refer to "software functions" in general, but the descriptions include software that would be considered CDS software. The FDA takes this a step further by using the criteria to *define* a CDS system as one that meets criteria 1 and 2 and is intended to support or provide recommendations about prevention, diagnosis, or treatment (i.e., part of criterion 3). Note that only the first three criteria are required to determine whether the software is defined as a CDS.

The other, perhaps simpler, way of thinking about the FDA qualification system (see Figure 6.9) is that a given piece of CDS software *is* a medical device if any of the above four criteria do *not* apply.

If the CDS software in question only meets criterion 1, 2, or 3, then it *is* a medical device (referred to as "device CDS") designed to be used by patients or caregivers and will therefore be subject to closer regulatory scrutiny by the FDA. Software that meets all four criteria (so is *not* a medical device) is referred to as "non-device CDS" and is not actively regulated by the FDA. Somewhat confusingly, the FDA also uses the term "Non-CDS Device" to describe a medical device that is not CDS.

As with other types of mobile apps, the FDA intends to exercise enforcement discretion regarding CDS software that qualifies as a medical device but is considered to represent a very low risk to patients. The method for risk assessment is

---

[28] "CDS software provides health care professionals (HCPs) and patients with knowledge and person-specific information, intelligently filtered or presented at appropriate times, to enhance health and health care".

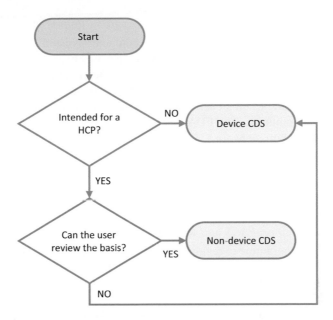

FIGURE 6.9 FDA schema for determining whether CDS software is a medical device. "Intended for a HCP" means that the software is designed for use *only* by a healthcare professional (HCP). The second decision box asks whether the HCP can *independently* review (i.e., verify) the basis of the recommendation made by the CDS software (part of criterion 4).

based on the IMDRF framework for SaMD, which depends on (a) the significance of the information provided by the SaMD and (b) the state of the patient's health or condition (Section 3.2.1).

6.5.8.7 Radiology Applications

Details of radiological equipment already classified by the FDA can be found on its respective PMA or 510(k) databases. Most diagnostic radiology imaging equipment (CT, MR, ultrasound, PET) has been classified as Class II, although a standard gamma camera is Class I. Radiological image analysis software is generally classified as a Class II but new applications may be initially designated as class III by default (see Section 6.5.3.4).

FDA guidance is available on the content of pre-market submissions for certain radiological imaging modalities, as well as radiological devices that contain quantitative imaging functions, such as standardised uptake values (in nuclear medicine imaging), calcium scoring (in CT imaging), and measurement of T1/T2 values (in MR imaging) [158]. The guidance document identifies many potential sources of error that manufacturers should consider in their risk analysis, under the headings of "patient characteristics", "imaging characteristics" and "image processing". It also includes requirements for proof of performance, including the use of both hardware and software phantoms for simulation purposes.

6.5.8.7.1   Guidance on CADe and CADx Software in Radiology

The FDA distinguishes software intended for computer-assisted *detection* of possible image abnormalities (CADe) from software designed to provide an *assessment* of a disease or condition in terms of its likelihood, differential diagnosis, or staging (CADx). An example of a CADx device would be a computer program designed to both identify lung nodules on a chest CT exam and *also* to provide a probability of malignancy to the clinician. The FDA has recently issued guidance on the content for PMN (510[k]) submissions for CADe devices [159]. In situations where substantial equivalence to a predicate device cannot be scientifically demonstrated (Section 6.5.4.1), a clinical performance assessment will be required and separate guidelines are available [160]. If the CADe or CADx software incorporates AI, the FDA provides additional guidance (Section 6.5.8.9).

6.5.8.7.2   Guidance on PACS and Related Systems

As part of a wide programme of regulatory and guidance amendments brought about by the change in the definition of [medical] device in the 21st Century Cures Act, the FDA recently reclassified three radiology-specific devices [161,162]:

> 21CFR892.2010: Medical Image Storage Device (MISD)
> 21CFR892.2020: Medical Image Communication Device (MICD)
> 21CFR892.2050: Picture Archiving and Communications System (PACS)

As the embedded software in a "medical image storage device" (e.g., to enable storage to, and retrieval from, a hardware device) is now excluded from the definition of a medical device, the relevant FDA regulation (21 CFR 892.2010) was amended to make clear that only the *hardware* elements of the device remain within the purview of the FDA.

The definition of a "medical image communication device" was also changed to include *simple* image processing and manipulation associated with display (e.g., greyscale windowing, pan/zoom). This type of image processing software was not excluded from regulation by the *Cures Act*, so an MICD will be qualified as a medical device.

The most significant amendment was to the old PACS regulation. SF for medical image storage and display were removed (i.e., moved to MISD), prompting the replacement of the term PACS with "medical image management and processing system" (MIMPS), defined as "a device that provides one or more capabilities relating to the review and digital processing of medical images for the purposes of interpretation by a trained practitioner of disease detection, diagnosis, or patient management". This type of image processing is referred to "advanced or complex" and includes multimodality image registration, 3D visualisation, and quantitation. The associated SF certainly meet the revised definition of a medical device, resulting in a class II classification for MIMPS (product code LLZ, 21 CFR 892.2050).

In summary, the software components of a modern old PACS system must now be viewed as separately regulated modules, with the software responsible for the basic storage, display[29] , and transfer of images and other data around a network no longer being considered a medical device under FDA rules. For the same reasons, proprietary PACS

---

[29] As for MICD.

viewer workstations[30] (or software emulation packages designed to run on personal computers and other hardware platforms) are also no longer classified as medical devices.

6.5.8.7.3   Radiology software that contains AI/ML technology

General guidance on FDA compliance is available for manufacturers of diagnostic radiology systems that contain AI/ML components [163].

6.5.8.8   Adoption and Use of IEC 62304 for Software Development

IEC 62304:2006/A1:2015 is formally recognised by the FDA as a means of complying with most of its regulatory requirements for device software, including SaMD [164]. IEC 62304 does not cover software validation, but the FDA has its own guidance for that activity (Section 6.5.8.2). Other FDA guidance documents to be used alongside IEC 62304 are listed on the FDA website [165]. A useful podcast is also available describing how IEC 62304 can be used to meet FDA SaMD requirements [166].

IEC 62304 software safety classifications A, B, and C (see Section 5.4.1.4) *roughly* correspond to the minor, moderate, and major "levels of concern" *previously* used by the FDA (Section 6.5.3.4.2). As a result, a good rule of thumb is to apply IEC 62304 (for the appropriate safety class), then apply the appropriate additional FDA requirements outlined in its guidance documents. The implementation of IEC 62304 is discussed in Section 5.4.1.

In a US context, the production of a traceability matrix is particularly important as it fulfils a basic FDA requirement, explicitly linking product requirements, design specifications, and testing requirements. It can also be used to link identified hazards to the testing of associated risk mitigations.

6.5.8.9   Devices Containing AI Technology

As explained in Chapter 3, modifications to AIaMD systems can take various forms. The regulatory framework for the algorithmic architecture type should be different from the continuous learning (adaptive) type since the latter can lead to more significant changes. For example, where the sensitivity of the output improves to the point where the manufacturer can claim a change in use from "aiding" diagnosis to providing a definitive diagnosis, or where the initial training population changes significantly, e.g., the inclusion of paediatric data.

Two types of AI/ML-based SaMD may be reviewed by FDA: "locked" and "adaptive" (see Chapter 3) [167]. Examples of locked algorithms are stated to include static look-up tables, decision trees and complex classifiers and any changes to this class of SaMD are likely to require a new pre-market submission. Adaptive technology (AT) is not as clearly defined, but devices containing AT can continue to learn and adjust using real-world data once distributed. Such changes would traditionally trigger the need for a new 510(K) submission, but the FDA recognises that this would hinder the development of AI/ML in medical devices and has instead proposed a new framework for dealing with adaptive AI/ML-based SaMD.

In essence, the FDA philosophy is that many "downstream" changes can be anticipated (i.e., predicted) at the time of pre-market submission (510(K), *De Novo* or PMA) by developing a Predetermined Change Control Plan (PCCP), to include SaMD

---

[30] For example, a ward-based PACS workstation (for use by senior nurses or junior medical staff) that provides basic display features but has no advanced/complex image processing facilities.

pre-specifications (SPS) and an associated algorithm change protocol (ACP). The SPS refers to the *type* of modifications anticipated (i.e., to performance, input, or intended use) and the ACP describes the methods to be used to achieve the anticipated modifications and to manage any new risks. Note that the PCCP is regarded as a technological characteristic of the device.

The FDA has issued draft guidance on the information to be included in the PCCP in a marketing submission for ML-enabled device software functions (ML-DSF) [168]. The guidance is applicable to ML-DSFs that the manufacturer intends to modify over time, whether automatically or manually.

Pre-market authorisation for an ML-DSF with a PCCP may be established via any of the main pathways (Section 6.5.4) but if the 510(k)-clearance route is used the demonstration of substantial equivalence (ref: comparison of technological characteristics) would be more straightforward if the predicate device was also authorised with a PCCP. In this case, however, the subject device must be compared to the version of the predicate device cleared or approved prior to any changes made under the PCCP.

Once the device is cleared, granted, or approved, the AI/ML SaMD will be deployed and begin to accumulate real-world data. Under the FDA's total product life cycle (TPLC) approach, the manufacturer continues to actively monitor the released SaMD by tracking its use and evaluating its performance. As the SaMD incorporates additional (real-world) data, it may need to be retrained, retuned, and possibly re-evaluated. If the manufacturer instigates or becomes aware of an actual change that is *outside* the scope of the FDA-reviewed SPS and ACP, he has two options depending on whether the change affects the device's intended use (Figure 6.10).

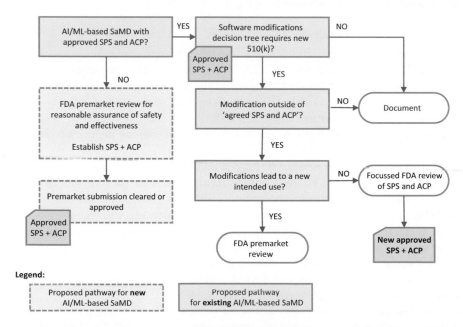

FIGURE 6.10 Flowchart to help decide whether a modification to previously approved AI/ML-enabled SaMD requires a new pre-market submission. For SPS, ACP meaning, see text. Adapted from Figure 5 of FDA discussion paper [167].

The manufacturer can also take advantage of the FDA's *pre-submission* programme [131], whereby advice can be obtained on whether a particular modification fits within a previously reviewed SPS.

The FDA has also published a list of over 500 AL/ML-enabled medical devices that received market authorisation between August 1995 and July 2022 [169], 94% of which were approved after 1 January 2016. All devices appear to have been cleared through the 510(k) route and 75% were in the radiology domain.

Initial experiences of manufacturers who have used the new AI/ML SaMD programme (including the PCCP) are limited, but the FDA recently announced its first authorisation (through the De Novo pathway) of an AI-enabled cardiac ultrasound software package designed to help the operator capture images of acceptable diagnostic quality [170].

The ways in which the FDA intends to develop its strategy for the future regulation of AI/ML-enabled medical devices, including its *Action Plan*, is considered further in Section 9.2.3.

6.5.8.10 Usability Engineering

The FDA prefers the term "human factors engineering" (HFE) to the more commonly used "usability engineering", but they mean the same thing. Current FDA guidance on the subject, published in 2016 [171], contains references to the relevant US regulatory requirements.

As with the EU regulations (Section 6.3.6.6), the FDA's focus is on identifying potential hazards related to usability and incorporating these into the risk management process. It describes what methods to use to analyse usability risks, how to mitigate them, the characteristics of the user and the user environment, and how to plan, implement, and document usability testing. UE is thus a key part of the medical device development process and is intertwined with risk management, quality management, and requirements engineering.

IEC 62366-1 is one of four standards relating to HFE and UE that are designated as a recognised consensus standards by the FDA in relation to medical devices, but compliance with IEC 62366-1 is not sufficient to demonstrate compliance with the FDA's extensive usability requirements [172]. Indeed, reference to IEC 62366-1 in the FDA guidance document is minimal and there is no mapping of clauses to FDA usability requirements. The Agency has, however, issued guidance on the minimum documentation that must accompany any declaration of conformance to the standard [173].

In December 2022 the FDA issued draft guidance on the type and amount of human factors (HF) documentation to be included in pre-market submissions (i.e., 510(K), De Novo, PMA, and HDE[31] applications) [174]. It is intended to complement rather than replace the 2016 guidance document, although chapters 3 (*Definitions*), 9 (*Documentation*), and Appendix A (*HFE/UE Report*) were updated.

It is stated that the purpose of including HFE information in a pre-marketing submission is "to ensure that the manufacturer meets the applicable legal standard by demonstrating that the UI of the device is appropriate for the intended users and for the use environment". The FDA introduced the notion of "HF submission categories"

---

[31] HDE: humanitarian device exemptions.

(1,2,3) to help determine the type of information to be included in the application.[32] The categorisation process is risk-based but is not directly related to the class of the device. A HF evaluation report is required, the content of which depends on the submission category. For category 1, corresponding to low-risk situations, a conclusion and high-level summary are sufficient, but more complex documentation is required for categories 2 and 3, including details of how the required HF validation activities (e.g., analysis of potential use errors, tests, etc.) were carried out.

The basic principles of usability testing are explained in Appendix F of the FDA guidance document on medical device patient labelling [175].

6.5.8.11 Cybersecurity Issues

Current FDA guidance on PMA relating to cybersecurity in medical devices dates to 2014, but new *draft* guidance was issued in April 2022: *Cybersecurity in Medical Devices: QS Considerations and Content of Pre-market Submissions* [176].

The draft guidance emphasises the importance of ensuring that devices are designed with security in mind and are therefore capable of mitigating emerging cybersecurity risks throughout the TPLC. The guidance includes the need for a software bill of materials (SBOM, see Section 8.5.1), which is particularly important if the finished software product contains numerous third-party/open-source components (Sections 2.2.1 and 7.6.1). The respective responsibilities of the medical device manufacturer and the healthcare provider regarding the SBOM are described in guidance produced by the IMDRF [177].

In December 2022 the FD&C Act was amended to include a new section (524B) on *Ensuring Cybersecurity of Devices*. As a result, the FDA issued guidance in March 2023 stating that, from October 2023, it would reserve the right to refuse pre-market submissions for "cyber devices" (Box 6.5) that do not contain plans to monitor and act on cybersecurity threats, including threat modelling, vulnerability assessment and the generation of an FDA-compliant SBOM [178]. The FDA also added IEC 81001-5-1 (Chapter 5, A.1.5.1) to its list of recognised consensus standards in December 2022.

BOX 6.5.   FDA DEFINITION OF 'CYBER DEVICE'

A cyber device is a [medical] device that:
1. Includes software validated, installed, or authorised by the sponsor as a device or in a device
2. Has the ability to connect to the internet
3. Contains any such technological characteristics validated, installed, or authorised by the sponsor that could be vulnerable to cybersecurity threats

---

Current FDA guidance on *PMS* of cybersecurity [179] is due for an update, but nonetheless contains useful information on the links between cybersecurity risk management and the QSR (Section 6.5.6), as well as specific methods for dealing

---

[32] Note that in common with FDA guidance for software in general, the HF guidance specifies the amount of documentation to be submitted rather than the amount to be created.

with identified vulnerabilities. The more recent IMDRF guidance on the cybersecurity of medical devices includes requirements for both pre-market and post-market activities [180].

6.5.8.12   Device Labelling and IFU

6.5.8.12.1   Instructions for Use

The purpose of IFU is to ensure the correct use of the device and, by the same token, also represents the manufacturer's first line of defence in a case of demonstrable misuse.

Medical device labelling and IFU are closely linked under US law. The term "label" is conventionally defined (under Section 201(k) of the FD&C Act, but the term "labelling" (Section 201[m]) is defined to include "accompanying printed or written materials" such as pamphlets, circulars, booklets, brochures, *and* instruction manuals. Labelling regulations pertaining to medical devices are found in various parts of Title 21 of the CFR, but mainly in 21 CFR Part 801. Device labelling and IFU relate to the wider issues of HFE and device usability (Section 6.5.8.10).

Original FDA guidance on labelling for medical devices was published in 1989 but was declared still current in August 2018 [181]. It contains information on various types of written instructions but it is distributed throughout the various section of the document. More up-to-date and coherent guidance was produced by the GHTF (the forerunner of the IMDRF) in 2011[33] [182]. The (adopted) IMDRF guidance specifies the minimum requirements for IFU content for both general medical devices and IVD medical devices and, importantly, covers all potential users, including professionals,[34] lay persons (e.g., caregivers), and patients.

The state-of-the-art *standard* for developing IFU content for medical devices is ANSI/AAMI HE75:2009 (R2018): *Human factors engineering – Design of medical devices*. General advice on *how* user instructions should be written (level, style, readability, etc.) is also available [182]

IFU aimed specifically at patients or lay persons are covered in FDA guidance on "medical device patient labelling" [183]. The guidance covers situations in which IFU should be provided, the way it should be written, and the general content. It also explains the circumstances in which risk/benefit information should also be provided. FDA guidance is also provided on acceptable media formats when IFU is provided in electronic form (eIFU) [184].

6.5.8.12.2   Labelling Requirements

Conventional device labelling does not apply to SaMD if it is provided to the user by electronic transfer rather than on physical media in a packaged container. However, it should be noted that any printed promotional materials or other forms of advertising may be considered "labelling" under US regulations [185].

---

[33] The USA was a participating member of the GHTF working group.
[34] The FDA often uses the term "product user manual" when referring to instructions aimed at professional users.

6.5.8.12.3   The UDI System

The US has a UDI system that is similar in principle to the one used in the EU (Section 6.3.14). The UDI is composed of a *device identifier* (the fixed, mandatory portion) and a *production identifier* (the conditional, variable portion). The UDI is issued by an FDA-accredited agent, and is uploaded to the GUDID.[35]

For physical devices, the UDI must appear on device labels, packaging and, in some cases, directly on the device [186]. Unless specifically exempt under regulation 21 CFR 801.30, all medical devices must bear a UDI.

Under the relevant device labelling regulation (21 CFR 801.50), standalone [medical device] software that is not distributed in packaged form (e.g., downloaded from a website) is deemed to meet the UDI labelling requirements if it (a) displays the UDI either on start-up (e.g., "splash screen") or via an "About" menu, and (b) conveys the version number in the production identifier [187].

6.5.9   Post-Market Studies

Post-market studies are a means by which FDA can collect safety and/or effectiveness data for a 510(k) cleared or pre-market approved device. The first type is a post-approval study, which is a condition of PMA.

In general, a post-approval study is a clinical study designed to collect long-term safety and/or effectiveness data for the approved device or to collect data that demonstrates the device's safety and/or effectiveness in a real-world clinical setting.

In contrast, Section 522 PMS studies are studies that may be mandated by FDA at any time after a device is 510(k) cleared or pre-market approved. For class II and class II devices, the need for a section 522 study arises in the following circumstances:

1. Device failure would be reasonably likely to have a serious adverse health consequence
2. Device is expected to have significant use in paediatric populations
3. Device is intended to be implanted in the body for more than one year
4. Device is intended to be a life-supporting device used outside of the user facility

Section 522 studies are typically designed to address specific questions. After completion of a post-approval study or a Section 522 PMS study, the labelling for the device is updated to reflect the findings.

6.5.9.1   Medical Device Tracking

Medical device tracking is an additional post-marketing tool that the FDA uses to ensure that a cleared/approved device remains safe and effective. The purpose of tracking, as with any other form, is to be able to contact the user as soon as possible in the event of a significant problem being detected, often through the medical

---

[35] The GUDID is the US equivalent of the EU's EUDAMED system.

device reporting programme (see below). Device tracking applies to class II or class III devices under the same circumstances as for post-market studies. For example, a replacement heart valve or a ventilator used in the person's home would be a tracked device.

6.5.9.2 Medical Device Reporting

The medical device reporting programme is essentially a system for reporting serious adverse incidents (involving death or serious injury) to the FDA, although certain other types of equipment malfunction must also be reported [188].

6.5.10 APPOINTMENT OF A US AGENT BY FOREIGN MANUFACTURERS

In addition to company registration and device listing (Section 6.5.1), manufacturers based outside the United States must appoint a US Agent who is familiar with the workings of the organisation [189]. The agent must either reside in the US or maintain a place of business in the US. The agent cannot use a post office box as an address, or just use a telephone answering service. The agent (or an employee) must be available to answer the phone during normal business hours. The FDA may wish to contact the manufacturer regarding inspections by an FDA field officer. Although an important link to the manufacturer, the US Agent has no responsibility for medical device reporting or adverse incident reporting.

6.5.11 INSPECTIONS BY THE FDA

There are four basic types of FDA inspection: Surveillance, pre-approval, compliance follow-up, and "for cause". Surveillance (or "routine") inspections can occur at any time after a device has been cleared/approved for market, but must (according to the FD&C Act) take place at least every two years for manufacturers of Class II and III devices [190]. Such inspections can also be triggered by public complaints. Inspections follow the QSIT approach and can be comprehensive or abbreviated [195], depending on how long the device has been on the market.

Pre-approval inspections take place as part of the PMA process (Section 6.5.4.3) [191]. If the PMA submission is approved, a follow-up visit will normally be conducted within 8–12 months, the main purpose of which is to check for any significant changes that may have been made to the device design, manufacturing process, or QS.

Compliance follow-up inspections are conducted to check for the completion of remedial actions recommended during a previous inspection, and "for cause" inspections are to investigate a specific problem that has been reported to the FDA.

The COVID-19 pandemic that started in early 2020 caused on-site inspections to be significantly delayed or suspended. Routine inspections resumed on 1 July 2021 but the FDA was faced with a backlog [192]. It conducted remote regulatory assessments (RRA) for manufacturers of "low risk" devices during the pandemic and has recently issued a draft consultation document on the proposed routine use of RRA as part of its wider inspection programme [193].

The draft guidance distinguishes between an RRA and a physical inspection of the manufacturer's premises. It also makes clear that the FDA does not consider an RRA to satisfy its statutory obligation to conduct inspections. When the guidance is finalised, the RRA scheme will complement the traditional inspection programme that the FDA is bound to resume. Like many organisations, the FDA discovered new ways of working during the COVID-19 pandemic so things will not simply go back to how they were. With the increasing use of electronic submission of requested documentation prior to an inspection, the implementation of an eQMS system (Section 5.2) is becoming more important.

Note that the proposed RRA system applies to all FDA-regulated industries, including drug manufacturers and food producers as well as medical device manufacturers. Guidance is available on how to prepare for an FDA inspection and how to conduct it [194].

Recently updated advice on "device establishment inspection processes and standards" [195] contains basic information about inspections (notice period, typical duration, required documents, etc.). The guidance also makes clear that, under 704(h)(1) of the FD&C Act, the FDA retains its authority to conduct unannounced "for-cause" inspections.

6.6   BENEFITS OF REGULATORY COMPLIANCE AND STANDARDS CERTIFICATION

For manufacturing activities covered by regulations, deliberate non-compliance is clearly not an option. However, organisations can run afoul of the law by a simple lack of awareness, as is potentially the case for medical software development in general and in-house medical software development in particular.

Some organisations regard regulatory compliance as a must-do chore but the process offers considerable benefits for improvement when approached in a positive manner. It should also be remembered that many medical device regulatory updates (as is the case for the EU MDR especially) are the direct result of previous irregularities that have had an impact on patient safety.

Some specific advantages to seeking and achieving regulatory compliance are listed below. The list is illustrative and is not meant to be exhaustive.

6.6.1   BENCHMARKING

The compliance process allows an organisation to measure itself against internationally recognised standards and "best practice" guidance in its area of activity.

6.6.2   IMPROVED QUALITY AND EFFICIENCY

There will always be shortcomings uncovered in a benchmarking process, even for the most highly respected departments/organisations, so the process represents a good opportunity for quality improvement. A quality improvement programme represents a "levelling up" process if employed across a national specialty (e.g., radiology),

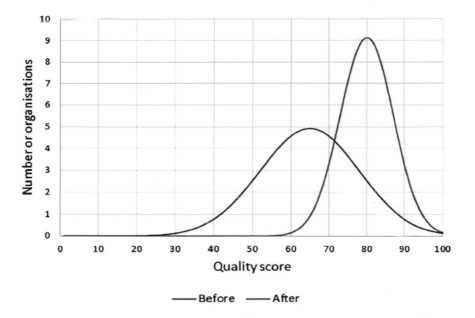

FIGURE 6.11 A pictorial (and hypothetical) representation of a quality improvement programme applied by a group of similar organisations. After successful application of the QM process, a significantly higher number of organisations achieved a higher quality score, with the mean increased from 65 to 80 and the standard deviation reduced from 13 to 7. In some quality circles, this is known as "chopping off the tail".

especially if encouraged and facilitated by the national professional body. Over time, more departments work close to the standards as the best and the variability between departments is reduced (Figure 6.11). The process also offers a realistic prospect of improved efficiency and reduced running costs.

6.6.3 ENHANCED REPUTATION

Achieving certification to a recognised international standard or regulation represents a considerable boost to staff morale, as well as providing a potential competitive advantage. It also improves staff retention and aids future recruitment.

6.6.4 PROVISION OF BUSINESS CASE 'AMMUNITION'

A request for additional resources, as would almost certainly be required for an organisation new to regulatory compliance, would usually be submitted as a business case for consideration by senior management. Gap analysis tools relating to specific standards or regulations can provide "hard evidence" of what is required. Also, the business case will usually be clear-cut; the answer to the usual pro-forma question "what would be the implications of *not* providing the requested resources?" being very simple: abandon the plan or stop the existing (non-compliant) service.

6.6.5   Reduced Clinical Risk

This is obviously the main purpose of regulatory compliance.

6.6.6   Reduced Corporate Risk

A reduction in corporate litigation risk is directly related to reduced clinical risk, but compliance with regulations and standards also provides mitigation if a serious problem occurs despite all the actions taken to ensure patient safety.

6.6.7   Increased Competency Levels

This tends to keep the individual performance of staff at a high level, by a combination of mandatory competency assessment and periodic re-audits by the assessment organisation(s)/certification bodies.

6.6.8   Keeping Up With Current Developments

Regulatory compliance helps an organisation keep abreast of modern methods and practices, as regulations change. To maintain its certification, an organisation must constantly update its procedures and staff training.

Appendix 1. Meaning of state of the art

MDR 17/745 refers to "taking into account the state of the art" (SOTA) no less than 12 times (e.g., software GSPR 17.2 [Section 6.3.6.1]) but does not define the term. However, MDCG guidance on standardisation for medical devices [196] contains a section on the interpretation of SOTA in the context of EU MDR. It quotes definitions from various sources; the one included in ISO Guide 63 (*Guide to the development and inclusion of aspects of safety in international standards for medical devices*) being typical: "Developed stage of technical capability at a given time as regards products, processes and services, based on the relevant consolidated findings of science, technology and experience". An added note states that:

> The 'state of the art' embodies what is currently and generally accepted as good practice in technology and medicine. The state of the art does not necessarily imply the most technologically advanced solution. The state of the art described here is sometimes referred to as the 'generally acknowledged state of the art'.

The MDCG guidance also makes a distinction between "taking into account" and compliance, adding that the term "state of the art" is "not a legally defined concept". Although the latest version of an international standard might be reasonably assumed to represent the current state of the art, adoption of such a standard does not automatically imply compliance with the relevant requirements of the applicable EU legislation unless it is cited in the *Official Journal of the European Union* (OJEU). Conversely, compliance with a *harmonised* standard (see Section 6.3.3) confers a "presumption of conformity", leading to the claim that "harmonised standards represent the current state of the art" with respect to EU regulations [197]. If there is no relevant harmonised standard, the manufacturer is required to use other standards, guidelines, and methodologies in its QMS.

Although often criticised for its general vagueness [198], the use of the term *SOTA* is an attempt to prolong the life of regulation by avoiding explicit reference to standards and their frequent updates. Supporting harmonised standards are generally "dated" but an updated version of the base standard could reasonably be argued to represent the new SOTA until such time that it is harmonised. Although implicit in its requirements, the FDA does not use the term "state-of-the-art" preferring to describe specific standards and its own guidelines.

REFERENCES

[1] C. Sorenson and M. Drummond, "Improving medical device regulation: The United States and Europe in perspective," *Milbank Quarterly,* vol. 92, no. 1, pp. 114–150, 2014
[2] R. A. Miller and R. M. Gardner, "Recommendations for responsible monitoring and regulation of clinical software systems," *Journal of the American Medical Informatics Association,* vol. 4, no. 6, pp. 442–457, 1997.

[3] UK House of Commons, "Regulation of medical implants in the UK," 17 October 2012. [Online]. Available: https://publications.parliament.uk/pa/cm201213/cmselect/cmsctech/163/163.pdf. [Accessed 20 September 2023].

[4] P. Baird and K. Cobbaert, "Software as a medical device: A comparison of the EU's approach with the US's approach," BSI, 2020. [Online]. Available: https://www.bsigroup.com/globalassets/localfiles/en-th/Medical%20devices/whitepapers/wp-software-th.pdf. [Accessed 20 September 2023].

[5] European Commission, "The 'Blue Guide' on the implementation of EU product rules 2022," 2022. [Online]. Available: https://eur-lex.europa.eu/legal-content/EN/TXT/?uri=uriserv%3AOJ.C_.2022.247.01.0001.01.ENG&toc=OJ%3AC%3A2022%3A247%3ATOC. [Accessed 20 September 2023].

[6] European Commission, "Flowchart to assist in deciding whether or not a device is covered by the extended MDR transitional period," 23 August 2023.[Online]. Available: https://health.ec.europa.eu/latest-updates/flowchart-assist-deciding-whether-or-not-device-covered-extended-mdr-transitional-period-2023-08-23_en. [Accessed 20 September 2023].

[7] Medical Device Regulation, "Harmonised standards list," 2023. [Online]. Available: https://www.medical-device-regulation.eu/mdr-resource-harmonized-standards-lis/. [Accessed 20 September 2023].

[8] European Commission, "C(2021)2406 – Standardisation request M/575," 14 April 2021. [Online]. Available: https://ec.europa.eu/growth/tools-databases/enorm/mandate/575_en. [Accessed 20 September 2023].

[9] MDCG, "MDCG 2019-11: Guidance on qualification and classification of software in regulation (EU) 2017/745 – MDR and Regulation (EU) 2017/746 – IVDR," 2019. [Online]. Available: https://health.ec.europa.eu/system/files/2020-09/md_mdcg_2019_11_guidance_qualification_classification_software_en_0.pdf. [Accessed 20 September 2023].

[10] MDCG, "MDCG 2020-6: Clinical evidence needed for medical devices previously CE marked under Directives 93/42/EEC or 90/385/EEC," April 2020. [Online]. Available: https://health.ec.europa.eu/system/files/2020-09/md_mdcg_2020_6_guidance_sufficient_clinical_evidence_en_0.pdf. [Accessed 20 September 2023].

[11] European Commission, "Manual on borderline and classification in the community regulatory framework for medical devices," 2019. [Online]. Available: https://health.ec.europa.eu/system/files/2020-08/md_borderline_manual_05_2019_en_0.pdf. [Accessed 21 September 2023].

[12] Apple Inc., "Apple watch Series 9," 2023. [Online]. Available: https://www.apple.com/uk/apple-watch-series-9/. [Accessed 21 September 2023].

[13] Australian Therapeutic Goods Administration, "Exemption for certain clinical decision support software," August 2022. [Online]. Available: https://www.tga.gov.au/sites/default/files/2022-08/exemption-for-certain-clinical-decision-support-software.pdf. [Accessed 21 September 2023].

[14] Medicines & Healthcare Products Agency, "Flowchart CIs - Studies under UKMDR2002 v1," 29 April 2022. [Online]. Available: https://assets.publishing.service.gov.uk/government/uploads/system/uploads/attachment_data/file/1072413/flowchart_CIs_-_Studies_under_UKMDR2002_v1_A4.pdf. [Accessed 21 September 2023].

[15] European Coordination Committee of the Radiological, Electromedical and Healthcare IT Industry, "COCIR: COCIR analysis on AI in medical device legislation - May 2021," 05 May 2021. [Online]. Available: https://www.cocir.org/media-centre/publications/article/cocir-analysis-on-ai-in-medical-device-legislation-may-2021. [Accessed 21 September 2023].

[16] MDCG, "MDCG 2021-24: Guidance on classification of medical devices," October 2021. [Online]. Available: https://health.ec.europa.eu/system/files/2021-10/mdcg_2021-24_en_0.pdf. [Accessed 21 September 2023].

[17] C. Johner, "MDR Rule 11: The classification nightmare," Johner Institute, 22 July 2017. [Online]. Available: https://www.johner-institute.com/articles/regulatory-affairs/and-more/mdr-rule-11-software/. [Accessed 21 September 2023].

[18] FME, "MDR guide for medical device software," 09 September 2021. [Online]. Available: https://www.fme.nl/system/files/publicaties/2021-09/MDR%20Guide.pdf. [Accessed 21 September 2023].

[19] C. Johner, "Klasse-I-Software," Johner Institute, 20 December 2022. [Online]. Available: https://www.johner-institut.de/blog/iec-62304-medizinische-software/klasse-i-software/. [Accessed 21 September 2023].

[20] O. Eidel, "How to classify software as a medical device under the MDR? (MDCG 2021–24)," Open Regulatory, 24 May 2023. [Online]. Available: https://openregulatory.com/mdcg-2021-24-examples-for-software-classification-of-software-as-a-medical-device-samd/. [Accessed 21 September 2023].

[21] Mindtech Store, "BILD test winner 2021: Mobile ECG devices," 06 July 2021. [Online]. Available: https://www.mindtecstore.com/BILD-test-winner-2021-of-the-mobile-ECG-devices-The-KardiaMobile-6L. [Accessed 21 September 2023].

[22] M. Kawalkowska, "The complete guide to EU Medical Device Regulation," Spyrosoft, [Online]. Available: https://spyro-soft.com/eu-mdr-regulation. [Accessed 21 September 2023].

[23] MHRA, "Medical devices: Software applications (apps)," 1 July 2023. [Online]. Available: https://www.gov.uk/government/publications/medical-devices-software-applications-apps. [Accessed 22 September 2023].

[24] European Commission, "Manual on borderline and classification in the community regulatory framework for medical devices (September 2022)," 07 September 2022. [Online]. Available: https://health.ec.europa.eu/latest-updates/manual-borderline-and-classification-community-regulatory-framework-medical-devices-september-2022-2022-09-07_en. [Accessed 21 September 2023].

[25] Institute of Physics and Engineering in Medicine, "Guidance for health institutions on in-house manufacture and use, including software (2nd Ed.)," 25 July 2022. [Online]. Available: https://www.ipem.ac.uk/resources/other-resources/statements-and-notices/guidance-for-in-house-manufacture-of-medical-devices-and-non-medical-devices-including-software-2nd-ed/. [Accessed 21 September 2023].

[26] Greenlight Guru, "SaMD gap assessment tool - Free download," Greenlight Guru, [Online]. Available: https://www.greenlight.guru/downloads/samd-gap-assessment-tool. [Accessed 21 September 2023].

[27] A. Murray, "Nuclear medicine software: Nothing is perfect," *Nuclear Medicine Communications,* vol. 35, no. 11, pp. 1093–1095, 2014.

[28] A. W. Murray, R. S. Lawson and S. C. Cade, "UK audit of glomerular filtration rate measurement from plasma sampling in 2013," *Nuclear Medicine Communications,* vol. 35, no. 11, pp. 1096–1106, 2014.

[29] Medicines and Healthcare products Regulatory Agency, "Guidance for manufacturers on reporting adverse incidents involving software as a medical device under the vigilance system - GOV.UK," Medicines and Healthcare products Regulatory Agency, [Online]. Available: https://www.gov.uk/government/publications/reporting-adverse-incidents-involving-software-as-a-medical-device-under-the-vigilance-system. [Accessed 20 September 2023].

[30] D. Reinsch, "Regulatorische Anforderungen an Medizinprodukte mit Machine Learning," Johner Institute, 07 September 2023. [Online]. Available: https://www.johner-institut.de/blog/iec-62304-medizinische-software/regulatorische-anforderungen-an-medizinprodukte-mit-machine-learning/. [Accessed 21 September 2023].

[31] British Standards Institute, "Machine learning AI in medical devices | BSI America," 2020. [Online]. Available: https://www.bsigroup.com/en-US/medical-devices/resources/Whitepapers-and-articles/machine-learning-ai-in-medical-devices/. [Accessed 21 September 2023].

[32] European Commission, "Guidance on significant changes regarding the transitional provision under Article 120 of the MDR with regard to devices covered by certificates according to MDD or AIMDD," 15 March 2020. [Online]. Available: https://ec.europa.eu/docsroom/documents/40301. [Accessed 21 September 2023].

[33] Johner Institute, "ai-guideline/Guideline-AI-Medical-Devices_EN.md at master · johner-institut/ai-guideline · GitHub," Johner Institute, 21 December 2021. [Online]. Available: https://github.com/johner-institut/ai-guideline/commits/master/Guideline-AI-Medical-Devices_EN.md. [Accessed 21 September 2023].

[34] B. North, "The growing role of human factors and usability engineering for medical devices," 09 February 2018. [Online]. Available: https://www.bsigroup.com/LocalFiles/de-de/Medizinprodukte/Growing-role-of-human-factors.pdf. [Accessed 21 September 2023].

[35] European Commission, "MDCG 2019-16 - Guidance on cybersecurity for medical devices," 06 January 2020. [Online]. Available: https://ec.europa.eu/docsroom/documents/41863. [Accessed 21 September 2023].

[36] European Commission, "C(2021)2406 – Standardisation request M/575," [Online]. Available: https://ec.europa.eu/growth/tools-databases/enorm/mandate/575_en. [Accessed 21 September 2023].

[37] Zvei, "Medical technology needs cybersecurity," 16 May 2023. [Online]. Available: https://www.zvei.org/presse-medien/publikationen/medizintechnik-braucht-cybersicherheit. [Accessed 21 September 2023].

[38] E. Biasin, "Medical devices cybersecurity: A growing concern?," Ku Leuven, 29 September 2019. [Online]. Available: https://www.law.kuleuven.be/citip/blog/medical-devices-cybersecurity-a-growing-concern/. [Accessed 21 September 2023].

[39] European Commission, "Regulation (EU) 2019/881 of the European Parliament and of the Council," 17 April 2019. [Online]. Available: https://eur-lex.europa.eu/eli/reg/2019/881/oj. [Accessed 21 September 2023].

[40] European Commission, "Commission Regulation (EU) No 207/2012 on electronic instructions for use (IFU) of medical devices," *OJ,* vol. 72, p. 28, 9 March 2012.

[41] Johner Institute, "SSRS checklist," [Online]. Available: https://www.johner-institute.com/ssrs-checklist/. [Accessed 21 September 2023].

[42] MHRA, "MHRA guidance on the health institution exemption (HIE) – IVDR and MDR (Northern Ireland)," 1 January 2021. [Online]. Available: https://www.gov.uk/government/publications/mhra-guidance-on-the-health-institution-exemption-hie-ivdr-and-mdr-northern-ireland. [Accessed 21 September 2023].

[43] I3CGlobal, "Person responsible for regulatory compliance," 3 October 2021. [Online]. Available: https://www.i3cglobal.com/person-responsible-for-regulatory-compliance/. [Accessed 21 September 2023].

[44] Medical Device Regulation, "Keep calm and start creating your MDR transition plan," [Online]. Available: https://www.medical-device-regulation.eu/. [Accessed 21 September 2023].

[45] i3cGlobal, "MDR technical documentation gap analysis," [Online]. Available: https://www.i3cglobal.com/mdr-technical-file-gap-analysis-checklist/. [Accessed 21 September 2023].

[46] Greenlight Guru, "SaMD gap assessment tool," [Online]. Available: https://www.greenlight.guru/downloads/samd-gap-assessment-tool. [Accessed 21 September 2023].

[47] Advisera, "How can ISO 13485 help with MDR compliance?," 9 March 2020. [Online]. Available: https://advisera.com/13485academy/blog/2020/03/09/how-can-iso-13485-help-with-mdr-compliance/. [Accessed 21 September 2023].

[48] M. Greenaway, "Medical device standards: ISO 13485, ISO 9001 or both?," Assent, 11 May 2020. [Online]. Available: https://www.assentriskmanagement.co.uk/iso-13485-iso-9001-or-both/. [Accessed 22 September 2023].

[49] E. Bills, "What does EN ISO 14971:2019's new amendment mean for harmonisation?," Med Device Online, 4 March 2022. [Online]. Available: https://www.meddeviceonline.com/doc/what-does-en-iso-s-new-amendment-mean-for-harmonisation-0001. [Accessed 22 September 2023].

[50] K. Larsson, "Software hazard identification based on IEC 80002-1 Annex B," Aligned Elements, 3 May 2021. [Online]. Available: https://www.aligned.ch/blog/product-news/664-software-hazard-identification-from-iec-80002-1-annex-b. [Accessed 22 September 2023].

[51] MDCG, "MDCG 2020-1: Guidance on clinical evaluation (MDR)/performance evaluation (IVDR) of medical device software," March 2020. [Online]. Available: https://health.ec.europa.eu/system/files/2020-09/md_mdcg_2020_1_guidance_clinic_eva_md_software_en_0.pdf. [Accessed 22 September 2023].

[52] MDCG, "MDCG 2020-5: Clinical evaluation - equivalence," 2020. [Online]. Available: https://health.ec.europa.eu/system/files/2020-09/md_mdcg_2020_5_guidance_clinical_evaluation_equivalence_en_0.pdf. [Accessed 22 September 2023].

[53] MDCG, "MDCG 2020-6: Regulation (EU) 2017/745: Clinical evidence needed for medical devices previously CE marked under Directives 93/42/EEC or 90/385/EEC," April 2020. [Online]. Available: https://health.ec.europa.eu/system/files/2020-09/md_mdcg_2020_6_guidance_sufficient_clinical_evidence_en_0.pdf. [Accessed 22 September 2023].

[54] A. Smirthwaite, "Clinical evaluation under EU MDR," BSI, 2020. [Online]. Available: https://www.bsigroup.com/globalassets/localfiles/en-gb/medical-devices/whitepapers/clinical-evaluation-white-paper/clinical-evaluation-under-eu-mdr.pdf. [Accessed 22 September 2023].

[55] Mantra Systems, "Clinical evaluation reports: CERs for medical devices," 2021. [Online]. Available: https://www.mantrasystems.co.uk/eu-mdr-compliance/clinical-evaluation-report-cer. [Accessed 22 September 2023].

[56] World Medical Association, "WMA declaration of Helsinki - Ethical principles for medical research involving human subjects," 6 September 2022. [Online]. Available: https://www.wma.net/policies-post/wma-declaration-of-helsinki-ethical-principles-for-medical-research-involving-human-subjects/. [Accessed 22 September 2023].

[57] J. Bergsteinsson, "Ultimate guide to ISO 14155:2020 for medical devices," Greenlight Guru, 2020. [Online]. Available: https://www.greenlight.guru/downloads/ultimate-guide-iso-14155-2020-compliant-clinical-investigations. [Accessed 22 September 2023].

[58] European Commission, "Guidance on the content and structure of the summary of the clinical investigation report," 2023. [Online]. Available: https://eur-lex.europa.eu/legal-content/EN/TXT/?uri=CELEX:52023XC0508(01). [Accessed 22 September 2023].

[59] MDCG, "MDCG 2023-1: Guidance on the Health Institution Exemption under Article 5(5) of Regulation (EU) 2017/745 and Regulation (EU) 2017/746," January 2023. [Online]. Available: https://health.ec.europa.eu/system/files/2023-01/mdcg_2023-1_en.pdf. [Accessed 22 September 2023].

[60] IPEM, "Best-practice guidance for the in-house manufacture of medical devices and non-medical devices, including software in both cases, for use within the same health institution," 25 July 2022. [Online]. Available: https://www.ipem.ac.uk/media/vp0ewy01/ipembe-1.pdf. [Accessed 22 September 2023].

[61] BSI, "MDR documentation submissions," May 2020. [Online]. Available: https://www.bsigroup.com/globalassets/meddev/localfiles/fr-fr/ressources/bsi-md-mdr-best-practice-documentation-submissions-en-gb1.pdf. [Accessed 22 September 2023].

[62] K. Colin, "STED is dead," Rimsys, 28 December 2022. [Online]. Available: https://www.rimsys.io/blog/sted-is-dead. [Accessed 22 September 2023].

[63] MDCG, "MDCG 2019-9 Rev.1: Summary of safety and clinical performance," March 2022. [Online]. Available: https://health.ec.europa.eu/system/files/2022-03/md_mdcg_2019_9_sscp_en.pdf. [Accessed 22 September 2023].

[64] International Medical Device Regulators Forum, "UDI guidance: Unique Device Identification (UDI) of medical devices," 18 December 2013. [Online]. Available: https://www.imdrf.org/documents/udi-guidance-unique-device-identification-udi-medical-devices. [Accessed 21 September 2023].

[65] B. Lentz, "The ultimate guide to the EU MDR/IVDR UDI," Rimsys, 22 June 2021. [Online]. Available: https://www.rimsys.io/blog/the-ultimate-guide-to-the-eu-mdr-ivdr-udi. [Accessed 21 September 2023].

[66] European Commission, "MDCG 2018-1 v3 guidance on BASIC UDI-DI and changes to UDI-DI," 15 March 2020. [Online]. Available: https://ec.europa.eu/docsroom/documents/40322. [Accessed 21 September 2023].

[67] MDCG, "MDCG 2021-19 - Guidance note integration of the UDI within an organisation's quality management system," 15 July 2021. [Online]. Available: https://health.ec.europa.eu/latest-updates/mdcg-2021-19-guidance-note-integration-udi-within-organisations-quality-management-system-2021-07-15_en. [Accessed 21 September 2023].

[68] MDCG, "MDCG 2018-5: UDI assignment to medical device software," 09 October 2018. [Online]. Available: https://ec.europa.eu/docsroom/documents/31926. [Accessed 21 September 2023].

[69] H. Lacalle, "UDI for Medical Device Software (MDSW) under EU MDR - Decomplix," Decomplix, 25 July 2021. [Online]. Available: https://decomplix.com/udi-medical-device-software-mdsw-eu-mdr/#. [Accessed 21 Software 2023].

[70] E. Nichols, "Post-market clinical follow-up under EU MDR: Your guide to PMCF activities," Greenlight Guru, 10 April 2023. [Online]. Available: https://www.greenlight.guru/blog/post-market-clinical-follow-up. [Accessed 22 September 2023].

[71] MDCG, "MDCG 2020-7: Post-market clinical follow-up (PMCF) plan template," April 2020. [Online]. Available: https://health.ec.europa.eu/system/files/2020-09/md_mdcg_2020_7_guidance_pmcf_plan_template_en_0.pdf. [Accessed 22 September 2023].

[72] Seleon, "Conformity assessment procedures for medical devices," [Online]. Available: https://www.seleon.com/en/regulatory-affairs/conformity-assessment-procedures-for-medical-devices/. [Accessed 22 September 2023].

[73] European Commission, "Single market compliance space," [Online]. Available: https://webgate.ec.europa.eu/single-market-compliance-space/#/home. [Accessed 22 September 2023].

[74] MDCG, "MDCG 2022-14: MDCG position paper - Notified body capacity and availability of medical devices and IVDs," August 2022. [Online]. Available: https://health.ec.europa.eu/system/files/2022-08/mdcg_2022-14_en.pdf. [Accessed 22 September 2023].

[75] MHRA, "Implementation of the future regulations," 27 July 2023. [Online]. Available: https://www.gov.uk/government/publications/implementation-of-the-future-regulation-of-medical-devices/implementation-of-the-future-regulations. [Accessed 22 September 2023].

[76] MHRA, "Regulating medical devices in the UK," 20 July 2023. [Online]. Available: https://www.gov.uk/guidance/regulating-medical-devices-in-the-uk. [Accessed 22 September 2023].

[77] UKMDR, "The medical devices (Amendment) (Great Britain) regulations 2023," 2023. [Online]. Available: https://ukmdr.com/regulations/. [Accessed 22 September 2023].

[78] Advena, "UK responsible person," [Online]. Available: https://advenamedical.com/services/uk-responsible-person/. [Accessed 22 September 2023].

[79] MEDDEV, "MEDDEV 2.1/6: Guidelines on the qualification and classification of standalone software used in healthcare within the regulatory framework of medical devices," 2012. [Online]. Available: http://www.meddev.info/_documents/2_1_6_ol_en.pdf. [Accessed 24 November 2023].

[80] MHRA, "Guidance on applying human factors to medical devices," 12 February 2021. [Online]. Available: https://www.gov.uk/government/publications/guidance-on-applying-human-factors-to-medical-devices. [Accessed 22 September 2023].

[81] MedTech Innovation, "The UK Medical Device Information System – A new resource for medtechs," 31 March 2021. [Online]. Available: https://www.med-technews.com/medtech-insights/medtech-regulatory-insights/the-uk-medical-device-information-system-%E2%80%93-a-new-resource-fo/. [Accessed 22 September 2023].

[82] MHRA, "Register medical devices to place on the market," 3 August 2023. [Online]. Available: https://www.gov.uk/guidance/register-medical-devices-to-place-on-the-market. [Accessed 22 September 2023].

[83] UK Department of Health and Social Care, "Independent medicines and medical devices safety review: update report on government implementation," 22 December 2022. [Online]. Available: https://www.gov.uk/government/publications/independent-medicines-and-medical-devices-safety-review-update-report-on-government-implementation/independent-medicines-and-medical-devices-safety-review-update-report-on-government-implementation. [Accessed 22 September 2023].

[84] MHRA, "Designated standards: Medical devices," 6 January 2022. [Online]. Available: https://www.gov.uk/government/publications/designated-standards-medical-devices. [Accessed 22 September 2023].

[85] NHS England, "Clinical risk management standards," [Online]. Available: https://digital.nhs.uk/services/clinical-safety/clinical-risk-management-standards. [Accessed 22 September 2023].

[86] NHS England, "Applicability of DCB 0129 and DCB 0160: Step by step guidance," [Online]. Available: https://digital.nhs.uk/services/clinical-safety/applicability-of-dcb-0129-and-dcb-0160/step-by-step-guidance. [Accessed 22 September 2023].

[87] AXREM, "DTAC and DCB 0129 problem statement," 4 July 2023. [Online]. Available: https://www.axrem.org.uk/axrem-dtac-and-dcb0129-problem-statement/. [Accessed 22 September 2023].

[88] IPEM, "Clinical risk management foundation course," June 2023. [Online]. Available: https://www.linkedin.com/posts/the-institute-of-physics-and-engineering-in-medicine-ipem-_clinical-risk-management-foundation-course-activity-7063439088007180288-yPQz/. [Accessed 22 September 2023].

[89] IPEM, "Panel discussion: Clinical risk management.," *Scope,* vol. 33, no. 4, pp. 16–19, 2022.

[90] IPEM, "Panel discussion: Clinical risk management – Part 2. *Scope*, 2023, 34:1:16–19," *Scope,* vol. 34, no. 1, pp. 16–19, 2023.

[91] FDA, "Overview of device regulation," 4 September 2020. [Online]. Available: https://www.fda.gov/medical-devices/device-advice-comprehensive-regulatory-assistance/overview-device-regulation. [Accessed 22 September 2023].

[92] B. Sutton, "Overview of regulatory requirements: Medical devices - Transcript," FDA, November 2011. [Online]. Available: https://www.fda.gov/training-and-continuing-education/cdrh-learn/overview-regulatory-requirements-medical-devices-transcript. [Accessed 22 September 2023].

[93] FDA, "Reclassification," 31 August 2018. [Online]. Available: https://www.fda.gov/medical-devices/classify-your-medical-device/reclassification. [Accessed 22 September 2023].

[94] FDA, "The 510(k) program: Evaluating substantial equivalence in premarket notifications [510(k)]," 28 July 2014. [Online]. Available: https://www.fda.gov/media/82395/download. [Accessed 22 September 2023].

[95] FDA, "Premarket approval (PMA)," 16 May 2019. [Online]. Available: https://www.fda.gov/medical-devices/premarket-submissions-selecting-and-preparing-correct-submission/premarket-approval-pma. [Accessed 22 September 2023].

[96] FDA, "Classify your medical device," 7 February 2020. [Online]. Available: https://www.fda.gov/medical-devices/overview-device-regulation/classify-your-medical-device. [Accessed 22 September 2023].

[97] FDA, "Device classification panels," 31 August 2018. [Online]. Available: https://www.fda.gov/medical-devices/classify-your-medical-device/device-classification-panels. [Accessed 22 September 2023].

[98] FDA, "Product classification," [Online]. Available: https://www.accessdata.fda.gov/scripts/cdrh/cfdocs/cfpcd/classification.cfm. [Accessed 22 September 2023].

[99] FDA, "CFR - Code of Federal Regulations Title 21," [Online]. Available: https://www.accessdata.fda.gov/scripts/cdrh/cfdocs/cfCFR/CFRSearch.cfm. [Accessed 22 September 2023].

[100] FDA, "Policy for device software functions and mobile medical applications," 28 September 2022. [Online]. Available: https://www.fda.gov/regulatory-information/search-fda-guidance-documents/policy-device-software-functions-and-mobile-medical-applications. [Accessed 22 September 2023].

[101] FDA, "Medical device data systems, medical image storage devices, and medical image communications devices," September 2022. [Online]. Available: https://www.fda.gov/regulatory-information/search-fda-guidance-documents/medical-device-data-systems-medical-image-storage-devices-and-medical-image-communications-devices. [Accessed 22 September 2023].

[102] FDA, "General wellness: Policy for low risk devices," September 2019. [Online]. Available: https://www.fda.gov/regulatory-information/search-fda-guidance-documents/general-wellness-policy-low-risk-devices. [Accessed 22 September 2023].

[103] FDA, "Content of premarket submissions for device software functions," June 2023. [Online]. Available: https://www.fda.gov/regulatory-information/search-fda-guidance-documents/content-premarket-submissions-device-software-functions. [Accessed 22 September 2023].

[104] E. Nichols, "Why class 1 medical device companies need design control," Quality Digest, 12 August 2022. [Online]. Available: https://www.greenlight.guru/blog/class-1-medical-device-design-controls. [Accessed 22 September 2023].

[105] M. Shneider, "FDA device approval pathways more complex than ever," Regulatory Focus, 3 August 2021. [Online]. Available: https://www.raps.org/news-and-articles/news-articles/2021/8/review-fda-device-approval-pathways-more-complex-t. [Accessed 22 September 2023].

[106] FDA, "510(k) Submission programs," 12 September 2019. [Online]. Available: https://www.fda.gov/medical-devices/premarket-notification-510k/510k-submission-programs. [Accessed 22 September 2023].

[107] FDA, "Premarket notification 510(k)," 3 October 2022. [Online]. Available: https://www.fda.gov/medical-devices/premarket-submissions-selecting-and-preparing-correct-submission/premarket-notification-510k. [Accessed 22 September 2023].

[108] FDA, "How to find and effectively use predicate devices," 4 September 2018. [Online]. Available: https://www.fda.gov/medical-devices/premarket-notification-510k/how-find-and-effectively-use-predicate-devices. [Accessed 22 September 2023].

[109] FDA, "FDA issues guidances and requests comments as a part of ongoing efforts to modernize the premarket notification [510(k)] program," 6 September 2023. [Online]. Available: https://content.govdelivery.com/accounts/USFDA/bulletins/36cccf3. [Accessed 22 September 2023].

[110] Drug Watch, "FDA 510(k) clearance process," 5 September 2023. [Online]. Available: https://www.drugwatch.com/fda/510k-clearance/. [Accessed 22 September 2023].

[111] J. Darrow, J. Avorn and A. Kesselheim, "FDA regulation and approval of medical devices: 1976-2020.," *JAMA,* vol. 326, no. 5, pp. 420–432, 2021.

[112] FDA, "Medical device exemptions 510(k) and GMP requirements," [Online]. Available: https://www.accessdata.fda.gov/scripts/cdrh/cfdocs/cfpcd/315.cfm.   [Accessed   22 September 2023].

[113] FDA, "Is a new 510(k) required for a modification to the device?," 31 October 2017. [Online]. Available: https://www.fda.gov/medical-devices/premarket-notification-510k/new-510k-required-modification-device. [Accessed 22 September 2023].

[114] FDA, "Product code classification database," 22 March 2018. [Online]. Available: https://www.fda.gov/medical-devices/classify-your-medical-device/product-code-classification-database. [Accessed 22 September 2023].

[115] FDA, "510(k) Premarket notification," [Online]. Available: https://www.accessdata.fda.gov/scripts/cdrh/cfdocs/cfpmn/pmn.cfm. [Accessed 22 September 2023].

[116] FDA, "Content of premarket submissions for device software functions," June 2023. [Online]. Available: https://www.fda.gov/regulatory-information/search-fda-guidance-documents/content-premarket-submissions-device-software-functions. [Accessed 22 September 2023].

[117] FDA, "510(k) Third party review program," 19 August 2022. [Online]. Available: https://www.fda.gov/medical-devices/premarket-submissions-selecting-and-preparing-correct-submission/510k-third-party-review-program.   [Accessed   22   September 2023].

[118] FDA, "How to prepare an abbreviated 510(k)," 23 January 2019. [Online]. Available: https://www.fda.gov/medical-devices/premarket-notification-510k/how-prepare-abbreviated-510k. [Accessed 22 September 2023].

[119] FDA, "Format for Traditional and Abbreviated 510(k)s," September 2019. [Online]. Available: https://www.tuvsud.com/ja-jp/-/media/regions/jp/ac/pdf-files/medical-info/2020/11/04_510k_guidance.pdf. [Accessed 22 September 2023].

[120] W. Schroeder, "Special 510(k) vs. Abbreviated 510(k) vs. Traditional 510(k): Which FDA program applies to my device?," Greenlight Guru, 21 February 2021. [Online]. Available: https://www.greenlight.guru/blog/special-510k-abbreviated-traditional.   [Accessed   23 September 2023].

[121] FDA, "Refuse to accept policy for 510(k)s," April 2022. [Online]. Available: https://www.fda.gov/regulatory-information/search-fda-guidance-documents/refuse-accept-policy-510ks. [Accessed 22 September 2023].

[122] J. Speer, "How to avoid being part of the 69% of 510(k) submissions that get rejected the first time," Greenlight Guru, 15 August 2016. [Online]. Available: https://www.greenlight.guru/blog/how-to-avoid-510-k-submission-rejected.   [Accessed   22   September 2023].

[123] T. Rish, "How to demonstrate substantial equivalence in 5 easy steps", 7 March 2021, Greenlight Guru. [Online]. Available: https://www.greenlight.guru/blog/substantial-equivalence. [Accessed 22 September 2023].

[124] J. Speer, "4 Reasons your 510(k) submission will be rejected (and how to avoid them)," Med Device Online, 19 September 2016. [Online]. Available: https://www.meddeviceonline.com/doc/reasons-your-k-submission-will-be-rejected-and-how-to-avoid-them-0001. [Accessed 22 September 2023].

[125] FDA, "eCopy medical device submissions," 3 October 2022. [Online]. Available: https://www.fda.gov/medical-devices/how-study-and-market-your-device/ecopy-medical-device-submissions. [Accessed 23 September 2023].

[126] FDA, "De Novo classification request," 3 October 2022. [Online]. Available: https://www.fda.gov/medical-devices/premarket-submissions-selecting-and-preparing-correct-submission/de-novo-classification-request. [Accessed 23 September 2023].

[127] W. Levine, "FDA PMA submission process: A beginner's guide," Rimsys, 27 April 2022. [Online]. Available: https://www.rimsys.io/blog/pma-submission-process-beginners-guide. [Accessed 23 September 2023].

[128] FDA, "PMA review process," 13 September 2021. [Online]. Available: https://www.fda.gov/medical-devices/premarket-approval-pma/pma-review-process. [Accessed 23 September 2023].

[129] FDA, "Breakthrough devices program," September 2023. [Online]. Available: https://www.fda.gov/regulatory-information/search-fda-guidance-documents/breakthrough-devices-program. [Accessed 23 September 2023].

[130] FDA, "Breakthrough devices program - Metrics," 30 June 2023. [Online]. Available: https://www.fda.gov/medical-devices/how-study-and-market-your-device/breakthrough-devices-program#metrics. [Accessed 23 September 2023].

[131] FDA, "Requests for feedback and meetings for medical device submissions: The Q-submission program," 2 June 2023. [Online]. Available: https://www.fda.gov/regulatory-information/search-fda-guidance-documents/requests-feedback-and-meetings-medical-device-submissions-q-submission-program.   [Accessed   23 September 2023].

[132] J. Kasic, "5 Key steps for FDA Q-submissions," Med Device Online, 18 April 2022. [Online]. Available: https://www.meddeviceonline.com/doc/key-steps-for-fda-q-submissions-0001. [Accessed 23 September 2023].

[133] US National Archives, "Title 21: Food and drugs," 21 September 2023. [Online]. Available: https://www.ecfr.gov/current/title-21/chapter-I/subchapter-H/part-820?toc=1. [Accessed 23 September 2023].

[134] FDA, "Acceptance of data from clinical investigations for medical devices," 16 April 2019. [Online]. Available: https://www.fda.gov/medical-devices/investigational-device-exemption-ide/acceptance-data-clinical-investigations-medical-devices. [Accessed 23 September 2023].

[135] FDA, "ISO 14155 Third edition 2020-07," 21 December 2020. [Online]. Available: https://www.accessdata.fda.gov/scripts/cdrh/cfdocs/cfStandards/detail.cfm?standard__identification_no=41711. [Accessed 23 September 2023].

[136] FDA, "Quality System (QS) regulation/medical device good manufacturing practices," 22 February 2022. [Online]. Available: https://www.fda.gov/medical-devices/postmarket-requirements-devices/quality-system-qs-regulationmedical-device-good-manufacturing-practices. [Accessed 23 September 2023].

[137] FDA, "Guide to inspection of quality systems," August 1999. [Online]. Available: https://www.fda.gov/media/73166/download. [Accessed 24 September 2023].

[138] E. Nichols, "The ultimate internal audit checklist every medical device company needs," Greenlight Guru, 25 October 2022. [Online]. Available: https://www.greenlight.guru/blog/internal-audit-checklist-medical-device. [Accessed 24 September 2023].

[139] E. Nichols, "QMSR explained: What FDA QSR & ISO 13485 harmonization means for medical device companies," Greenlight Guru, 21 July 2023. [Online]. Available: https://www.greenlight.guru/blog/qmsr-quality-management-system-regulation. [Accessed 24 September 2023].

[140] Authenticated US Government Information (GPO), "Federal register: 21 CFR parts 4 and 820," 23 February 2022. [Online]. Available: https://www.govinfo.gov/content/pkg/FR-2022-02-23/pdf/2022-03227.pdf. [Accessed 24 September 2023].

[141] E. Nichols, "ISO 14971 risk management for medical devices: The definitive guide," Greenlight Guru, 11 May 2023. [Online]. Available: https://www.greenlight.guru/blog/iso-14971-risk-management. [Accessed 24 September 2023].

[142] OrielStat, "How medical device risk management and ISO 14971:2019 work," 21 March 2023. [Online]. Available: https://www.orielstat.com/blog/iso-14971-risk-management-basics/. [Accessed 24 September 2023].

[143] FDA, "Deciding when to submit a 510(k) for a software change to an existing device," October 2017. [Online]. Available: https://www.fda.gov/regulatory-information/search-fda-guidance-documents/deciding-when-submit-510k-software-change-existing-device. [Accessed 24 September 2023].

[144] FDA, "FDASIA health IT report," 18 November 2020. [Online]. Available: https://www.fda.gov/about-fda/cdrh-reports/fdasia-health-it-report. [Accessed 24 September 2023].

[145] L. Tsang and V. Pollard, "EU and US regulation of health information technology, software and mobile apps," Thomson Reuters - Practical Law, 1 August 2014. [Online]. Available: https://uk.practicallaw.thomsonreuters.com/3-518-3154. [Accessed 24 September 2023].

[146] FDA, "General principles of software validation," 15 May 2019. [Online]. Available: https://www.fda.gov/regulatory-information/search-fda-guidance-documents/general-principles-software-validation. [Accessed 24 September 2023].

[147] J. Lyons, "CSV vs. CSA: Exploring FDA's new software validation approach," Greenlight Guru, 4 June 2023. [Online]. Available: https://www.greenlight.guru/blog/csa-vs-csv. [Accessed 24 September 2023].

[148] FDA, "Computer software assurance for production and quality system software," September 2022. [Online]. Available: https://www.fda.gov/regulatory-information/search-fda-guidance-documents/computer-software-assurance-production-and-quality-system-software. [Accessed 24 September 2023].

[149] FDA, "CFR - Code of Federal Regulations title 21 - Part 820," 7 June 2023. [Online] Available: http://www.accessdata.fda.gov/scripts/cdrh/cfdocs/cfCFR/CFRSearch.cfm?fr=820.3. [Accessed 24 September 2023].

[150] J. Lyons, "Beginner's guide to design verification & design validation for medical devices," Greenlight Guru, 10 February 2023. [Online]. Available: https://www.greenlight.guru/blog/design-verification-and-design-validation. [Accessed 24 September 2023].

[151] FDA, "What are examples of Software as a Medical Device?," 6 December 2017. [Online]. Available: https://www.fda.gov/medical-devices/software-medical-device-samd/what-are-examples-software-medical-device. [Accessed 24 September 2023].

[152] J. Smith, "Medical imaging: The basics of FDA regulation," MD+DI, 1 August 2006. [Online]. Available: https://www.mddionline.com/radiological/medical-imaging-basics-fda-regulation. [Accessed 24 September 2023].

[153] FDA, "Developing a software precertification program," January 2019. [Online]. Available: https://www.fda.gov/media/119722/download. [Accessed 24 September 2023].

[154] FDA, "Software as a Medical Device (SAMD): Clinical evaluation," December 2017. [Online]. Available: https://www.fda.gov/regulatory-information/search-fda-guidance-documents/software-medical-device-samd-clinical-evaluation. [Accessed 24 September 2023].

[155] FDA, "Device software functions including mobile medical applications," 29 September 2022. [Online]. Available: https://www.fda.gov/medical-devices/digital-health-center-excellence/device-software-functions-including-mobile-medical-applications. [Accessed 24 September 2023].

[156] US Federal Trade Commission, "Mobile health app interactive tool," December 2022. [Online]. Available: https://www.ftc.gov/business-guidance/resources/mobile-health-apps-interactive-tool. [Accessed 24 September 2023].

[157] FDA, "Clinical decision support software," 28 September 2022. [Online]. Available: https://www.fda.gov/regulatory-information/search-fda-guidance-documents/clinical-decision-support-software. [Accessed 24 September 2023].

[158] FDA, "Technical performance assessment of quantitative imaging in radiological device premarket submissions," 16 June 2022. [Online]. Available: https://www.fda.gov/media/123271/download. [Accessed 24 September 2023].

[159] FDA, "Computer-assisted detection devices applied to radiology images and radiology device data - Premarket notification [510(k)] submissions," 28 September 2022. [Online]. Available: https://www.fda.gov/media/77635/download. [Accessed 24 September 2023].

[160] FDA, "Clinical performance assessment: Considerations for computer-assisted detection devices applied to radiology images and radiology device data in premarket notification (510(k)) submissions," September 2022. [Online]. Available: https://www.fda.gov/regulatory-information/search-fda-guidance-documents/clinical-performance-assessment-considerations-computer-assisted-detection-devices-applied-radiology. [Accessed 24 September 2023].

[161] DICOM Director, "What you need to know about the recent FDA device reclassification and medical imaging," 23 March 2022. [Online]. Available: https://www.dicomdirector.com/recent-fda-device-reclassifications/. [Accessed 24 September 2023].

[162] RamSoft, "MIMPS and PACS: A quick overview on recent changes from the FDA," 31 May 2021. [Online]. Available: https://www.ramsoft.com/mimps-and-pacs-a-quick-overview-on-recent-changes-from-the-fda/. [Accessed 24 September 2023].

[163] F. Van Leeuwen, "A 101 guide to the FDA regulatory process for AI radiology software," Quantib, 20 November 2019. [Online]. Available: https://www.quantib.com/blog/a-101-guide-to-the-fda-regulatory-process-for-ai-radiology-software. [Accessed 24 September 2023].

[164] FDA, "Standards and conformity assessment program," 19 September 2023. [Online]. Available: https://www.fda.gov/medical-devices/premarket-submissions-selecting-and-preparing-correct-submission/standards-and-conformity-assessment-program. [Accessed 24 September 2023].

[165] FDA, "Recognized consensus standards: Medical devices: IEC 62304," 14 January 2019. [Online]. Available: https://www.accessdata.fda.gov/scripts/cdrh/cfdocs/cfStandards/detail.cfm?standard__identification_no=38829. [Accessed 24 September 2023].

[166] N. Tippmann, "How to leverage IEC 62304 to improve SaMD development processes," Greenlight Guru, 18 March 2020. [Online]. Available: https://www.greenlight.guru/blog/how-to-leverage-iec-62304-to-improve-samd-development-processes. [Accessed 24 September 2023].

[167] FDA, "Artificial Intelligence and Machine Learning in Software as a Medical Device", 22 September 2021. [Online]. Available: https://www.fda.gov/medical-devices/software-medical-device-samd/artificial-intelligence-and-machine-learning-software-medical-device. [Accessed 24 September 2023].

[168] FDA, "Predetermined Change Control Plans for Machine Learning-Enabled Medical Devices: Guiding Principles", 24 October 2023. [Online]. Available: https://www.fda.gov/medical-devices/software-medical-device-samd/predetermined-change-control-plans-machine-learning-enabled-medical-devices-guiding-principles. [Accessed 24 November 2023].

[169] FDA, "Artificial Intelligence and Machine Learning (AI/ML)-enabled medical devices," 5 October 2022. [Online]. Available: https://www.fda.gov/medical-devices/software-medical-device-samd/artificial-intelligence-and-machine-learning-aiml-enabled-medical-devices. [Accessed 24 September 2023].

[170] FDA, "FDA authorizes marketing of first cardiac ultrasound software that uses artificial intelligence to guide user," 7 February 2020. [Online]. Available: https://www.fda.gov/news-events/press-announcements/fda-authorizes-marketing-first-cardiac-ultrasound-software-uses-artificial-intelligence-guide-user. [Accessed 23 September 2023].

[171] FDA, "Applying human factors and usability engineering to medical devices," February 2016. [Online]. Available: https://www.fda.gov/regulatory-information/search-fda-guidance-documents/applying-human-factors-and-usability-engineering-medical-devices. [Accessed 24 September 2023].

[172] Seleon, "Usability engineering & the IEC 62366-1 for medical devices," 15 August 2021. [Online]. Available: https://www.seleon.com/en/regulatory-affairs/usability-engineering-the-iec-62366-1-for-medical-devices/. [Accessed 24 September 2023].

[173] FDA, "Human factors: Premarket information - device design and documentation processes," 10 July 2018. [Online]. Available: https://www.fda.gov/medical-devices/human-factors-and-medical-devices/human-factors-premarket-information-device-design-and-documentation-processes. [Accessed 25 September 2023].

[174] FDA, "Content of human factors information in medical device marketing submissions," December 2022. [Online]. Available: https://www.fda.gov/regulatory-information/search-fda-guidance-documents/content-human-factors-information-medical-device-marketing-submissions. [Accessed 24 September 2023].

[175] FDA, "Guidance on medical device patient labeling," 31 August 2018. [Online]. Available: https://www.fda.gov/regulatory-information/search-fda-guidance-documents/guidance-medical-device-patient-labeling. [Accessed 24 September 2023].

[176] FDA, "Cybersecurity in medical devices: Quality system considerations and content of premarket submissions," April 2022. [Online]. Available: https://www.fda.gov/regulatory-information/search-fda-guidance-documents/cybersecurity-medical-devices-quality-system-considerations-and-content-premarket-submissions. [Accessed 24 September 2023].

[177] IMDRF, "Principles and practices for software bill of materials for medical device cybersecurity," 13 April 2023. [Online]. Available: https://www.imdrf.org/documents/principles-and-practices-software-bill-materials-medical-device-cybersecurity. [Accessed 24 September 2023].

[178] FDA, "Cybersecurity in medical devices. Refuse to accept policy for cyber devices and related systems under Section 524B of the FD&C Act," March 2023. [Online]. Available: https://digirepo.nlm.nih.gov/master/borndig/9918662283106676/9918662283106676.pdf. [Accessed 24 September 2023].

[179] FDA, "Postmarket management of cybersecurity in medical devices," December 2016. [Online]. Available: https://www.fda.gov/regulatory-information/search-fda-guidance-documents/postmarket-management-cybersecurity-medical-devices. [Accessed 24 September 2023].

[180] IMDRF, "Principles and practices for medical device cybersecurity," 20 April 2020. [Online]. Available: https://www.imdrf.org/documents/principles-and-practices-medical-device-cybersecurity. [Accessed 24 September 2023].

[181] FDA, "Labeling - Regulatory requirements for medical devices (FDA 89-4203)," 31 August 2018. [Online]. Available: https://www.fda.gov/regulatory-information/search-fda-guidance-documents/labeling-regulatory-requirements-medical-devices-fda-89-4203. [Accessed 24 September 2023].

[182] IMDRF, "Label and instructions for use for medical devices," 16 September 2011. [Online]. Available: https://www.imdrf.org/sites/default/files/docs/ghtf/archived/sg1/technical-docs/ghtf-sg1-n70-2011-label-instruction-use-medical-devices-110916.pdf. [Accessed 24 September 2023].

[183] Research Collective, "Human factors and FDA: Instructions for use (IFU)," 15 November 2021. [Online]. Available: https://research-collective.com/fda-medical-device-ifu/. [Accessed 24 September 2023].

[184] FDA, "Acceptable media for electronic product user manuals," 18 March 2010. [Online]. Available: https://www.fda.gov/media/78332/download. [Accessed 24 September 2023].

[185] FDA, "Device labeling," 23 October 2020. [Online]. Available: https://www.fda.gov/medical-devices/overview-device-regulation/device-labeling. [Accessed 24 September 2023].

[186] FDA, "Unique Device Identification System (UDI System)," 22 July 2022. [Online]. Available: https://www.fda.gov/medical-devices/device-advice-comprehensive-regulatory-assistance/unique-device-identification-system-udi-system. [Accessed 24 September 2023].

[187] US National Archives, "Code of Federal regulations:," 19 September 2023. [Online]. Available: https://www.ecfr.gov/current/title-21/chapter-I/subchapter-H/part-801/subpart-B. [Accessed 24 September 2023].

[188] FDA, "Mandatory reporting requirements: Manufacturers, importers and device user facilities," 22 May 2020. [Online]. Available: https://www.fda.gov/medical-devices/postmarket-requirements-devices/mandatory-reporting-requirements-manufacturers-importers-and-device-user-facilities. [Accessed 24 September 2023].

[189] FDA, "U.S. agents," 23 December 2017. [Online]. Available: https://www.fda.gov/medical-devices/device-registration-and-listing/us-agents. [Accessed 24 September 2023].

[190] QA Consulting, "Overview of the Different Types of FDA Inspections for Medical Devices", 3 November 2023. [Online]. Available: https://qaconsultinginc.com/types-of-fda-inspections-for-medical-devices/. [Accessed 10 November 2023].

[191] FDA, "Medical device premarket approval and postmarket inspections - Part III: Inspectional," 4 December 2017. [Online]. Available: https://www.fda.gov/medical-devices/quality-and-compliance-medical-devices/medical-device-premarket-approval-and-postmarket-inspections-part-iii-inspectional. [Accessed 24 September 2023].

[192] OrielStat, "When will FDA resume medical device inspections?," 16 August 2021. [Online]. Available: https://www.orielstat.com/blog/when-will-fda-inspections-resume/. [Accessed 24 September 2023].

[193] FDA, "Conducting remote regulatory assessments," July 2022. [Online]. Available: https://www.fda.gov/media/160173/download. [Accessed 24 September 2023].

[194] J. Speer, "How to prepare for an FDA inspection," Greenlight Guru, 5 June 2017. [Online]. Available: https://www.greenlight.guru/blog/how-to-prepare-for-an-fda-inspection. [Accessed 24 September 2023].

[195] FDA, "Review and update of device establishment inspection processes and standards," 29 June 2020. [Online]. Available: https://www.fda.gov/media/139466/download. [Accessed 24 September 2023].

[196] MDCG, "MDCG 2021-5: Guidance on standardisation for medical devices," April 2021. [Online]. Available: https://health.ec.europa.eu/system/files/2021-04/md_mdcg_2021_5_cn_0.pdf. [Accessed 24 September 2023].

[197] Med Tech Europe, "Recommendations on the use of guidance documents related to the Medical Device Regulation (MDR) and In vitro Diagnostics Regulation (IVDR)," 30 June 2022. [Online]. Available: https://www.medtecheurope.org/resource-library/recommendations-on-the-use-of-guidance-documents-related-to-the-medical-device-regulation-mdr-and-in-vitro-diagnostics-regulation-ivdr/. [Accessed 24 September 2023].

[198] Johner Institute, "State of the art: It's worse than you think," 11 September 2020. [Online]. Available: https://www.johner-institute.com/articles/regulatory-affairs/and-more/state-of-the-art-its-worse-than-you-think/. [Accessed 24 September 2023].

7 Best Practice and Legal Liability

"If people are good only because they fear punishment, and hope for reward, then we are a sorry lot indeed."

Albert Einstein

7.1 OVERVIEW

Concerns about legal liability have historically been a significant deterrent for in-house developers writing software for medical applications. Raising the subject with high-level corporate managers (e.g., Risk Managers, Legal Advisors) has tended to be met with extreme caution. Finance Managers may take a different view, but only if there is potential for the health institution to generate significant income through sales of the resultant products.

Under national regulations derived from the old EU MDD, there was no legal liability for in-house medical software producers if the software was used only within the developer's own institution, but the situation changed significantly with the introduction of the EU Medical Device Regulations. Although in-house developers are exempt from the full rigour of the Regulations (provided the device is used only in-house), they must now comply with several strict conditions in order to qualify under the exemption (Section 6.3.11).

For legal purposes, the terms 'best practice' and 'state of the art' should be considered synonymous, even though their technical definitions may be subtly different. EU MDR 17 makes numerous references to "taking into account the current state of the art" and "manufactured in according with the state of the art" (Chapter 6, Appendix 1), so, for regulatory compliance, implementation of best practice techniques (as represented by harmonised standards and/or official best practice guides) is *effectively* mandatory (Section 6.3.3).

Furthermore, failure to comply with best practice techniques recommended for the manufacture of medical devices not only creates liability under MDR 17/745 but also leaves the manufacturer and supplier open to prosecution under other laws.

7.2 EUROPEAN UNION REGULATIONS

Apart from the EU Medical Device Regulations MDR 17/745, several other EU Directives and Regulations are relevant to the general issue of product safety and liability. The main one is the EU Product Liability Directive (PLD, EU 85/374/EEC) but others may be relevant, including:

- EU General Product Safety Directive (2001/95/EC)
- EU Data Protection Directive (95/46/EC)
- EU Consumer Rights Directive (2011/83/EC)

Product liability can arise either under the Tort of negligence, the strict liability imposed by the EU PLD, or contract law, as expressed in the EU Consumer Rights Directive. The General Product Safety Directive (GPSD) relates to "consumer goods", but some medical products (e.g., health apps) may be interpreted as consumer goods if sold directly to the general public. The GPSD is due to be replaced by the EU General Product Safety *Regulation* (GSPR), which is designed to establish a "safety net" for non-food consumer goods that are not regulated elsewhere. In particular, the GPSR will cover the liability of AI-based systems that are not covered under the forthcoming EU Artificial Intelligence Act (AI Act) (Section 7.2.3).

The GPSR proposals contain several new provisions for general consumer products, including product recall, information for consumers, and post-market surveillance [1]. Medical devices are not exempt from the GDSR, but product-specific legislation (i.e., medical device regulations) takes precedence over GPS regulation in areas where the provisions have similar objectives [2].

The EU Data Protection Directive was replaced by the EU General Data Protection Regulation (GDPR), which became national law in all EU member states in May 2018. The GDPR's wide scope includes "data concerning health" and is applicable to aspects of the medical device development procedure (e.g., clinical investigation) as well as the routine clinical use of the final product [3]. While most of the GDPR affects "back-end" data handling facilities (e.g., database storage and data transportation), some aspects of the GDPR affect data handling within medical devices themselves. Some items of sensitive personal information cannot be collected/processed without explicit consent [4], but these types of data are not usually collected by medical devices. Furthermore, some individual rights under the GDPR (e.g., to object to data processing and to request data deletion) do not apply to healthcare data needed for treatment. Irrespective of any consent requirements, the manufacturer has a legal obligation to protect personally identifiable patient data (e.g., medical images), which clearly involves adequate security measures (see Chapter 8). The provisions of the EU GDPR are *similar* to those contained in the US Health Insurance Portability and Accountability Act (HIPAA) [5].

Directive 2011/83/EC on consumer rights applies when an individual purchases a typical lifestyle/well-being app from an app store. Such a purchase will generally form a "distance contract" between the trader and consumer, and various rules governing cancellation and information requirements apply.

7.2.1 MEDICAL DEVICE REGULATIONS

The EU Medical Device Regulations MDR 17/745 came into force in EU member states in May 2017 and became applicable (following a permitted transition period) on 26 May 2021. Enforcement of the regulations is the responsibility of national governments, usually through their appointed competent authorities. In Germany, this is the Federal Institute for Drugs and Medical Devices (BfArM), and in France, it is the National Agency for the Safety of Medicine and Health Product (ANSM) [6].

Article 10.16 of MDR 17/745 states (under *General obligations of manufacturers*) that

> Natural or legal persons may claim compensation for damage caused by a defective device in accordance with applicable Union and national law. Manufacturers shall, in a manner that is proportionate to the risk class, type of device and the size of the enterprise, have measures in place to provide sufficient financial coverage [i.e., insurance] in respect of their potential liability under Directive 85/374/EEC, without prejudice to more protective measures under national law.

There is a similar wording in Legislative Act (LA)31.

Regarding harm caused to a human subject during a medical device clinical investigation (Section 6.3.10.2), any resultant civil or criminal liability of the investigator or the sponsor (including issues of causality and the level of damages and sanctions), shall be dealt with under relevant *national* laws (MDR17, LA 66).

7.2.1.1 Responsibilities of the Authorised Representative

Medical device manufacturers not established in an EU member state must appoint/ designate an EU-based Authorised Representative (AR) to act on their behalf regarding specific aspects of the regulation (Section 6.3.7.1.4). The definition of AR is given in Article 2(32). The tasks listed should be detailed in a written mandate issued to and formally accepted by the AR. As a minimum, the tasks should include those listed in Article 11, which include responsibilities relating to the Declaration of Conformity (Section 6.3.16). The minimum requirements for an AR should be clearly stated (in the mandate or elsewhere) and, in terms of training and qualifications, would be similar to those required for the person responsible for regulatory compliance (Section 6.3.7.1).

According to Legislative Act 35, the AR should be "made legally liable for defective devices in the event that a manufacturer established outside the Union has not complied with its general obligations". The liability of the AR specified in MDR17 is without prejudice to the provisions of EU PLD 85/374/EEC (see below), and, accordingly, the AR would be jointly and severally liable, along with the manufacturer and (where relevant) the importer.

The EU requirement for an AR is superficially similar to the US FDA requirement for a US Agent (Section 6.5.10), but the latter is essentially a local contact with whom the FDA can easily communicate and pass messages regarding site inspections, etc. to the foreign manufacturer.

7.2.2 EU PRODUCT LIABILITY DIRECTIVE 85/374/EEC

Directive 85/374/EEC is known as the EU PLD. Published in 1985, it introduced the concept of "strict liability" in respect of defective products, whereby a claimant must only prove:

1. That the product was defective
2. That damage was suffered
3. A causal link between 1 and 2

Unlike the common law of negligence, the claimant does not have to prove that the producer breached his duty of care or was in any way at fault (i.e., provides "no-fault liability"). The Directive applies whether a product was supplied to an individual consumer or to a business.

7.2.2.1 Key Definitions

7.2.2.1.1 Product

Under the PLD, a producer is liable for damages caused by a defect in its product. For these purposes, a product is defined as "all movables, even if incorporated into another movable or into an immovable", and this definition includes electricity (Article 2, PLD). A "movable" is interpreted as a movable object, that corresponds to a physical or tangible product [7].

The position of so-called "intangibles", such as software, has been much less clear. Although embedded software in a hardware device would probably be construed as a component product under the EU PLD, the position of *standalone* software (and therefore standalone medical software, including apps) has always been in doubt [7]. The doubts will, however, be removed if the EC's plans to radically revise the 1985 PLD are enacted [8].

As well as increasing the scope of product liability law to include "loss or corruption of data", the proposals include a new definition of a product as "All movables, even if integrated into another movable or into an immovable", with a rider that "Product" includes electricity, digital manufacturing files, *and* software.

The proposed PLD is designed to complement the EU AI Act (Section 7.2.3), which aims to ensure that "high-risk" AI systems (including medical devices) comply with safety and fundamental rights requirements (e.g., data governance, transparency, and human oversight). It is claimed that the PLD proposal:

> will ensure that when AI systems are defective and cause physical harm, property damage or data loss it is possible to seek compensation from the AI system provider or from any manufacturer that integrates an AI system into another product [9].

7.2.2.1.2 Defect

A product is defective if "the safety of the product is not such that persons are generally entitled to expect". In determining this, the following factors are taken into consideration:

1. The manner and purposes for which the product has been marketed, for instance, the packaging, the use of a mark, any warnings on the product, and instructions will be considered.
2. What might reasonably be expected to be done with or in relation to the product.
3. The time when the product was supplied by its producer.

Manufacturers can therefore protect themselves (to some extent) by placing appropriate warnings on their products and including adequate instructions for use.

It should be noted, however, that the Court of Justice of the European Union (CJEU) has held that, for *certain products* (including medical devices), the safety level that the consumer is entitled to expect is particularly high, due to the "inherent function of the product, the vulnerability of the typical user and its abnormal potential for damage that the product presents" [10].

7.2.2.1.3 Damage

Harm is established under the PLD when there has been "any damage", which means that any person who suffers damage as a result of the defective product is entitled to claim compensation, irrespective of whether they purchased the product.

Damage can be personal injury (or even death), or material damage to property. The degree of personal injury is not specified but the threshold for financial compensation (for any type of action) is currently 500 Euros, thereby avoiding trivial claims. The Directive allows member states to impose a maximum compensation limit, which may not be less than €70 million. The injured person has three years within which to seek compensation, starting from the date on which they became aware of the damage, the defect, and the identity of the producer. The damage must have been caused wholly or partly by the defect, meaning that it must at least have been a significant contributory factor.

7.2.2.1.4 Producer

A "producer" would usually be the manufacturer or the product, including any business or organisation involved in the manufacturing process. This means that more than one party could be held liable. The producer is only liable (under the PLD) for a period of ten years after the product in question was placed on the market.

7.2.2.2 Development Risk Defence

Several legitimate defences are permitted under the EU PLD but the development risk defence is the most controversial. Its purpose was to strike a balance between protecting the consumer without discouraging innovative research, but some argue that it undermines the principle of strict liability [11]. In short, a producer will not be held liable for damages caused by his product if he can successfully invoke the development risk defence.

The phrases "development risk defence" and "state-of-the-art (SOTA) defence" are often used interchangeably but they relate to different aspects of the legal liability issue. Development risk relates to undiscoverable defects, whereas SOTA (see Chapter 6, Appendix 1) relates more to the question of defectiveness. The development risk defence is set out in Article 7(e) of the European Directive on Product Liability as follows:

> "The producer shall not be liable ... if he proves that the state of scientific and technical knowledge at the time when he put the product into circulation was not such as to enable the existence of the defect to be discovered." It could be optionally omitted by EU member states in the process of transposition into national law, but all except one country chose to incorporate it. However, different interpretations were placed on the word "knowledge" (see Section 7.4.2).

7.2.2.3 Summary

Taken together, the proposed changes for a new EU PLD would undoubtedly *increase* the potential for product liability litigation within EU member states. The proposals have been opposed by MedTech Europe (the European trade association representing the medical technology industries), on the basis that nearly all the new issues raised in the EC proposals could be dealt with under the existing PLD legislation [12].

More information on the scope of applicable product liability legislation, including relevant judgements made in the German courts and in the European Court of Justice (ECJ), can be viewed on the Johner Institute website [13].

7.2.3 EU AI Act

The new EU AI Act has been touted as a groundbreaking piece of legislation that will lay the legal foundations of all AI-based products and services within the EU [14]. It passed through the first important Parliamentary stage of the adoption process on 14 June 2023 and is set to become law during 2024 [15].

The Act is generic in nature, grouping all AI product types into one of three risk classes: *Unacceptable risk,*[1] *high risk, and limited risk*. The mandatory requirements of the Act will apply *only* to high-risk systems. Title IX of the Act describes a framework for the creation of voluntary *codes of conduct* that "aim to encourage providers of *non-high-risk* AI systems to apply voluntarily the mandatory requirements for high-risk AI systems (as laid out in Title III)".

Products that qualify as medical devices (under the EU MDR) are defined as "high risk", while other health-related devices (e.g., fitness trackers, wellbeing apps) are classed as "limited risk". According to the draft of the EC's 2020 White paper on AI [16], high-risk devices will be subject to *general* requirements (e.g., quality management system, pre-market conformity assessment, post-market surveillance system) as well as AI-specific ones related to training data governance, information provided to users, human oversight, robustness/cybersecurity, technical documentation, and risk management.

The AI Act is designed to be consistent with existing EU legislation covering sectors in which AI-based systems are already used – a task that always presents problems of overlap and contradiction. Several trade associations published strong views on the draft legislation, including representatives of the European medical device industry.

In the Explanatory Memorandum that accompanied the draft legislation, it was stated (Section 2.3: Proportionality) that

> ...for high-risk AI systems, the requirements of high quality data, documentation and traceability, transparency, human oversight, accuracy and robustness, are strictly necessary to mitigate the risks to fundamental rights and safety posed by AI and that are not covered by other existing legal frameworks.

---

[1] AI-based products/applications deemed to constitute an "unacceptable risk", based on infringement of civil liberties or other basic human rights will simply be banned from the EU market.

However, when these requirements are covered, to some degree, in sectorial legislation then questions of legal precedence arise. In fact, the lack of clarity on issues of precedence was one of the concerns expressed by MedTech Europe[2] in its assessment of the draft AI Act, along with concerns regarding the definition of AI and the assessment of existing notified bodies [17].

Furthermore, a report by the European Coordination Committee of the Radiological, Electromedical, and Healthcare IT Industry (COCIR)[3] concluded that the provisions of the existing EU medical device regulations are sufficient to ensure the general objectives stated in the European Commission's 2020 White Paper on AI. Future implications of the EU AI Act for medical device manufacturers are discussed further in Section 9.5.5.

7.2.4 VICARIOUS LIABILITY

There is usually no question of any individual software developer being prosecuted under the medical device or product liability legislation, as the employer will normally be held vicariously liable for the actions of its employees. The important condition is that the employee was performing an authorised task or duty when the incident occurred.

The legal doctrine of vicarious liability will exist in all EU countries (and most other countries in the world), but the wording of the relevant Tort, common, or civil laws may vary, particularly regarding the nature of the relationship between employer and employee.

The proviso that the employee was engaged in an approved activity at the time of the incident is an interesting one for in-house developers, as it relates directly to the content of job descriptions (Sections 2.3 and 2.6). In short, any healthcare scientist engaged in software development that could give rise to a legal liability issue should have the responsibility clearly stated in their job description. Otherwise, the employer may be able to argue that the member of staff was acting outside his/her area of competence (i.e., in an unauthorised manner).

7.3 US REGULATIONS

7.3.1 MEDICAL DEVICE REGULATIONS

Under the power invested in it by Section 1003 of the Federal Food, Drug, and Cosmetic Act (FD&C Act), the FDA can take or recommend corrective action against a device manufacturer, importer, distributor, or other registrant if the agency finds that such registrant is in violation of FD&C Act requirements or FDA regulations. However, while the FDA has significant authority to promote compliance with and to investigate violations of the FD&C Act (including the issuing of warning letters), it does not have independent litigating authority [18].

---

[2] MedTech Europe is the European trade association for the medical technology industry, including diagnostics, medical devices, and digital health.

[3] COCIR is the European trade association representing the medical imaging, radiotherapy, health ICT and electromedical industries.

The FDA must therefore coordinate with the US Department of Justice (DOJ) to enforce the Act through product seizures, injunctions, civil penalty proceedings, or (in extreme cases) criminal prosecutions. Other federal agencies may play a role in enforcing discrete parts of the FD&C Act but individuals have no right of redress through private lawsuits.

Note that FDA guidance documents do not establish legally enforceable responsibilities (Section 6.5.3.1).

7.3.2 PRODUCTS LIABILITY LAW

Products liability claims can be based on negligence, strict liability, or breach of warranty. This will typically depend on the jurisdiction within which the claim is based since there is no federal products liability law. This lack of uniformity has prompted the US Department of Commerce to publish the Model Uniform Products Liability Act (MUPLA), which attempts to encourage more standardisation in the application of products liability legislation.

The question of whether embedded or standalone medical software constitutes a product under US products legislation is still contentious. Some argue that software embedded in a physical medical device sufficiently resembles a tangible device to be considered a product under strict liability law, but the law is unsettled [19]. Clearly, the position of standalone software, including medical apps, is even more contentious in this regard. Most wellness apps are not considered medical devices by the FDA (Section 6.5.3.4.1) but apps that *are* medical devices (and may thus be regarded as products) may fall under the purview of products liability legislation [20].

Proponents of product liability for software medical devices (including AI-based devices) claim that it would help fill the gaps in medical device legislation and help incentivise quality improvement and accountability amongst device software producers [21]. Plaintiffs in the US have successfully brought product liability claims against medical device manufacturers but so far only for traditional hardware devices, such as cardiac pacemakers.

With no definitive case law and arguments for and against, the legal position on product liability for SaMD and AIiMD is fluid. However, if a claim based on strict liability is not possible, a claim under negligence is still possible, albeit more difficult to prove.

The definition of negligence in US law is similar but not identical to that used in UK law: Namely, "A failure to behave with the level of care that someone of ordinary prudence would have exercised under the same circumstances" [22]. The behaviour usually consists of actions, but can also consist of omissions when there is some duty to act.

For developers of medical software products generally, and mobile medical apps in particular, there are a number of other US federal laws and regulations law that might apply – to do with data access, protection, and security (Section 6.5.8.5). As stated above, most wellness apps are exempt from FDA regulation but compliance with GMP requirements outlined in the QSR (Section 6.5.6) may offer some defence against products liability claims, or claims of negligence or breach of warranty [23].

7.4   UK REGULATIONS

The UK has three separate legal systems (one for England and Wales, one for Scotland, and one for Northern Ireland) but Acts of Parliament made in Westminster (including the laws referred to below) apply to all constituent parts of the UK. Definitions and interpretations made under common law (i.e., that arising from case law) may vary between jurisdictions.

7.4.1   UK Medical Device Regulations 2002

The UK Medical Devices Regulations 2002 (SI 2002 No 618, as amended) (UK MDR) implemented the EU Directives relating to implantable medical devices, medical devices, and in vitro diagnostic medical devices (IVDs). Pending the issuance of new medical device regulations (expected July 2025) the UK MDR 2002 continues to have effect in Great Britain (Section 6.4.1).

Apart from the Medical Devices Regulations 2002, the MHRA also has enforcement powers under the Consumer Protection Act 1987 and the General Product Safety Regulations 2005 [24]. If the MHRA considers that a manufacturer has committed a serious offence by failing to comply with any of the above regulations, or the conditions of a notice issued, the manufacturer may then be subject to prosecution, which could carry a penalty of an unlimited fine and/or six months' imprisonment.

7.4.2   UK Consumer Protection Act 1987

Part 1 of the UK Consumer Protection Act (CPA87) implemented EU PLD 85/374/EEC (Section 7.2.2) by introducing a regime of strict liability for damage arising from defective products. Part 2 created government powers to regulate the safety of consumer products through statutory instruments and Part 3 defined the giving of misleading price information as a criminal offence. Some consumer advice agencies state categorically that standalone software is not covered as a product under CPA87 [25] but this has not yet been proven in case law.

The essential principles of the Consumer Protection Act 1987 are the same as the EU PLD. Namely, that the injured party only must prove that a defective product caused harm/damage, not that the producer was negligent – which is more difficult to prove (Section 7.4.3).

7.4.2.1   Development Risk Defence

The UK CPA 87 implemented the "development risk defence" allowed by the EU PLD (Section 7.2.2.2), but the interpretation was relatively narrow. In short, a defence was created "if the state of scientific and technical knowledge at the time the product was manufactured was not such that the *producer of a similar product* might have been expected to discover the defect". Clearly, this interpretation gives the defence a better chance of success compared with the wording of the law at the European level, which deals with the state of scientific and technical knowledge generally.

7.4.3   Negligence and Common Law

Although a claim of negligence is unlikely to occur in the context of medical device *software*, it is important for software producers to understand the basic principles as there remains considerable doubt whether software represents a product under the 1985 EU PLD, and therefore CPA87. If software were to be regarded as a *service*, CPA87 would not apply, but a person suffering injury could pursue an action in negligence or breach of contract [26].

National laws based on the 1985 EU PLD place a "no-fault liability" on the producer of a product, whereas a claim made in negligence is based on "at-fault liability", where the claimant must prove that the manufacturer/supplier was negligent according to national law.

7.4.3.1   Definitions of Negligence

We tend to think of negligence in terms of "gross negligence" (involving reckless or irresponsible behaviour) but in English common law[4] it is simply defined as "Any act or omission which falls short of the standard to be expected of the reasonable person". However, for a claim of negligence to succeed, it is necessary to establish (a) that a duty of care was owed by the defendant to the claimant, (b) that the duty was breached, (c) that the claimant's loss was caused by the breach of duty and (d) that the loss fell within the defendant's scope of duty and was a foreseeable consequence of the breach of duty [27].

Definitions used in healthcare tend to be more specific and usually relate to the treatment of a patient by a healthcare professional (HCP). For example, clinical (or medical) negligence is deemed to have occurred when a HCP deviates from the care standards of their profession and causes injury to a patient [28]; the expected standard of care being judged by a HCP working in the same field with an ordinary level of skill and competence.

For staff working within the UK NHS, clinical negligence is defined as:

> a breach of duty of care by members of the health care professions or others consequent on decisions or judgments made by members of those professions acting in their professional capacity in the course of their employment, and which are admitted as negligent by the employer or are determined as such through the legal process [29].

7.4.4   UK Consumer Rights Act 2015

The UK Consumer Rights Act 2015 is an instrument of contract law. It was not directly derived from EU Directive 2011/83/EC but was a consolidation and extension of UK consumer protection laws derived, in part, from the earlier (1999) EU Directive on Consumer Rights (1999/44/EC) [30]. The Act contains new provisions for digital content.

---

[4] English common law applies to England and Wales. Variations may apply in Scotland and Northern Ireland.

7.4.5   Vicarious Liability

In UK common law, an employer can be held responsible for the wrongful actions or omissions of an employee if it can be shown that they took place "in the course of their employment". That is, where there is sufficient connection between the employee's position and the wrongful conduct to make it appropriate for the employer to be held responsible. In other words, was the employee acting in an officially authorised manner?

As is often the case with common law, it has taken a recent judgement by the UK Supreme Court to confirm that an employer will *not* generally be held vicariously liable for the actions of an employee if that employee acted in an unauthorised, irresponsible, or malicious manner [31]. In such cases, an individual criminal or civil action may be brought against the employee.

The UK NHS has its own rules (derived from national law) on full liability and vicarious liability, given the high probability of expensive clinical negligence claims that occur in certain branches of healthcare. NHS bodies are held vicariously liable for the acts and/or omissions of their employees and remain liable for any clinical negligence and other negligent harm to individuals [e.g., patients] covered by the duty of care owed to them. This is mainly because NHS bodies will be easier to successfully sue than individual employees, especially in cases where life-changing personal injury claims can run into £millions. As a result, NHS bodies need to have insurance to cover such large financial liabilities (Section 7.4.6).

In the unlikely event of a fault in an in-house developed medical device leading to a prosecution under medical device or product liability legislation, the employer would therefore be held liable if the employee in question was acting in an *authorised manner*. In deciding this, a court would probably look, amongst other things, at the content of the person's job description and the way the person was managed within the organisation.

Most roles and responsibilities within the job description of a given grade of HCP (e.g., Radiographer, Rehabilitation Engineer) will be standard but some roles will be non-standard. For most healthcare scientists working in Medical Physics and Clinical Engineering, medical software development would be a non-standard role. For non-standard roles that may give rise to legal liability issues, it may be prudent for staff carrying out those roles to obtain official confirmation of their vicarious liability protection from the Chief Executive or nominated deputy.

The documentation often obtained by staff undertaking certain recognised "extended roles"[5] may serve as a model. For example, senior clinical scientists and radiographers may undertake clinical reporting of medical images, subject to suitable training and ongoing supervision by a Consultant Radiologist. In this case, the letter of authorisation from the Chief Executive to the employee would typically state that the employing authority duly accepts vicarious liability for the individual's clinical reporting activities (e.g., in the event of a claim arising from an incorrect patient diagnosis due to an error in a clinical report), *provided that* the individual adheres strictly to the conditions for unsupervised reporting laid down (in writing) by the named Radiologist.

---

[5] A role extension recognised by the appropriate professional body for this grade of staff.

It is acknowledged that medical software development may not be considered a recognised extended role for most healthcare scientists in the same way as clinical reporting, but it is nonetheless a non-standard or atypical role that may benefit from the same approach. Clearly, vicarious liability would not be an issue for dedicated software development staff working within scientific computing departments (Section 2.6) as they would be *specifically employed* to develop and manage clinical software.

7.4.6 Insuring Against Product Liability Claims

NHS indemnity is the process by which NHS bodies provide indemnity for liabilities, based on Department of Health Circular HSG(96)48. NHS Trusts may carry the risk themselves or insure against it through the Clinical Negligence Scheme for Trusts (CNST), which is part of the risk pooling scheme for NHS Trusts [32]. The Scottish NHS equivalent is the Clinical Negligence and Other Risks Indemnity Scheme (CNORIS) [33].

If the employing hospital Trust is signed up to the Liabilities to Third Parties Scheme (LTPS), run by the NHS Litigation Authority (NHSLA), this indemnifies it and its employees for their legal liability in the event of claims arising from "non-clinical risks" (e.g., public and product liability and "professional negligence", amongst other things). It appears that the scheme covers medical software transfer within the NHS (whether sold or not), but does not cover supply to non-NHS bodies. For the latter, the trust would need to take out separate commercial professional indemnity insurance.

The NHSLA has indicated that an NHS Trust supplying a medical device to another trust should state in the associated contract/disclaimer that it can only be held responsible for any claim for which it is legally responsible under its NHSLA participation. That is, it cannot accept responsibility for the use, interpretation, and application of the software in other NHS Trusts or outside establishments, thus putting the onus on the receiving hospital to do its own thorough testing/validation prior to any routine clinical use.

7.5 BEST PRACTICE

The terms "best practice" and "state-of-the-art"[6] may be considered synonymous from a strict legal perspective, but it is helpful to think of a best practice guide (BPG) as an expression of the state of the art on a given subject or technique. The adoption of best practice advice for medical device manufacturing can provide a measure of legal protection for producers but is clearly desirable for purely professional reasons.

At the more basic level, registered healthcare scientists working in public healthcare institutions have a *professional obligation* to maintain and develop knowledge and competence[7] and only undertake work that they are competent to perform [34].

---

[6] As used in EU MDR 17, the term 'state of the art' does not necessarily imply the most technologically advanced approach (Chapter 6, Appendix 1).

[7] Competence relates to a person's ability to perform a task/role to a satisfactory or safe standard. It does not *necessarily* involve the use of state-of-the-art techniques. For example, a young person who has just passed his/her driving test is judged competent to drive a car on public roads.

The American Association of Physicists in Medicine (AAPM) Code of Ethics is more specific on the question of competence, stating that members "must undertake only work that they are *qualified* to perform" [35].

An international standard is arguably the ultimate expression of a good practice guide (Chapter 5), so adherence to relevant standards and associated official guidance produced by professional bodies and government agencies is important for all manufacturers, but particularly for in-house medical software developers working in public healthcare for whom it is often not a core responsibility (Section 2.6.1). In this context, IPEM has published a comprehensive BPG for in-house medical device development, aimed at medical physicists and clinical engineers working in the UK health service [36].

Software-related BPGs are available for other healthcare sectors, but most are produced by consortia of industry representatives. For example, the GAMP® 5 Guide (*A Risk-Based Approach to Compliant GxP Computerized Systems*) issued by the (US-based) International Society for Pharmaceutical Engineering (ISPE) [37].

Policy statements issued by European national professional bodies on the roles and responsibilities of healthcare scientists generally focus on acceptance testing and general quality assurance of *commercial* medical software [38], whereas those outlining recognised activities of healthcare scientists working in dedicated clinical scientific computing departments/units will tend to include reference to in-house software development.

At the pan-European level, the European Federation of Organisations for Medical Physics (EFOMP) referred to the in-house development of medical device software development in its 2014 policy document on education and training [39] but did not provide guidance on how it should be conducted.

In the US, best practice recommendations by the AAPM on computer-based applications in healthcare focus on performance assessment and quality control of commercial software [40].

For in-house medical software developers, BPG on in-house manufacture of medical devices produced by national professional bodies or other recognised expert groups should be regarded in the same way as an Approved Code of Practice issued in support of radiation protection regulations: They are essential voluntary procedures, but professionals working in the field would need a very good reason not to follow them. BPGs are especially useful as they contain practical advice on *how* to comply with mandatory legal requirements that are often missing from the regulations themselves.

An appraisal of relevant BPGs should be included in the department's software development policy, along with the rationale behind the selection of the adopted guides (Chapter 2, Appendix 1).

7.6 INTELLECTUAL PROPERTY

This Chapter has so far concentrated on the legal liabilities of the medical software producer, but intellectual property rights (IPR) are concerned with *protecting* the developer. Ownership rights are generally well covered in commercial organisations for obvious reasons, but medical software producers working in public-sector organisations (e.g., healthcare institutions) will need to obtain help and advice from their parent organisation.

There are several types of IP (including trademarks and patents) but the one most relevant to all in-house developers is copyright [41]. Most large hospitals will have a policy on IPR (usually written by the Research & Development Department if one exists) and further advice is available centrally in most European countries. In England, for example, this is provided by the NHS Innovation Service [42].

The strict legal position on IP is that anything produced by an employee within the scope of his or her duties will belong to the employer. The position with external consultants is the reverse, so advice needs to be taken if non-employees are to have any involvement in the creation of the software (Section 2.2.5). If a user-developer undertakes work on a project out of normal working hours an arrangement may be made whereby any proceeds from commercial exploitation of the IP (if that is intended) can be shared between the developer (employee) and the Trust on a basis typically described in the IPR policy.

Some copyright considerations associated with the use of AI technology are discussed briefly in Section 9.5.5.

7.6.1 OPEN-SOURCE SOFTWARE LICENSING

The potential use of free and open-source software (FOSS) in the in-house development of medical device software was briefly discussed in Chapter 2, but we now consider the broader legal issues. FOSS is an umbrella term encompassing "free software" and "open-source software": two closely related and much-confused terms [43]. For simplicity, we refer to open-source software (OSS), but most of the comments also apply to free software.

In terms of medical device regulations and associated standards, FOSS should be treated as third-party off-the-shelf software (OTSS), so the requirements for incorporation of SOUP described in ISO 62304 apply. For the US market specifically, FDA guidelines on the use of OTTS in medical devices are applicable (Section 5.4.1.11). For FOSS used in production or quality systems software, Section 6 of FDA software validation guidelines applies, but these are set to be replaced by the computer software assurance (CSA) guidelines (Section 6.5.8.3).

It is sometimes claimed that the nature of commonly used open-source licences may limit the legal liability of the originating author, but this is contentious. For example, MDR17 applies to both FOSS distribution methods, since applicability depends only on the product being "placed on the market" (i.e., not necessarily sold). In regulatory terms, a "computer program" includes OSS, and may also include un-compiled software generally, if the information required for installation is provided by the original producer(s) [44].

OSS licences are essentially concerned with copyright and how the legal rights of the originating developer are transferred when the software (in the form of source code) is distributed. Traditionally, copyright was something that creators of original works (in whatever area) wished to protect and commercially exploit, but the open-source movement runs contrary to this, being founded on a share-and-share-alike principle for the benefit of society as a whole. With conventional proprietary software, ownership remains with the producer or creator, as does the copyright and any related IP. All use of such software is controlled by an end-user licence agreement (EULA). Although there is a *conceptual* waiving of copyright in the case of OSS, organisations representing the open-source community ensure, through the provision of open-source licences, that the author and their copyright is duly recognised and acknowledged whenever such OSS is redistributed or shared with other users, with or without modification [45]. In summary, most OSS is still effectively copyright protected, and infringement of its terms and conditions stated in the accompanying license may result in legal copyright infringement.

There are several non-profit organisations, such as the Apache Software Foundation, the Open-Source Initiative (OSI), and the Free Software Foundation (FSF), that oversee the open-source market and determine what can be declared an open-source license under the terms of the open-source definition [46].

Licences differ considerably in how amendments and 'derivative works' (i.e., derived software products) are handled, so it is important to choose one most suited to your philosophy and working practices. Most open-source licences are of the "copyleft" (or restrictive) variety,[8] which essentially means that derivative works must be distributed using the same license as the original.

In contrast, permissive open-source licences allow for derived software products to be (a) proprietary and (b) commercially exploited. The Berkley Software Distribution (BSD) license and the Massachusetts Institute of Technology (MIT) license are examples of permissive open-source licences.

However, to further complicate the issue, there are two types of copyleft licences – referred to as "strong copyleft" and "weak copyleft". For software distributed under a strong copyleft license (e.g., the GNU General Public License, GPL) any derivative work must be distributed under the *same* open license. There are several weak (i.e., less restrictive) copyleft licences, the most notable being the GNU Lesser General Public License (LGPL), which effectively straddles the line between strong copyleft and permissive licences.

The way in which collaborative open-source projects are managed and controlled is defined in legalistic terms by the use of "contributor agreements", which specify the mechanism by which contributions are accepted and the distribution conditions for derived products. The two main types of contributor agreements are the Contributor Assignment Agreement (CAA) and the Contributor License Agreement (CLA), the latter being generally recommended for public sector projects [47].

Under such formal arrangements "the project" must be a legal entity, although it can also be represented by certain umbrella organisations (e.g., Apache Software Foundation). CLA templates and instructions for use are available online [48].

There are two distinct situations relating to the use of OSS in a medical device setting: Releasing a "finished" software product under an open-source license agreement, and simply *using* open-source components as part of the overall software build.

---

[8] The term "copyleft" is a deliberate subversion of the word "copyright"; the "left" just implies the "opposite direction of travel" to traditional (protective) copyright. It is not a reference to "something being left behind".

Releasing software under an open-source licence involves an implicit legal liability for the authors, just as for proprietary or non-FOSS software, and may even present a more complicated scenario in situations where it is difficult to determine individual or collective responsibility for defective code. This is a particular concern for medical and other safety-related applications where, unlike general consumer goods, the potential liability is much greater than a simple refund of the purchase price. Under EU medical devices regulation, the identity of the "producer" must be clear, mainly (as for general product liability legislation) to make the legal redress process for any injured party as straightforward as possible.

The second (more common) situation is the incorporation of open-source components (typically library functions) into a medical device that predominately comprises proprietary software written by the medical device manufacturer. In this case, selecting OSS available under a permissive or semi-permissive licence will make the integration process more straightforward from a *general* legal perspective [49].

Open-source licences may be slightly different in intent to EULAs associated with *general purpose* commercial software such as Microsoft Office® [50], but they still contain warranty disclaimers and statements about limitation of liability. For example, the GNU GPL licence states that the software comes without warranty of any kind and that "the entire risk as to the quality and performance of the program is with you" [the user].

It is useful to contrast the above terms and conditions with those typically associated with commercial proprietary medical software. Here, the manufacturer may warranty that the software is fit for purpose (in a specific medical context) and provide ongoing maintenance and support, thus accepting responsibility for it. This implies that trust can be placed on the quality of the software, but commercial manufacturers still emphasise (in their license agreements) that the software should be tested locally. For diagnostic medical software, it is also generally stated that the output from the software should not be used as the sole means of diagnosing a particular disease or condition (Section 2.4.1).

Having expressed justified caution regarding the use of OSS, its use in the Med Tech industry is certainly increasing, with some notable large manufacturers adopting the open-source development model with enthusiasm [51]. There are also those who make the case for medical software to be developed "in the open", where problematic issues such as transparency and security may be better handled [52,53].

In the US, specific recommendations for the much wider use of FOSS in medical devices have been made by the Software Freedom Law Centre (SFLC), with calls for the FDA to require medical device manufacturers to publish the source code for implantable medical devices, thus making it open to public and regulatory scrutiny.

Ultimately, the medical device software producer is legally responsible for the whole product, including any carefully selected OS components, so the choice is essentially a risk management issue. Under current US and EU medical device regulations, it is probably preferable to limit the use of OS components to the relatively low-risk parts of the device software, as this will make their inclusion easier to justify (Chapter 2, Appendix1).

REFERENCES

[1] R. Freeman and T. Bischofberger, "Consumer product safety reforms one step closer in Europe – Productwise," Cooley, 23 December 2022. [Online]. Available: https://products.cooley.com/2022/12/23/consumer-product-safety-reforms-one-step-closer-in-europe/. [Accessed 20 September 2023].

[2] DBIS, "Product safety for manufacturers," Department for Business, Innovation and Skills. [Online]. Available: https://www.gov.uk/product-safety-for-manufacturers, 2013.

[3] FME, "MDR guide for medical device software," 27 September 2021. [Online]. Available: https://www.fme.nl/system/files/publicaties/2021-09/MDR%20Guide.pdf. [Accessed 20 September 2023].

[4] J. K. Barchie, "What is GDPR's effect on medical devices," Med Device Online, 30 April 2018. [Online]. Available: https://www.meddeviceonline.com/doc/what-is-gdpr-s-effect-on-medical-devices-0001. [Accessed 20 September 2023].

[5] P. Cosgriff and J. Åtting, "Regulatory considerations when deploying your software in a clinical environment," in *Diagnostic Radiology Physics with MATLAB*, London: CRC Press, 2021, pp. 121–125.

[6] European Medicines Agency, "National competent authorities (human) | European Medicines Agency," [Online]. Available: https://www.ema.europa.eu/en/partners-networks/eu-partners/eu-member-states/national-competent-authorities-human. [Accessed 20 September 2023].

[7] A. Krause, O. Becker, "Liability for software under the current Product Liability Directive," 18 March 2022. [Online]. Available: https://www.linklaters.com/en/insights/blogs/productliabilitylinks/2022/march/liability-for-software-under-the-current. [Accessed 20 September 2023].

[8] J. Leadley, K. Corby, J. Redmond and L. Gest, "EU: Modernised Product Liability Directive proposal finally arrives - Baker McKenzie InsightPlus," Baker McKenzie InsightPlus, 10 October 2022. [Online]. Available: https://insightplus.bakermckenzie.com/bm/consumer goods-retail_1/eu-modernised-product-liability-directive-proposal-finally-arrives. [Accessed 20 September 2023].

[9] European Union, "Proposal for a DIRECTIVE OF THE EUROPEAN PARLIAMENT AND OF THE COUNCIL on liability for defective products," 28 September 2022. [Online]. Available: https://eur-lex.europa.eu/legal-content/EN/TXT/?uri=CELEX%3A52022PC0495. [Accessed 20 September 2023].

[10] R. Freeman, C. Temple, C. Bischofberger, S. Dobson and C. Roberts, "Product liability and safety in the EU: Overview," Cooley LLP, 01 August 2020. [Online]. Available: https://uk.practicallaw.thomsonreuters.com/w-013-0379. [Accessed 20 November 2023].

[11] LexisNexis, "'Development risks' or 'state of the art' defence to defective product liability," [Online]. Available: https://www.lexisnexis.co.uk/legal/commentary/efp/sale-of-goods-vol-34/388-scientific-technical-knowledge-defence-to-defective-product-liability. [Accessed 20 November 2023].

[12] MedTech Europe, "Product liability rules and the medical technology sector," 07 July 2022. [Online]. Available: https://www.medtecheurope.org/wp-content/uploads/2022/09/20220712_position-paper_final.pdf. [Accessed 20 September 2023].

[13] S. Seubert, "Product liability: Medical device manufacturers pay attention!," Johner Institute, 11 February 2021. [Online]. Available: https://www.johner-institute.com/articles/regulatory-affairs/and-more/product-liability/. [Accessed 20 September 2023].

[14] European Union, "Proposal for a REGULATION OF THE EUROPEAN PARLIAMENT AND OF THE COUNCIL LAYING DOWN HARMONISED RULES ON ARTIFICIAL INTELLIGENCE (ARTIFICIAL INTELLIGENCE ACT) AND AMENDING

CERTAIN UNION LEGISLATIVE ACTS," 21 April 2021. [Online]. Available: https://eur-lex.europa.eu/legal-content/EN/TXT/?uri=celex%3A52021PC0206. [Accessed 20 September 2023].

[15] European Parliament, "EU AI Act: First regulation on artificial intelligence | News | European Parliament," 08 June 2023. [Online]. Available: https://www.europarl.europa.eu/news/en/headlines/society/20230601STO93804/eu-ai-act-first-regulation-on-artificial-intelligence. [Accessed 20 September 2023].

[16] European Commission, "White paper on artificial intelligence: A European approach to excellence and trust," 19 February 2020. [Online]. Available: https://commission.europa.eu/publications/white-paper-artificial-intelligence-european-approach-excellence-and-trust_en. [Accessed 20 September 2023].

[17] MedTech Europe, "MedTech Europe's reaction to the EU Council's General Approach on the AI Act", 7 December 2022. [Online]. Available: https://www.medtecheurope.org/resource-library/medtech-europes-reaction-to-the-eu-councils-general-approach-on-the-ai-act/. [Accessed 20 September 2023].

[18] Congressional Research Service, "Enforcement of the food, drug, and cosmetic act: Select legal issues," 09 February 2018. [Online]. Available: https://crsreports.congress.gov/product/pdf/R/R43609/10. [Accessed 20 September 2023].

[19] S. E. Dyson, "Medical device software & products liability: An overview (Part I) - MedTech Intelligence," MedTech Intelligence, 15 September 2017. [Online]. Available: https://medtechintelligence.com/feature_article/medical-device-software-products-liability-overview-part/. [Accessed 20 September 2023].

[20] S. E. Dyson, "Medical device software & products liability: The homefront (Part II) - MedTech Intelligence," MedTech Intelligence, 27 November 2017. [Online]. Available: https://medtechintelligence.com/feature_article/medical-device-software-products-liability-homefront-part-ii/. [Accessed 20 September 2023].

[21] Barbara J. Evans and Frank Pasquale, "Product liability suits for FDA-regulated AI/ML software," in *The Future of Medical Device Regulation*, Cambridge University Press, Cambridge, UK, 2022, pp. 22–35.

[22] Cornell Law School, "Negligence | Wex | US Law | LII/Legal Information Institute," [Online]. Available: https://www.law.cornell.edu/wex/negligence. [Accessed 20 September 2023].

[23] K. Crobar, "General wellness v. medical device considerations - NYS Science & Technology Law Center – Syracuse University," Syracuse University, 09 April 2021. [Online]. Available: https://nysstlc.syr.edu/general-wellness-v-medical-device-considerations/. [Accessed 20 September 2023].

[24] Medicines & Healthcare Products Regulatory Agency, "Medical devices: The regulations and how we enforce them - GOV.UK," 01 July 2023. [Online]. Available: https://www.gov.uk/government/publications/report-a-non-compliant-medical-device-enforcement-process/how-mhra-ensures-the-safety-and-quality-of-medical-devices. [Accessed 20 September 2023].

[25] Which?, "Consumer Protection Act 1987 - Which?," 04 August 2022. [Online]. Available: https://www.which.co.uk/consumer-rights/regulation/consumer-protection-act-1987-a5xTL3w6L9OI. [Accessed 20 September 2023].

[26] S. Silver, I. Hobbs, P. Margolis and M. Naidoo, "Chambers UK: Product Liability & Safety 2021 - Trends and developments," Kennedys Law, 28 June 2021. [Online]. Available: https://kennedyslaw.com/en/thought-leadership/article/chambers-uk-product-liability-safety-2021-trends-and-developments/. [Accessed 20 September 2023].

[27] Thomson Reuters, "Negligence | Practical Law," [Online]. Available: https://uk.practicallaw.thomsonreuters.com/0-107-6876. [Accessed 20 November 2023].

[28] National Accident Healthline, "What is medical negligence? | National accident helpline," National Accident Healthline, [Online]. Available: https://www.national-accident-helpline.co.uk/medical-negligence/what-is-medical-negligence. [Accessed 20 September 2023].

[29] NHS Indemnity, "NHS indemnity - Arrangements for clinical negligence claims in the NHS," [Online]. Available: https://resolution.nhs.uk/wp-content/uploads/2018/10/NHS-Indemnity.pdf. [Accessed 20 September 2023].

[30] The Stationary Office, "Consumer Rights Act 2015 - Explanatory notes," 2015. [Online]. Available: https://www.legislation.gov.uk/ukpga/2015/15/notes/annex/2#. [Accessed 20 September 2023].

[31] A. Sanders, "Vicarious liability - The UK Supreme Court hands down two important decisions. | Global Workplace Insider," Norton Rose Fulbright, 02 April 2020. [Online]. Available: https://www.globalworkplaceinsider.com/2020/04/vicarious-liability-the-uk-supreme-court-hands-down-two-important-decisions/. [Accessed 20 September 2023].

[32] NIIS Resolution, "Clinical negligence scheme for trusts - NHS resolution," [Online]. Available: https://resolution.nhs.uk/services/claims-management/clinical-schemes/clinical-negligence-scheme-for-trusts/. [Accessed 20 September 2023].

[33] Scottish Government, "A study of medical negligence claiming in Scotland," Scot. gov, 07 June 2012. [Online]. Available: https://www.gov.scot/publications/study medical-negligence-claiming-scotland/pages/2/. [Accessed 20 September 2023].

[34] Institute of Physics and Engineering in Medicine, "Code of professional and ethical conduct," 25 January 2018. [Online]. Available: https://www.ipem.ac.uk/media/ogrip byz/03-07-05-0217-08-00-code-of-professional-and-ethical-conduct.pdf. [Accessed 23 September 2023].

[35] American Association of Physicists in Medicine, "AAPM position statements, policies and procedures Details," 19 November 2020. [Online]. Available: https://www.aapm.org/org/policies/details.asp?id=2564#GeneralWorkEthics. [Accessed 20 September 2023].

[36] IPEM, "Best-practice guidance for the in-house manufacture of medical devices and non-medical devices, including software in both cases, for use within the same health institution," 25 July 2022. [Online]. Available: https://www.ipem.ac.uk/media/vp0ewy01/ipembe-1.pdf. [Accessed 22 September 2023].

[37] International Society for Pharmaceutical Engineering, "Pharmaceutical facility publications and guidance documents | ISPE | International Society for Pharmaceutical Engineering," [Online]. Available: https://ispe.org/publications/guidance-documents. [Accessed 20 September 2023].

[38] L. Fraser, N. Parkar, K. Adamson et al, "Guidance on medical physics expert support for nuclear medicine," *The British Journal of Radiology,* vol. 95, no. 1135, 2022.

[39] C. Caruana, S. Christofides and G. Hartmann, "European Federation of Organisations for Medical Physics (EFOMP) policy statement 12.1: Recommendations on medical physics education and training in Europe 2014," *Physica Medica,* vol. 30, no. 6, pp. 598–603, 2014.

[40] L. Hadjiiski, "AAPM task group report 273: Recommendations on best practices for AI and machine learning for computer-aided diagnosis in medical imaging," *Medical Physics,* vol. 50, no. 2, pp. e1–e24, 2022.

[41] M. Miquel, "Copyright revisited," *Scope,* vol. 20, no. 1, pp. 12–17, 2011.

[42] NHS Innovation Service, "Your gateway to innovation in the NHS - Innovation Service," [Online]. Available: https://innovation.nhs.uk/. [Accessed 20 September 2023].

[43] S. K. Peterson, "What's the difference between open source software and free software?," opensource.com, 7 November 2017. [Online]. Available: https://opensource.com/article/17/11/open-source-or-free-software. [Accessed 20 September 2023].

[44] Medicines & Healthcare Products Regulatory Agency, "MHRA software flowchart," [Online]. Available: https://assets.publishing.service.gov.uk/government/uploads/system/uploads/attachment_data/file/1168485/Medical_device_stand-alone_software_including_apps__including_IVDMDs_.pdf. [Accessed 20 September 2023].

[45] S. Mahawar, "Intellectual property issues relating to open source software - iPleaders," iPleaders, 18 March 2022. [Online]. Available: https://blog.ipleaders.in/intellectual-property-issues-relating-open-source-software/. [Accessed 20 September 2023].

[46] Open Source Initiative, "Licenses – Open source initiative," [Online]. Available: https://opensource.org/licenses/. [Accessed 20 September 2023].

[47] Civic Commons, "Contributor agreements: How to accept code and documentation contributions legally," Civic Commons. [Online]. Available: http://wiki.civiccommons.org/Contributor_Agreements, 2011.

[48] Apache Software Foundation, "ASF contributor agreements," [Online]. Available: https://www.apache.org/licenses/contributor-agreements.html. [Accessed 20 September 2023].

[49] Synopsys, "Guide to open source licenses: Use, obligations, and risk," 06 October 2016. [Online]. Available: https://www.synopsys.com/blogs/software-security/open-source-licenses.html. [Accessed 20 September 2023].

[50] T. Holwerda, "The difference between EULAs and Open source licenses – OSnews," OSnews, 25 09 2009. [Online]. Available: https://www.osnews.com/story/22233/the-difference-between-eulas-and-open-source-licenses/. [Accessed 20 September 2023].

[51] S. Morrison, "Quality Considerations of Open-Source Software for Medical Devices," Siemens, 17 January 2022. [Online]. Available: https://blogs.sw.siemens.com/embedded-software/2022/01/17/quality-considerations-of-open-source-software-for-medical-devices/. [Accessed 20 September 2023].

[52] K. MacCallum, "Should you use open source software in medical devices?," StarFish Medical, 19 March 2018. [Online]. Available: https://starfishmedical.com/blog/open-source-software-medical-devices/. [Accessed 20 September 2023].

[53] C. Eastham, "Is open source technology the healthy option for medical devices?," FieldFisher, 11 November 2022. [Online]. Available: https://www.fieldfisher.com/en/insights/is-open-source-technology-the-healthy-option-for-medical-devices#_ftn1. [Accessed 20 September 2023].

8 Security of Medical Devices

"The only truly secure system is one that is powered off, cast in a block of concrete and sealed in a lead-lined room with armed guards".

Bruce Schneier

8.1 OVERVIEW

Any discussion of the security of healthcare computer systems quickly gravitates to the topical issue of cybersecurity, but there are other more mundane security risks that need to be considered when producing medical device software designed for different users. This chapter covers current methods designed to protect medical systems against cyberattacks but also refers to simple access control measures that are designed to protect the application and its stored data during routine clinical use.

In the past, it was common for device manufacturers to rely solely on risk control measures instigated by the customer's IT department, but the security of devices is now recognised as a shared responsibility between the medical device manufacturer (MDM) and the end-user (healthcare provider) [1].

The MDM has a responsibility to design the software in such a way as to minimise vulnerabilities and to provide the user with the information and tools to fully implement the recommended security measures. The latter requirement led to the concept of the Software Bill of Materials (SBOM, Section 8.5.1), the generation of which is now a regulatory requirement for software medical devices in the US (Section 6.5.8.11).

With recent technological developments, increased use of networked devices, remote access to and from medical devices, the use of cloud-based services, and the seemingly constant stream of phishing attempts within a hospital environment, the issue of cybersecurity has become a significant issue when developing and deploying medical software. It is also an issue set to grow in importance as connectivity between healthcare establishments is seen as a route to more efficient healthcare. For example, the UK NHS is committed to "ensure that clinicians can access and interact with patient records and care plans wherever they are" [2].

Numerous recent security breaches have prompted medical systems designers to pay more attention to the vulnerabilities that elite hackers can exploit. For example, the 2017 WannaCry ransomware attack in the UK not only caused irreversible encrypting of medical data but also caused health institutions' IT contingency plans to swing into action, shutting down entire hospital networks with significant disruption to clinics and patient safety. The financial cost to the NHS was estimated at £92m [3]. More recently, a national cyberattack affecting all five public radiotherapy centres in the Republic of Ireland caused extensive disruption to critical oncology services [4].

DOI: 10.1201/9781003301202-8

The 2023 *Global Threat Intelligence Report*, compiled by Blackberry, noted that:

The healthcare and financial services industries were among the most targeted sectors. In healthcare, the combination of valuable data and critical services presents a lucrative target for cybercriminals, resulting in ransomware gangs directly targeting healthcare organizations and in the proliferation of information stealing malware, or info stealers [5].

This chapter explores the concepts surrounding medical device cybersecurity from the UK, EU, and US perspectives with an emphasis on practical advice.

8.2   GENERAL CONCEPTS AND DEFINITIONS

The EU Agency for Network and Information Security (ENISA) suggests that the term "cybersecurity" be considered as comprising a set of "domains"; those relevant to SaMD being Communications Security, Operations Security, and Information Security [6].

Communications security is defined as "protection against a threat to the technical infrastructure of a cyber system, which may lead to an alteration of its characteristics in order to carry out activities that were not intended by its owners, designers or users". In the context of medical devices, this relates to the confidentiality of information stored locally and in transit, the accuracy and integrity of the data, and the availability of data, systems, and devices. In terms of data accuracy and integrity, accepted standards for the transmission of patient data should be considered when communicating between systems. In the imaging domain, the DICOM standard is widely accepted, whilst the HL7 Version 2 is the current *de facto* standard for the exchange of sensitive data.

Operational security is defined as "protection against the intended corruption of procedures or workflows that will have results that were unintended by its owners, designers or users". The operating security of IT infrastructure surrounding medical devices is referred to in both the EU MDR and IVDR, under sections 17.4, 18.8, and 16.4 respectively. A useful checklist for those developing or managing a system can be found in the US Code of Federal Regulations, Part 164, Subpart C – Security Standards for the Protection of Electronic Protected Health Information (Table 8.1).

Information security is defined as "protection against the threat of theft, deletion or alteration of stored or transmitted data within a cyber system". In the UK, the NHS has an overarching Information Security Policy that outlines the requirements of NHS Trusts and their informatics teams to protect information, including the roles and responsibilities of the various stakeholders (Chief Executive, Data Protection Officer, and general users).

8.2.1   SAFETY, SECURITY, AND EFFECTIVENESS

Annex I of the EU MDR states that devices "shall be safe and effective whilst not compromising the clinical condition or the safety of patients, or the safety and health of users", meaning that an acceptable balance often has to be struck. MDCG 2019-16 [7] cites an example of an implanted cardiac pacemaker, for which strong security measures need to be in place during the normal operation of the device, but where the

---

TABLE 8.1

Extract from US Code of Federal Regulations, Part 164, Subpart C – *Security Standards for the Protection of Electronic Protected Health Information,* **detailing operational security issues to consider in the implementation and or design of software in the healthcare setting**

Standards	Implementation specifications
Administrative safeguards	
Workforce security	Authorisation and/or supervision
Information access management	Access authorisation
Security awareness and training	Security reminders
	Protection from malicious software
	Login monitoring
	Password management
Security incident procedures	Response and reporting
Contingency plan	Data backup plan
	Disaster recovery plan
	Applications and data criticality analysis
Physical safeguards	
Facility access controls	Contingency operations
	Facility security plan
	Access control and validation procedures
	Maintenance records
Device and media controls	Disposal
	Media re-use
	Accountability
	Data backup and storage
Technical safeguards	
Access control	Unique user identification
	Emergency access procedure
	Automatic logoff
	Encryption and decryption
Audit controls	
Transmission security	Encryption

---

system must also allow medical staff to access the operating software without undue restriction during an emergency.

8.2.2 Reasonably Foreseeable Misuse

As part of a risk management process guided by standards such as ISO 14971 and AAMI TIR57, manufacturers should identify and evaluate any potential exploits or vulnerabilities that may arise from reasonably foreseeable misuse of the system. As part of the subsequent design process, manufacturers should ensure that a medical device is designed and manufactured in such a way that ensures that these risks are mitigated, or their impacts minimised. Mitigations would include active monitoring of any potential vulnerabilities as part of post-market surveillance (PMS).

8.2.3 OPERATING ENVIRONMENT

Manufacturers of devices need to consider the variation in the IT infrastructure of different healthcare providers. Such networks should be under a risk management process, taking into account the following cybersecurity best practices:

- Prevention of unauthorised physical access to the device or network access points
- Prevention of unauthorised access via control measures to ensure only authorised personnel are able to access the network elements, data, and applications
- Limit device communication to segmented areas of the network
- Good management of security and patch updates
- Prevention of malicious code execution from malware
- Training of end users to raise awareness of cybersecurity
- Audit processes to determine user actions and changes to the system

Clearly, the more connections that a medical device has to other medical devices, the local area network, and the wider internet, the greater the risk that it may be affected directly or indirectly by a cyberattack or security breach. In this regard, there is always a trade-off between cybersecurity and interoperability [8], but the increasing need for remote access and telemedicine means that cybersecurity will always be an activity that needs to keep pace with ever-growing connectivity requirements.[1] The increased use of cloud computing by large organisations as a means of reducing IT capital costs and increasing accessibility brings some potential security benefits but also has its own set of risks that need to be managed by staff with appropriate cyber-security training [11].

8.2.4 SHARED RESPONSIBILITY

Whilst regulatory instruments place legal obligations on MDMs, cybersecurity is ultimately a shared responsibility of the MDM and the healthcare provider (HCPR). The HCPR will have its own IT security policy that any networked medical device will need adhere. Such policies may require a Data Protection Impact Assessment (DPIA) or other risk-related procedures.

---

[1] The collection of internet-connected medical devices and healthcare information systems is known as the Internet of Medical Things (IoMT) or the Healthcare Internet of Things (HIoT) [9,10].

8.2.5 TRANSPARENCY AND INFORMATION SHARING

The concepts of transparency and information sharing are now promoted as antidotes to the old practice of "security through obscurity". It is therefore important that users have access to information on the device's cybersecurity controls, and potential risks, amongst other relevant information.

User manuals should include information on how to securely configure and update the device, and supplementary documentation/software should contain information on third-party components, usually in the form of an SBOM (Section 8.5.1). All known security vulnerabilities should also be disclosed to the end-user (Section 8.3.3).

The FDA encourages all responsible stakeholders to participate as Information Sharing Analysis Organizations (ISAOs) to aid in the communication of cybersecurity incidents, threats, and vulnerabilities that may affect the safety, performance, integrity, and security of medical devices and connected healthcare infrastructure. On a global scale, regulators are also encouraged to share information with other regulators to help protect and maintain patient safety.

IMDRF guidance document N60 contains further information on the nature of shared cybersecurity responsibilities and the types of information sharing between MDM and HCPR [12].

The MDCG guidance includes a section on information that should be provided to healthcare providers by MDMs regarding the intended use environment, including instructions for virus protection, backup/restore, and a list of network ports (for hardware devices) and interfaces, etc. [7].

8.2.6 TOTAL PRODUCT LIFE CYCLE (TPLC)

As part of the *secure-by design* approach promoted by EU regulators and the FDA (Section 8.3.1), the risks posed by cybersecurity threats and vulnerabilities should be addressed throughout the entire life of a medical device, including design, manufacture, testing, and PMS activities. The FDA and the IMDRF refer to this as the TPLC.

IEC 81001-5-1:2021 (Chapter 5, A.1.5.1) uses the TPLC as a framework for discussion of the principles of information security risk management and represents the current state of the art. It is expected to become a harmonised standard under MDR 17 in 2024 (Section 6.3.6.7). There is no equivalent of IEC 62304's software safety classification, so IEC 81001-5-1's basic requirements are applicable to all software classes.

8.3 PRE-MARKET CONSIDERATIONS

Under both the EU MDR and US FDA regulatory frameworks, manufacturers are required to conduct pre-market security measures that include risk management, secure design, clinical evaluation, and conformity assessment.

8.3.1 Secure by Design

The notion of "secure-by-design" is central to both EU and FDA approaches to medical device security. For devices aimed at the US market, the FDA recommends that manufacturers adopt its suggested Secure Product Development Framework (SPDF) [13] as one possible way of complying with the security requirements laid out in the quality system regulation (QSR). The other option is to use IEC 81001-5-1:2021 (Chapter 5, A.1.5.1), which is widely used in Europe as a means of demonstrating compliance with the security requirements of MDR 17.

The IMDRF has also proposed a list of basic principles and control measures that should be integral to any secure-by-design process [12]:

- Secure communication (with other devices and networks)
- Data protection
- Device integrity
- User authentication
- Software maintenance
- Physical access
- Reliability and availability

8.3.2 Security Risk Management

The general approach to cybersecurity risk management follows the well-established principles of *safety* risk management established by ISO 14971 (Section 5.3.1). In specific medical device security standards such as AAMI TIR57 (Chapter 5, A.1.5.2), the (safety) risk processes are essentially replaced by *security* risk processes (Figure 8.1).

The UK National Cyber Security Centre (NCSC) has produced a useful guidance document on cybersecurity risk management that covers all stages of the process and distinguishes between system-driven and component-driven methods [14].

8.3.3 Threat Modelling and Testing

An important part of any *system* risk assessment process will be the identification of any vulnerabilities. These would usually arise from connections with the outside world via internet links, but internal connections with other organisation sub-systems should also be considered. As defined by the FDA [13] threat modelling includes a process for identifying security objectives, risks, and vulnerabilities across a system. These are then used to design countermeasures to prevent, or mitigate the effects of, threats to the system throughout its life cycle. As a minimum, the threat model should:

- Identify system risks and mitigations as well as inform the pre- and post-mitigation risks considered as part of the initial security risk assessment
- State any assumptions about the system or environment of use

- Capture cybersecurity risks that might be introduced through the supply chain, manufacturing, deployment, interoperation with other devices, maintenance/update activities, and decommission activities

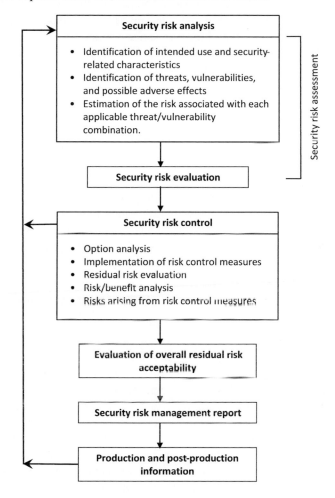

FIGURE 8.1 Schematic representation of the security risk management process. Adapted with permission from AAMI TIR57: *Principles for medical device security – Risk management* © 2016 by the Association for the Advancement of Medical Instrumentation.

The UK NCSC provides practical guidance on how to undertake threat modelling [15], which is also covered in Annex C of IEC 81001-5-1 (Chapter 5, A.1.5.1).

The general issues of identifying and disclosing vulnerabilities are addressed in ISO/IEC 30111:2019: (*Information technology – Security techniques – Vulnerability handling processes*) and ISO/IEC 29147:2018 (*Information technology – Security techniques – Vulnerability disclosure*), respectively.

8.4   POST-MARKET CONSIDERATIONS

There is an acknowledgement that cybersecurity risks will change and evolve throughout the life cycle of the product and, as such, it is not possible to completely mitigate risks through pre-market controls alone. Appropriate post-market security activities include modification of risk control measures, performing further risk assessments, and updating PMS plans/systems as necessary. The FDA requires manufacturers to update their *security risk management report* as new information, threats or vulnerabilities arise (Section 6.5.8.11).

AAMI TIR97 (Chapter 5, A.1.5.3) covers post-market risk management for medical device manufacturers and is intended to be used in conjunction with AAMI TIR57 (Section 8.3.2)

Despite all reasonable efforts, there is an acknowledgement that medical devices cannot be completely secured if they are connected to a wider IT network. Vulnerabilities may be inadvertently incorporated at any stage of the system development/integration process, resulting from poor design decisions, lack of technical understanding, or the nature of the software technology. Even if an identified security risk is assessed as not presenting a patient safety issue, a future change to the software or environment may change its impact so it must continue to be monitored as part of PMS.

8.5   CODING IMPLICATIONS AND SYSTEM MANAGEMENT

Most security issues that a medical device software manufacturer needs to be concerned about relate to the way in which the application is accessed and the way in which it connects to other devices and networks. Adhering to accepted coding standards (Section 5.4.4) for the medical device itself will improve testability and aid future maintainability, but it is the software interfaces that require particular attention. Most cyberattacks exploit operating systems weaknesses so it is important for the developers to understand how these weaknesses may be exploited and to ensure that all security patches are in place and up to date. This will normally be the job of an IT systems manager (usually in a separate corporate IT department) so some collaboration will be necessary. If there is no requirement for the device software to be remotely accessed (i.e., from outside the organisation's LAN) then the corporate firewall port that allows connection to the departmental sub-network should be permanently blocked.

It should be remembered that loss (inadvertent deletion or corruption) or theft of patient data is the biggest security concern for a medical device software manufacturer so building secure systems that (a) protect the data as far as reasonably possible and (b) allow rapid recover from any loss of data should it occur are important design considerations. As such, a recovery plan that covers all foreseeable eventualities (derived from the security risk analysis) should be part of the general software maintenance process (i.e., the data recovery procedure should be regularly practiced).

For the application itself, the main security design decisions relate to basic access controls (login, logout) and the protection of the application and its data once accessed. The latter particularly applies to spreadsheet applications (Section 5.4.5) for which it is necessary to protect cells that contain formulae to prevent them from being inadvertently over-written by the user.

The current version (and only the current version) of the application should reside in the appropriate folder on a departmental server (i.e., not be installed on a single workstation/PC) so the user will require a network login[2] as well as a separate login to the application. Also, only staff who are trained and authorised to use the application should be given access. All passwords should be changed (usually a forced change) according to organisational/departmental policy.

Many of these security aspects come under the general heading of "system management" and a System Manager (for the medical device software) should be appointed to take responsibility for ensuring that all the elements are under control [17], including:

- User training and authorisation
- Application backup
- Data file backup
- Configuration management (version control, etc.)
- Documentation (user documentation, application development documentation)
- Certification (proof of standards compliance, etc.)

With regard to the requirements gathering stage of the SDLC, security requirements should be listed and treated the same as the more obvious user requirements in terms of implementation and traceability [18].

8.5.1   OFF-THE-SHELF (OTS) SOFTWARE

It is common for medical devices to incorporate third-party software in their products, which could be commercial OTS (COTS) or open source in nature. The evaluation of the risks associated with these third-party components inevitably adds extra procedures to the risk management process. The FDA provides guidance on how to assess the risk posed by third-party software in its guidance document "Cybersecurity for networked medical devices containing off-the-shelf (OTS) software" [19]. Indeed, it is a requirement of the US QSR (part 21 CFR 820 of the Current Good Manufacturing Practice (CGMP) regulations) that all third-party software incorporated by medical device manufacturers be assessed for cybersecurity and that these risks should be addressed as part of the overall risk management plan.

Processes and controls should also be implemented to ensure that these third-party providers (commercial or open source) conform to the requirements of the manufacturer and this information should be included in design documentation. To allow users to be informed and able to manage these associated risks, the FDA now requires manufacturers to provide an SBOM (Section 6.5.8.11), which is also mentioned in MDGC guidance in relation to EU MDR 17 (Section 6.3.6.7).

In the post-market phase of implementation, there is an expectation that manufacturers will have a process for managing any change (update) in the incorporated third-party software that is subsequently re-integrated into the medical device.

---

[2] In a hospital environment, logging into the main hospital network will also provide access (usually via separate login) to the departmental sub-net in which the employee works.

BOX 8.1 WHAT IS AN SBOM?

An SBOM is a standardised machine-readable inventory of a finished software product's components (especially third-party components) and their inter-dependencies. There are currently three accepted SBOM formats (software package data exchange (SPDE), CycloneDX (CDX), and software identification tags (SWID) [20]), with data arranged as key-value pairs in a JSON (JavaScript Object Notation) file. An SBOM can be produced directly from source code using a variety of open-source and commercial software tools [21]. *As a minimum*, the SBOM should contain the name of the software manufacturer, the name of the component, the version number, the level of support provided by the component manufacturer, and any known vulnerabilities.

8.6. SPECIAL REQUIREMENTS FOR AI/ML-ENABLED MEDICAL DEVICES

The presence of AI technology in a *medical device* adds another layer of vulnerability in terms of cybersecurity, so assessing the nature of the vulnerability and designing control measures will become more important as the number of medical devices containing AI grows.

The European Union Agency for Cybersecurity (ENISA) has produced a generic report detailing how existing and planned standards may support the cybersecurity of AI-enabled devices [22]. It assesses the scope of the respective standards and identifies gaps in the total coverage. ENISA adopts a broad view of cybersecurity, encompassing both the "traditional" *confidentiality-integrity-availability* paradigm as well as the wider concept of *AI trustworthiness*. Finally, the report examines how standardisation can support the implementation of the cybersecurity requirement aspects of the EU AI Act (see Section 7.2.3).

REFERENCES

[1] D. Wilkerson, "2023 predictions for medical device product development," Jama Software, 22 December 2022. [Online]. Available: https://www.jamasoftware.com/blog/2023-predictions-for-medical-device-product-development. [Accessed 19 September 2023].

[2] NHS, "NHS long term plan," [Online]. Available: https://www.longtermplan.nhs.uk/. [Accessed 19 September 2023].

[3] National Health Executive, "WannaCry cyber-attack cost the NHS £92m after 19,000 appointments were cancelled," 12 October 2018. [Online]. Available: https://www.nationalhealthexecutive.com/articles/wannacry-cyber-attack-cost-nhs-ps92m-after-19000-appointments-were-cancelled. [Accessed 19 September 2023].

[4] A. Flavin, E. O'Toole and L. Murphy, "A national cyberattack affecting radiation therapy: The Irish experience," *Advances in Radiation Oncology,* vol. 7, no. 5, pp. 2452–1094, 2022.

[5] BlackBerry, "BlackBerry quarterly global threat report — August," August 2023. [Online]. Available: https://www.blackberry.com/us/en/solutions/threat-intelligence/threat-report. [Accessed 19 September 2023].

[6] ENISA, "Definition of cybersecurity - Gaps and overlaps in standardisation — ENISA," 1 July 2016. [Online]. Available: https://www.enisa.europa.eu/publications/definition-of-cybersecurity. [Accessed 19 September 2023].

[7] Medical Device Coordination Group, "MDCG 2019-16 - Guidance on cybersecurity for medical devices," 06 January 2020. [Online]. Available: https://ec.europa.eu/docsroom/documents/41863. [Accessed 19 September 2023].

[8] S. Domas, "Balancing cybersecurity and interoperability in medical devices," Med Device Online, 26 May 2017. [Online]. Available: https://www.meddeviceonline.com/doc/balancing-cybersecurity-and-interoperability-in-medical-devices-0001. [Accessed 19 September 2023].

[9] B. Lutkevich and A. DelVecchio, "What is the Internet of Medical Things (IoMT)? I Definition from TechTarget," TechTarget, [Online]. Available: https://www.techtarget.com/iotagenda/definition/IoMT-Internet-of-Medical-Things. [Accessed 19 September 2023].

[10] Deloitte, "Medtech and the internet of medical things," Deloitte, July 2018. [Online]. Available: https://www2.deloitte.com/content/dam/Deloitte/global/Documents/Life-Sciences-Health-Care/gx-lshc-medtech-iomt-brochure.pdf. [Accessed 19 September 2023].

[11] Skyhigh Security, "Cloud computing security issues - Skyhigh Security," [Online]. Available: https://www.skyhighsecurity.com/cybersecurity-defined/cloud-computing-security-issues.html. [Accessed 19 September 2023].

[12] International Medical Device Regulators Forum, "Principles and practices for medical device cybersecurity I International Medical Device Regulators Forum," 20 April 2020. [Online]. Available: https://www.imdrf.org/documents/principles-and-practices-medical-device-cybersecurity. [Accessed 19 September 2023].

[13] Food and Drug Administration, "Cybersecurity in medical devices: Quality system considerations and content of premarket submissions I FDA," April 2022. [Online]. Available. https://www.fda.gov/regulatory-information/search-fda-guidance-documents/cybersecurity-medical-devices-quality-system-considerations-and-content premarket-submissions. [Accessed 19 September 2023].

[14] National Cyber Security Centre, "Risk management - NCSC.GOV.UK," 09 June 2023. [Online]. Available: https://www.ncsc.gov.uk/collection/risk-management. [Accessed 19 September 2023].

[15] National Cyber Security Centre, "Threat modelling - NCSC.GOV.UK," 09 June 2023. [Online]. Available: https://www.ncsc.gov.uk/collection/risk-management/threat-modelling. [Accessed 19 September 2023].

[16] AAMI, "AAMI TIR97:2019 (R2023) - Principles for medical device security - Postmarket risk management for device manufacturers," 27 September 2019. [Online]. Available: https://webstore.ansi.org/standards/aami/aamitir972019r2023. [Accessed 19 September 2023].

[17] D. Tran, "Secure software development best practices I Perforce," Perforce, 31 March 2023. [Online]. Available: https://www.perforce.com/blog/sca/best-practices-secure-software-development. [Accessed 19 September 2023].

[18] Ø. Forsbak, "10 Best practices for software development security," Orient, 29 November 2021. [Online]. Available: https://www.orientsoftware.com/blog/software-development-security/. [Accessed 19 September 2023].

[19] Food and Drug Administration, "Cybersecurity for networked medical devices containing Off-the-Shelf (OTS) software," January 2005. [Online]. Available: https://www.fda.gov/regulatory-information/search-fda-guidance-documents/cybersecurity-networked-medical-devices-containing-shelf-ots-software. [Accessed 19 September 2023].

[20] J. Martin, "A guide to standard SBOM formats," mend.io, 04 May 2023. [Online]. Available: https://www.mend.io/blog/guide-to-standard-sbom-formats/. [Accessed 19 September 2023].

[21] E. Kaminski, "2023 FDA CyberSecurity standards & guidance best practice - Ketryx Software Compliance Platform," Ketryx, 19 July 2023. [Online]. Available: https://www.ketryx.com/blog/fda-drops-an-sbom. [Accessed 19 September 2023].

[22] ENISA, "Cybersecurity of AI and standardisation," 14 March 2023. [Online]. Available: https://www.enisa.europa.eu/publications/cybersecurity-of-ai-and-standardisation. [Accessed 19 September 2023].

9 Future Regulation of Medical Device Software

"The future is already here, it's just not evenly distributed"

William Gibson (2003)

9.1 OVERVIEW

In August 2011 a landmark article appeared in the Wall Street Journal entitled "Why Software is Eating the World" [1]. Twelve years on, it could be argued that software produced by a few giant corporations has *eaten* the world, although the effect of this software revolution on medical device regulation has so far been limited. For *device software*, it was not until the publication of EC Directive 2007/47/EC in September 2007 that standalone software was even recognised as a medical device (Section 6.3.5) and, in terms of *supporting software*, the move to fully computerised quality management systems has been slow (Section 5.2). Things are now changing more rapidly, however, and the process of "digital transformation" is explored in Section 9.5.2.

All major regulatory systems are undergoing a period of rapid development as regulators seek to clarify the boundary between medical devices and other health IT products. Furthermore, the hugely increased use of artificial intelligence/machine learning in healthcare has prompted a general rethink on the way that all medical devices should be regulated. At present, the legal oversight of SaMD and AIaMD operates within regulatory regimes that were drafted before the recent developments in software engineering generally and AI/ML in particular.

This book is mainly concerned with medical device software and, unsurprisingly, this is the area of medical device regulation most likely to see dramatic change over the next decade. Most device software is still constructed using traditional software engineering methodologies, although agile techniques are starting to gain a foothold in the industry. However, these modern techniques need to be significantly adapted to comply with existing medical device regulations and associated standards (Section 5.4.1.12), so there is a pressing need for some standards to be updated.

The rapidly expanding use of AI/ML technologies in medical devices has raised concerns about the ability of current regulatory practices to adequately deal with the unique characteristics of adaptive technology. All regulators are currently grappling with the issues presented by AI-enabled medical devices, but initial strategies are starting to emerge (Sections 6.3.6.5, 6.4.4.3 and 6.5.8.9). This chapter looks ahead to consider how the regulation of medical device software may change over the next five years.

DOI: 10.1201/9781003301202-9

9.2 UNITED STATES

9.2.1 GENERAL AND ORGANISATIONAL ISSUES

9.2.1.1 The Approval System

The FDA has been more proactive than EU medical device regulators in addressing concerns about medical device regulation generally, especially regarding issues of transparency and engagement with medical device manufacturers. The Agency takes a "least burdensome" approach to all its guidance, to ensure safety without imposing undue bureaucracy. All draft FDA guidance is subject to public consultation and, where practical, pilot schemes are established to "road test" new requirements.

Nonetheless, the FDA has identified some problems with its approval systems and has started a comprehensive modernisation programme. Its aim is to make the product review/approval system more streamlined and the electronic submission of pre-market applications (Section 6.5.4.1.7) is part of that process.

The FDA has also signalled its intent to focus its limited resources on higher-risk devices. Specific steps in this direction include the deregulation of some types of "health-related" software (e.g., wellness apps), a policy of "enforcement discretion" towards some types of low-risk medical device software (Sections 6.5.8.5, 6.5.8.6), and the use of approved third-party organisations to undertake the initial review of some types of pre-market submissions for class I and class II devices (Section 6.5.4.1.4). The use of third-party organisations is expected to increase over the next few years, possibly leading to their involvement in other areas of the Agency's work.

9.2.1.2 Connecting with Industry

There is expected to be increased collaboration between the FDA and medical device manufacturers, including the expanded use of voluntary pilot schemes to test out proposed regulatory changes. As an example of its outreach strategy, the FDA is a participant in the Medical Devices Innovation Consortium (MDIC), which is an independent public-private partnership with representatives from both large and small manufacturers, as well as patient advocacy groups and other stakeholders [2].

In 2018 the FDA participated in a pilot *voluntary improvement programme* facilitated by the MDIC to allow medical device manufacturers to assess their performance using third-party appraisals based on an established capability maturity model. This successful pilot scheme has now transitioned into the *Case for Quality Voluntary Improvement Programme* (CfQVIP) and the FDA has published guidance on how it intends to engage with it [3].

9.2.1.3 Alignment of the Quality System Regulation with ISO 13485

In February 2022, following concerted pressure from the US medical device industry, the FDA published a proposed rule change in connection with the relationship between the Quality System Regulation (QSR) and ISO 13485:2016. In a form of partial adoption, the FDA proposes to "incorporate ISO 13485:2016 by reference", which would involve replacing the majority of the QSR's existing requirements for establishing and maintaining a quality system, and placing a greater emphasis on risk management throughout the development life cycle. If finalised, the new regulation will be referred to as the *Quality Management System Regulation* (QMSR) to distinguish it from the present QSR.

The FDA suggests that total reliance on ISO 13485 without clarification or modifications "would create inconsistencies", so it is proposing "additional definitions, clarifying concepts, and additional requirements", all of which would require compliance within a manufacturer's QMS *in addition to* ISO 13485. Some long-standing QSR documentation terminology (e.g., Device Master Record, Design History File) will disappear (those elements are deemed to be covered by Clause 4.2 of ISO 13485:2016), but other basic requirements will remain [4].

In areas that the FDA considers ISO 13485 to be lacking, existing QSR provisions will be incorporated into the QMSR. For device labelling, for example, manufacturers would need to comply with Clause 7.5.1 of ISO 13485 and the additional requirements specified in the proposed section §820.45 of the QMSR. Where a direct conflict exists between the QMSR and ISO 13485:2016, the QMSR will prevail.

The draft regulation includes a table giving a mapping between existing QSR requirements and clauses of ISO 13485. It will have a 12-month transition period once finalised. It will mainly affect the approximately 25% of US Med Tech companies that only sell into the US market since most of the remainder will probably already be ISO 13485 compliant.

There is some pressure from within the US for the FDA to *formally* adopt ISO 13485 (i.e., accept ISO 13485 conformance certificates as proof, in themselves, of a QMS suitable for a medical device manufacturer marketing products in the US) [5] but these are being resisted for the time being. Nonetheless, it makes sense for US medical device manufacturers to have a single QMS that is compliant with ISO 13485 and the QSR/QMSR.

9.2.2 Software-Related

It is expected that the increasing use of agile/flexible development techniques will drive changes in the QSR and AAMI technical report TIR45 represents a step in this direction (Section 5.4.1.12) [6]. FDA guidance on the principles of validation (Section 6.5.8.2) for device software is expected to be revised to bring it more in line with the draft guidance on software assurance of production and quality system software (Section 6.5.8.3).

FDA plans for its software pre-certification (Pre-Cert) programme (Section 6.5.8.4.1) to be used as a new streamlined pathway for the pre-market review of SaMD products have had to be put "on hold" as the envisaged programme cannot be realised under the FDA's current statutory authority [7]. The Agency may seek additional authority through Congress, but this would be a lengthy process with no guarantee of success. In the meantime, a different strategy may be required [8].

9.2.3 AI/ML-Enabled Medical Devices

AIaMD is *effectively* a SaMD sub-type but is afforded special consideration due to the unique nature in which it is developed and maintained, thereby adding another layer of regulatory complexity. Initial proposals are being trialled (Section 6.5.8.9) but the effective regulation of adaptive AI technology will require a new paradigm.

Most AI/ML-based medical devices cleared by the FDA over the last decade have not involved new clinical testing [9] so more rigorous pre-market assessment is indicated.

However, for adaptive devices, it is *post-market* surveillance that is likely to be prioritised to ensure that such devices remain safe and effective as they change automatically. Several different schemes have been suggested, including regular pre-defined audits to be performed by the FDA itself or its approved agents [10]. Whether the FDA has the staffing resources to embark on such a large undertaking is an open question, so the alternative of only allowing certain types of adaptive changes is also likely to be pursued and expanded.

The FDA published a discussion paper in 2019 outlining its proposals for a new regulatory framework for dealing with modifications to AI/ML-based SaMD [11]. Following industry feedback, an *Action Plan* for the future regulation of AI/ML-based SaMD followed in January 2021 [12], based on the use of its predetermined change control programme, PCCP (Section 6.5.8.9).

Associated draft guidance on the content of pre-market submissions for AI/ML-enabled device software functions that contain a PCCP [13] is expected to be finalised in 2024. This draft guidance may be contrasted with the recently finalised guidance on the content of premarket submissions for more straightforward device software functions/SaMD (Section 6.5.3.4.2).

The 2019 FDA discussion paper on AI/ML-based SaMD [11] suggested that the recently piloted Software Pre-Cert Programme may also be a possible regulatory pathway for AI/ML-based SaMD, but the realisation of that programme is now in some doubt (see Section 9.2.2).

9.3   EUROPEAN UNION

9.3.1   GENERAL AND ORGANISATION ISSUES

The transition from the old Medical Devices Directives to the new Medical Device Regulations has not been a smooth one, although plans were disrupted by the COVID-19 pandemic during 2020–21. There are fewer Notified Bodies under the new regime, so the process of getting a device approved for the EU market has taken considerably longer. The problems with the approval system have been officially acknowledged [14] but some of the proposed actions have not been universally welcomed.

Some legal academics have expressed strong views on how the EU medical device regulations need to change, but relatively few of these suggestions will make it into statute.

The process of harmonising numerous standards formally recognised under the old MDD will continue, but progress is expected to be slow as it depends on CEN/CENELEC accepting the request to undertake the required work and also being in a position to do it. It is expected that MDCG will continue its work producing guidelines aimed at clarifying the interpretation of the current EU medical device regulations.

9.3.2 SOFTWARE-RELATED

The future direction for EU regulation of general medical device software (i.e., not AI-driven) is unclear, as specific guidance was last issued by the MDCG in 2019 (Section 6.3.5.2.1). MDCG general guidance on medical device classification published in 2021 ([15], see Section 6.3.5.2.3) provided further examples of medical device software classification according to the controversial Rule 11 of MDR 17, but further, more comprehensive, guidance is needed.

Compliance with the EU MDR's software requirements is dependent on harmonised standards, so the fact that the most important software standard (IEC 62304:2015) is overdue for revision is a problematic issue. However, the "saving grace" of IEC 62304 (Section 5.4.1) is that it is a *framework* standard that specifies what needs to be done rather than exactly how to do it. For example, the software development plan (Clause 5.1.1) can reference existing software processes *or* define new ones. For example, if the software has an AI component, an "AI algorithm process" can be assembled and added to the software development plan. In this case, the new process would comprise deliverables (of the associated activities/tasks), management of algorithmic changes, and known biases [16]. An AI algorithm verification plan would also be required under Clause 5.1.6. There are, of course, other *processes* in IEC 62304 for which a new component would need to be described, including the software risk management process (Clause 7).

9.3.3 AI-ENABLED MEDICAL DEVICES

Regarding future changes to the ways in which AI/ML-enabled medical devices are regulated, the EU starts from a similar baseline as the US. Between 2015 and 2020, more than half of all approvals were for radiological devices (53% in the EU, 58% in the US), and very few devices were classified as high risk (1% in the US, 2% in the EU) [17].

In late 2022 the European Commission requested ten generic standards for AI (covering aspects such as risk management, transparency, human oversight, etc.), all of which are relevant to medical device manufacture (Sections 6.3.3 and 6.3.6.5). The requested standards have a target completion date of 31 January 2025, subject to acceptance by CEN/CENELEC [18]. Guidance on the application of the respective standards to medical device manufacturing will then be required from the EC and/or MDCG.

The implications of the introduction of the EU AI Act (Section 7.2.3) on medical device manufacturers are yet unclear, but it may represent an additional regulatory layer [19].

A recent report commissioned by the European Parliamentary Research Service (EPRS) on artificial intelligence in healthcare in 2022 [20] identified seven potential risks arising from the use of AI in healthcare, which largely reflect those identified in the preparation of the EU AI Act.

1. Patient harm due to AI errors
2. The misuse of medical AI tools
3. Bias in AI and the perpetuation of existing inequities

4. Lack of transparency
5. Privacy and security issues
6. Gaps in accountability
7. Obstacles in implementation

The EPRS paper proposes some possible mitigations to the identified risks but calls for more research on, amongst other things, the technical robustness of medical AI.

Numerous standards for AI systems are under development by ISO and national standards organisations. For example, ISO 23894:2023 and BS AAMI 34971:2023 address the risk management of AI systems, both based on ISO 14971. These are generic "framework" standards, which will require some adaptation for application in the medical field.

9.4 UNITED KINGDOM

9.4.1 GENERAL AND ORGANISATIONAL ISSUES

The modernisation of the medical device regulatory system in the UK was hugely disrupted by the combined effects of the COVID-19 pandemic in 2020 and the UK's exit from the European Union in January 2021. Due to a 12-month Brexit delay caused by the COVID-19 pandemic, the deadline for full implementation of the EU MDR did not take effect during the Brexit transition period, so it did not automatically pass into UK law as retained EU law under the European Union (Withdrawal) Act 2018.

The situation was further complicated by the position of Northern Ireland, which was subject to special arrangements under the Northern Ireland Protocol when the UK withdrew from the EU. As a result of the 2021 *Medical Devices (Northern Ireland Protocol) Regulations*, the EU MDR applies in Northern Ireland and the new arrangements that the UK government is currently putting in place will apply in Great Britain (England, Scotland, and Wales). The *Northern Ireland Protocol Bill* (introduced in Parliament on 13 June 2022) seeks to remove EU Court of Justice jurisdiction and bring Northern Ireland under the UK's control but has significant hurdles to overcome before becoming law [21].

On behalf of the UK government, the MHRA conducted a consultation process on proposals for new UK medical device legislation between September and November 2021, with an official response published in June 2022 [22]. It was announced in 2022 that new legislation would come into force in July 2023 but this was subsequently put back until July 2025 [23].

This further delay meant that the transitional arrangements for allowing CE-marked medical devices onto the GB market had to be significantly extended. As a result, general medical devices compliant with the EU MDR can continue to be placed on the GB market until 30 June 2030. There are slightly different transitional arrangements for devices CE-marked under the old EU MDD.

Prior to full implementation of new UK regulations, the government intends to introduce specific legislation during 2023 (planned to come into force in mid-2024) that will strengthen post-market surveillance requirements ahead of the wider changes [23].

It was announced in the Spring 2023 Budget Report that the MHRA would move to a different regulatory model from 2024, which:

> will allow rapid, often near-automatic sign-off for medicines and technologies already approved by trusted regulators in other parts of the world such as the United States, Europe, and Japan. At the same time, it will set up a swift new approval process for the most cutting-edge medicines and devices to ensure that the UK becomes a global centre for their development. With an extra £10 million of funding over the next two years, they will put in place the quickest, simplest regulatory approval in the world for companies seeking rapid market access [24].

The details of this plan are awaited.

9.4.2 IN-HOUSE MANUFACTURING AND USE

It was expected that new UK medical device regulations would largely mirror the so-called "Health Institution Exemption" (HIE) described in EU MDR 17 (Section 6.3.11) but the UK government's response to the 2021 consultation process suggests that the UK requirements may be more stringent than at EU level.

The scope and conditions attached to any exemptions are yet to be confirmed, but the indications are that in-house manufacturers in the UK will need to comply with all the relevant essential requirements of the (new) UK medical devices regulations,[1] including those applying to technical documentation retention and adverse incident reporting. In-house developers will also be required to register devices with the MHRA, which will have the continued right of inspection. It was emphasised that the exemption will *not* apply in cases where services/products are provided for commercial or profitable purposes [22].

In summary, the future specific exemptions for in-house producers may be limited to the UKCA marking of devices and the requirement for *certified* QMS (although a QMS would still be required).

UK in-house medical software producers are advised to assume that most, if not all, of the proposals contained in the government's response to the consultation process will be translated into medical devices legislation.

9.4.3 SOFTWARE-RELATED

The MHRA published its *"Software and AI as a Medical Device Change Programme"* in September 2012, most recently updated in June 2023 [25]. The original eleven work packages have been reduced to eight, of which five relate to general SaMD (WPs 1–5) and three specifically to AIaMD (WPs 9–11).

The plan was to publish the first tranche of deliverables (WP1-02, WP4-01, WP9-02, WP9-05, WP11-01) before the end of 2022 but this deadline was missed. WP1 relates to the qualification of SaMD so the MHRA clearly considers that this has not been adequately defined by the International Medical Device Regulators Forum (IMDRF) or MDCG (see Sections 6.3.4.1 and 6.3.5.2.1).

---

[1] Expected to roughly correspond to the General Safety and Performance Requirements (GSPR) found in Annex I of EU MDR 17 (see Section 6.3.2).

Most of the deliverables are in the form of (non-binding) guidance documents rather than actual regulatory change, although some of the promised changes will be brought about through secondary legislation [23].

9.4.4   AI-ENABLED MEDICAL DEVICES

The UK's current position regarding the regulation of AIaMD was recently summarised in a report by the Regulatory Horizons Council (RHC) [26], an independent body set up by the UK government to advise it on the implications of technical innovation [27]. The gaps and weaknesses identified in the RHC report should serve as a basis for future improvements in the way that AI-enabled medical devices are approved for the UK market. The regulation of medical AI should also fit with the UK government's "pro-innovation approach" to AI regulation generally [28].

The MHRA's future programme for software and AI (Section 9.4.3) contains three specific work packages for AIaMD, related to rigour, interpretability, and adaptivity of AIaMD.

The UK National Health Service (NHS) has its own plans for the introduction of AI-enabled technology in healthcare, but progress has thus far been slow – partly due to organisational changes. The "AI Lab" was initially part of NHS-X, which merged with NHS Digital in 2021; the latter subsequently being absorbed into NHS England in February 2023. The AI Lab's future programme includes work packages on AI Imaging, AI Ethics, and AI Regulation [29].

A recent summary of MHRA guidance on the regulation of medical software and AI [30] lists several bodies with whom the MRHA is collaborating, including three groups within NHS England.

The new UK medical device regulations are now due to come into force in mid-2025 (Section 6.4.1). Based on the UK government's response to the 2021 consultation process [31], the UK approach to the regulation of AIaMD is likely to broadly reflect that taken in EU MDR guidance (Section 9.3.3), but may also include a proposal based on the FDA's Predetermined Change Control Plan (Section 6.5.8.9).

9.5   COMMON ISSUES AND OBJECTIVES

Keeping up to date with the fast-moving world of medical device regulations is a major challenge for any manufacturer, but especially for small teams with limited staffing resources. It is therefore useful to subscribe to an authoritative service that provides updates by way of weekly notifications. It is beneficial to European manufacturers to choose a service that is focused on the EU MDR, but that also provides updates on FDA and other guidance from around the world [32]. For US-based manufacturers, there are several companies that offer a corresponding service [33].

9.5.1   GLOBAL HARMONISATION

The IMDRF is a voluntary international organisation comprised of medical device regulators attempting to harmonise national and regional regulations by developing guidance documents and templates for such organisation to use. Current membership of the IMDRF management committee has representatives from Australia, Brazil, Canada, China, the European Union (EC), Japan, Russia, Singapore, South Korea, the UK, and the US [34]. Each participating regulatory authority will generally produce a publicly available document explaining its role within the IMDRF and its policies for using and adopting IMDRF guidance documents [35].

Much of the medical device regulation that we see today (especially for SaMD) is based on work done by the IMDRF and its forerunner the Global Harmonisation Task Force (GHTF). There is clearly a huge practical benefit of regulatory harmonisation for medical device manufacturers selling their products in more than one market. It is part of the IMDRF's role to identify good practices in national/regional regulatory systems and to promote them in other jurisdictions.

The IMDRF currently has eight active working groups on various topics, including AI, cybersecurity, and SaMD [36]. The IMDRF's strategic plan for 2021–25 was published in September 2020 [37], with a progress report published in May 2023 [38].

9.5.2   Digital Transformation

Digital transformation is the final step in the process of moving from systems that are reliant, or partially reliant, on paper-based records to a point where a whole organisation is "totally" digital. An eQMS (Section 5.2) is certainly part of this process, but all software used in the design and production processes needs to be compatible and suitably integrated (see Section 6.5.8.3).

Subject only to political barriers, the respective IT systems of registered manufacturers, Notified Bodies and regulatory authorities could be connected in such a way that product conformity could be automatically checked (e.g., if regulatory interpretation changes), thus avoiding the need for any electronic documents to be exchanged/manually verified [39]. In principle at least, there is no reason why such a networked compliance system could not operate in real-time [40], which would make the process of regulatory intelligence much simpler for manufacturers [41]. Clearly, the automatic searching of relevant online databases would be considerably enhanced by the use of AI technology (Section 9.5.5.5).

9.5.3   Regulation as Code

In a radical departure from the way we think about regulatory compliance, it is possible to imagine a system based on algorithms rather than published regulations, official guidelines, and court rulings. In other words, a system in which the regulations *themselves* are distilled into codes. The potential advantages are enormous (e.g., the end of badly worded or ambiguous regulations), but the challenges are also enormous, as every single regulatory requirement would need to be reviewed and expressed in formal terms [42].

9.5.4   Medical Apps and Wearable Devices

As previously described in Chapter 6, regulators in the US, EU, and UK are taking slightly different approaches to the regulation of mobile medical apps generally and "wellness apps" in particular. And some wearable devices are already blurring the boundary between so-called activity trackers ("measurements for wellness") and true medical devices [43]. A wearable device that produces alerts and recommendations (e.g., to contact a doctor) is a rapidly expanding sub-group that can already monitor an individual's ECG, blood pressure, and blood oxygen level, amongst other physiological parameters (Section 6.3.4.5).

Some of the promotional material for such devices is aimed directly at doctors, with claims that the devices can "support you and your patients across multiple aspects of health including heart health, mobility, activity, medications, and more" [44].

While companies such as Fitbit Inc. and Apple Inc. point out (in the small print) that their wearable products are *not* medical devices and are "only designed for general fitness and wellness purposes" [45], there is growing evidence that public confusion and "inadvertent misuse" can lead to significant health anxiety issues in vulnerable/susceptible individuals [43]. So, while the manufacturers are clear about how *not* to use their products, there is pressure from the medical community for device makers to be more explicit about how their devices *should* be used. The use of wearable technologies offers huge potential benefits for public health research purposes but their use in the context of direct selling needs to be carefully monitored.

Given the disparity that may exist between the intended use of a health app and its *actual* use, it has been suggested that the EU MDR's requirement for a proactive post-market surveillance (PMS) plan could be used to require manufacturers to acquire knowledge on the actual use of a medical apps and wearable devices. However, MDR 17 is not particularly clear on the extent of the manufacturer's PMS obligation for low-risk devices, so new official guidance would be required [46]. Furthermore, if an unintended use of a device led to harm, any product liability claim (Section 7.2.2) would be strengthened if such use had been previously identified by the manufacturer as a "reasonably foreseeable misuse" (Section 5.3.1.3) at the design stage. It is expected that regulatory guidance documents and standards such as IEC 82304-2:2021 (Chapter 5, A.1.3.7) will need to be regularly updated to keep pace with rapidly advancing technology.

9.5.5   ARTIFICIAL INTELLIGENCE

Apart from the initial responses to the challenge of AI-based medical devices discussed above (Sections 9.2.3, 9.3.3, and 9.4.4), there are some emerging issues that all regulators will need to address over the next few years. Given the rate at which AI/ML is developing, regulators need to get "ahead of the curve" (in terms of foreseeable applications) in order to achieve a degree of futureproofing. At present, nearly all *medical device* applications represent some form of assisted diagnosis/prognosis, based on either personal data (including data from diagnostic and genetic tests) or Big Data, respectively, but the next frontier is *AI for Treatment* [47], which of course carries much greater risks. This is analogous to the quantum leap being contemplated from current "driver assist" technology in new cars (that can usually be "muted" or switched off) to fully autonomous driving.

9.5.5.1   The Definition of AI

Perhaps the most fundamental issue facing the widespread adoption and public acceptance of AI technology in healthcare generally surrounds the term "artificial intelligence" itself – mainly because the technology that we now refer to as AI is neither artificial nor intelligent [48]. It is a term originally coined during the Cold War years of the 1950s when scientists and engineers aspired to build computing machines with "human-level intelligence". That aspiration still exists today (in some quarters[2]), but what has been developed over the last ten years under the banner of "artificial intelligence" is very different.

The term "artificial intelligence" is thus ladened with inappropriate meaning and attempts to define it tend to further confuse the issue. In Chapter 3 we quoted the same rudimentary definition of AI as used by the FDA [11], but the lack of a unified definition has already hindered some comparative studies on the different regulatory approaches to AI/ML-based medical devices in the US and the EU [17].

Despite problems with underlying meaning, current definitions of AI quoted in "top-level" AI legislation in the US and the EU are similar. The US National AI Initiative Act (2020) states that the term "artificial intelligence" means "a machine-based system that can, for a given set of human-defined objectives, make predictions, recommendations or decisions influencing real or virtual environments" [49]. By comparison, the new EU AI Act (Section 7.2.3) states that:

> 'Artificial intelligence system' (AI system) means software that is developed with one or more of the techniques and approaches listed in Annex I and can, for a given set of human-defined objectives, generate outputs such as content, predictions, recommendations, or decisions influencing the environments they interact with.

The reference to Annex I of the Act is important since it allows the technologies listed there to be updated over time, thus avoiding the need to change the basic definition. However, some of the modelling and statistical techniques listed in Annex I are not specific to AI, so weaken the latter's definition. It is anticipated that some of these issues will need to be resolved after the Act becomes law. To that end, and as part of the Act itself (Recital 76), the EC is to establish a European AI Board (EAIB) that will be responsible for several advisory tasks, including issuing guidance on matters related to the implementation of the regulation and providing advice to the Commission on specific questions related to AI.

The recent explosion in the interest in AI applications such as ChatGPT means that it may be difficult to change the terminology in the short term, but it is interesting to note that the American Medical Association (AMA) uses the term *augmented intelligence* in its guidance rather than AI [50]. The AMA does not define "augmented intelligence" as such, but describes it as "a conceptualisation of artificial intelligence that focuses on AI's assistive role, emphasizing that its design enhances human intelligence rather than replaces it".

At a global level, a recent guidance document published by the Artificial Intelligence Medical Device (AIMD) Working Group of the IMDRF effectively

---

[2] The term artificial *general* intelligence (AGI) is used to describe hypothetic AI systems that would possess human-like cognitive abilities.

sidestepped the issue of "AI-based medical devices" by restricting its advice on terminology to "ML-enabled medical devices" (MLMD) [51]; referring to the definition of machine learning given in ISO 22989:2022.[3] Namely, "the process of optimising model parameters through computational techniques, such that the model's behaviour reflects the data or experience". The IMDRF guidance is referenced in a Special Report by the AAMI on medical device AI [52].

The foregoing discussion should serve to illustrate the rather confused and confusing situation that the practical application of AI has got into; a situation summed up succinctly in a 2023 report by the European Union Agency for Cybersecurity (ENISA) [53]:

> A clear definition and scope of AI have proven to be elusive. The concept of AI is evolving and the debate over what it is, and what it is not, is still largely unresolved – partly due to the influence of marketing behind the term 'AI'. Even at the scientific level, the exact scope of AI remains very controversial. In this context, numerous forums have adopted/proposed definitions of AI.

Unless there is a rapid optimisation and subsequent standardisation of AI terminology used in global healthcare regulation, the combination of an inappropriate title and ongoing debate about the scope and categorisation of the underlying technologies will make it difficult to explain "AI-enabled medical technology" to the very people it is meant to help [54]. The implications of the new EU AI Act on medical device regulation are as yet unclear, but the generic legislation will have trickle-down effects.

9.5.5.2   Importance of Data Quality

Ironically, one of the biggest concerns about the application of machine learning in medicine does not relate to the implementation of AI software, but to the training data sets from which the underlying algorithm is taught. Inadvertent systematic bias is one of the main potential problems with ML-based systems, which is why one of the *guiding principles* for AI-based medical devices outlined by regulators is that the data sets employed need to be representative of the target patient population for the device. Future regulation of AI/ML-based medical devices will undoubtedly contain specific requirements for data accuracy and integrity.

A proposal has been made to place meaningful transparency obligations on AI systems covered by the EU AI Act (Section 7.2.3) to ensure the lawful use of copyright-protected content in situations where AI systems rely on using protected materials as input. It is recommended that AI systems comply with the EU copyright framework, and that developers and deployers keep detailed records of third-party works used, including the basis of access, to enable copyright holders to enforce their rights [55].

For adaptive systems, this oversight will need to extend to PMS, in situations where the input clinical data is no longer under the control of the manufacturer. Data quality is one of the main characteristics of medical AI systems that is proposed as a major "review point" by regulatory authorities [56].

---

[3] ISO 22989. *Information technology – Artificial intelligence – Artificial Intelligence concepts and terminology.*

In order to produce AI-specific regulatory requirements for medical device software, it is likely that the risk presented by such a system will need to be graded independently of the (generic) software safety classification in IEC 62304 (Section 5.4.1.4). Various AIaMD classification systems have been proposed that are generally based on the degree of adaptivity and/or autonomy [57,58].

9.5.5.3 Explainable AI (XAI)

Explainable AI (XAI) – also known as interpretable AI – is a form of AI that can be readily understood by the humans who use it. The understanding comes not from the technical expertise of the user, but from the fact the explanation or the inner workings of the highly complex model is provided (in simple language) by the application itself. It is meant to address some of the trust issues associated with the "black-box" nature of most AI systems.

Numerous groups have stressed the importance of employing human-centred design principles when developing medical AI systems and some guidelines have been developed [59]. Furthermore, the related concepts of explainability, transparency, and human oversight are among the basic requirements for "high-risk" AI systems as defined in the draft EU AI Act (Sections 9.3.3 and 7.2.3).

XAI systems are therefore bound to become important in the medical field, given that a medical professional needs to understand (and be able to challenge) the reasoning behind a decision made by an AI-based clinical decision support (CDS) system or other medical application [60,61].

XAI systems currently have some significant limitations [62,63] but most of these will be overcome in the next few years. The transparency provided by XAI fosters confidence and trust in the technology, facilitating its adoption and subsequent clinical validation.

9.5.5.4 Ethical and Clinical Validation Issues

Notwithstanding reservations regarding data privacy and cybersecurity, the main concerns of the medical profession undoubtedly revolve around AI's ethical and clinical validation issues.

At a global level, the World Health Organization (WHO) has produced a comprehensive report describing the main ethical issues surrounding the application of AI in healthcare [64]. The report identifies six key ethical principles and makes detailed recommendations. It is expected that medical device regulators will refer to this report when producing their own guidance on AI/ML-enabled devices.

At the medical specialty level, a joint European and North American multisociety statement on the ethics of AI in Radiology emphasised the attributes of dependability, transparency, and accountability [65]. Similar statements have appeared relating to other specialties, notably cardiology and oncology.

Numerous articles have appeared in medical journals calling for improved clinical validation of medical devices generally, and for AI-enabled devices in particular [66,67]. Some groups have also suggested standard criteria by which the clinical validation of predictive AI-based medical systems should be judged [68]. It is notable that some of the criteria are either not addressed, or only partially addressed, in current EU/US regulatory proposals. Clinical validation is also one of the cornerstones of professional body policy statements relating to acceptable conditions for the introduction of AI technology into routine clinical practice [69].

9.5.5.5   Use of Generative AI Apps Such as ChatGPT

There is much current interest within the medical profession in OpenAI's Generative Pre-Trained Transformer (GPT) technology, especially ChatGPT, its large language model (LLM). ChatGPT is not a medical device itself (whatever question it is asked) [70] but may have to be treated as SOUP (5.4.1.11) if incorporated into a SaMD product as a third-party component.

Most of the proposed "administrative" applications of ChatGPT (e.g., summarising recent medical interventions to produce patient discharge summaries) would not, in any case, qualify as medical devices, but a few suggested applications come close to the domain boundary. There are reservations about the use of LLMs generally (Section 9.5.5.6), particularly in medical research publishing [71], but experimentation with the technology is bound to increase, especially as OpenAI now provides a relatively simple means for the app to be incorporated (via an application programming interface, API) into a host application [72].

If incorporated into a SaMD product as a third-party component, the chatbot would be treated as SOUP and be subject to the relevant requirements of ISO 62304 (Section 5.2.4). However, this is likely to be problematic as the SOUP verification would include a requirement to confirm the appropriateness of the dataset on which the chatbot has been trained (Section 9.5.5.2) and this is generally unknown.

9.5.5.6   Using AI to Generate Computer Code

Generative AI systems based on OpenAI's GPT-4 LLM can be used to produce impressive high-level computer code in an array of programming languages [73], so its future use by software developers working in all industrial sectors is almost inevitable.

It is difficult to predict what further advances (in coding ability) the next revisions of the LLM will bring, but regulatory systems for AI in healthcare are bound to require LLM-generated code to be independently reviewed and tested by an expert software developer – even though the methods for doing this are as yet unspecified.

However, the coding phase represents a relatively small part of the entire software development process so the other SDLC phases will, for the foreseeable future, need to be considered, conducted, and overseen by suitably qualified persons well-versed in the discipline of software engineering. In particular, the traceability of *all* individual requirements (through to specification and code) [74] will need to be confirmed by existing methods. LLM-generated code is likely to be viewed as off-the-shelf (OTS) software and would thus be considered as SOUP under ISO 62304 (Section 5.4.1.11) [75].

9.5.5.7   Using AI to Improve Regulatory Systems

AI is usually viewed as representing a challenge to regulators but it also holds considerable promise for improving the efficiency and reliability of regulatory systems.

In the problematic area of PMS – especially, and ironically, for AI-enabled devices – AI technology could potentially be used to *continuously* search global databases (media, industry journals, medical journals, etc.) for adverse events and trends, to be reviewed by qualified professionals. AI technology may also provide suggestions on what additional information may be required for a jurisdiction-specific report based on previous reports of a similar nature.

In preparing for pre-market evaluation, AI technology could provide the manufacturer with a succinct list of regulations and standards relevant to product design, based on global and/or national requirements driven by product type, risk class, and the target country for the launch. Such a system could also be designed to provide useful information on what additional documentation may be required for marketing the device in a different country/region. This might be seen as a more comprehensive and sophisticated version of the FTC's online flowchart for determining the US regulations relevant to mobile health apps (Section 6.5.8.5).

These are just two examples of how AI technology could be used to improve regulatory oversight and speed up regulatory approval systems. It is expected that many other applications of AI's so-called "digital eye" will follow.

9.5.5.8   Incorporating AI into QMS Software

A QMS software package (eQMS) is an essential tool for the development of regulated medical products (Section 5.2). As generative AI products such as ChatGPT become popular for a variety of search-based applications, it is inevitable that eQMS producers will incorporate them into their products. AI-based eQMS offers many *potential* advantages over conventional QMS software [76] but it remains for this approach to be scientifically proven.

REFERENCES

[1] M. Andreessen, "Why software is eating the World," 20 August 2011. [Online]. Available: https://a16z.com/2011/08/20/why-software-is-eating-the-world/.
[2] Medical Device Innovation Consortium, "Medical Device Innovation Consortium | Regulatory Science Advancement," Medical Device Innovation Consortium, 18 September 2023. [Online]. Available: https://mdic.org/. [Accessed 18 September 2023].
[3] Food and Drug Administration, "Fostering medical device improvement: FDA activities and engagement with the voluntary improvement program," 14 September 2023. [Online]. Available: https://www.fda.gov/media/158180/download. [Accessed 18 September 2023].
[4] Food and Drug Administration, "Medical devices; Quality system regulation amendments," *Federal Register,* vol. 87, no. 36, pp. 10119–10134, 23 February 2022.
[5] G. Ramaley, "Quality Digest - It's time for the FDA to fully embrace ISO 13485," Quality Digest, 16 August 2022. [Online]. Available: https://www.qualitydigest.com/inside/healthcare-column/its-time-fda-fully-embrace-iso-13485-072922.html. [Accessed 2023 September 2023].
[6] E. Nichols, "Greenlight Guru - AAMI TIR45: Closing the gap between agile software development & medical device regulations," Greenlight Guru, 11 September 2022. [Online]. Available: https://www.greenlight.guru/blog/aami-tir45. [Accessed 18 September 2023].
[7] F. Al-Faruque, "Regulatory focus," Regulatory Affairs Professionals Society, 03 October 2022. [Online]. Available: https://www.raps.org/news-and-articles/news-articles/2022/10/fda-acknowledges-shortcomings-of-pre-cert-pilot-in. [Accessed 18 September 2023].

[8] Food and Drug Administration, "The Software Precertification (Pre-Cert) Pilot Program: Tailored total product lifecycle approaches and key findings," September 2022. [Online]. Available: https://www.fda.gov/media/161815/download. [Accessed 18 September 2023].

[9] T. Hwang, A. Kesselheim and K. Vokinger, "Lifecycle regulation of artificial intelligence- and machine learning-based software devices in medicine," *JAMA,* vol. 322, no. 23, pp. 2285–2286, 2019.

[10] R. Parikh, Z. Obermeyer and A. Navathe, "Regulation of predictive analytics in medicine," *Science,* vol. 363, no. 6429, pp. 810–812, 2019.

[11] Food and Drug Administration, "US FDA Artificial Intelligence and Machine Learning discussion paper," 04 February 2019. [Online]. Available: https://www.fda.gov/files/medical%20devices/published/US-FDA-Artificial-Intelligence-and-Machine-Learning-Discussion-Paper.pdf. [Accessed 18 September 2023].

[12] Food and Drug Administration, "Artificial Intelligence/Machine Learning (AI/ML)-based Software as a Medical Device (SaMD) action plan," January 2021. [Online]. Available: https://www.fda.gov/media/145022/download. [Accessed 18 September 2023].

[13] Food and Drug Administration, "Marketing submission recommendations for a predetermined change control plan for Artificial Intelligence/Machine Learning (AI/ML)-enabled device software functions," 03 April 2023. [Online]. Available: https://www.fda.gov/media/166704/download. [Accessed 18 September 2023].

[14] European Commission, "MDCG 2022-14 - Transition to the MDR and IVDR - Notified body capacity and availability of medical devices and IVDs," 26 August 2022. [Online]. Available: https://health.ec.europa.eu/system/files/2022-08/mdcg_2022-14_en.pdf. [Accessed 18 September 2023].

[15] European Commission, "Guidance on qualification and classification of software in regulation (EU) 2017/745 – MDR and regulation (EU) 2017/746 – IVDR," 10 October 2019. [Online]. Available: https://ec.europa.eu/docsroom/documents/37581?locale=en. [Accessed 18 September 2023].

[16] R. De La Cruz, "The application of IEC 62304 for AI and other technologies: It's not rocket science, it's computer science," AAMI Array, 13 February 2023. [Online]. Available: https://array.aami.org/content/news/application-iec-62304-ai-and-other-technologies-s-not-rocket-science-s-computer-science. [Accessed 18 September 2023].

[17] U. Muehlematter, P. Daniore and K. Vokinger, "Approval of artificial intelligence and machine learning-based medical devices in the USA and Europe (2015–20): A comparative analysis," *Lancet Digit Health,* vol. 3, no. 3, pp. e195–e203, 2021.

[18] European Commission, "Draft standardisation request to the European Standardisation Organisations in support of safe and trustworthy artificial intelligence," 05 December 2022. [Online]. Available: https://ec.europa.eu/docsroom/documents/52376?locale=en. [Accessed 18 September 2023].

[19] MedTech Europe, "MedTech Europe's reaction to the EU Council's general approach on the AI Act," MedTech Europe, 07 December 2022. [Online]. Available: https://www.medtecheurope.org/resource-library/medtech-europes-reaction-to-the-eu-councils-general-approach-on-the-ai-act/. [Accessed 18 September 2023].

[20] European Parliamentary Research Service, "Artificial intelligence in healthcare - Applications, risks, and ethical and societal impacts," June 2022. [Online]. Available: https://www.europarl.europa.eu/RegData/etudes/STUD/2022/729512/EPRS_STU(2022)729512_EN.pdf. [Accessed 18 September 2023].

[21] P. Rudd-Clarke and A. Lundy, "The UK medical devices regime and the impact of the Northern Ireland Protocol," Osborne Clarke, 22 July 2022. [Online]. Available: https://www.osborneclarke.com/insights/uk-medical-devices-regime-and-impact-northern-ireland-protocol. [Accessed 18 September 2023].

[22] Department of Health and Social Care, "Consultation on the future regulation of medical devices in the United Kingdom," 26 June 2022. [Online]. Available: https://www.gov.uk/government/consultations/consultation-on-the-future-regulation-of-medical-devices-in-the-united-kingdom. [Accessed 18 September 2023].

[23] Medicines & Healthcare Products Regulatory Agency, "Implementation of the future regulations," 27 July 2023. [Online]. Available: https://www.gov.uk/government/publications/implementation-of-the-future-regulation-of-medical-devices-and-extension-of-standstill-period/implementation-of-the-future-regulations. [Accessed 18 September 2023].

[24] UK House of Commons, "Medical technology regulations and the NHS," 27 March 2023. [Online]. Available: https://commonslibrary.parliament.uk/research-briefings/cdp-2023-0077/. [Accessed 18 September 2023].

[25] Department of Health and Social Care, "Software and AI as a medical device change programme - Roadmap," 14 June 2023. [Online]. Available: https://www.gov.uk/government/publications/software-and-ai-as-a-medical-device-change-programme/software-and-ai-as-a-medical-device-change-programme-roadmap. [Accessed 18 September 2023].

[26] Department for Health and Social Care, "Regulatory horizons council: The regulation of artificial intelligence as a medical device," 30 November 2022. [Online]. Available: https://www.gov.uk/government/publications/regulatory-horizons-council-the-regulation-of-artificial-intelligence-as-a-medical-device. [Accessed 18 September 2023].

[27] HM Government, "Regulatory Horizons Council (RHC)," July 2023. [Online]. Available: https://www.gov.uk/government/groups/regulatory-horizons-council-rhc. [Accessed 18 September 2023].

[28] Department for Science, Innovation and Technology, "A pro-innovation approach to AI regulation," 3 August 2023. [Online]. Available: https://www.gov.uk/government/publications/ai-regulation-a-pro-innovation-approach/white-paper. [Accessed 18 September 2023].

[29] NHS Artificial Intelligence Laboratory, "The NHS AI Lab," [Online]. Available: https://transform.england.nhs.uk/ai-lab/. [Accessed 18 September 2023].

[30] Medicines & Healthcare Products Regulatory Agency, "Software and Artificial Intelligence (AI) as a medical device," 26 July 2023. [Online]. Available: https://www.gov.uk/government/publications/software-and-artificial-intelligence-ai-as-a-medical-device/software-and-artificial-intelligence-ai-as-a-medical-device. [Accessed 18 September 2023].

[31] MHRA, "Consultation on the future regulation of medical devices in the United Kingdom," 26 June 2022. [Online]. Available: https://www.gov.uk/government/consultations/consultation-on-the-future-regulation-of-medical-devices-in-the-united-kingdom. [Accessed 18 September 2023].

[32] Johner Institute, [Online]. Available: https://www.johner-institute.com/. [Accessed 18 September 2023].

[33] Greenlight Guru, [Online]. Available: https://www.greenlight.guru/blog. [Accessed 18 September 2023].

[34] International Medical Device Regulators Forum, "About IMDRF - International Medical Device Regulators Forum," [Online]. Available: https://www.imdrf.org/about. [Accessed 18 September 2023].

[35] Food and Drug Administration, "International Medical Device Regulators Forum (IMDRF) | FDA," [Online]. Available: https://www.fda.gov/medical-devices/cdrh-international-programs/international-medical-device-regulators-forum-imdrf. [Accessed 18 September 2023].

[36] International Medical Device Regulators Forum, "Working Groups | International Medical Device Regulators Forum (IMDRF)," [Online]. Available: https://www.imdrf.org/working-groups. [Accessed 18 September 2023].

[37] International Medical Device Regulators Forum, "IMDRF Strategic Plan 2021–2025 | International Medical Device Regulators Forum (IMDRF)," [Online]. Available: https://www.imdrf.org/documents/imdrf-strategic-plan-2021-2025. [Accessed 18 September 2023].

[38] International Medical Device Regulators Forum, "IMDRF Strategic Plan 2021–2025 - Progress Report Card | International Medical Device Regulators Forum (IMDRF)," [Online]. Available: https://www.imdrf.org/documents/imdrf-strategic-plan-2021-2025-progress-report-card. [Accessed 18 September 2023].

[39] Johner Institute, "7 tips for the successful digital transformation of medical device manufacturers," 1 June 2023. [Online]. Available: https://www.johner-institut.de/blog/gesundheitswesen/digitale-transformation/. [Accessed 18 September 2023].

[40] Johner Institute, "Real-time Compliance System (RCS)," [Online]. Available: https://www.johner-institut.de/produkte/realtime-compliance-system/. [Accessed 18 September 2023].

[41] Johner Institute, "Regulatory intelligence - A core task of regulatory affairs?," 28 June 2023. [Online]. Available: https://www.johner-institute.com/articles/regulatory-affairs/regulatory-intelligence/. [Accessed 18 September 2023].

[42] Johner Institute, "Regulation as code: The end of regulation as we know it," [Online]. Available: https://www.johner-institute.com/articles/regulatory-affairs/regulations-as-code/. [Accessed 18 September 2023].

[43] L. Eadicicco, "Fitbit and Apple know their smartwatches aren't medical devices. But do you?," CNET, 14 January 2022. [Online]. Available: https://www.cnet.com/tech/mobile/features/fitbit-apple-know-smartwatches-arent-medical-devices-but-do-you/. [Accessed 18 September 2023].

[44] Apple Inc., "Healthcare - Apple watch - Apple," [Online]. Available: https://www.apple.com/healthcare/apple-watch/. [Accessed 18 September 2023].

[45] Apple Inc., "Apple watch series 8 - Technical specifications," Apple, 2022. [Online]. Available: https://support.apple.com/kb/SP878?locale=en_GB. [Accessed 18 November 2023].

[46] H. Yu, "Regulation of digital health technologies in the European Union," in *The Future of Medical Device Regulation*, Cambridge, Cambridge University Press, 2022, pp. 103–114.

[47] T. Bowe, "Demystifying the nuances of AI & ML for your regulated medical product," Med Device Online, 14 June 2023. [Online]. Available: https://www.meddeviceonline.com/doc/demystifying-the-nuances-of-ai-ml-for-your-regulated-medical-product-0001. [Accessed 18 September 2023].

[48] K. Pretz, "Stop calling everything AI, machine-learning pioneer says," IEEE Spectrum, 31 March 2021. [Online]. Available: https://spectrum.ieee.org/stop-calling-everything-ai-machinelearning-pioneer-says#toggle-gdpr. [Accessed 18 September 2023].

[49] US Government, "The National Artificial Intelligence Initiative (NAII)," [Online]. Available: https://www.ai.gov/. [Accessed 18 September 2023].

[50] American Medical Association (AMA), "Augmented intelligence in medicine," [Online]. Available: https://www.ama-assn.org/practice-management/digital/augmented-intelligence-medicine#. [Accessed 18 September 2023].

[51] International Medical Device Regulators Forum, "Machine learning-enabled medical devices: Key terms and definitions," 09 May 2022. [Online]. Available: https://www.imdrf.org/documents/machine-learning-enabled-medical-devices-key-terms-and-definitions. [Accessed 18 September 2023].

[52] M. Vockley, "AAMI releases special report on Artificial Intelligence," AAMI Array, 13 April 2023. [Online]. Available: https://array.aami.org/content/news/aami-releases-special-report-artificial-intelligence. [Accessed 18 September 2023].

[53] European Union Agency for Cybersecurity, "Cybersecurity of AI and standardisation," 14 Marh 2023. [Online]. Available: https://www.enisa.europa.eu/publications/cybersecurity-of-ai-and-standardisation. [Accessed 18 September 2023].

[54] J. Worth, "Stop calling it Artificial Intelligence," 02 October 2016. [Online]. Available: https://joshworth.com/stop-calling-in-artificial-intelligence/. [Accessed 18 September 2023].

[55] IFPI, "European creators and right holders call for meaningful transparency obligations on AI systems to ensure the lawful use of copyright-protected content," 19 July 2023. [Online]. Available: https://www.ifpi.org/european-creators-and-right-holders-call-for-meaningful-transparency-obligations-on-ai-systems-to-ensure-the-lawful-use-of-copyright-protected-content/ [Accessed 18 September 2023].

[56] Pharmaceuticals and Medical Device Agency (Japan), "Regulatory process of artificial intelligence," 01 March 2023. [Online]. Available: https://www.pmda.go.jp/files/000226223.pdf. [Accessed 18 September 2023].

[57] K. Chinzei, "Regulatory science on AI-based medical devices and systems," *Advanced Biomedical Engineering,* vol. 7, pp. 118–123, 2018.

[58] S. Beale, "Small regulatory steps for AI in SaMD," Med Device Online, 28 December 2021. [Online]. Available: https://www.meddeviceonline.com/doc/small-regulatory-steps-for-ai-in-samd-0001. [Accessed 18 September 2023].

[59] H. Chen, C. Gomez and C. Huang, "Explainable medical imaging AI needs human-centered design: Guidelines and evidence from a systematic review," *NPJ Digital Medicine,* vol. 5, p. 156, 2022.

[60] S. Ready, "Explainability and artificial intelligence in medicine," *The Lancet Digital Health,* vol. 4, no. 4, pp. E214–E215, 2022.

[61] B. Solaiman and M. Bloom, "AI, explainability, and safeguarding patient safety in Europe," in *The Future of Medical Device Regulation,* Cambridge, Cambridge University Press, 2022, pp. 91–102.

[62] V. Turri, "What is explainable AI?," Carnegie Mellon University Software Engineering Institute, 17 January 2022. [Online]. Available: https://insights.sei.cmu.edu/blog/what-is-explainable-ai/. [Accessed 18 September 2023].

[63] The Lancet Digital Health, "The false hope of current approaches to explainable artificial intelligence in health care," *The Lancet Digital Health,* vol. 3, no. 11, pp. E745–E750, 2021.

[64] World Health Organisation, "Ethics and governance of artificial intelligence for health," 28 June 2021. [Online]. Available: https://www.who.int/publications/i/item/9789240029200. [Accessed 18 September 2023].

[65] J. R. Geis, "Ethics of artificial intelligence in radiology: Summary of the joint European and North American multisociety statement," *Radiology,* vol. 293, no. 2, pp. 436–440, 2019.

[66] A. Aristidou, R. Jena and E. Topol, "Bridging the chasm between AI and clinical implementation," *The Lancet,* vol. 399, no. 10325, pp. 12–18, 2022.

[67] C. McCague, "Position statement on clinical evaluation of imaging AI," *The Lancet Digital Health,* vol. 5, no. 7, pp. e400–e402, 2023.

[68] R. Parikh, Z. Obermeyer and A. Navathe, "Regulation of predictive analytics in medicine," *Science,* vol. 363, no. 6429, pp. 810–812, 2019.

[69] AMA-ASSN, "2018 AI Board report summary," 2019. [Online]. Available: https://www.ama-assn.org/system/files/2019-08/ai-2018-board-policy-summary.pdf. [Accessed 18 September 2023].

[70] D. Tietjen and E. Schwind, "AI software ChatGPT – Actually a medical device?," Taylor Wessing, 27 March 2023. [Online]. Available: https://www.taylorwessing.com/en/insights-and-events/insights/2023/03/ki-software-chatgpt. [Accessed 18 September 2023].

[71] The Lancet Digital Health, "ChatGPT: Friend or foe?," *The Lancet Digital Health,* vol. 5, no. 3, E102, March 2023.

[72] OpenAI, "OpenAI API," [Online]. Available: https://platform.openai.com/. [Accessed 18 September 2023].

[73] S. Bubeck, "Sparks of artificial general intelligence: Early experiments with GPT-4," [Online]. Available: https://arxiv.org/abs/2303.12712. [Accessed 20 November 2023].

[74] International Standards Organisation, "IEC 62304:2006 Medical device software — Software life cycle processes," May 2006. [Online]. Available: https://www.iso.org/standard/38421.html. [Accessed 18 September 2023].

[75] BSI Group, "What regulators expect from medical device manufacturers of software with artificial intelligence (AI) & machine learning (ML)," 04 March 2021. [Online]. Available: https://www.bsigroup.com/globalassets/meddev/localfiles/en-gb/documents/bsi-md-de-qa-medical-webinar-samd-uk-en.pdf. [Accessed 18 September 2023].

[76] Dot Compliance, "Resource blocks archive," [Online]. Available: https://www.dotcompliance.com/resources/. [Accessed 18 September 2023].

10 Summary

The acknowledgement by regulators that standalone software can constitute a medical device in its own right has had major repercussions for health-related software and mobile app developers.

Keeping up with medical device regulations represents an obvious challenge to all medical device manufacturers but especially so for in-house developers and small start-ups. Also, achieving regulatory compliance is just the beginning, as manufacturers must accept that the "goalposts" are constantly moving as new guidance and standards are issued.

Current procedures required for regulatory compliance of medical device software within three different jurisdictions are described in this book, but the need for proactive surveillance of relevant guidelines and standards cannot be overemphasised. The main steps involved in bringing a medical device to market in the EU, UK, and US are described in Sections 6.3.1, 6.4.1 and 6.5.1 respectively.

Writing medical device software in compliance with EU/UK/US regulations involves adherence to many of the general requirements applicable to all medical devices and, as such, the adoption of software-specific standards such as IEC 62304 needs to be integrated into a wider quality management system based on ISO 13485 and ISO 14971. This strategy is appropriate in the US as well as Europe, given the FDA's long-standing recognition of ISO 14971 combined with the Agency's plans to incorporate ISO 13485 into its quality system regulation.

IEC 62304 is a framework standard for software life cycle processes that needs to be supported by specific software engineering methodologies. These *best practice techniques* (Chapters 5 and 7) are indirectly referenced in the EU regulations by a requirement that states that software medical devices should be "developed and manufactured in accordance with the state-of-the-art …", subsequently defined as a technique or process that "embodies what is currently and generally accepted as good practice in technology and medicine".

All medical device regulations are now risk-based, meaning that the degree of regulatory oversight is dependent on the potential risk that the device presents to the patient or operator. The estimation of the different types of risk associated with a given medical device is therefore central to the whole process of regulation and must be performed according to a recognised standard (ISO 14971). A thorough understanding of the basic concepts of risk and safety (Chapter 3) and a detailed knowledge of ISO 14971 (Chapter 5) are both crucial to successful regulatory compliance.

Within the EU, medical device software developed for purely in-house use is subject to less exacting regulatory requirements than commercial software requiring full CE marking, but the tasks and responsibilities placed on developers working in health institutions are no less onerous. Similar requirements for in-house manufacturing are expected in the forthcoming major revision of the UK medical device regulations, which may result in software development activities being gradually concentrated in dedicated clinical computing departments, to be undertaken by staff with formal qualifications in software engineering. Relationships would then need to be established with clinical departments, such as radiology and radiotherapy, if those front-line departments do not have their own clinical computing sections. If implemented, this would slowly replace the historic situation of computer-savvy healthcare professionals developing medical software as a sideline to their core duties.

In the US, the FDA has generally done a good job of anticipating technological changes (e.g., mobile medical apps, AI/ML-based medical devices) and has engaged with manufacturers prior to issuing specific guidance. Manufacturers can also engage directly with the FDA for advice before making pre-market submissions, which helps avoid basic administrative errors. There is much that the EU could learn from the way that FDA enforces US medical device regulations (and vice versa) so it is anticipated that there will be further global harmonisation of regulatory requirements facilitated by the International Medical Device Regulators Forum.

Index